*Sources of*

# THE MAKING O



## PEOPLES AND CULTURES

## A CONCISE HISTORY

Volume I: To 1740

*Sources of*
# The Making of the West

## Peoples and Cultures

### A Concise History

Second Edition

Volume I: To 1740

Katharine J. Lualdi
University of Southern Maine

BEDFORD/ST. MARTIN'S Boston ◆ New York

**For Bedford/St. Martin's**

*Publisher for History:* Mary V. Dougherty
*Executive Editor:* Katherine Meisenheimer
*Director of Development for History:* Jane Knetzger
*Developmental Editor:* Sara Wise
*Senior Production Supervisor:* Dennis J. Conroy
*Executive Marketing Manager:* Jenna Bookin Barry
*Project Management:* DeMasi Design and Publishing Services
*Text Design:* Wanda Kossak
*Cover Design:* Billy Boardman
*Cover Art:* Workshop of Filippino Lippi, *The Worship of the Egyptian Bull God, Apis,* ca. 1500. Oil and egg (identified) on wood. National Gallery, London.
*Composition:* LinMark Design
*Printing and Binding:* RR Donnelley & Sons Company

*President:* Joan E. Feinberg
*Editorial Director:* Denise B. Wydra
*Director of Marketing:* Karen Melton Soeltz
*Director of Editing, Design, and Production:* Marcia Cohen
*Manager, Publishing Services:* Emily Berleth

Library of Congress Control Number: 2006923856



Manufactured in the United States of America.

2 1 0 9 8 7
f e d c b a

*For information, write:* Bedford/St. Martin's, 75 Arlington Street, Boston, MA 02116
(617-399-4000)

ISBN-10: 0-312-41593-1
ISBN-13: 978-0-312-41593-8

**Acknowledgments**
*Acknowledgments and copyrights are continued at the back of the book on pages 263–67, which constitute an extension of the copyright page.*

# Preface

COMPILED SPECIFICALLY TO accompany *The Making of the West: Peoples and Cultures, A Concise History,* second edition, *Sources of The Making of the West* is intended to help instructors bring the history of Western civilization to life for their students. This collection—newly expanded to five documents per chapter—is organized to parallel the chapters in *The Making of the West,* and thereby offer instructors varied opportunities to ignite a dialogue in the classroom between the past and present. With this goal in mind, I have added a broad range of new sources, both written and visual, to complement the thematic and chronological framework of the textbook. The intellectual, emotional, and visual landscapes of people living at the time enrich facts and chronology, revealing that the study of history is not fixed, but is an ongoing process of evaluation and interpretation.

The criteria governing the selection of sources reflect historians' changing understanding of Western civilization. Although the collection includes traditional political sources, these views are broadened by less conventional documents illuminating not only social and cultural life but also Europe's increasing interconnectedness with the world beyond its borders. The voices of women and minorities were also granted a special place in the selection process because of their crucial and often underappreciated role in shaping the course of Western history both from within and outside the corridors of power. In Volume II, Chapter 16, for instance, students can hear the collective voice of the National Assembly as it launched the French Revolution (Document 2) alongside that of female political activist Olympe de Gouges (Document 3).

Of course asking the right questions and finding the right answers lie at the heart of "doing" history. For this reason, this edition of *Sources of The Making of the West* begins with a new introduction on how to interpret written and visual primary sources that leads students step by step through the process of historical analysis. It opens with a brief overview of what this process entails, followed by an extended discussion of the process at work in the analysis of a source drawn specifically from this collection. I adopted this integrated approach for the introduction to help students move easily from abstract concepts to concrete examples. As a result, the introduction does not rely on telling students what to do but rather on showing them how to do it for themselves based on the raw data of history.

The inclusion of visual primary sources in this second edition adds an exciting new dimension to students' ability to see and interpret the past. These documents visually enrich traditional written documents while challenging students to read the past in new ways. Along with training their minds to analyze texts for meaning, students will learn to view images and their spatial arrangement as an equally valuable window into the past. Examples range from a Roman blueprint (Chapter 5), to a photograph of young victims of the Vietnam War (Chapter 23), to a political cartoon (Chapter 24). Throughout the collection, I chose written and nonwritten sources that work well together to elucidate important events and opinions of a specific historical era.

Each source was also selected based on its accessibility and appeal to students. When necessary, I have carefully edited documents—without impairing the documents' overall sense and tone—to speak to specific themes. I have also included documents of varying lengths to increase their utility for both short class exercises and outside writing assignments.

To assist students with their journey into the past, I have revised the chapter summaries to situate the sources within their broader historical context and address their relationship to one another. An explanatory headnote accompanies each source to provide fundamental background information on the author or artist and the source while highlighting its significance. Revised and expanded discussion questions help students examine key points and issues in greater depth. Finally, each chapter concludes with new comparative questions intended to encourage students to see both the harmony and discordance among the sources. Although these editorial features intentionally strengthen the coherence of each chapter as a unit, they also allow instructors to choose sources and questions that best suit their specific goals and methods.

## Acknowledgments

Many people deserve thanks for helping to bring this second edition to fruition. First among them are the authors of *The Making of the West,* Lynn Hunt, Thomas Martin, Barbara Rosenwein, R. Po-chia Hsia, and Bonnie Smith. Many thanks as well to the instructors who provided valuable insights and suggestions when I revised the second edition of *Sources of The Making of the West:* Alexandra Cuffel, University of Massachusetts; Patricia Franz, John Jay College; James Jaffe, University of Wisconsin–Whitewater; Kathleen Kamerick, University of Iowa; Michael Kulikowski, University of Tennessee, Knoxville; Eileen Lyon, State University of New York at Fredonia; Michael Maher, St. Louis University; Shannon McSheffrey, Concordia University; Joelle Neulander, The Citadel; Justin Pettegrew, Loyola University Chicago; Jeff Plaks, University of Central Oklahoma; and Dakota Hamilton, Humboldt State University. I would also like to thank Larissa Juliet Taylor at Colby College and also Christine Pennypacker, who was my undergraduate research assistant at Colby College while I was a visiting professor there, for their help and encouragement. I also owe a huge debt of gratitude to Ashley Waddell for her invaluable assistance in selecting and editing many of the excellent new sources included in Volume II, and to Jilana Ordman for reviewing the selections so carefully and providing helpful suggestions.

# Introduction: Working with Historical Sources

THE LONG HISTORY of Western civilization encompasses a broad range of places and cultures. Textbooks provide an essential chronological and thematic framework for understanding the formation of the West as a cultural and geographical entity. Yet the process of historical inquiry extends beyond textbook narratives into the thoughts, words, images, and experiences of people living at the time. Primary sources expose this world so that you can observe, analyze, and interpret the past as it unfolds before you. History is thus not a static collection of facts and dates. Rather, it is an ongoing attempt to make sense of the past and its relationship to the present through the lens of both written and visual primary sources.

*Sources of The Making of the West, A Concise History,* second edition, provides this lens for you, with a wide range of engaging documents—from an Egyptian chronicle to a political cartoon to firsthand accounts of student revolts. When combined, the sources reflect historians' growing appreciation of the need to examine Western civilization from different conceptual angles—political, social, cultural, economic—and geographic viewpoints. The composite picture that emerges reveals a variety of historical experiences that shaped each era both from within and outside of Europe's borders. Furthermore, the documents here demonstrate that the most historically significant of these experiences are not always those of people in formal positions of power. Men and women from all walks of life have influenced the course of Western history.

The written and visual sources in this reader were selected with an eye toward their ability not only to capture the multifaceted dimensions of the past but also to ignite your intellectual curiosity. Each document is a unique product of human endeavor and as such is often colored by the personal concerns, biases, and objectives of the author or the artist. Among the most exciting challenges facing you is to sift through such nuances for what they reveal about the source and its links to the broader historical context.

## INTERPRETING WRITTEN SOURCES

Understanding a written document and its connection to larger historical issues depends on knowing which questions to ask and how to find the right answers. The first step in this process of discovery is to identify who wrote the source and when and where it was written. This basic information will allow you to situate the document and its author within a specific geographical and chronological context. With this basic groundwork laid, you should then consider the document's type and its intended audience. The answers to these questions will guide you to a deeper level of analysis: What are the main points of the document? What does it reveal about the society in which the document was created? As you work through each question, you will progress from identifying basic facts contained directly within the document to inferring their broader meanings. Thus, at its very heart, the study of primary sources centers on the interplay between "facts" and "interpretation." To help you engage in this interplay, let's examine an actual historical document. Read it carefully, keeping the questions just outlined at the front of your mind. In this way, you will gain insight into this particular text while training yourself how to interpret written primary sources in general.

## 1
## Henry IV
## *Edict of Nantes*
### 1598

*The promulgation of the Edict of Nantes in 1598 by King Henry IV (r. 1589–1610) marked the end of the French Wars of Religion by recognizing French Protestants as a legally protected religious minority. Drawing largely on earlier edicts of pacification, the Edict of Nantes was composed of ninety-two general articles, fifty-six secret articles, and two royal warrants. The two series of articles represented the edict proper and were registered by the highest courts of law in the realm* (parlements). *The following excerpts from the general articles reveal the triumph of political concerns over religious conformity on the one hand, and the limitations of religious tolerance in early modern France on the other.*

Henry, By the Grace of God, King of *France,* and *Navarre,* To all Present, and to Come, greeteth. Among the infinite Mercies that God hath pleased to bestow upon us, that most Signal and Remarkable is, his having given us Power and Strength not to yield to the dreadful Troubles, Confusions, and Disorders, which were found at our coming to this Kingdom, divided into so many Parties and Factions, that the most Legitimate was almost the least, enabling us with Constancy in such manner to oppose the Storm, as in the end to surmount it, reducing this Estate to Peace and Rest. . . . For the general difference among our good Subjects, and the particular evils of the soundest parts of the State, we judged might be easily cured, after the Principal cause (the continuation of the Civil Wars) was taken away, in which we have, by the blessing of God, well and happily succeeded, all Hostility and Wars through the Kingdom being now ceased, and we hope he will also prosper us in our other affairs, which remain to be composed, and that by this means we shall arrive at the establishment of a good Peace, with tranquility and rest. . . . Amongst our said affairs . . . one of the principal hath been, the many complaints we received from divers of our Provinces and Catholick Cities, for that

From English text of "The Edict" as in Edmund Everard, *The Great Pressures and Grievances of the Protestants in France,* London, 1681, appendix 4 in Roland Mousnier, *The Assassination of Henry IV,* trans. Joan Spencer (London: Faber and Faber, 1973), 316–25, 333, 343, 347.

the exercise of the Catholick Religion was not universally re-established, as is provided by Edicts or Statutes heretofore made for the Pacification of the Troubles arising from Religion; as also the Supplications and Remonstrances which have been made to us by our Subjects of the reformed Religion, as well upon the execution of what hath been granted by the said former Laws, as that they desire to have some addition for the exercise of their Religion, the liberty of their Consciences and the security of their Persons and Fortunes; presuming to have just reasons for desiring some inlargement of Articles, as not being without great apprehensions, because their Ruine hath been the principal pretext and original foundation of the late Wars, Troubles, and Commotions. Now not to burden us with too much business at once, as also that the fury of War was not compatible with the establishment of Laws, how good soever they might be, we have hitherto deferred from time to time giving remedy herein. But now that it hath pleased God to give us a beginning of enjoying some Rest, we think we cannot imploy our self better, than to apply to that which may tend to the glory and service of his holy name, and to provide that he may be adored and prayed unto by all our Subjects: and if it hath not yet pleased him to permit it to be in one and the same form of Religion, that it may at the least be with one and the same intention, and with such rules that may prevent amongst them all troubles and tumults. . . . For this cause . . . we have upon the whole judged it necessary to give to all our said Subjects one general Law, Clear, Pure, and Absolute, by which they shall be regulated in all differences which have heretofore risen among them, or may hereafter rise, wherewith the one and other may be contented, being framed according as the time requires: and having had no other regard in this deliberation than solely the Zeal we have to the service of God, praying that he would henceforward render to all our subjects a durable and Established peace. . . . We have by this Edict or Statute perpetual and irrevocable said, declared, and ordained, saying, declaring, and ordaining;

That the memory of all things passed on the one part and the other, since the beginning of the month of *March,* 1585. Until our coming to the Crown, and also during the other precedent troubles, and the occasion of the same, shall remain extinguished and suppressed, as things that had never been. . . .

We prohibit to all our Subjects of what State and Condition soever they be, to renew the memory thereof, to attaque, resent, injure, or provoke one the other by reproaches for what is past, under any pretext or cause whatsoever, by disputing, contesting, quarrelling, reviling, or offending by factious words; but to contain themselves, and live peaceably together as Brethren, Friends, and fellow-Citizens, upon penalty for acting to the contrary, to be punished for breakers of Peace, and disturbers of the public quiet.

We ordain, that the Catholick Religion shall be restored and re-established in all places, and quarters of this Kingdom and Countrey under our obedience, and where the exercise of the same hath been intermitted, to be there again, peaceably and freely exercised without any trouble or impediment. . . .

And not to leave any occasion of trouble and difference among our Subjects, we have permitted and do permit to those of the Reformed Religion, to live and dwell in all the Cities and places of this our Kingdom and Countreys under our obedience, without being inquired after, vexed, molested, or compelled to do any thing in Religion, contrary to their Conscience. . . .

We permit also to those of the said Religion to hold, and continue the Exercise of the same in all the Cities and Places under our obedience, where it hath by them been Established and made public by many and divers times, in the Year 1586, and in 1597, until the end of the Month of *August*. . . .

In like manner the said Exercise may be Established, and re-established in all the Cities and Places where it hath been established, or ought to be by the Statute of Pacification, made in the Year 1577. . . .

As also not to exercise the said Religion in our Court, nor in our Territories and Countries beyond the Mountains, nor in our City of *Paris*, nor within five Leagues of the said City. . . .

We prohibit all Preachers, Readers, and others who speak in public, to use any words, discourse, or propositions tending to excite the People to Sedition; and we enjoin them to contain and comport themselves modestly, and to say nothing which shall not be for the instruction and edification of the Auditors, and maintaining the peace and tranquillity established by us in our said Kingdom. . . .

They [French Protestants] shall also be obliged to keep and observe the Festivals of the Catholick Church, and shall not on the same dayes work, sell, or keep open shop, nor likewise the Artisans shall not work out of their shops, in their chambers or houses privately on the said Festivals, and other dayes forbidden, of any trade, the noise whereof may be heard without by those that pass by, or by the Neighbors. . . .

We ordain, that there shall not be made any difference or distinction upon the account of the said Religion, in receiving Scholars to be instructed in the Universities, Colledges, or Schools, nor of the sick or poor into Hospitals, sick houses or public Almshouses. . . .

We Will and Ordain, that all those of the Reformed Religion, and others who have followed their party, of what State, Quality or Condition soever they be, shall be obliged and constrained by all due and reasonable wayes, and under the penalties contained in the said Edict or Statute relating thereunto, to pay tythes to the Curates, and other Ecclesiasticks, and to all others to whom they shall appertain. . . .

To the end to re-unite so much the better the minds and good will of our Subjects, as is our intention, and to take away all complaints for the future; We declare all those who make or shall make profession of the said Reformed Religion, to be capable of holding and exercising all Estates, Dignities, Offices, and public charges whatsoever. . . .

We declare all Sentences, Judgments, Procedures, Seisures, Sales, and Decrees made and given against those of the Reformed Religion, as well living as dead, from the death of the deceased King *Henry* the Second our most honored Lord and Father in Law, upon the occasion of the said Religion, Tumults and Troubles since happening, as also the execution of the same Judgments and Decrees, from henceforward cancelled, revoked, and annulled. . . .

Those also of the said Religion shall depart and desist henceforward from all Practices, Negotiations, and Intelligences, as well within as without our Kingdom;

and the said Assemblies and Councels established within the Provinces, shall readily separate, and also all the Leagues and Associations made or to be made under what pretext soever, to the prejudice of our present Edict, shall be cancelled and annulled, . . . prohibiting most expresly to all our Subjects to make henceforwards any Assesments or Leavy's of Money, Fortifications, Enrolments of men, Congregations and Assemblies of other than such as are permitted by our present Edict, and without Arms. . . .

We give in command to the People of our said Courts of Parliaments, Chambers of our Courts, and Courts of our Aids, Bayliffs, Chief-Justices, Provosts and other our Justices and Officers to whom it appertains, and to their Leivetenants, that they cause to be read, published, and Registred this present Edict and Ordinance in their Courts and Jurisdictions, and the same keep punctually, and the contents of the same to cause to be injoyned and used fully and peaceably to all those to whom it shall belong, ceasing and making to cease all troubles and obstructions to the contrary, for such is our pleasure: and in witness hereof we have signed these presents with our own hand; and to the end to make it a thing firm and stable for ever, we have caused to put and indorse our Seal to the same. Given at *Nantes* in the Month of *April* in the year of Grace 1598. and of our Reign the ninth

Signed

HENRY

## ■ Who wrote this document, when and where?

The "doing" of history depends on historical records, the existence of which in turn depends on the individuals who composed them at a particular time and place with a specific goal in mind. Therefore before you can begin to understand a document and its significance, you need to determine who wrote it and when and where it was written. Although many documents will not answer these questions directly, whereupon you will have to look elsewhere for clues, here the internal evidence is clear. The author is Henry IV, king of France and Navarre, who issued the document in the French town of Nantes in 1598. This information will help shape your interpretation, for, as you may have already guessed, the language of documents often reflects their authors' social and/or political status. One of the most obvious examples in this document of Henry IV's status is his use of the first-person plural when referring to himself, a grammatical choice that accentuated his royal stature.

## ■ What type of document is this?

Because all genres have their own defining characteristics, identifying the type of document at hand is vital to elucidating its meaning. In this source, you do not have to look far for an answer. Henry IV describes the document as an "edict," "statute," and "ordinance." These designations reveal the public and official nature of the document, echoing their use in society today. Think of the statute of limitations governing the prosecution of certain crimes or city ordinances prohibiting public nudity. Even if you do not know exactly what an edict, statute, or ordinance meant in late sixteenth-century terms, the document itself points the way: "we

[Henry IV] have upon the whole judged it necessary to give to all our said Subjects one general Law, Clear, Pure, and Absolute. . . ." Now you know that the document is a body of law issued by King Henry IV in 1598, which helps to explain its formality as well as the predominance of legal language.

## ■ Who is the intended audience of the document?

The type or genre of a source often goes hand in hand with the intended audience. For instance, popular songs in the vernacular are designed to reach people across the socioeconomic spectrum whereas papal bulls written in Latin are directed to a tiny, educated, and predominantly male elite. Moreover, an author often crafts the style and content of a source to appeal to a particular audience and to enhance the effectiveness of his or her message. Henry IV begins by addressing "all Present," which, when combined with the edict's formality and legal language, suggests his audience is some form of political and/or legal body. The final paragraph supports this conclusion. Here Henry IV commands the "People of our said Courts" to register and implement the edict.

Reading between the lines, you can detect a mixture of power and dependency in Henry IV's tone. Look carefully at his verb choices: *prohibit, ordain, will, declare, command.* Each of these verbs casts Henry IV as the leader and his audience as his followers. This strategy was essential because without the courts' compliance, an edict would be nothing but empty words. Imagine for a moment that Henry IV was not the king of France but rather a soldier writing a letter to his wife or a merchant preparing a contract. In either case, the language chosen would have been changed to suit the audience. Thus, identifying the relationship between author and audience can help you to understand both what the document does and does not say.

## ■ What are the main points of this document?

All primary sources contain stories—whether in numbers, words, and/or images. Before you can begin to analyze their meanings, you need to have a good command of a document's main points. For this reason, while reading you should mark words, phrases, and passages that strike you as particularly important to create visual and mental markers that will help you navigate the document. Don't worry about mastering all of the details; you can work through them later once you have sketched out the basic content. The preamble of this source makes your job somewhat easier because it explains why the edict was issued in the first place: to replace the "dreadful Troubles, Confusions, and Disorders" in France with "one general Law, Clear, Pure, and Absolute, by which they [our said subjects] shall be regulated in all differences which have heretofore risen among them. . . ." But what differences specifically? Even with no knowledge of the circumstances surrounding the formulation of the edict, you would notice the numerous references to "the Catholick Religion," "the reformed Religion," and "the said religion." With this in mind, read the preamble again.

Here we learn that Henry IV had received complaints and supplications from French Catholics and Protestants ("those of the reformed Religion") regarding the exercise of their respective religions. Furthermore, as the text continues, since "it hath pleased God to give us a beginning of enjoying some Rest, we think we cannot imploy our self better, than to apply to that which may tend to the glory and service of his holy name . . . and if it hath not yet pleased him to permit it [France] to be in one and the same form of Religion, that it may at the least be with one and the same intention, and with such rules that may prevent amongst them [our subjects] all troubles and tumults. . . ." Now the details of the document fall into place. Each of the articles addresses specific "rules" governing the legal rights and obligations of French Catholics and Protestants, ranging from where they could worship to where they could work.

## ■ Why was this document written?

The simplicity of this question masks the complexity of the possible answers. Historical records are never created in a vacuum; they were produced for a reason, whether public or private, pragmatic or fanciful. Sometimes a source will state outright why it was created, as is the case with the Edict of Nantes. Yet with or without such direct cues, you should look for less obvious signs of the author's intent and strategies for success, as reflected in word choice, for example, or by the way in which a point is communicated. As we have already seen, Henry IV relied on the written word to convey information and, at the same time, to express his "power" and "strength." The legalistic and formal nature of the edict aided him in this effort. Yet, as Henry IV knew all too well, the gap between law and action could be large, indeed. Thus Henry IV compiled the edict not simply to tell people what to do but to persuade them to do it by delineating the terms of religious coexistence point by point and presenting them as the best safeguard against the return of religious war.

## ■ What does this document reveal about the particular society and period in question?

This question strikes at the heart of historical analysis and interpretation. Whether intentionally or not, every source opens a window onto its author and time period. Often your view through this window will be obscured, but it is important, and fascinating, to look as closely as possible. Perhaps the most striking thing about the Edict of Nantes is what it reveals about the role of religion in society at the time. Our contemporary notion of the separation of church and state had no place in the world of Henry IV and his subjects. As he proclaims in the opening lines, he was king "[b]y the Grace of God" who had given him "Power" and "Strength." Furthermore, you might stop to consider why religious differences were the subject of royal legislation in the first place. Note Henry IV's statement that "if it hath not yet pleased him to permit it [France] to be in one and the same form of Religion, that it may at the least be with one and the same intention. . . ." What does this suggest about sixteenth-century attitudes toward religious difference and tolerance? You cannot answer this question simply by reading the document in black-and-white terms; you need to look beyond the words and between the lines to draw out the document's broader meanings.

## INTERPRETING VISUAL SOURCES

Historians do not rely on written records alone to reconstruct the past; they also turn to nonwritten sources, which are equally varied and rich. Historians have reconstructed the material dimensions of everyday life in centuries long past by drawing on archeological evidence, for example; still others have used church sculpture to explore popular religious beliefs. This book includes a range of pictorial representations to enliven your view of history while enhancing your interpretive skills. Interpreting a visual document is very much like interpreting a nonvisual one. You begin with a set of questions similar to the ones you have already applied to the Edict of Nantes, and move from there to a more complex level of interpretation. With this goal in mind, start by identifying the artist or creator, what type of image it is, and when and where it was produced. Because many pictorial representations provide little explicit guidance in this respect, the headnotes accompanying each image will help you to piece together this basic information. You can then consider who the intended viewers were, and what message the image is trying to convey. Since artists use images, color, and space to communicate with their audience, you must train your eyes to look for visual rather than verbal cues. Here it is important to evaluate all of the features of a particular image as well as the relationship among them. In doing so, you can better understand the image on its own terms as well as the ways in which it speaks to the broader historical context.

## CONCLUSION

Through your analysis of historical sources, you will not only learn details about the world in which the sources were created but also become an active contributor to our understanding of these details' broader significance. Written documents and pictorial representations don't just "tell" historians what happened; they require them to step into their own imaginations as they strive to reconstitute the past. In this regard, historians' approach is exactly that described here: They determine the basics of the source—who created it and when and where—as a springboard for increasingly complex levels of analysis. Each level builds on the other, just like rungs on a ladder. If you take the time to climb each rung in sequence, you will be able to master the content of a source and to use it to bring history to life. The written and visual primary documents included in this second edition of *Sources of The Making of the West, A Concise History* will allow you to participate firsthand in the process of historical inquiry by exploring the people, places, and sights of the past, and how they shaped their world and continue to shape ours today.

# Contents

## CHAPTER 5
## The Roman Empire, c. 44 B.C.E.–284 C.E. 83



## CHAPTER 6
## The Transformation of the Roman Empire, c. 284–600 C.E. 105



## CHAPTER 7
## The Heirs of the Roman Empire, 600–750 122



## CHAPTER 8
## Unity and Diversity in Three Societies, 750–1050 138



## CHAPTER 9
## Renewal and Reform, 1050–1200 154

Chapter

# 1

# Foundations of Western Civilization, to 500 B.C.E.

THE ROOTS OF WESTERN CULTURE cut across distant lands and ancient societies. The first two documents in this chapter expose fundamental features of these early civilizations between the twentieth and tenth centuries B.C.E. The evidence reveals that on the one hand, peoples then living in the Near East, Africa, and the Mediterranean developed distinctive cultural identities. On the other, they shared many attributes, such as large urban populations, the use of writing, devotion to religion, and economies based on trade and agriculture. This unique mixture of cross-cultural similarities and differences forged the path for the future as the Near East and Mediterranean endured dire economic conditions and foreign invasions from 1200 to 1000 B.C.E., followed by a remarkable period of recovery. The last three documents illuminate the course of renewal in the Persian kingdom and Greece. Between the sixth and fifth centuries B.C.E., Persian rulers enhanced the traditional Near Eastern model of monarchical government through military conquest. Among the eventual targets of Persia's imperial ambitions was Greece, where its people rebuilt Greek social, cultural, and political life in innovative ways, ranging from the creation of the city-state to lyric poetry, that left permanent imprints on Western civilization.

## 1.
## King Hammurabi
## *The Code of Hammurabi*
### Early Eighteenth Century B.C.E.

*The law code promulgated by King Hammurabi (r. c. 1792–1750 B.C.E.) of Babylon elucidates the inner workings of Mesopotamian society, the cradle of the world's first civilization. The copy of the code excerpted here is inscribed on a stone pillar, crowned by a sculptural relief depicting the god of justice commissioning Hammurabi to write*

---

From James B. Pritchard, ed., *Ancient Near Eastern Texts Relating to the Old Testament,* 3d ed. (Princeton: Princeton University Press, 1969), 164–78.

*the laws. This image embodies the Mesopotamian belief that kings were divinely appointed and thereby responsible for imparting justice and promoting their subjects' well-being. As a messenger of the divine will, King Hammurabi influenced both the public and private lives of his people. The following selection reveals that he was especially concerned with protecting property rights and the social hierarchy, with slaves at the bottom and free persons at the top. By codifying laws in writing, Hammurabi helped set an enduring precedent in the Western tradition.*

When lofty Anum,[1] king of the Anunnaki,[2]
(and) Enlil, lord of heaven and earth,
the determiner of the destinies of the land,
determined for Marduk,[3] the first-born of Enki,[4]
the Enlil functions over all mankind,
made him great among the Igigi,[5]
called Babylon by its exalted name,
made it supreme in the world,
established for him in its midst an enduring kingship,
whose foundations are as firm as heaven and earth—
at that time Anum and Enlil named me
to promote the welfare of the people,[6]
me, Hammurabi, the devout, god-fearing prince,
to cause justice to prevail in the land,
to destroy the wicked and the evil,
that the strong might not oppress the weak,
to rise like the sun over the black-headed (people),[7]
and to light up the land. . . .

(v)

When Marduk commissioned me to guide the people aright,
to direct the land,

---

[1]The sky-god, the leader of the pantheon, worshiped especially in the temple of Eanna in Uruk, along with the goddess Inanna.

[2]In this inscription the Anunnaki are the lesser gods attendant upon Anum, and the Igigi are the lesser gods attendant on Enlil.

[3]The storm-god, the chief executive of the pantheon, worshiped especially in the temple of Ekur in Nippur in central Babylonia, modern Nuffar.

[4]The son of Enki and consort of Sarpanit; the god of Babylon and in Hammurabi's time the god of the Babylonian Empire with the functions of Enlil delegated to him; worshiped especially in the temple of Esagila in Babylon.

[5]Lord of the earth and the mass of life-giving waters within it, issuing in streams and fountains; the father of Marduk; worshiped especially in the temple of Eabzu in Eridu, in southern Babylonia, modern Abu Shahrein.

[6]Lit., "to make good the flesh of the people."

[7]The late-Sumerian expression for men in general.

I established law and justice in the language of the land,
thereby promoting the welfare of the people.
At that time (I decreed):

## THE LAWS

If a seignior[8] accused a(nother) seignior and brought a charge of murder against him, but has not proved it, his accuser shall be put to death.[9]

If a seignior brought a charge of sorcery against a(nother) seignior, but has not proved it, the one against whom the charge of sorcery was brought, upon going to the river,[10] shall throw himself into the river, and if the river has then overpowered him, his accuser shall take over his estate; if the river has shown that seignior to be innocent and he has accordingly come forth safe, the one who brought the charge of sorcery against him shall be put to death, while the one who threw himself into the river shall take over the estate of his accuser.

If a seignior came forward with false testimony in a case, and has not proved the word which he spoke, if that case was a case involving life, that seignior shall be put to death. . . .

If a seignior has purchased or he received for safe-keeping either silver or gold or a male slave or a female slave or an ox or a sheep or an ass or any sort of thing from the hand of a seignior's son or a seignior's slave without witnesses and contracts, since that seignior is a thief, he shall be put to death.

If a seignior stole either an ox or a sheep or an ass or a pig or a boat, if it belonged to the church (or) if it belonged to the state, he shall make thirtyfold restitution; if it belonged to a private citizen, he shall make good tenfold. If the thief does not have sufficient to make restitution, he shall be put to death. . . .

If a seignior has stolen the young son of a(nother) seignior, he shall be put to death.[11]

If a seignior has helped either a male slave of the state or a female slave of the state or a male slave of a private citizen or a female slave of a private citizen to escape through the city-gate, he shall be put to death.

---

[8]The word *awēlum,* used here, is literally "man," but in the legal literature it seems to be used in at least three senses: (1) sometimes to indicate a man of the higher class; (2) sometimes to suggest a free man of any class; and (3) occasionally, to indicate a man of any class. For the last, I use the inclusive word *man,* but for the first two, since it is seldom clear which of the two is intended in a given context, I follow the ambiguity of the original and use the rather general term *seignior* in Italian and Spanish, to indicate any free man of standing, and not in the strict feudal sense, although the ancient Near East did have something approximating the feudal system, and that is another reason for using *seignior.*

[9]With this law and the three following, cf. Deut. 5:20, 19:16 ff.; and Exod. 23:1–3.

[10]The word for "river" throughout this section has the determinative of deity, indicating that the Euphrates river, as judge in the case, was regarded as god.

[11]Cf. Exod. 21:16 and Deut. 24:7.

If a seignior has harbored in his house either a fugitive male or female slave belonging to the state or to a private citizen and has not brought him forth at the summons of the police, that householder shall be put to death. . . .

If a seignior made a breach in a house, they shall put him to death in front of that breach and wall him in.[12]

If a seignior committed robbery and has been caught, that seignior shall be put to death.

If the robber has not been caught, the robbed seignior shall set forth the particulars regarding his lost property in the presence of god, and the city and governor, in whose territory and district the robbery was committed, shall make good to him his lost property.

If it was a life (that was lost), the city and governor shall pay one mina[13] of silver to his people. . . .[14]

If a seignior rented a field for cultivation, but has not produced grain in the field, they shall prove that he did no work on the field and he shall give grain to the owner of the field on the basis of those adjoining it.

If he did not cultivate the field, but has neglected (it), he shall give grain to the owner of the field on the basis of those adjoining it; furthermore, the field which he neglected he shall break up with mattocks, harrow and return to the owner of the field. . . .

If a shepherd has not come to an agreement with the owner of a field to pasture sheep on the grass, but has pastured sheep on the field without the consent of the owner of the field, when the owner of the field harvests his field, the shepherd who pastured the sheep on the field without the consent of the owner of the field shall give in addition twenty *kur* of grain per eighteen *iku* to the owner of the field. . . .

If a merchant lent grain, wool, oil, or any goods at all to a trader to retail, the trader shall write down the value and pay (it) back to the merchant, with the trader obtaining a sealed receipt for the money which he pays to the merchant.

If the trader has been careless and so has not obtained a sealed receipt for the money which he paid to the merchant, the money with no sealed receipt may not be credited to the account.

If a trader borrowed money from a merchant and has then disputed (the fact) with his merchant, that merchant in the presence of god and witnesses shall prove that the trader borrowed the money and the trader shall pay to the merchant threefold the full amount of money that he borrowed.

When a merchant entrusted (something) to a trader and the trader has returned to his merchant whatever the merchant gave him, if the merchant has then disputed with him whatever the trader gave him, that trader shall prove it against the merchant in the presence of god and witnesses and the merchant shall pay to the trader sixfold whatever he received because he had a dispute with his trader.

---

[12]Cf. Exod. 22:2, 3a.

[13]A weight of about 500 grams, divided into 60 shekels.

[14]For this and the preceding law, cf. Deut. 21:1 ff.

If a woman wine seller, instead of receiving grain for the price of a drink, has received money by the large weight and so has made the value of the drink less than the value of the grain, they shall prove it against that wine seller[15] and throw her into the water.

If outlaws have congregated in the establishment of a woman wine seller and she has not arrested those outlaws and did not take them to the palace, that wine seller shall be put to death. . . .

If a seignior pointed the finger at a nun or the wife of a(nother) seignior, but has proved nothing, they shall drag that seignior into the presence of the judges and also cut off half his (hair).

If a seignior acquired a wife, but did not draw up the contracts for her, that woman is no wife.

If the wife of a seignior has been caught while lying with another man, they shall bind them and throw them into the water. If the husband[16] of the woman wishes to spare his wife, then the king in turn may spare his subject.[17]

If a seignior bound the (betrothed) wife of a(nother) seignior, who had had no intercourse with[18] a male and was still living in her father's house, and he has lain in her bosom and they have caught him, that seignior shall be put to death, while that woman shall go free.[19]

If a seignior's wife was accused by her husband,[20] but she was not caught while lying with another man, she shall make affirmation by god and return to her house.

If the finger was pointed at the wife of a seignior because of another man, but she has not been caught while lying with the other man, she shall throw herself into the river[21] for the sake of her husband.[22]

If a seignior was taken captive, but there was sufficient to live on in his house, his wife [shall not leave her house, but she shall take care of her person by not] entering [the house of another].[23]

If that woman did not take care of her person, but has entered the house of another, they shall prove it against that woman and throw her into the water.[24]

If the seignior was taken captive and there was not sufficient to live on in his house, his wife may enter the house of another, with that woman incurring no blame at all.

---

[15]This has also been translated as "they shall bind that wine seller."
[16]Lit., "owner, master."
[17]Lit., "his slave." With this law cf. Deut. 22:22.
[18]Lit., "had not known."
[19]Cf. Deut. 22:23–27.
[20]Lit., "If with respect to a seignior's wife *(casus pendens)* her husband accused her."
[21]I.e., submit to the water ordeal, with the river as divine judge; cf. note 10.
[22]Cf. Num. 5:11–31.
[23]I.e., in order to live there as another man's wife.
[24]I.e., to be drowned.

If, when a seignior was taken captive and there was not sufficient to live on in his house, his wife has then entered the house of another before his (return) and has borne children, (and) later her husband has returned and has reached his city, that woman shall return to her first husband, while the children shall go with their father.

If, when a seignior deserted his city and then ran away, his wife has entered the house of another after his (departure), if that seignior has returned and wishes to take back his wife, the wife of the fugitive shall not return to her husband because he scorned his city and ran away. . . .

If a seignior wishes to divorce his wife who did not bear him children, he shall give her money to the full amount of her marriage-price and he shall also make good to her the dowry which she brought from her father's house and then he may divorce her.

If there was no marriage-price, he shall give her one mina of silver as the divorce-settlement.

If he is a peasant, he shall give her one-third mina of silver.

If a seignior's wife, who was living in the house of the seignior, has made up her mind to leave in order that she may engage in business, thus neglecting her house (and) humiliating her husband, they shall prove it against her; and if her husband has then decided on her divorce, he may divorce her, with nothing to be given her as her divorce-settlement upon her departure.[25] If her husband has not decided on her divorce, her husband may marry another woman, with the former woman[26] living in the house of her husband like a maidservant.

If a woman so hated her husband that she has declared, "You may not have me," her record shall be investigated at her city council, and if she was careful and was not at fault, even though her husband has been going out and disparaging her greatly, that woman, without incurring any blame at all, may take her dowry and go off to her father's house.

If she was not careful, but was a gadabout, thus neglecting her house (and) humiliating her husband, they shall throw that woman into the water. . . .

When a seignior married a woman and a fever[27] has then seized her, if he has made up his mind to marry another, he may marry (her), without divorcing his wife whom the fever seized; she shall live in the house which he built and he shall continue to support her as long as she lives.

If that woman has refused to live in her husband's house, he shall make good her dowry to her which she brought from her father's house and then she may leave.

If a seignior, upon presenting a field, orchard, house, or goods to his wife, left a sealed document with her, her children may not enter a claim against her after (the death of) her husband, since the mother may give her inheritance to that son of hers whom she likes, (but) she may not give (it) to an outsider. . . .

---

[25]Lit., "her journey," a noun in the adverbial accusative of manner.

[26]Lit., "that woman."

[27]The exact meaning of the word used here, *la'bum,* is not known.

If a seignior's wife has brought about the death of her husband because of another man, they shall impale that woman on stakes. . . .

If, when a seignior acquired a wife, she bore him children and that woman has then gone to (her) fate, her father may not lay claim to her dowry, since her dowry belongs to her children.

If a seignior acquired a wife and that woman has gone to (her) fate without providing him with children, if his father-in-law has then returned to him the marriage-price which that seignior brought to the house of his father-in-law, her husband may not lay claim to the dowry of that woman, since her dowry belongs to her father's house. . . .

If a member of the artisan class[28] took a son as a foster child and has taught him his handicraft, he may never be reclaimed. . . .

If a son has struck his father, they shall cut off his hand.[29]

If a seignior has destroyed the eye of a member of the aristocracy,[30] they shall destroy his eye.[31]

If he has broken a(nother) seignior's bone, they shall break his bone.[32]

If he has destroyed the eye of a commoner or broken the bone of a commoner, he shall pay one mina of silver.

If he has destroyed the eye of a seignior's slave or broken the bone of a seignior's slave, he shall pay one-half his value.

If a seignior has knocked out a tooth of a seignior of his own rank, they shall knock out his tooth.[33]

If he has knocked out a commoner's tooth, he shall pay one-third mina of silver.

If a seignior has struck the cheek of a seignior who is superior to him, he shall be beaten sixty (times) with an oxtail whip in the assembly.

If a member of the aristocracy has struck the cheek of a(nother) member of the aristocracy who is of the same rank as[34] himself, he shall pay one mina of silver.

If a commoner has struck the cheek of a(nother) commoner, he shall pay ten shekels of silver.

If a seignior's slave has struck the cheek of a member of the aristocracy, they shall cut off his ear.

---

[28]Lit., "the son of an artisan," where "son" is used in the technical sense of "belonging to the class or species of," which is so common in the Semitic languages.

[29]Cf. Exod. 21:15. For the whole collection of laws dealing with personal injuries (laws 195–214), cf. the similar collection in Exod. 21:12–27.

[30]Lit., "the son of a man," where "son" is used in the technical sense explained before and "man" is used in the sense of "noble or aristocrat." It is also possible that "son" here is intended to be taken in its regular sense to indicate a person younger than the assailant.

[31]Cf. Exod. 21:23–25.

[32]Cf. Lev. 24:19f.

[33]Cf. Deut. 19:21.

[34]Lit., "who is like."

If a seignior has struck a(nother) seignior in a brawl and has inflicted an injury on him, that seignior shall swear, "I did not strike him deliberately";[35] and he shall also pay for the physician.

If he has died because of his blow, he shall swear (as before), and if it was a member of the aristocracy, he shall pay one-half mina of silver.

If it was a member of the commonalty, he shall pay one-third mina of silver.

If a seignior struck a(nother) seignior's daughter and has caused her to have a miscarriage,[36] he shall pay ten shekels of silver for her fetus.

If that woman has died, they shall put his daughter to death.

If by a blow he has caused a commoner's daughter to have a miscarriage, he shall pay five shekels of silver.

If that woman has died, he shall pay one-half mina of silver.

If he struck a seignior's female slave and has caused her to have a miscarriage, he shall pay two shekels of silver.

If that female slave has died, he shall pay one-third mina of silver. . . .

If an ox, when it was walking along the street, gored a seignior to death,[37] that case is not subject to claim.

If a seignior's ox was a gorer and his city council made it known to him that it was a gorer, but he did not pad its horns (or) tie up his ox, and that ox gored to death a member of the aristocracy, he shall give one-half mina of silver.[38]

If it was a seignior's slave, he shall give one-third mina of silver. . . .

## The Epilogue

The laws of justice, which Hammurabi, the efficient king, set up,
and by which he caused the land to take the right way and have good government.
I, Hammurabi, the perfect king,
was not careless (or) neglectful of the black-headed (people),
whom Enlil had presented to me,
(and) whose shepherding Marduk had committed to me;
I sought out peaceful regions for them;
I overcame grievous difficulties;
I caused light to rise on them.
With the mighty weapon which Zababa and Inanna entrusted to me,
with the insight that Enki allotted to me,
with the ability that Marduk gave me,
I rooted out the enemy above and below;
I made an end of war;
I promoted the welfare of the land;

---

[35]Lit., "while I was aware of (it)."

[36]Lit., "caused her to drop that of her womb (her fetus)." With this and the following five laws, cf. Exod. 21:22–25.

[37]Lit., "and has caused his death."

[38]Cf. Exod. 21:28–36.

I made the peoples rest in friendly habitations;
I did not let them have anyone to terrorize them.
The great gods called me,
so I became the beneficent shepherd whose scepter is righteous;
my benign shadow is spread over my city.
In my bosom I carried the peoples of the land of Sumer and Akkad;
they prospered under my protection;
I always governed them in peace;
I sheltered them in my wisdom.
In order that the strong might not oppress the weak,
that justice might be dealt the orphan (and) the widow,
in Babylon, the city whose head Anum and Enlil raised aloft,
in Esagila, the temple whose foundations stand firm like heaven and earth,
I wrote my precious words on my stela,
and in the presence of the statue of me, the king of justice,
I set (it) up in order to administer the law of the land,
to prescribe the ordinances of the land,
to give justice to the oppressed.

### Discussion Questions

1. What do the Prologue and Epilogue indicate about the status of Mesopotamian rulers?
2. What values or ideals governing the code are expressed in these excerpts?
3. What does the code reveal in particular about women's position in Mesopotamian society?
4. Historians traditionally view cities, formal political systems, knowledge of writing, and diverse crafts as defining features of civilization. Which of these features are reflected in the code?

## 2.
## *The Book of Exodus, Chapters 19–24*
### c. Tenth–Sixth Centuries B.C.E.

*This excerpt from the second book of the Hebrew Bible, Exodus, exposes an important trait shared by Hammurabi's Code and other ancient laws: perpetrators of acts defined as unlawful must endure a specified punishment. In its account of the flight of the Hebrews from Egypt in the thirteenth century* B.C.E.*, the book of Exodus includes what was believed to be the first proclamation by their God about the divine laws governing his relations with them and with one another. The Hebrews agreed to follow the rules in exchange for God's promise to make them his chosen people. Although they did not yet deny the existence of other gods, their covenant with him was a crucial stage in the development of monotheism. The biblical story casts the Hebrew* *leader Moses in much the same role as that of Hammurabi in his code: both are agents of divine justice and protection.*

## III. THE COVENANT AT SINAI

### A. The Covenant and the Decalogue

***The Israelites Come to Sinai*** 19 Three months after they came out of the land of Egypt . . . on that day the sons of Israel came to the wilderness of Sinai.[1] From Rephidim they set out again; and when they reached the wilderness of Sinai, there in the wilderness they pitched their camp; there facing the mountain Israel pitched camp.

***Yahweh Promises a Covenant*** Moses then went up to God, and Yahweh called to him from the mountain, saying, "Say this to the House of Jacob, declare this to the sons of Israel, 'You yourselves have seen what I did with the Egyptians, how I carried you on eagle's wings and brought you to myself. From this you know that now, if you obey my voice and hold fast to my covenant, you of all the nations shall be my very own for all the earth is mine. I will count you a kingdom of priests, a consecrated nation.' Those are the words you are to speak to the sons of Israel." So Moses went and summoned the elders of the people, putting before them all that Yahweh had bidden him. Then all the people answered as one, "All that Yahweh has said, we will do." And Moses took the people's reply back to Yahweh.

***Preparing for the Covenant*** Yahweh said to Moses, "I am coming to you in a dense cloud so that the people may hear when I speak to you and may trust you always." And Moses took the people's reply back to Yahweh.

Yahweh said to Moses, "Go to the people and tell them to prepare themselves today and tomorrow. Let them wash their clothing and hold themselves in readiness for the third day, because on the third day Yahweh will descend on the mountain of Sinai in the sight of all the people. You will mark out the limits of the mountain and say, 'Take care not to go up the mountain or to touch the foot of it. Whoever touches the mountain will be put to death. No one must lay a hand on him: he must be stoned or shot down by arrow, whether man or beast; he must not remain alive.' When the ram's horn sounds a long blast, they are to go up the mountain."

So Moses came down from the mountain to the people and bade them prepare themselves; and they washed their clothing. Then he said to the people, "Be ready for the third day; do not go near any woman."

---

From *The Jerusalem Bible: Reader's Edition* (New York and London: Doubleday, 2000), 80–86.

[1]According to tradition, Mount Sinai was at Jebel Musa in the southern region of the Sinai peninsula.

***The Theophany on Sinai*** Now at daybreak on the third day there were peals of thunder on the mountain and lightning flashes, a dense cloud, and a loud trumpet blast, and inside the camp all the people trembled. Then Moses led the people out of the camp to meet God; and they stood at the bottom of the mountain. The mountain of Sinai was entirely wrapped in smoke, because Yahweh had descended on it in the form of fire. Like smoke from a furnace the smoke went up, and the whole mountain shook violently. Louder and louder grew the sound of the trumpet. Moses spoke, and God answered him with peals of thunder. Yahweh came down on the mountain of Sinai, on the mountain top, and Yahweh called Moses to the top of the mountain; and Moses went up. Yahweh said to Moses, "Go down and warn the people not to pass beyond their bounds to come and look on Yahweh, or many of them will lose their lives. The priests, the men who do approach Yahweh, even these must purify themselves, or Yahweh will break out against them." Moses answered Yahweh, "The people cannot come up the mountain of Sinai because you warned us yourself when you said, 'Mark out the limits of the mountain and declare it sacred.'" "Go down," said Yahweh to him "and come up again bringing Aaron with you. But do not allow the priests or the people to pass beyond their bounds to come up to Yahweh, or he will break out against them." So Moses went down to the people and spoke to them. . . .

***The Decalogue*** 20 Then God spoke all these words. He said, "I am Yahweh your God who brought you out of the land of Egypt, out of the house of slavery.

"You shall have no gods except me.

"You shall not make yourself a carved image or any likeness of anything in heaven or on earth beneath or in the waters under the earth; you shall not bow down to them or serve them. For I, Yahweh your God, am a jealous God and I punish the father's fault in the sons, the grandsons, and the great-grandsons of those who hate me; but I show kindness to thousands of those who love me and keep my commandments.

"You shall not utter the name of Yahweh your God to misuse it,[2] for Yahweh will not leave unpunished the man who utters his name to misuse it.

"Remember the Sabbath day and keep it holy. For six days you shall labor and do all your work, but the seventh day is a Sabbath for Yahweh your God. You shall do no work that day, neither you nor your son nor your daughter nor your servants, men or women, nor your animals nor the stranger who lives with you. For in six days Yahweh made the heavens and the earth and the sea and all that these hold, but on the seventh day he rested; that is why Yahweh has blessed the Sabbath day and made it sacred.

"Honor your father and your mother so that you may have a long life in the land that Yahweh your God has given to you.

"You shall not kill.

"You shall not commit adultery.

---

[2] Either in a false oath or irreverently.

"You shall not steal.

"You shall not bear false witness against your neighbor.

"You shall not covet your neighbor's house. You shall not covet your neighbor's wife, or his servant, man or woman, or his ox, or his donkey, or anything that is his."

All the people shook with fear at the peals of thunder and the lightning flashes, the sound of the trumpet, and the smoking mountain; and they kept their distance. "Speak to us yourself" they said to Moses "and we will listen; but do not let God speak to us, or we shall die." Moses answered the people, "Do not be afraid; God has come to test you, so that your fear of him, being always in your mind, may keep you from sinning." So the people kept their distance while Moses approached the dark cloud where God was.

## B. The Book of the Covenant

***Law Concerning the Altar*** Yahweh said to Moses, "Tell the sons of Israel this, 'You have seen for yourselves that I have spoken to you from heaven. You shall not make gods of silver or gods of gold to stand beside me; you shall not make things like this for yourselves.

'You are to make me an altar of earth, and sacrifice on this the holocausts and communion sacrifices from your flocks or herds. In every place in which I have my name remembered I shall come to you and bless you. If you make me an altar of stone, do not build it of dressed stones; for if you use a tool on it, you profane it. You shall not go up to my altar by steps for fear you expose your nakedness.' "

***Laws Concerning Slaves*** 21 "This is the ruling you are to lay before them: 'When you buy a Hebrew slave, his service shall be for six years. In the seventh year he may leave; he shall be free, with no compensation to pay. If he came single, he shall leave single; if he came married, his wife shall leave with him. If his master gives him a wife and she bears him sons and daughters, wife and children shall belong to her master, and the man must leave alone. But if the slave declares, 'I love my master and my wife and children; I renounce my freedom,' then his master shall take him to God, leading him to the door or the door post. His master shall pierce his ear with an awl, and he shall be in his service for all time. If a man sells his daughter as a slave, she shall not regain her liberty like male slaves. If she does not please her master who intended her for himself, he must let her be bought back: he has not the right to sell her to foreigners, thus treating her unfairly. If he intends her for his son, he shall deal with her according to the ruling for daughters. If he takes another wife, he must not reduce the food of the first or her clothing or her conjugal rights. Should he cheat her of these three things she may leave, freely, without having to pay any money.

***Homicide*** 'Anyone who strikes a man and so causes his death, must die. If he has not lain in wait for him but God has delivered him into his hands,[3] then I will appoint you a place where he may seek refuge. But should a man dare to kill his

[3]Accidents are attributed to God.

fellow by treacherous intent, you must take him even from my altar to be put to death.

'Anyone who strikes his father or mother must die. Anyone who abducts a man—whether he has sold him or is found in possession of him—must die. Anyone who curses father or mother must die.

***Blows and Wounds*** 'If men quarrel and one strikes the other a blow with stone or fist so that the man, though he does not die, must keep his bed, the one who struck the blow shall not be liable provided the other gets up and can go about, even with a stick. He must compensate him, however, for his enforced inactivity, and care for him until he is completely cured.

'If a man beats his slave, male or female, and the slave dies at his hands, he must pay the penalty. But should the slave survive for one or two days, he shall pay no penalty because the slave is his by right of purchase.

'If, when men come to blows, they hurt a woman who is pregnant and she suffers a miscarriage, though she does not die of it, the man responsible must pay the compensation demanded of him by the woman's master; he shall hand it over, after arbitration. But should she die, you shall give life for life, eye for eye, tooth for tooth, hand for hand, foot for foot, burn for burn, wound for wound, stroke for stroke.

'When a man strikes at the eye of his slave, male or female, and destroys the use of it, he must give him his freedom to compensate for the eye. If he knocks out the tooth of his slave, male or female, he must give him his freedom to compensate for the tooth.

'When an ox gores a man or woman to death, the ox must be stoned. Its flesh shall not be eaten, and the owner of the ox shall not be liable. But if the ox has been in the habit of goring before, and if its owner was warned but has not kept it under control, then should this ox kill a man or woman, the ox must be stoned and its owner put to death. If a ransom is imposed on him, he must pay whatever is imposed, to redeem his life. If the ox gores a boy or a girl, he must be treated in accordance with this same rule. If the ox gores a slave, male or female, the owner must pay over to their master a sum of money—thirty shekels—and the ox must be stoned.

'When a man leaves a pit uncovered, or when he digs one but does not cover it, should an ox, or donkey, fall into it, then the owner of the pit shall make up for the loss: he must pay its owner money, and the dead animal shall be his own. If one man's ox harms another's so that it dies, the owners must sell the live ox and share the price of it; they shall also share the dead animal. But if it is common knowledge that the ox has been in the habit of goring before, and its owner has not kept it under control, he must repay ox for ox; the dead animal shall be his own.

***Theft of Animals*** 'If a man steals an ox or a sheep and then slaughters or sells it, he must pay five oxen for the ox, four sheep for the sheep.

22 'If a thief is caught breaking in and is struck a mortal blow, there is to be no blood-vengeance for him, but there shall be blood-vengeance for him if it was after dawn. Full restitution must be made; if he has not the means, he must be sold to pay for what he has stolen. If the stolen animal is found alive in his possession, ox or donkey or sheep, he must pay double.

***Offences Demanding Compensation*** 'When a man puts his animals out to graze in a field or vineyard and lets his beasts graze in another's field, he must make restitution for the part of the field that has been grazed in proportion to its yield. But if he has let the whole field be grazed, he must make restitution in proportion to the best crop recorded in the injured party's field or vineyard.

'When a fire spreads, setting light to thorn bushes and destroying stacked or standing corn or the field itself, the man responsible for the fire must make full restitution.

'When a man has entrusted money or goods to another's keeping and these are stolen from his house, the thief, if he can be caught, must repay double. Should the thief not be caught, the owner of the house must swear before God that he has not laid hands on the other man's property.

'Whenever there is breach of trust in the matter of ox, donkey, sheep, clothing, or any lost property for which it is claimed "Yes, this is it," the dispute shall be brought before God. The person whom God pronounces guilty[4] must pay double to the other.

'When a man has entrusted to another's keeping a donkey, ox, sheep, or any beast whatever, and this dies or is injured or carried off, without a witness, an oath by Yahweh shall decide between the two parties whether one man has laid hands on the other's property or not. The owner shall take what remains, the other shall not have to make good the loss. But if the animal has been stolen from him, he must make restitution to the owner. If it has been savaged by wild beasts, he must bring the savaged remains of the animal as evidence, and he shall not be obliged to give compensation.

'When a man borrows an animal from another, and it is injured or dies in the owner's absence, the borrower must make full restitution. But if the owner has been present, the borrower will not have to make good the loss. If the owner has hired it out, he shall settle for the price of its hire.

***Violation of a Virgin*** 'If a man seduces a virgin who is not betrothed and sleeps with her, he must pay her price[5] and make her his wife. If her father absolutely refuses to let him have her, the seducer must pay a sum of money equal to the price fixed for a virgin.

***Moral and Religious Laws*** 'You shall not allow a sorceress to live.

'Anyone who has intercourse with an animal must die.

'Anyone who sacrifices to other gods shall come under the ban.

'You must not molest the stranger or oppress him, for you lived as strangers in the land of Egypt. You must not be harsh with the widow, or with the orphan; if you are harsh with them, they will surely cry out to me, and be sure I shall hear their cry; my anger will flare and I shall kill you with the sword, your own wives will be widows, your own children orphans.

---

[4]Through trial by ordeal, or oracle, or oath.

[5]The "bride-price," *mohar,* paid by a betrothed man to the family of his future wife.

'If you lend money to any of my people, to any poor man among you, you must not play the usurer with him: you must not demand interest from him.

'If you take another's cloak as a pledge, you must give it back to him before sunset. It is all the covering he has; it is the cloak he wraps his body in; what else would he sleep in? If he cries to me, I will listen, for I am full of pity.

'You shall not revile God nor curse a ruler of your people.

***First-Fruits and First-Born*** 'Do not be slow to make offering from the abundance of your threshing-floor and your winepress. You must give me the first-born of your sons; you must do the same with your flocks and herds. The first-born must remain with its mother for seven days; on the eighth day you must give it to me.

'You are to be men consecrated to me. You must not eat the flesh of an animal that has been savaged by wild beasts; you must throw it to the dogs.

***Justice. Duties towards Enemies*** 23 'You must not make false assertions. You must not support a guilty man by giving malicious evidence. You must not take the side of the greater number in the cause of wrong-doing nor side with the majority and give evidence in a lawsuit in defiance of justice; nor in a lawsuit must you show partiality to the poor.

'If you come on your enemy's ox or donkey going astray, you must lead it back to him. If you see the donkey of a man who hates you fallen under its load, instead of keeping out of his way, go to him to help him.

'You must not cheat any poor man of yours of his rights at law. Keep out of trumped-up cases. See that the man who is innocent and just is not done to death, and do not acquit the guilty. You must not accept a bribe, for a bribe blinds clear-sighted men and is the ruin of the just man's cause.

'You must not oppress the stranger; you know how a stranger feels, for you lived as strangers in the land of Egypt.

***The Sabbatical Year and the Sabbath*** 'For six years you may sow your land and gather its produce, but in the seventh year you must let it lie fallow and forego all produce from it. Those of your people who are poor may take food from it, and let the wild animals feed on what they leave. You shall do the same with your vineyard and your olive grove.

'For six days you shall do your work, but stop on the seventh day, so that your ox and your donkey may rest and the son of your slave girl have a breathing space, and the stranger too.

'Take notice of all I have told you and do not repeat the name of other gods: let it not be heard from your lips.

***The Great Feasts*** 'Three times a year you are to celebrate a feast in my honor. You must celebrate the feast of Unleavened Bread: you must eat unleavened bread, as I have commanded you, at the appointed time in the month of Abib, for in that month you came out of Egypt. And no one must come before me empty-handed. The feast of Harvest, too, you must celebrate, the feast of the first-fruits of the produce of your sown fields; the feast of Ingathering also, at the end of the year when you gather in the fruit of your labors from the fields. Three times a year all your menfolk must present themselves before the Lord Yahweh.

'You must not offer unleavened bread with the blood of the victim sacrificed to me, nor put by the fat of my festal victim for the following day.

'You must bring the best of the first-fruits of your soil to the house of Yahweh your God.

'You must not boil a kid in its mother's milk.[6]

***Preparatory Promises and Instructions for the Entry into Canaan*** 'I myself will send an angel before you to guard you as you go and to bring you to the place that I have prepared. Give him reverence and listen to all that he says. Offer him no defiance; he would not pardon such a fault, for my name is in him. If you listen carefully to his voice and do all that I say, I shall be enemy to your enemies, foe to your foes. My angel will go before you and lead you to where the Amorites are and the Hittites, the Perizzites, the Canaanites, the Hivites, the Jebusites; I shall exterminate these. You must not bow down to their gods or worship them; you must not do as they do: you must destroy their gods utterly and smash their standing-stones.[7] You are to worship Yahweh your God, and I shall bless your bread and water, and remove sickness from among you. In your land no woman will miscarry, none be barren. I shall give you your full term of life.

'I shall spread panic ahead of you; I shall throw into confusion all the people you encounter; I shall make all your enemies turn and run from you. I shall send hornets in front of you to drive Hivite and Canaanite and Hittite from your presence. I shall not drive them out before you in a single year, or the land would become a desert where, to your cost, the wild beasts would multiply. Little by little I will drive them out before you until your numbers grow and you come into possession of the land. For your frontiers I shall fix the Sea of Reeds and the Philistine sea, the desert and the river;[8] yes, I shall deliver the inhabitants of the country into your hands, and you will drive them out before you. You must make no pact with them or with their gods. They must not live in your country or they will make you sin against me; you would come to worship their gods, and that would be a snare for you indeed!' "

## C. The Covenant Ratified

24 To Moses he had said, "Come up to Yahweh, yourself and Aaron, Nadab and Abihu, and seventy of the elders of Israel and bow down in worship at a distance. Moses alone must approach Yahweh; the others must not, nor must the people go up with him."

Moses went and told the people all the commands of Yahweh and all the ordinances. In answer, all the people said with one voice, "We will observe all the com-

---

[6]A Canaanite custom.

[7]*Stelae,* stones or pillars with a phallic significance in the Canaanite cult.

[8]The Arabian desert and the river Euphrates. The boundaries mentioned are those of Solomon's kingdom.

mands that Yahweh has decreed." Moses put all the commands of Yahweh into writing, and early next morning he built an alter at the foot of the mountain, with twelve standing-stones for the twelve tribes of Israel. Then he directed certain young Israelites to offer holocausts and to immolate bullocks to Yahweh as communion sacrifices. Half of the blood Moses took up and put into basins, the other half he cast on the altar. And taking the Book of the Covenant he read it to the listening people, and they said, "We will observe all that Yahweh has decreed; we will obey." Then Moses took the blood and cast it towards the people. "This" he said "is the blood of the Covenant that Yahweh has made with you, containing all these rules."

Moses went up with Aaron, Nadab and Abihu, and seventy elders of Israel. They saw the God of Israel beneath whose feet there was, it seemed, a sapphire pavement pure as the heavens themselves. He laid no hand on these notables of the sons of Israel: they gazed on God. They ate and they drank.

***Moses on the Mountain*** Yahweh said to Moses, "Come up to me on the mountain and stay there while I give you the stone tablets—the law and the commandments—that I have written for their instruction." Accordingly Moses rose, he and his servant Joshua, and they went up the mountain of God. To the elders he had said, "Wait here for us until we come back to you. You have Aaron and Hur with you; if anyone has a difference to settle, let him go to them." And Moses went up the mountain.

The cloud covered the mountain, and the glory of Yahweh settled on the mountain of Sinai; for six days the cloud covered it, and on the seventh day Yahweh called to Moses from inside the cloud. To the eyes of the sons of Israel the glory of Yahweh seemed like a devouring fire on the mountain top. Moses went right into the cloud. He went up the mountain, and stayed there for forty days and forty nights.

### ■ Discussion Questions

1. What does God mean by his "covenant," and what is its significance for the Hebrew people?
2. What do the Ten Commandments and the other laws delineated here reveal about the Hebrews' way of life?
3. How does the book of Exodus cast light on the development of Hebrew monotheism?

## 3.
## *Inscription Honoring Cyrus, King of Persia*
**r. c. 557–530 B.C.E.**

*The Persian king Cyrus founded the third in a series of powerful kingdoms that emerged from the shadows of the Dark Age in the Near East. Following the example of his Babylonian and Assyrian counterparts, Cyrus embraced imperial monarchy as a model of government while striving to expand his wealth and territorial holdings. The inscription that follows, etched originally on a clay barrel, recounts a pivotal event in Cyrus's reign, his conquest of Babylon in 539 B.C.E. The inscription also exposes the foundations of Cyrus's success: military might, cultural tolerance, and the belief in his divine right to rule. Following his lead, his successors built an even more formidable empire that threatened everything in its path, including the Greek city-states.*

(one line destroyed)
. . . [r]ims (of the world) . . . a weakling has been installed as the *enû*[1] of his country; [the correct images of the gods he removed from their thrones, imi]tations he ordered to place upon them. A replica of the temple Esagila he has . . . for Ur and the other sacred cities inappropriate rituals . . . daily he did blabber [incorrect prayers]. He (furthermore) interrupted in a fiendish way the regular offerings, he did . . . he established within the sacred cities. The worship of Marduk, the king of the gods, he [chang]ed into abomination, daily he used to do evil against his (i.e., Marduk's) city. . . . He [tormented] its [inhabitant]s with corvé-work (lit.: a yoke) without relief, he ruined them all.

Upon their complaints the lord of the gods became terribly angry and [he departed from] their region, (also) the (other) gods living among them left their mansions, wroth that he had brought (them) into Babylon. (But) Marduk [who does care for] . . . on account of (the fact that) the sanctuaries of all their settlements were in ruins and the inhabitants of Sumer and Akkad had become like (living) dead, turned back (his countenance) [his] an[ger] [abated] and he had mercy (upon them). He scanned and looked (through) all the countries, searching for a righteous ruler willing to lead him (i.e., Marduk) (in the annual procession). (Then) he pronounced the name of Cyrus, king of Anshan,[2] declared him (lit.: pronounced [his] name) to be(come) the ruler of all the world. He made the Guti country and all the Manda-hordes bow in submission to his (i.e., Cyrus') feet. And he (Cyrus) did always endeavour to treat according to justice the black-headed whom he (Marduk) has made him conquer. Marduk, the great lord, a protector of his people/worshipers, beheld with pleasure his (i.e., Cyrus') good deeds and his upright mind (lit.: heart) (and therefore) ordered him to march against his city Babylon. He made him set out on the road to Babylon going at his side like a real friend. His widespread troops—their number, like that of the water of a river,

---

From James B. Pritchard, ed., *Ancient Near Eastern Texts Relating to the Old Testament,* 3d ed. (Princeton: Princeton University Press, 1969), 315–16.

[1]The old Sumerian title appears here in a context that seems to indicate that the primitive concept concerning the intimate connection between the physical vitality of the ruler and the prosperity of the country was still valid in the political speculations of the Babylonian clergy.

[2]Persia.

could not be established—strolled along, their weapons packed away. Without any battle, he made him enter his town Babylon, sparing Babylon any calamity. He delivered into his (i.e., Cyrus') hands Nabonidus, the king who did not worship him (i.e., Marduk). All the inhabitants of Babylon as well as of the entire country of Sumer and Akkad, princes and governors (included), bowed to him (Cyrus) and kissed his feet, jubilant that he (had received) the kingship, and with shining faces. Happily they greeted him as a master through whose help they had come (again) to life from death (and) had all been spared damage and disaster, and they worshiped his (very) name.

I am Cyrus, king of the world, great king, legitimate king, king of Babylon, king of Sumer and Akkad, king of the four rims (of the earth), son of Cambyses, great king, king of Anshan, grandson of Cyrus, great king, king of Anshan, descendant of Teipes, great king, king of Anshan, of a family (which) always (exercised) kingship; whose rule Bel and Nebo love, whom they want as king to please their hearts.

When I entered Babylon as a friend and (when) I established the seat of the government in the palace of the ruler under jubilation and rejoicing, Marduk, the great lord, [induced] the magnanimous inhabitants of Babylon [to love me], and I was daily endeavouring to worship him. My numerous troops walked around in Babylon in peace, I did not allow anybody to terrorize (any place) of the [country of Sumer] and Akkad. I strove for peace in Babylon and in all his (other) sacred cities. As to the inhabitants of Babylon, [who] against the will of the gods [had/were . . . , I abolished] the corvé (lit.: yoke) which was against their (social) standing. I brought relief to their dilapidated housing, putting (thus) an end to their (main) complaints. Marduk, the great lord, was well pleased with my deeds and sent friendly blessings to myself, Cyrus, the king who worships him, to Cambyses, my son, the offspring of [my] loins, as well as to all my troops, and we all [praised] his great [godhead] joyously, standing before him in peace.

All the kings of the entire world from the Upper to the Lower Sea, those who are seated in throne rooms, (those who) live in other [types of buildings as well as] all the kings of the West land living in tents, brought their heavy tributes and kissed my feet in Babylon. (As to the region) from . . . as far as Ashur and Susa, Agade, Eshnunna, the towns Zamban, Me-Turnu, Der as well as the region of the Gutians, I returned to (these) sacred cities on the other side of the Tigris, the sanctuaries of which have been ruins for a long time, the images which (used) to live therein and established for them permanent sanctuaries. I (also) gathered all their (former) inhabitants and returned (to them) their habitations. Furthermore, I resettled upon the command of Marduk, the great lord, all the gods of Sumer and Akkad whom Nabonidus has brought into Babylon to the anger of the lord of the gods, unharmed, in their (former) chapels, the places which make them happy.

May all the gods whom I have resettled in their sacred cities ask daily Bel and Nebo for a long life for me and may they recommend me (to him); to Marduk, my lord, they may say this: "Cyrus, the king who worships you, and Cambyses, his son, . . ." . . . all of them I settled in a peaceful place . . . ducks and doves, . . . I endeavored to fortify/repair their dwelling places.

## ■ Discussion Questions

1. According to the inscription, why did Cyrus conquer Babylon? What does this reveal about the relationship between political and religious beliefs at the time?
2. How did the residents of the city and the neighboring regions respond to the Persian conquest, and why?
3. What specific examples does the inscription provide of Cyrus's religious tolerance?
4. What might have been the purpose of this inscription, and who was its intended audience?

# 4.
# Tyrtaeus of Sparta and Solon of Athens
## *Poems*
### Seventh–Sixth Centuries B.C.E.

*Among the most remarkable products of Greece's recovery from its Dark Age was the creation of a new social and political entity, the city-state. These poems elucidate the values shaping two of these communities, Sparta and Athens. The author of the first, Tyrtaeus of Sparta (originally from Athens, according to some ancient sources), was active when Sparta launched the Second Messenian War in the mid-sixth century* B.C.E. *His poem reveals the preeminent importance of military glory to the Spartans' communal identity. The author of the second work, the Athenian statesman Solon, emphasizes shared justice as the ideal basis of society. Democratic reforms instituted in the late sixth century* B.C.E. *transformed his vision into reality. Both poems are written in the elegiac meter, a style often used at the time to instruct the public.*

### TYRTAEUS

It is a beautiful thing when a good man falls
    and dies fighting for his country.
The worst pain is leaving one's city and fertile
    fields for the life of a beggar,
wandering with mother, old father, little
    children, and wedded wife.
The man beaten by need and odious poverty
    is detested everywhere he goes,
a disgrace to his family and noble appearance, trailed
    by every dishonor and evil.

---

From *Early Greek Lyric Poetry,* trans. David Mulroy (Ann Arbor: University of Michigan Press, 1992), 48–49, 68–69.

If no one takes care of the wanderer or gives him
honor, respect, or pity,
we must fight to the death for our land and children, giving
no thought to lengthening life.
Fight in a stubborn, close array, my boys!
Never waver or retreat!
Feel your anger swell. There is no place
in combat for love of life.
Older soldiers, whose knees are not so light,
need you to stand and protect them.
An aging warrior cut down in the vanguard of battle
disgraces the young. His head
is white, his beard is grey, and now he is spilling
his powerful spirit in dust,
naked, clutching his bloody groin: a sight
for shame and anger. But youthful
warriors always look good, until the blossom
withers. Men gape
at them in life and women sigh, and dying
in combat they are handsome still.
Now is the time for a man to stand, planting
his feet and biting his lip.

## Solon

Our city will never perish by decree of Zeus
or whim of the immortals; such
is the great-hearted protector, child of thunder, who holds
her hands over us: Athena.
But by thoughtless devotion to money, the citizens are willing
to destroy our great city.
Our leaders' minds are unjust; soon they will suffer
The pangs of great arrogance.
They cannot control their greed and enjoy the cheerful
feast at hand in peace . . .[1]
Their wealth depends on crime. . . .
They seize and steal at random
without regard for the holy, the public good,
or the sacred foundations of Justice,
who is silent but knows present and past, and comes
for full retribution in time.
The deadly infection spreads throughout the city,
rushing it into slavery,

[1]Fragment of text ends at this point. [Ed.]

which wakens internal strife and war that kills
so many beautiful youths.
Malicious conspiracies easily ruin a city,
though the people love it dearly.
These are the evils stalking the people: many
impoverished leave for foreign
soil, bound and sold in chains of disgrace.
The public evil visits every home;
undeterred by courtyard gates,
it leaps the high hedge and finds its man,
though he runs to his bedroom to hide.
My heart bids me to teach the Athenians that lawless
behavior is the bane of a city,
but respect for law spreads order and beauty;
it shackles the legs of the unjust,
smooths and moderates, diminishes arrogance and withers
delusion's burgeoning blossoms;
it straightens crooked judgments, humbles pride,
halts partisanship and the anger
born of fraction. Everything righteous and wise
depends on respect for the law.

### ■ Discussion Questions

1. What does Tyrtaeus reveal about the values and conduct that Spartan warriors were expected to embody?
2. How does Tyrtaeus describe warriors who do not live up to these expectations? What do his criticisms reveal about Spartan culture?
3. Why does Solon think Athenian citizens pose a threat to the polis?
4. What message does Solon seek to convey to Athenian citizens in this poem?

## 5.
## Sappho of Lesbos
## *Poems*
### Sixth Century B.C.E.

*The poetry of Sappho of Lesbos offers a woman's voice emanating from Greece during the Archaic Age. While many claims have been made about the poet and her sexuality, her poetry provides the only direct record of her life and literary legacy. Despite their fragmentary form, the rhythm of her poems, their use of the first person, and*

From Mary R. Lefkowitz and Maureen B. Fant, eds., *Women's Life in Greece and Rome,* 2d ed. (Baltimore: Johns Hopkins University Press, 1992), 2–4.

*their emphasis on the personal reflect the cultural innovations characteristic of the period. The fact that so few female voices survive from ancient Greece, which like many ancient societies was male dominated, further enhances Sappho's importance to the historical record. Her poems were revered throughout the ancient world, and they established an influential precedent for later lyric poets.*

## To Aphrodite (Fr. 1. G)

Aphrodite on your intricate throne, immortal, daughter of Zeus, weaver of plots, I beg you, do not tame me with pain or my heart with anguish

but come here, as once before when I asked you, you heard my words from afar and listened, and left your father's golden house and came

you yoked your chariot, and lovely swift sparrows brought you, fast whirling over the dark earth from heaven through the midst of the bright air

and soon they arrived. And you, O blessed goddess, smiled with your immortal face and asked what was wrong with me, and why did I call now,

and what did I most want in my maddened heart to have for myself. "Whom now am I to persuade to your love, who, Sappho, has done you wrong? For if she flees, soon she'll pursue you, and if she won't take gifts, soon she'll give them, and if she won't love, soon she will love you, even if she doesn't want to."

Come to me now again, release me from my cruel anxiety, accomplish all that my heart wants accomplished. You yourself join my battle.

## When I Look at You (Fr. 31. G)

The man seems to me strong as a god, the man who sits across from you and listens to your sweet talk nearby

and your lovely laughter—which, when I hear it, strikes fear in the heart in my breast. For whenever I glance at you, it seems that I can say nothing at all

but my tongue is broken in silence, and that instant a light fire rushes beneath my skin, I can no longer see anything in my eyes and my ears are thundering,

and cold sweat pours down me, and shuddering grasps me all over, and I am greener than grass, and I seem to myself to be little short of death

But all is endurable, since even a poor man . . . [1]

[1]Fragment of text ends at this point. [Ed.]

## Anactoria (Fr. 16. G)

Some would say an army of cavalry, others of infantry, others of ships, is the fairest thing on the dark earth, but I say it's whatever you're in love with

It's completely easy to make this clear to everyone, for Helen, who far surpassed other people in beauty, left behind the most aristocratic

of husbands and went to Troy. She sailed away, and did not remember at all her daughter or her beloved parents, but [Aphrodite] took her aside

*(3 lines missing)* which makes me remember Anactoria who is no longer near,

her lovely step and the brilliant glancing of her face I would rather see than the Lydians' chariots or their infantry fighting in all their armour.

## Parting (Fr. 94. G)

"The truth is, I wish I were dead." She left me, weeping often, and she said this, "Oh what a cruel fate is ours, Sappho, yes, I leave you against my will."

And I answered her: "Farewell, go and remember me, for you know how we cared for you.

"If you do remember, I want to remind you . . . and were happy . . . of violets . . . you set beside me and with woven garlands made of flowers around your soft neck

"and with perfume, royal, rich . . . you anointed yourself and on soft beds you would drive out your passion

"and then . . . sanctuary . . . was . . . from which we were away." . . .

## Remembering the Girl Atthis (Fr. 96. G)

. . . you, like a goddess renowned, in your song she took most joy. Now she is unique among Lydian women, as the moon once the sun sets

stands out among all the stars, and her light grasps both the salt sea and the flowering meadows

and fair dew flows forth, and soft roses and chervil and fragrant melilot bloom.

Often as she goes out, she remembers gentle Atthis, and her tender heart is eaten by grief . . .

## THE WEDDING OF HECTOR AND ANDROMACHE (FR. 44. G)

". . . Hector and his comrades are bringing a girl with dark eyes from holy Thebes and . . . Plakia, soft Andromache in their ships across the salt sea; many curved bands of gold and purple robes and intricate playthings, countless silver cups and ivory." So he spoke. And [Hector's] beloved father quickly got up, and the story went out to his friends throughout the city [of Troy] with its wide dancing places. Then the Trojan women led mules to wheeled carts and a crowd of women came out, and also of . . . -ankled maidens, and separately the daughters of Priam and men brought horses with chariots *(unknown number of lines missing)* . . . and the sweet-sounding *aulos* was mixed with the noise of castanets, and the maidens sang a sacred song and the holy sound reached heaven . . . bowls and goblets . . . perfume and cassia and incense were mixed and all the older women shouted out, and all the men cried out a fair loud song, calling on Paean, the far-shooter, the lyre player, to sing of Hector and Andromache, who were like gods. . . .

### ■ Discussion Questions

1. How might Sappho's status as a woman have shaped the content of her poetry?
2. What are Sappho's primary interests and concerns as a poet?
3. From reading these poems, what, if anything, can you learn about Sappho's life and/or the broader historical context in which she lived?

### ■ Comparative Questions

1. Despite their common ground, how do the laws delineated in the first two documents differ, and why?
2. Based on Cyrus's inscription and Solon's poem, how did Near Eastern and Greek social and political organizations differ?
3. What are the similarities between the Spartan and Persian cultures as revealed in Cyrus's inscription and Tyrtaeus's poem?
4. How would you compare the content and function of the poems by Tyrtaeus, Solon, and Sappho? What does this comparison suggest about the differences between the status of men and women in Greek society?
5. Based on evidence from all five sources, what characteristics defined political, social, and religious life in ancient civilizations? If and how did these characteristics change as the eastern Mediterranean emerged from its "Dark Age" in 1000 B.C.E.?

Chapter

# 2

# The Greek Golden Age, c. 500–400 B.C.E.

IN THE FIFTH CENTURY B.C.E., Athens entered a period of extraordinary prosperity and achievement. Its economy was booming and its culture flourishing while at the same time its male citizens developed the first democracy in history. Under their guidance, Athens became the leader of the Greek world. The first two documents explain the dynamism of the times in a variety of related arenas, all of which attest to Athens's enduring legacy to Western civilization. They also reveal that even as innovation fueled the city-state's rise to glory, the pull of traditional beliefs remained strong. Such beliefs were especially influential in demarcating the boundaries of the lives of Athenian women. As the last three documents demonstrate, a woman's status was inextricably linked to her roles as wife and mother. To put either in jeopardy threatened the very foundations of Athenian society.

## 1.
## Thucydides
## *The Funeral Oration of Pericles*
### 429 B.C.E.

*The most renowned Athenian politician in his day, Pericles (c. 495–429 B.C.E.) contributed greatly to the brilliance of Athens's Golden Age. Not only did he help to build the city-state's empire abroad, but he also devoted much of his career to strengthening democracy at home. In his* History of the Peloponnesian War, *Thucydides brings Pericles to life in a description of a speech he delivered to honor those who had died during the first year of fighting. The Peloponnesian War pitted Athens against its authoritarian rival, Sparta, from 431 to 404 B.C.E., ending ultimately with Athens's defeat. Pericles' words reveal, however, that at the time of his speech, Athens was still brimming with confidence in the greatness of its people and government.*

From Thucydides, *The Peloponnesian Wars,* trans. Benjamin Jowett (New York: Twayne Publishers, 1963), 65–72.

During the same winter, in accordance with traditional custom, the funeral of those who first fell in this war was celebrated by the Athenians at the public charge. . . .

Over the first who were buried, Pericles was chosen to speak. At the fitting moment he advanced from the sepulcher to a lofty stage, which had been erected in order that he might be heard as far away as possible by the crowd, and spoke somewhat as follows: . . .

"I will speak of our ancestors first, for it is right and seemly that on such an occasion as this we should also render this honor to their memory. Men of the same stock, ever dwelling in this land, in successive generations to this very day, by their valor handed it down as a free land. They are worthy of praise, and still more are our fathers, who added to their inheritance, and after many a struggle bequeathed to us, their sons, the great empire we possess. . . . But before I praise the dead, I shall first proceed to show by what kind of practices we attained to our position, and under what kind of institutions and manner of life our empire became great. For I conceive that it would not be unsuited to the occasion that this should be told, and that this whole assembly of citizens and foreigners may profitably listen to it.

"Our institutions do not emulate the laws of others. We do not copy our neighbors: rather, we are an example to them. Our system is called a democracy, for it respects the majority and not the few; but while the law secures equality to all alike in their private disputes, the claim of excellence is also recognized; and when a citizen is in any way distinguished, he is generally preferred to the public service, not in rotation, but for merit. Nor again is there any bar in poverty and obscurity of rank to a man who can do the state some service. It is as free men that we conduct our public life, and in our daily occupations we avoid mutual suspicions; we are not angry with our neighbor if he does what he likes; we do not put on sour looks at him which, though harmless, are not pleasant. While we give no offense in our private intercourse, in our public acts we are prevented from doing wrong by fear; we respect the authorities and the laws, especially those which are ordained for the protection of the injured as well as those unwritten laws which bring upon the transgressor admitted dishonor.

"Furthermore, none have provided more relaxations for the spirit from toil; we have regular games and sacrifices throughout the year; our homes are furnished with elegance; and the delight which we daily feel in all these things banishes melancholy. Because of the greatness of our city, the fruits of the whole earth flow in upon us so that we enjoy the goods of other countries as freely as our own.

"Then, again, in military training we are superior to our adversaries, as I shall show. Our city is thrown open to the world, and we never expel a foreigner or prevent him from seeing or learning anything which, if not concealed, it might profit an enemy to see. We rely not so much upon preparations or stratagems, as upon our own courage in action. And in the matter of education, whereas from early youth they are always undergoing laborious exercises which are to make them brave, we live at ease and yet are equally ready to face perils to which our strength is equal. And here is the evidence. The Lacedaemonians march against our land not by themselves, but with all their allies: we invade a neighbor's country alone;

and although our opponents are fighting for their homes and we are on a foreign soil, we seldom have any difficulty in overcoming them. . . .

"Nor is this the only cause for marveling at our city. We are lovers of beauty without extravagance and of learning without loss of vigor. Wealth we employ less for talk and ostentation than when there is a real use for it. To avow poverty with us is no disgrace: the true disgrace is in doing nothing to avoid it. The same persons attend at once to the concerns of their households and of the city, and men of diverse employments have a very fair idea of politics. If a man takes no interest in public affairs, we alone do not commend him as quiet but condemn him as useless; and if few of us are originators, we are all sound judges of a policy. In our opinion action does not suffer from discussion but, rather, from the want of that instruction which is gained by discussion preparatory to the action required. For we have an exceptional gift of acting with audacity after calculating the prospects of our enterprises, whereas other men are bold from ignorance but hesitate upon reflection. But it would be right to esteem those men bravest in spirit who have the clearest understanding of the pains and pleasures of life and do not on that account shrink from danger. . . .

"This is why I have dwelt upon the greatness of Athens, showing you that we are contending for a higher prize than those who enjoy no like advantages, and establishing by manifest proof the merit of these men whom I am now commemorating. Their loftiest praise has been already spoken; for in descanting on the city, I have honored the qualities which earned renown for them and for men such as they. And of how few Hellenes can it be said as of them, that their deeds matched their fame! In my belief an end such as theirs proves a man's worth; it is at once its first revelation and final seal. For even those who come short in other ways may justly plead the valor with which they have fought for their country; they have blotted out evil with good, and their public services have outweighed the harm they have done in their private actions. . . . And when the moment for fighting came, they held it nobler to suffer death than to yield and save their lives; it was the report of dishonor from which they fled, but on the battlefield their feet stood fast; and while for a moment they were in the hands of fortune, at the height, less of terror than of glory, they departed.

"Such was the conduct of these men; they were worthy of Athens. The rest of us must pray for a safer issue to our courage and yet disdain to show any less daring towards our enemies. We must not consider only what words can be uttered on the utility of such a spirit. Anyone might discourse to you at length on all the advantages of resisting the enemy bravely, but you know them just as well yourselves. It is better that you should actually gaze day by day on the power of the city until you are filled with the love of her; and when you are convinced of her greatness, reflect that it was acquired by men of daring who knew their duty and feared dishonor in the hour of action, men who if they ever failed in an enterprise, even then disdained to deprive the city of their prowess but offered themselves up as the finest contribution to the common cause. . . .

"To you who are the sons and brothers of the departed, I see that the struggle to emulate them will be arduous. For all men praise the dead; and, however preeminent your virtue may be, you would hardly be thought their equals, but somewhat inferior. The living have their rivals and detractors; but when a man is out of the way, the honor and good will which he receives is uncontested. And, if I am also to speak of womanly virtues to those of you who will now be widows, let me sum them up in one short admonition: 'Your glory will be great if you show no more than the infirmities of your nature, a glory that consists in being least the subjects of report among men, for good or evil.'

"I have spoken in obedience to the law, making use of such fitting words as I had. The tribute of deeds has been paid in part, for the dead have been honorably interred; it remains only that their children shall be maintained at the public charge until they are grown up: this is the solid prize with which, as with a garland, Athens crowns these men and those left behind after such contests. For where the rewards of virtue are greatest, there men do the greatest services to their cities. And now, when you have duly lamented, everyone his own dead, you may depart."

### ■ Discussion Questions

1. According to Pericles, what sets Athens apart from its neighbors and adversaries?
2. As described here, what are the guiding principles of Athenian democracy?
3. How does Pericles characterize his fellow Athenians and their contributions to the city's glory?
4. What obligations does Pericles believe Athenian citizens have to the state?

## 2.
## Plato
## *The Apology of Socrates*
### 399 B.C.E.

*Political innovation was not the only distinctive feature of fifth-century* B.C.E. *Athens. Socrates (469–399* B.C.E.*) was a famous philosopher of the day, and his views on ethics and morality challenged conventional values while steering Greek philosophy in new directions. Unlike the sophists, Socrates offered no classes and did not write his ideas down. He relied instead on conversation and critical questioning to draw people into his way of thinking. In this document, we hear Socrates speaking for himself before a jury as described by his pupil Plato. At the time, Socrates was on trial for impiety, and he spoke these words to convince his fellow citizens of his innocence. Sadly, his efforts were in vain; he was convicted and sentenced to death.*

---

From J. D. Kaplan, ed., *Dialogues of Plato,* trans. Benjamin Jowett (New York: Pocket Books, 1950), 5–14, 21–24, 39–40.

How you, O Athenians, have been affected by my accusers, I cannot tell; but I know that they almost made me forget who I was—so persuasively did they speak; and yet they have hardly uttered a word of truth. But of the many falsehoods told by them, there was one which quite amazed me;—I mean when they said that you should be upon your guard and not allow yourselves to be deceived by the force of my eloquence. To say this, when they were certain to be detected as soon as I opened my lips and proved myself to be anything but a great speaker, did indeed appear to me most shameless—unless by the force of eloquence they mean the force of truth; for if such is their meaning, I admit that I am eloquent. But in how different a way from theirs! Well, as I was saying, they have scarcely spoken the truth at all; but from me you shall hear the whole truth: not, however, delivered after their manner in a set oration duly ornamented with words and phrases. No, by heaven! but I shall use the words and arguments which occur to me at the moment; for I am confident in the justice of my cause. . . .

I will begin at the beginning, and ask what is the accusation which has given rise to the slander of me, and in fact has encouraged Meletus to prefer this charge against me. Well, what do the slanderers say? They shall be my prosecutors, and I will sum up their words in an affidavit: "Socrates is an evildoer, and a curious person, who searches into things under the earth and in heaven, and he makes the worse appear the better cause; and he teaches the aforesaid doctrines to others." Such is the nature of the accusation: it is just what you have yourselves seen in the comedy of Aristophanes, who has introduced a man whom he calls Socrates, going about and saying that he walks in air, and talking a deal of nonsense concerning matters of which I do not pretend to know either much or little—not that I mean to speak disparagingly of any one who is a student of natural philosophy. I should be very sorry if Meletus could bring so grave a charge against me. But the simple truth is, O Athenians, that I have nothing to do with physical speculations. Very many of those here present are witnesses to the truth of this, and to them I appeal. . . .

Men of Athens, this reputation of mine has come of a certain sort of wisdom which I possess. If you ask me what kind of wisdom, I reply, wisdom such as may perhaps be attained by man, for to that extent I am inclined to believe that I am wise; whereas the persons of whom I was speaking have a superhuman wisdom, which I may fail to describe, because I have it not myself; and he who says that I have, speaks falsely, and is taking away my character. And here, O men of Athens, I must beg you not to interrupt me, even if I seem to say something extravagant. For the word which I will speak is not mine. I will refer you to a witness who is worthy of credit; that witness shall be the God of Delphi—he will tell you about my wisdom, if I have any, and of what sort it is. You must have known Chaerephon; he was early a friend of mine, and also a friend of yours, for he shared in the recent exile of the people, and returned with you. Well, Chaerephon, as you know, was very impetuous in all his doings, and he went to Delphi and boldly asked the oracle to tell him whether—as I was saying, I must beg you not to interrupt—he asked the oracle to tell him whether any one was wiser than I was, and the Pythian prophetess answered, that there was no man wiser. Chaerephon is dead himself; but his brother, who is in court, will confirm the truth of what I am saying.

Why do I mention this? Because I am going to explain to you why I have such an evil name. When I heard the answer, I said to myself, What can the God mean? and what is the interpretation of his riddle? for I know that I have no wisdom, small or great. What then can he mean when he says that I am the wisest of men? And yet he is a god, and cannot lie; that would be against his nature. After long consideration, I thought of a method of trying the question. I reflected that if I could only find a man wiser than myself, then I might go to the god with a refutation in my hand. I should say to him, "Here is a man who is wiser than I am; but you said that I was the wisest." Accordingly I went to one who had the reputation of wisdom, and observed him—his name I need not mention; he was a politician whom I selected for examination—and the result was as follows: When I began to talk with him, I could not help thinking that he was not really wise, although he was thought wise by many, and still wiser by himself; and thereupon I tried to explain to him that he thought himself wise, but was not really wise; and the consequence was that he hated me, and his enmity was shared by several who were present and heard me. So I left him, saying to myself, as I went away: Well, although I do not suppose that either of us knows anything really beautiful and good, I am better off than he is,—for he knows nothing, and thinks that he knows; I neither know nor think that I know. In this latter particular, then, I seem to have slightly the advantage of him. Then I went to another who had still higher pretensions to wisdom, and my conclusion was exactly the same. Whereupon I made another enemy of him, and of many others besides him.

Then I went to one man after another, being not unconscious of the enmity which I provoked, and I lamented and feared this: but necessity was laid upon me,—the word of God, I thought, ought to be considered first. And I said to myself, Go I must to all who appear to know, and find out the meaning of the oracle. And I swear to you, Athenians, by the dog I swear!—for I must tell you the truth—the result of my mission was just this: I found that the men most in repute were all but the most foolish; and that others less esteemed were really wiser and better. I will tell you the tale of my wanderings and of the "Herculean" labors, as I may call them, which I endured only to find at last the oracle irrefutable. After the politicians, I went to the poets; tragic, dithyrambic, and all sorts. And there, I said to myself, you will be instantly detected; now you will find out that you are more ignorant than they are. Accordingly I took them some of the most elaborate passages in their own writings, and asked what was the meaning of them—thinking that they would teach me something. Will you believe me? I am almost ashamed to confess the truth, but I must say that there is hardly a person present who would not have talked better about their poetry than they did themselves. Then I knew that not by wisdom do poets write poetry, but by a sort of genius and inspiration; they are like diviners or soothsayers who also say many fine things, but do not understand the meaning of them. The poets appeared to me to be much in the same case; and I further observed that upon the strength of their poetry they believed themselves to be the wisest of men in other things in which they were not wise. So I departed, conceiving myself to be superior to them for the same reason that I was superior to the politicians.

At last I went to the artisans, I was conscious that I knew nothing at all, as I may say, and I was sure that they knew many fine things; and here I was not mistaken, for they did know many things of which I was ignorant, and in this they certainly were wiser than I was. But I observed that even the good artisans fell into the same error as the poets;—because they were good workmen they thought that they also knew all sorts of high matters, and this defect in them overshadowed their wisdom; and therefore I asked myself on behalf of the oracle, whether I would like to be as I was, neither having their knowledge nor their ignorance, or like them in both; and I made answer to myself and to the oracle that I was better off as I was.

This inquisition has led to my having many enemies of the worst and most dangerous kind, and has given occasion also to many calumnies. And I am called wise, for my hearers always imagine that I myself possess the wisdom which I find wanting in others: but the truth is, O men of Athens, that God only is wise; and by his answer he intends to show that the wisdom of men is worth little or nothing; he is not speaking of Socrates, he is only using my name by way of illustration, as if he said, He, O men, is the wisest, who, like Socrates, knows that his wisdom is in truth worth nothing. And so I go about the world obedient to the god, and search and make enquiry into the wisdom of any one, whether citizen or stranger, who appears to be wise; and if he is not wise, then in vindication of the oracle I show him that he is not wise; and my occupation quite absorbs me, and I have no time to give either to any public matter of interest or to any concern of my own, but I am in utter poverty by reason of my devotion to the god.

There is another thing:—young men of the richer classes, who have not much to do, come about me of their own accord; they like to hear the pretenders examined, and they often imitate me, and proceed to examine others; there are plenty of persons, as they quickly discover, who think that they know something, but really know little or nothing; and then those who are examined by them instead of being angry with themselves are angry with me: This confounded Socrates, they say; this villainous misleader of youth!—and then if somebody asks them, Why, what evil does he practice or teach? they do not know, and cannot tell; but in order that they may not appear to be at a loss, they repeat the ready-made charges which are used against all philosophers about teaching things up in the clouds and under the earth, and having no gods, and making the worse appear the better cause; for they do not like to confess that their pretence of knowledge has been detected—which is the truth; and as they are numerous and ambitious and energetic, and are drawn up in battle array and have persuasive tongues, they have filled your ears with their loud and inveterate calumnies. And this is the reason why my three accusers, Meletus and Anytus and Lycon, have set upon me; Meletus, who has a quarrel with me on behalf of the poets; Anytus, on behalf of the craftsmen and politicians; Lycon, on behalf of the rhetoricians: and, as I said at the beginning, I cannot expect to get rid of such a mass of calumny all in a moment. And this, O men of Athens, is the truth and the whole truth; I have concealed nothing, I have dissembled nothing. And yet, I know that my plainness of speech makes them hate me, and what is their hatred but a proof that I am speaking the truth? Hence has arisen the prejudice against me; and this is the reason of it....

Some one will say: And are you not ashamed, Socrates, of a course of life which is likely to bring you to an untimely end? To him I may fairly answer: There you are mistaken: a man who is good for anything ought not to calculate the chance of living or dying; he ought only to consider whether in doing anything he is doing right or wrong—acting the part of a good man or of a bad....

For the fear of death is indeed the pretence of wisdom, and not real wisdom, being a pretence of knowing the unknown; and no one knows whether death, which men in their fear apprehend to be the greatest evil, may not be the greatest good. Is not this ignorance of a disgraceful sort, the ignorance which is the conceit that a man knows what he does not know? And in this respect only I believe myself to differ from men in general, and may perhaps claim to be wiser than they are:—that whereas I know but little of the world below, I do not suppose that I know: but I do know that injustice and disobedience to a better, whether God or man, is evil and dishonorable, and I will never fear or avoid a possible good rather than a certain evil. And therefore if you let me go now, and are not convinced by Anytus, who said that since I had been prosecuted I must be put to death; (or if not that I ought never to have been prosecuted at all); and that if I escape now, your sons will all be utterly ruined by listening to my words—if you say to me, Socrates, this time we will not mind Anytus, and you shall be let off, but upon one condition, that you are not to enquire and speculate in this way any more, and that if you are caught doing so again you shall die;—if this was the condition on which you let me go, I should reply: Men of Athens, I honor and love you; but I shall obey God rather than you, and while I have life and strength I shall never cease from the practice and teaching of philosophy, exhorting any one whom I meet and saying to him after my manner: You, my friend,—a citizen of the great and mighty and wise city of Athens,—are you not ashamed of heaping up the greatest amount of money and honor and reputation, and caring so little about wisdom and truth and the greatest improvement of the soul, which you never regard or heed at all? And if the person with whom I am arguing, says: Yes, but I do care; then I do not leave him or let him go at once; but I proceed to interrogate and examine and cross-examine him, and if I think that he has no virtue in him, but only says that he has, I reproach him with undervaluing the greater, and overvaluing the less. And I shall repeat the same words to every one whom I meet, young and old, citizen and alien, but especially to the citizens, inasmuch as they are my brethren. For know that this is the command of God; and I believe that no greater good has ever happened in the State than my service to the God. For I do nothing but go about persuading you all, old and young alike, not to take thought for your persons or your properties, but first and chiefly to care about the greatest improvement of the soul. I tell you that virtue is not given by money, but that from virtue comes money and every other good of man, public as well as private. This is my teaching, and if this is the doctrine which corrupts the youth, I am a mischievous person. But if any one says that this is not my teaching, he is speaking an untruth. Wherefore, O men of Athens, I say to you, do as Anytus bids or not as

Anytus bids, and either acquit me or not; but whichever you do, understand that I shall never alter my ways, not even if I have to die many times. . . .

Wherefore, O judges, be of good cheer about death, and know of a certainty, that no evil can happen to a good man, either in life or after death. He and his are not neglected by the gods; nor has my own approaching end happened by mere chance. But I see clearly that the time had arrived when it was better for me to die and be released from trouble; wherefore the oracle gave no sign. For which reason, also, I am not angry with my condemners, or with my accusers; they have done me no harm, although they did not mean to do me any good; and for this I may gently blame them.

Still, I have a favor to ask of them. When my sons are grown up, I would ask you, O my friends, to punish them; and I would have you trouble them, as I have troubled you, if they seem to care about riches, or anything, more than about virtue; or if they pretend to be something when they are really nothing,—then reprove them, as I have reproved you, for not caring about that for which they ought to care, and thinking that they are something when they are really nothing. And if you do this, both I and my sons will have received justice at your hands.

The hour of departure has arrived, and we go our ways—I to die, and you to live. Which is better God only knows.

### ■ Discussion Questions

1. According to Socrates, what accusations have been levied against him, and why?
2. In refuting these accusations, what does Socrates reveal about his fundamental intellectual beliefs and methods?
3. Why do you think many of Socrates' contemporaries found his views so threatening?
4. What impressions do Socrates' words give you of him as a man?

## 3.
## Euphiletus
## *A Husband Speaks in His Own Defense*
### c. 400 B.C.E.

*In contrast to the trial of Socrates, that of an ordinary Athenian recounted next illuminates the more mundane aspects of life in fifth-century* B.C.E. *Athens. It also indicates that despite the momentous changes of the age, ancient traditions retained their grip on much of society, especially women. The testimony is that of a man*

---

From Kathleen Freeman, ed., *The Murder of Herodes and Other Trials from the Athenian Law Courts* (London: MacDonald & Co., 1946), 43–52.

*named Euphiletus who was put on trial for murdering his wife's lover. He presented the following arguments in his own defense, as prepared for him by the speech-writer Lysias (c. 440–380 B.C.E.). Although the outcome of the trial is unknown, Euphiletus's testimony opens a window onto domestic routines at the time and the ways in which they were expected to serve as the anchor of a woman's identity and her husband's honor.*

I would give a great deal, members of the jury, to find you, as judges of this case, taking the same attitude towards me as you would adopt towards your own behavior in similar circumstances. I am sure that if you felt about others in the same way as you did about yourselves, not one of you would fail to be angered by these deeds, and all of you would consider the punishment a small one for those guilty of such conduct.

Moreover, the same opinion would be found prevailing not only among you, but everywhere throughout Greece. This is the one crime for which, under any government, democratic or exclusive, equal satisfaction is granted to the meanest against the mightiest, so that the least of them receives the same justice as the most exalted. Such is the detestation, members of the jury, in which this outrage is held by all mankind.

Concerning the severity of the penalty, therefore, you are, I imagine, all of the same opinion: not one of you is so easy-going as to believe that those guilty of such great offenses should obtain pardon, or are deserving of a light penalty. What I have to prove, I take it, is just this: that Eratosthenes seduced my wife, and that in corrupting her he brought shame upon my children and outrage upon me, by entering my home; that there was no other enmity between him and me except this; and that I did not commit this act for the sake of money, in order to rise from poverty to wealth, nor for any other advantage except the satisfaction allowed by law.

I shall expound my case to you in full from the beginning, omitting nothing and telling the truth. In this alone lies my salvation, I imagine—if I can explain to you everything that happened.

Members of the jury: when I decided to marry and had brought a wife home, at first my attitude towards her was this: I did not wish to annoy her, but neither was she to have too much of her own way. I watched her as well as I could, and kept an eye on her as was proper. But later, after my child had been born, I came to trust her, and I handed all my possessions over to her, believing that this was the greatest possible proof of affection.

Well, members of the jury, in the beginning she was the best of women. She was a clever housewife, economical and exact in her management of everything. But then, my mother died; and her death has proved to be the source of all my troubles, because it was when my wife went to the funeral that this man Eratosthenes saw her; and as time went on, he was able to seduce her. He kept a look-out for our maid who goes to market; and approaching her with his suggestions, he succeeded in corrupting her mistress.

Now first of all, gentlemen, I must explain that I have a small house which is divided into two—the men's quarters and the women's—each having the same space, the women upstairs and the men downstairs.

After the birth of my child, his mother nursed him; but I did not want her to run the risk of going downstairs every time she had to give him a bath, so I myself took over the upper story, and let the women have the ground floor. And so it came about that by this time it was quite customary for my wife often to go downstairs and sleep with the child, so that she could give him the breast and stop him from crying.

This went on for a long while, and I had not the slightest suspicion. On the contrary, I was in such a fool's paradise that I believed my wife to be the chastest woman in all the city.

Time passed, gentlemen. One day, when I had come home unexpectedly from the country, after dinner, the child began crying and complaining. Actually it was the maid who was pinching him on purpose to make him behave so, because—as I found out later—this man was in the house.

Well, I told my wife to go and feed the child, to stop his crying. But at first she refused, pretending that she was so glad to see me back after my long absence. At last I began to get annoyed, and I insisted on her going.

"Oh, yes!" she said. "To leave *you* alone with the maid up here! You mauled her about before, when you were drunk!"

I laughed. She got up, went out, closed the door—pretending that it was a joke—and locked it. As for me, I thought no harm of all this, and I had not the slightest suspicion. I went to sleep, glad to do so after my journey from the country.

Towards morning, she returned and unlocked the door.

I asked her why the doors had been creaking during the night. She explained that the lamp beside the baby had gone out, and that she had then gone to get a light from the neighbors.

I said no more. I thought it really was so. But it did seem to me, members of the jury, that she had done up her face with cosmetics, in spite of the fact that her brother had died only a month before. Still, even so, I said nothing about it. I just went off, without a word.

After this, members of the jury, an interval elapsed, during which my injuries had progressed, leaving me far behind. Then, one day, I was approached by an old hag. She had been sent by a woman—Eratosthenes' previous mistress, as I found out later. This woman, furious because he no longer came to see her as before, had been on the look-out until she had discovered the reason. The old crone, therefore, had come and was lying in wait for me near my house.

"Euphiletus," she said, "please don't think that my approaching you is in any way due to a wish to interfere. The fact is, the man who is wronging you and your wife is an enemy of ours. Now if you catch the woman who does your shopping and works for you, and put her through an examination, you will discover all. The culprit," she added, "is Eratosthenes from Oea. Your wife is not the only one he has seduced — there are plenty of others. It's his profession."

With these words, members of the jury, she went off.

At once I was overwhelmed. Everything rushed into my mind, and I was filled with suspicion. I reflected how I had been locked into the bedroom. I remembered how on that night the middle and outer doors had creaked, a thing that had never happened before; and how I had had the idea that my wife's face was rouged. All these things rushed into my mind, and I was filled with suspicion.

I went back home, and told the servant to come with me to market. I took her instead to the house of one of my friends; and there I informed her that I had discovered all that was going on in my house.

"As for you," I said, "two courses are open to you: either to be flogged and sent to the tread-mill, and never be released from a life of utter misery; or to confess the whole truth and suffer no punishment, but win pardon from me for your wrong-doing. Tell me no lies. Speak the whole truth."

At first she tried denial, and told me that I could do as I pleased — she knew nothing. But when I named Eratosthenes to her face, and said that he was the man who had been visiting my wife, she was dumbfounded, thinking that I had found out everything exactly. And then at last, falling at my feet and exacting a promise from me that no harm should be done to her, she denounced the villain. She described how he had first approached her after the funeral, and then how in the end she had passed the message on, and in course of time my wife had been overpersuaded. She explained the way in which he had contrived to get into the house, and how when I was in the country my wife had gone to a religious service with this man's mother, and everything else that had happened. She recounted it all exactly.

When she had told all, I said:

"See to it that nobody gets to know of this; otherwise the promise I made you will not hold good. And furthermore, I expect you to show me this actually happening. I have no use for words. I want the *fact* to be exhibited, if it really is so."

She agreed to do this.

Four or five days then elapsed, as I shall prove to you by important evidence. But before I do so, I wish to narrate the events of the last day.

I had a friend and relative named Sôstratus. He was coming home from the country after sunset when I met him. I knew that as he had got back so late, he would not find any of his own people at home; so I asked him to dine with me. We went home to my place, and going upstairs to the upper story, we had dinner there. When he felt restored, he went off; and I went to bed.

Then, members of the jury, Eratosthenes made his entry; and the maid wakened me and told me that he was in the house.

I told her to watch the door; and going downstairs, I slipped out noiselessly.

I went to the houses of one man after another. Some I found at home; others,

I was told, were out of town. So collecting as many as I could of those who were there, I went back. We procured torches from the shop near by, and entered my house. The door had been left open by arrangement with the maid.

We forced the bedroom door. The first of us to enter saw him still lying beside my wife. Those who followed saw him standing naked on the bed.

I knocked him down, members of the jury, with one blow. I then twisted his hands behind his back and tied them. And then I asked him why he was committing this crime against me, of breaking into my house.

He answered that he admitted his guilt; but he begged and besought me not to kill him—to accept a money-payment instead.

But I replied:

"It is not I who shall be killing you, but the law of the State, which you, in transgressing, have valued less highly than your own pleasures. You have preferred to commit this great crime against my wife and my children, rather than to obey the law and be of decent behavior."

Thus, members of the jury, this man met the fate which the laws prescribe for wrong-doers of his kind.

Eratosthenes was not seized in the street and carried off, nor had he taken refuge at the altar, as the prosecution alleges. The facts do not admit of it: he was struck in the bedroom, he fell at once, and I bound his hands behind his back. There were so many present that he could not possibly escape through their midst, since he had neither steel nor wood nor any other weapon with which he could have defended himself against all those who had entered the room.

No, members of the jury: you know as well as I do how wrong-doers will not admit that their adversaries are speaking the truth, and attempt by lies and trickery of other kinds to excite the anger of the hearers against those whose acts are in accordance with Justice.

*(To the Clerk of the Court):*

Read the Law.

*(The Law of Solon is read, that an adulterer may be put to death by the man who catches him.)*

He made no denial, members of the jury. He admitted his guilt, and begged and implored that he should not be put to death, offering to pay compensation. But I would not accept his estimate. I preferred to accord a higher authority to the law of the State, and I took that satisfaction which you, because you thought it the most just, have decreed for those who commit such offenses.

Witnesses to the preceding, kindly step up.

*(The witnesses come to the front of the Court, and the Clerk reads their depositions. When the Clerk has finished reading, and the witnesses have agreed that the depositions are correct, the defendant again addresses the Clerk):*

Now please read this further law from the pillar of the Court of the Areopagus:

*(The Clerk reads another version of Solon's law, as recorded on the pillar of the Areopagus Court.)*

You hear, members of the jury, how it is expressly decreed by the Court of the Areopagus itself, which both traditionally and in your own day has been granted the right to try cases of murder, that no person shall be found guilty of murder who catches an adulterer with his wife and inflicts this punishment. The Lawgiver was so strongly convinced of the justice of these provisions in the case of married women, that he applied them also to concubines, who are of less importance. Yet obviously, if he had known of any greater punishment than this for cases where married women are concerned, he would have provided it. But in fact, as it was impossible for him to invent any more severe penalty for corruption of wives, he decided to provide the same punishment as in the case of concubines.

*(To the Clerk of the Court):*

Please read me this Law also.

*(The Clerk reads out further clauses from Solon's laws on rape.)*

You hear, members of the jury, how the Lawgiver ordains that if anyone debauch by force a free man or boy, the fine shall be double that decreed in the case of a slave. If anyone debauch a woman—in which case it is *permitted* to kill him—he shall be liable to the same fine. Thus, members of the jury, the Lawgiver considered violators deserving of a lesser penalty than seducers: for the latter he provided the death-penalty; for the former, the doubled fine. His idea was that those who use force are loathed by the persons violated, whereas those who have got their way by persuasion corrupt women's minds, in such a way as to make other men's wives more attached to themselves than to their husbands, so that the whole house is in their power, and it is uncertain who is the children's father, the husband or the lover. These considerations caused the Lawgiver to affix death as the penalty for seduction.

And so, members of the jury, in my case the laws not only hold me innocent, but actually order me to take this satisfaction; but it depends on you whether they are to be effective or of no moment. The reason, in my opinion, why all States lay down laws is in order that, whenever we are in doubt on any point, we can refer to these laws and find out our duty. And therefore it is the laws which in such cases enjoin upon the injured party to exact this penalty. I exhort you to show yourselves in agreement with them; otherwise you will be granting such impunity to adulterers that you will encourage even burglars to declare themselves adulterers, in the knowledge that if they allege this reason for their action and plead that this was their purpose in entering other men's houses, no one will lay a finger on them. They will all realize that they need not bother about the law on adultery, but need only fear your verdict, since this is the supreme authority in the State.

Consider, members of the jury, their accusation that it was I who on that day told the maid to fetch the young man. In my opinion, gentlemen, I should have been justified in using any means to catch the seducer of my wife. If there had been only words spoken and no actual offense, I should have been doing wrong; but when by that time they had gone to all lengths and he had often gained entry into my house, I consider that I should have been within my rights whatever means I employ to catch him. But observe that this allegation of the prosecution is also false. You can easily convince yourselves by considering the following:

I have already told you how Sôstratus, an intimate friend of mine, met me coming in from the country around sunset, and dined with me, and when he felt refreshed, went off. Now in the first place, gentlemen, ask yourselves whether, if on that night I had had designs on Eratosthenes, it would have been better for me that Sôstratus should dine elsewhere, or that I should take a guest home with me to dinner. Surely in the latter circumstances Eratosthenes would have been less inclined to venture into the house. Further, does it seem to you probable that I would have let my guest go, and been left alone, without company? Would I not rather have urged him to stay, so that he could help me to punish the adulterer?

Again, gentlemen, does it not seem to you probable that I would have passed the word round among my friends during the daytime, and told them to assemble at the house of one of my friends who lived nearest, rather than have started to run round at night, as soon as I found out, without knowing whom I should find at home and whom away? Actually, I called for Harmodius and certain others who were out of town — I did not know it — and others, I found, were not at home, so I went along taking with me whomever I could. But if I had known beforehand, does it not seem to you probable that I would have arranged for servants and passed the word round to my friends, so that I myself could go in with the maximum of safety — for how did I know whether he too might not have had a dagger or something? — and also in order that I might exact the penalty in the presence of the greatest number of witnesses? But in fact, since I knew nothing of what was going to happen on that night, I took with me whomever I could get.

Witnesses to the preceding, please step up.

*(Further witnesses come forward, and confirm their evidence as read out by the Clerk.)*

You have heard the witnesses, members of the jury. Now consider the case further in your own minds, inquiring whether there had ever existed between Eratosthenes and myself any other enmity but this. You will find none. He never brought any malicious charge against me, nor tried to secure my banishment, nor prosecuted me in any private suit. Neither had he knowledge of any crime of which I feared the revelation, so that I desired to kill him; nor by carrying out this act did I hope to gain money. So far from ever having had any dispute with him, or drunken brawl, or any other quarrel, I had never even set eyes on the man before that night. What possible object could I have had, therefore, in running so great a risk, except that I had suffered the greatest of all injuries at his hands? Again, would I myself have called in witnesses to my crime, when it was possible for me, if I desired to murder him without justification, to have had no confidants?

It is my belief, members of the jury, that this punishment was inflicted not in my own interests, but in those of the whole community. Such villains, seeing the rewards which await their crimes, will be less ready to commit offenses against others if they see that you too hold the same opinion of them. Otherwise it would be far better to wipe out the existing laws and make different ones, which will penalize those who keep guard over their own wives, and grant full immunity to those who criminally pursue them. This would be a far more just procedure than to set a trap for citizens by means of the laws, which urge the man who catches an adulterer to do with him whatever he will, and yet allow the injured party to undergo a trial far more perilous than that which faces the law-breaker who seduces other men's wives. Of this, I am an example—I, who now stand in danger of losing life, property, everything, because I have obeyed the laws of the State.

### ■ Discussion Questions

1. What does Euphiletus's testimony reveal about the position of married women in Athenian society?
2. How does the husband justify his actions?
3. Why does he think adultery is especially worthy of severe punishment?

## 4.

## *Overhead Views of a House on the Slope of the Areopagus*

### Fifth Century B.C.E.

*Classical Athenian society had strictly prescribed rules for females that began at birth. The political and legal rights of females of all ages in Athenian society were limited, and girls were more frequently victims of infanticide—that is, abandoned to die at birth—than boys. Most women spent a significant part of their lives segregated in their own quarters* (gynakeion), *usually on the second floor of the house to limit access to the street. Men's quarters* (andron) *were on the first floor and were furnished with couches for symposia, banquets, and entertainment. Defined by their roles as daughters, wives, and widows, women were closely supervised. The drawings show the first floor of an excavated house on the Slope of Areopagus, a rocky hill west of the Acropolis in Athens, where an important council met.*

---

From Susan Walker, "Women and Housing in Classical Greece: The Archaeological Evidence," in *Images of Women in Antiquity,* ed. Averil Cameron and Amélie Kuhrt (London: Routledge, 1983), 87. Reproduced by permission of International Thomson Publishing Services Ltd. on behalf of Routledge. Courtesy Crook Helm, London.

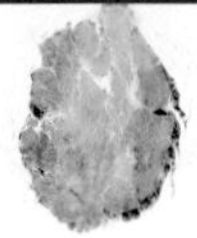

**Probable Functions of Rooms**

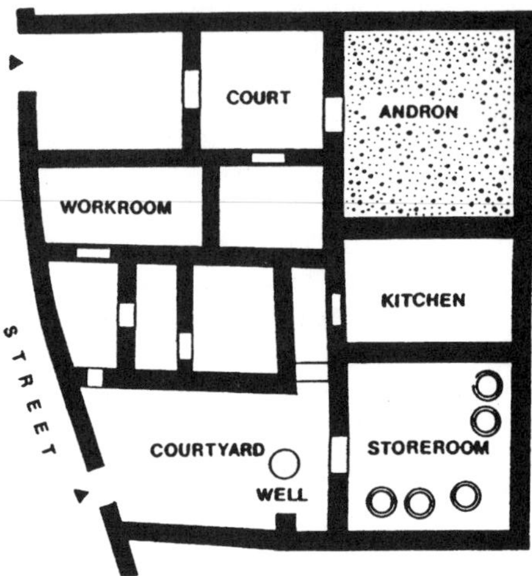


House on the North Slope of the Areopagus (Fifth Century B.C.E.)

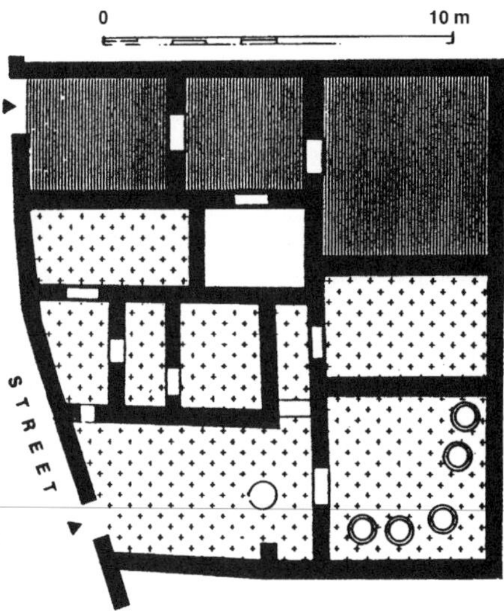


Areas Traditionally Used by Women and Men

*Areas used by women are marked +; those used by men are shaded. Entrances to houses from the street are marked with arrows*

## ■ Discussion Questions

1. Looking at the rooms used by women, describe the role of women in Athenian family life.
2. How much contact would there have been between the women who lived in this house and men of the family and male visitors?

3. If the goal of the architecture of Athenian houses was to limit women from appearing in public spaces, are there any potential weaknesses? If so, where?

# 5.
# Aristophanes
# *Lysistrata*
## 411 B.C.E.

*The plays of Aristophanes (455–385 B.C.E.) were the only comedies to survive from the Greek Golden Age. Although he was a wellborn Athenian, Aristophanes held the leaders of his city-state responsible for starting the Peloponnesian War (431–404 B.C.E.) and refusing to make peace, and he produced* Acharnians, *the first antiwar play, in 425 B.C.E.* Lysistrata, *Aristophanes' most famous comedy, describes a meeting of women who come together to decide how to end the war. The group's Athenian leader, Lysistrata, tells the gathering that women are about to seize the Acropolis—the geographical, political, and religious center of Athens's power. She suggests a bold strategy to force the men to desist from war and make peace: a sex strike. Although the work was satiric, Aristophanes' antiwar stance signaled increasing dissatisfaction with conditions in Athens as a result of the war. His message in* Lysistrata *is so powerful and timeless that it is still performed through the world.*

LAMPITO: Who has gathered together this company of women?

LYSISTRATA: I have.

LAMPITO: Speak up, then. What do you want?

LYSISTRATA: . . . before I speak, let me ask you a little question.

MYRRHINE: Anything you like.

LYSISTRATA [*earnestly*]: Tell me: don't you yearn for the fathers of your children, who are away at the wars? I know you all have husbands abroad.

CALONICE: Why, yes; mercy me! my husband's been away for five months in Thrace keeping guard on—Eucrates.[1]

MYRRHINE: And mine for seven whole months in Pylus.

LAMPITO: And mine, as soon as ever he returns from the fray, readjusts his shield and flies out of the house again.

LYSISTRATA: And as for lovers, there's not even a ghost of one left. Since the Milesians revolted from us, I've not even seen an eight-inch dingus to be a leather consolation for us widows.[2] Are you willing, if I can find a way, to help me end the war?

---

From Whitney Jennings Oates and Charles T. Murphy, *Greek Literature in Translation.* (London: Longman Publishing Group, 1944).

[1]**Eucrates:** An Athenian general of questionable loyalty.

[2]**leather . . . widows:** The Milesians, former allies of Athens, manufactured a leather dildo.

MYRRHINE: Goodness, yes! I'd do it, even if I had to pawn my dress and—get drunk on the spot!

CALONICE: And I, even if I had to let myself be split in two like a flounder.

LAMPITO: I'd climb up Mt. Taygetus[3] if I could catch a glimpse of peace.

LYSISTRATA: I'll tell you, then, in plain and simple words. My friends, if we are going to force our men to make peace, we must do without—

MYRRHINE: Without what? Tell us.

LYSISTRATA: Will you do it?

MYRRHINE: We'll do it, if it kills us.

LYSISTRATA: Well then, we must do without sex altogether. [*general consternation*] Why do you turn away? Where go you? Why turn so pale? Why those tears? Will you do it or not? What means this hesitation?

MYRRHINE: I won't do it! Let the war go on.

CALONICE: Nor I! Let the war go on.

LYSISTRATA: So, my little flounder? Didn't you say just now you'd split yourself in half?

CALONICE: Anything else you like. I'm willing, even if I have to walk through fire. Anything rather than sex. There's nothing like it, my dear.

LYSISTRATA [*to* MYRRHINE]: What about you?

MYRRHINE [*sullenly*]: I'm willing to walk through fire, too.

LYSISTRATA: Oh vile and cursed breed! No wonder they make tragedies about us: we're naught but "love-affairs and bassinets." But you, my dear Spartan friend, if you alone are with me, our enterprise might yet succeed. Will you vote with me?

LAMPITO: 'Tis cruel hard, by my faith, for a woman to sleep alone without her nooky; but for all that, we certainly do need peace.

LYSISTRATA: O my dearest friend! You're the only real woman here.

CALONICE [*wavering*]: Well, if we do refrain from—[*shuddering*] what you say (God forbid!), would that bring peace?

LYSISTRATA: My goodness, yes! If we sit at home all rouged and powdered, dressed in our sheerest gowns, and neatly depilated, our men will get excited and want to take us; but if you don't come to them and keep away, they'll soon make a truce. . . .

CALONICE: What if the men give us up?

LYSISTRATA: "Flay a skinned dog," as Pherecrates says.

CALONICE: Rubbish! These make-shifts are no good. But suppose they grab us and drag us into the bedroom?

LYSISTRATA: Hold on to the door.

CALONICE: And if they beat us?

LYSISTRATA: Give in with a bad grace. There's no pleasure in it for them when they have to use violence. And you must torment them in every possible way. They'll give up soon enough; a man gets no joy if he doesn't get along with his wife.

MYRRHINE: If this is your opinion, we agree.

---

[3]**Mt. Taygetus:** A mountain near Sparta.

LAMPITO: As for our own men, we can persuade them to make a just and fair peace; but what about the Athenian rabble? Who will persuade them not to start any more monkey-shines?

LYSISTRATA: Don't worry. We guarantee to convince them.

LAMPITO: Not while their ships are rigged so well and they have that mighty treasure in the temple of Athene.

LYSISTRATA: We've taken good care for that too: we shall seize the Acropolis today. The older women have orders to do this, and while we are making our arrangements, they are to pretend to make a sacrifice and occupy the Acropolis.

LAMPITO: All will be well then. That's a very fine idea.

LYSISTRATA: Let's ratify this, Lampito, with the most solemn oath. . . . Place all your hands on the cup, and one of you repeat on behalf of all what I say. Then all will swear and ratify the oath. *I will suffer no man, be he husband or lover,*

CALONICE: *I will suffer no man, be he husband or lover,*

LYSISTRATA: *To approach me all hot and horny.* [*as* CALONICE *hesitates*] . . . *I will remain at home unmated, . . . Wearing my sheerest gown and carefully adorned, . . . That my husband may burn with desire for me. . . . And if he takes me by force against my will, . . . I shall do it badly and keep from moving. . . . Nor will I take the posture of the lioness on the knife-handle. . . .*

[*A shout is heard from off-stage.*]

LAMPITO: What's that shouting?

LYSISTRATA: That's what I was telling you: the women have just seized the Acropolis. Now, Lampito, go home and arrange matters in Sparta; and leave these two ladies here as hostages. We'll enter the Acropolis to join our friends and help them lock the gates.

CALONICE: Don't you suppose the men will come to attack us?

LYSISTRATA: Don't worry about them. Neither threats nor fire will suffice to open the gates, except on the terms we've stated.

CALONICE: I should say not! Else we'd belie our reputation as unmanageable pests.

## ■ Discussion Questions

1. According to Aristophanes, how do women in the Greek Golden Age feel about sex? What, if anything, is surprising about Lysistrata's proposal to the group?
2. How does the play reflect the role of women in Greek society? Does the satirical and comedic intent of the playwright affect your interpretation?
3. How does Aristophanes use defined gender roles to make a political statement?

## ■ Comparative Questions

1. How might Socrates have reacted to Pericles' description of the role of wealth in Athenian society?
2. Are there any similarities between Pericles' and Euphiletus's understanding of the relationship between the individual and the state?

3. How did Socrates challenge this relationship?
4. How does the archaeological plan of a house on the Areopagus help you understand the story told by Euphiletus?
5. Both Euphiletus's defense and Aristophanes' comedy suggest that the attempt to enforce the segregation and/or seclusion of women did not always work. Compare the actual women mentioned in the defense with the heroines of the play. What do they have in common? What does Aristophanes exaggerate or make up to advance his antiwar position?

Chapter

# 3

# From the Classical to the Hellenistic World, c. 400–30 B.C.E.

FOLLOWING THE END of the Peloponnesian War in 404 B.C.E., the Greek city-states fell victim to internal squabbling and disunity as each vied to dominate Greece. Macedonian kings seized this opportunity to become masters of the eastern Mediterranean and beyond. Their successors capitalized on their legacy, carving out individual kingdoms from the Macedonian empire. Immigrant Greeks and Macedonians helped to keep the wheels of royal rule running smoothly at the local level. In the first document, we see the Hellenistic world through the eyes of one such official working in Egypt. The second document helps us better understand where women fit into this new landscape, which was colored by both change and tradition, while the map of Alexandria (Document 3) shows an early version of urban planning. Against this backdrop, the once mighty Greek city-states became second-rate powers, prompting many Greek thinkers, including Epicurus (Document 4), to reexamine the role of fate and chance in human life. The final document demonstrates the increasing power of Rome at the time, and its appeal as a political ally.

## 1. Zeno, Egyptian Official *Records* 259–250 B.C.E.

*Although Alexander the Great's imperial glory was short-lived, it opened the door to a new, more international eastern Mediterranean world. Upon his death in 323 B.C.E., Alexander's army commanders divided his empire into separate kingdoms*

From *Select Papyri,* trans. A. S. Hunt and C. C. Edgar, vol. 1 (London and New York: William Heinemann Ltd., 1932), 269–77, 397–99, 409–15.

*over which they assumed control. To rule effectively, these new kings and their successors relied on a hierarchial bureaucracy staffed by Greeks and local administrators to oversee local affairs. This document illuminates the busy life of a Greek named Zeno, who was an agent for Apollonius, the financial minister for Ptolemy Philadelphus of Egypt (r. 285–246 B.C.E. and the employer of the camel trader mentioned in the beginning of Chapter 3 in the* Making of the West, A Concise History*). At the time, Egypt was home to both Greeks and indigenous peoples who contributed to a vibrant urban culture and economy. These extracts include instructions from Apollonius, requests for help, a desk diary, and other records of Zeno's daily affairs.*

## Letter from Hierocles (257 B.C.E.)

Hierocles to Zeno greeting. If you are well, it would be excellent. I too am in good health. You wrote to me about Pyrrhus, telling me to train[1] him if I am quite certain of his success, but if not, to avoid incurring useless expense and distracting him from his studies. Now as for my being certain, the gods should know best, but it seems to Ptolemaeus, as far as a man can tell, that Pyrrhus is much better than those now being trained, though they started long before him, and that in a very short time he will be far ahead of them; moreover he is pursuing his other studies as well; and to speak with the gods' leave, I hope to see you crowned. Make haste to send him a bathing-apron, and if possible let it be of goatskin or, if not, of thin sheepskin, and a tunic and cloak, and the mattress, coverlet and pillows, and the honey. You wrote to me that you were surprised at my not understanding that all these things are subject to toll. I know it, but you are well able to arrange for them to be sent in perfect security.[2] (Addressed) To Zeno. (Docketed) Hierocles about Pyrrhus. Year 29, Xandicus 3, at Memphis.

## Letter from Promethion (256 B.C.E.)

Promethion[3] to Zeno greeting. I suffered anxiety when I heard of your long protracted illness, but now I am delighted to hear that you are convalescent and already on the point of recovery. I myself am well. I previously gave your agent Heraclides 150 drachmae in silver from your account, as you wrote to me to do, and he is bringing you now 10 *hins* of perfume in 21 vases which have been sealed with my finger-ring. For though Apollonius wrote to me to buy and give him also 300 wild pomegranate wreaths, I did not manage to give him these at the same time, as they were not ready, but Pa . . . will bring them to him at Naucratis; for they will be finished before the 30th. I have paid the price both of these and of the perfume from your account, as Apollonius wrote. I have also paid a charge of 10 drachmae in copper for the boat in which he is sailing up. And 400 drachmae in

[1]For competition in the public games.
[2]That is, by using his influence as an agent of the financial minister.
[3]A banker in Mendes.

silver have been paid to Iatrocles for the papyrus rolls which are being manufactured in Tanis for Apollonius. Take note then that these affairs have been settled thus. And please write yourself if ever you need anything here. Goodbye. Year 29, Choiach 28. (Addressed) To Zeno. (Docketed) Year 29, Peritius 3. Promethion about what he has paid.

## LETTER FROM APOLLONIUS THE DIOECETES (256 B.C.E.)

Apollonius to Zeno greeting. From the dry wood put on board a boat as many of the thickest logs as possible and send them immediately to Alexandria that we may be able to use them for the festival of Isis. Goodbye. Year 30, Dius 3, Phaophi 23. (Addressed) To Zeno. At once.[4] (Docketed by Zeno) Year 30, Dius 18, Hathur 18. Apollonius about wood for the Isis festival. (Docketed by sender) Wood for the Isis festival.

## LETTER FROM PLATON (255 B.C.E.)

Platon to Zeno greeting. The father of Demetrius the bearer of this letter happens, it seems, to be residing in the Arsinoite nome,[5] and the lad therefore wishes to find employment there himself. On hearing of your kindly disposition some of his friends asked me to write to you about him, begging you to give him a post in your service. Please then do me a favour and provide some employment for him, whatever you may think suitable, and otherwise look after him, if you find him useful. As a token (of goodwill) I have sent you, from Sosus, 2 artabae[6] of chick-peas bought at 5 drachmae each, and if there are any at Naucratis, I will try to buy you about 20 artabae more and bring them up to you myself. Goodbye. Year 31, Dius 12. (Addressed) To Zeno.

## LETTER FROM ARTEMIDORUS (252 B.C.E.)

Artemidorus[7] to Zeno greeting. If you are well, it would be excellent. I too am well and Apollonius is in good health and other things are satisfactory. As I write this, we have just arrived in Sidon after escorting the princess[8] to the frontier, and I expect that we shall soon be with you. Now you will do me a favor by taking care of your own health and writing to me if you want anything done that I can do for you. And kindly buy me, so that I may get them when I arrive, 3 metretae[9] of the best honey and 600 artabae of barley for the animals, and pay the cost of them out of

[4]An admonition to the persons concerned to send the letter immediately.
[5]**nome:** Region. [Ed.]
[6]**artabae:** Baskets. [Ed.]
[7]A physician in the service of the dioecetes.
[8]The princess Berenice, who was escorted to Syria by Apollonius on the occasion of her marriage to Antiochus II.
[9]**metretae:** Jars. [Ed.]

the produce of the sesame and croton,[10] and also see to the house in Philadelphia in order that I may find it roofed when I arrive. Try also as best you can to keep watch on the oxen and the pigs and the geese and the rest of the stock there; I shall have a better supply of provisions if you do. Also see to it that the crops are harvested somehow, and if any outlay is required, do not hesitate to pay what is necessary. Goodbye. Year 33, intercalary Peritius 6. (Addressed) To Zeno. To Philadelphia. (Docketed) Year 33, Phamenoth 6. Artemidorus.

## LETTER FROM AN INVALID (259–257 B.C.E.)

Memorandum to Zeno from Cydippus. If in accordance with the doctors' orders I could have purchased any of the following things in the market, I should not have troubled you; but as it is I have written you a note of what I require, as Apollonius thought I ought to do. So if you have them in store, send me a jar of wine, either Lesbian or Chian, of the very sweetest, and if possible a chous[11] of honey or, if not, as much as you can; and order them to fill me the vessel with salt fish. For both these things they consider to be most needful. And if my health improves and I go abroad to Byzantium, I will bring you back some excellent salt fish. (On the back) Memorandum from Cydippus.

## LETTER FROM A HOUSE-PAINTER (c. 255 B.C.E.)

Memorandum to Zeno from Theophilus the . . . About the work in the house of Diotimus: for the portico, [I undertake] to have the cornice painted with a purple border, the upper part of the wall variegated, the lower course like vetch-seed,[12] and the pediment with circular veining, providing myself with all materials, for 30 drachmae. For the dining-room with seven couches, I will do the vault according to the pattern which you saw, and give the lower course an agreeable tint and paint the Lesbian cornice, providing myself with all materials, for 20 drachmae. And for the dining-rooms with five couches, I will paint the cornices, providing myself with all materials, for 3 drachmae. The sum total is 53 drachmae. But if you provide everything, it will come to 30 drachmae. Goodbye.

## ZENO'S AGENDA (c. 250 B.C.E.)

To ask Herodotus about the goat hair. To ask Aminias at how much mina he sold it. The letter to Dioscurides about the boat. To make an agreement with Timaeus about the pigs. To draft the contract with Apollodorus and write to him to hand over. To load the boat with wool. To write to Jason to let Dionysius put the wool on board and take it down the river when cleaned; the fourth part of the Arabian

[10]The two oils chiefly used in Egypt at this period were made from sesame and croton (the castor-oil plant), the former for food and the latter for lamps.
[11]**chous:** Container. [Ed.]
[12]**vetch-seed:** Pea-colored. [Ed.]

wool; to let him take down the sour wine. To write to Meliton to plant shoots of the *bumastus* vine belonging to Neoptolemus, and to Alcimus to do likewise if he approves. To Theogenes about twelve yokes of bulls. To give Apollodorus and Callippus . . . [f]rom Metrodorus to Athenagoras about the same year's produce. To Theophilus granting a favor and about the state of the work. To write about corn to Iatrokles and Theodorus before the water from the canal. . . .

## ZENO'S AGENDA (c. 250 B.C.E.)

To get the olive kernels. The oil from Heragoras. To buy for the horses 4 strigils, 4 rubbing cloths, 4 scrapers, and for Phatres 1 strigil. To get shoots of the walnut trees. To ascertain the registration of the wine carried down, for which nome it has been registered. To receive Hermon's boy.

## LIST OF FOREIGN GOODS (257 B.C.E.)

Year 29, Xandicus 11, at Hermopolis.[13] We have left behind these articles which Charmus has handed over to Apollodotus: in a basket 5 small bags of nard sealed and 1 small wallet sealed, 1 small wallet, sealed, containing dice of gazelle bone; purple dye in one pillow-case; 1 strip of variegated cloth; 3 half-strips of variegated cloth; 2 strips of white cloth; 4 strips of purple cloth; 3 bags and 1 small bag of frankincense sealed; 3 small bags of myrrh sealed; 1 wallet containing dice of gazelle bone; 1 small wallet of purple dye sealed; 1 small wallet of saffron sealed.

## LIST OF ZENO'S CLOTHES (c. 257 B.C.E.)

Zeno's trunk in which are contained: 1 linen wrap, washed; 1 clay-colored cloak, for winter, washed, and 1 worn, 1 for summer, half-worn, 1 natural-colored, for winter, washed, and 1 worn, 1 vetch-colored, for summer, new; 1 white tunic for winter, with sleeves, washed, 1 natural-colored, for winter, with sleeves, worn, 1 natural-colored, for winter, worn, 2 white, for winter, washed, and 1 half-worn, 3 for summer, white, new, 1 unbleached, 1 half-worn; 1 outer garment, white, for winter, washed; 1 coarse mantle; 1 summer garment, white, washed, and 1 half-worn; 1 pair of Sardian pillow-cases; 2 pairs of socks, clay-colored, new, 2 pairs of white, new; 2 girdles, white, new. (Endorsed) From Pisicles, a list of Zeno's clothes.

### ■ Discussion Questions

1. If you had to write a job description for Zeno based on these records, what responsibilities would it include?
2. What do Zeno's records reveal about the local economy?
3. What evidence do you find in Zeno's records of cross-cultural influences within the Hellenistic world?

[13]Hermopolis Parva in the Delta.

## 2.
## *Funerary Inscriptions and Epitaphs*
### Fifth–First Centuries B.C.E.

*These inscriptions and epitaphs provide a glimpse of women's place in the Classical and Hellenistic worlds as described by family members and admirers after their deaths. The words preserved in this form do not simply mark each woman's passing from this world to the next, but they hold her up as an exemplar of female behavior. As in the past, a woman's identity revolved principally around her roles as daughter, wife, and mother. Yet not all women's lives were confined to domestic duties. Some were royal attendants, priestesses, and even physicians, whose daily activities extended into the public sphere.*

### ARCHEDICE, ATHENS, FIFTH CENTURY B.C.E.

This dust hides Archedice, daughter of Hippias, the most important man in Greece in his day. But though her father, husband, brothers, and children were tyrants, her mind was never carried away into arrogance.

### ASPASIA, CHIOS, C. 400 B.C.E.

Of a worthy wife this is the tomb—here, by the road that throngs with people—of Aspasia, who is dead; in response to her noble disposition Euopides set up this monument for her; she was his consort.

### DIONYSIA, ATHENS, FOURTH CENTURY B.C.E.

It was not clothes, it was not gold that this woman admired during her lifetime; it was her husband and the good sense that she showed in her behavior. But in return for the youth you shared with him, Dionysia, your tomb is adorned by your husband Antiphilus.

### CLAUDIA, ROME, SECOND CENTURY B.C.E.

Friend, I have not much to say; stop and read it. This tomb, which is not fair, is for a fair woman. Her parents gave her the name Claudia. She loved her husband in her heart. She bore two sons, one of whom she left on earth, the other beneath it. She was pleasant to talk with, and she walked with grace. She kept the house and worked in wool. That is all. You may go.

---

From Mary R. Lefkowitz and Maureen B. Fant, eds., *Women's Life in Greece and Rome,* 2d ed. (Baltimore: Johns Hopkins University Press, 1992), 16–17, 190, 206, 219, 221–22, 263, 266–67, 274.

## An Accomplished Woman, Sardis, First Century B.C.E.

[An inscription set up by the municipality of Sardis in honor of Menophila, daughter of Hermagenes.] This stone marks a woman of accomplishment and beauty. Who she is the Muses' inscriptions reveal: Menophila. Why she is honored is shown by a carved lily and an alpha, a book and a basket, and with these a wreath. The book shows that you were wise, the wreath that you wore on your head shows that you were a leader; the letter alpha that you were an only child; the basket is a sign of your orderly excellence; the flower shows the prime of your life, which Fate stole away. May the dust lie light on you in death. Alas; your parents are childless; to them you have left tears.

## Posilla Senenia, Monteleone Sabino, First Century B.C.E.

Posilla Senenia, daughter of Quartus and Quarta Senenia, freedwoman of Gaius.

Stranger, stop and, while you are here, read what is written: that a mother was not permitted to enjoy her only daughter, whose life, I believe, was envied by some god.

Since her mother was not allowed to adorn her while she was alive, she does so just the same after death; at the end of her time, [her mother] with this monument honors her whom she loved.

## Xenoclea, Piraeus, c. 360 B.C.E.

Leaving two young girls, Xenoclea, daughter of Nicarchus, lies here dead; she mourned the sad end of her son, Phoenix, who died out at sea when he was eight years old.

There is no one so ignorant of grief, Xenoclea, that he doesn't pity your fate. You left behind two young girls and died of grief for your son, who has a pitiless tomb where he lies in the dark sea.

## Handiwork, Athens, after 350 B.C.E.

I worked with my hands; I was a thrifty woman, I, Nicarete who lie here.

## A Storeroom Attendant, Cape Zoster, near Athens, 56–55 B.C.E.

[An epitaph by a mother for a daughter who worked for Cleopatra at the royal court of Alexandria.] Her mother, an Athenian woman, raised her to be an attendant of foreign storerooms. She too rushed for her child's sake to come to the palace of the king who had set her over his rich possessions. Yet still she could not bring her daughter back alive. But the daughter has a tomb in Athens instead of on Libyan sand.

## Epitaph for a Woman Who Died while Pregnant, Egypt, Second–First Centuries B.C.E.

Dosithea, daughter of—. Look at these letters on the polished rock. Thallo's son Chaeremon married me in his great house. I die in pain, escaping the pangs of childbirth, leaving the breath of life when I was twenty-five years old; from a disease which he died of before, I succumbed after. I lie here in Schedia. Wayfarers, as you go by, all of you, say: "Beloved Dosithea, stay well, also among the dead."

## A Midwife and Physician, Athens, Fourth Century B.C.E.

[The memorial tablet represents two women, one seated, one standing, surrounded by infants of both sexes.] Phanostrate, a midwife and physician, lies here. She caused pain to none, and all lamented her death.

## A Nurse, Athens, after 350 B.C.E.

[Epitaph for] Apollodorus the immigrant's daughter, Melitta, a nurse. Here the earth covers Hippostrate's good nurse; and Hippostrate still misses you. "I loved you while you were alive, nurse, I love you still now even beneath the earth and now I shall honor you as long as I live. I know that for you beneath the earth also, if there is reward for the good, honors will come first to you, in the realm of Persephone and of Pluto."

## Epitaph for a Priestess, Miletus, Third Century B.C.E.

Bacchae[1] of the City, say, "Farewell you holy priestess." This is what a good woman deserves. She led you to the mountain and carried all the sacred objects and implements, marching in procession before the whole city. Should some stranger ask for her name: Alcmeonis, daughter of Rhodius, who knew her share of the blessings.

### ■ Discussion Questions

1. Judging from these inscriptions and epitaphs, what particular qualities did people admire in women, and why?
2. Scholars have described Greek society at the time as patriarchal. Do the epitaphs and inscriptions support this view?
3. What do the epitaphs and inscriptions reveal about the social and economic standing of the women they describe?

[1]**Bacchae:** Women worshipers of Dionysus. [Ed.]

# 3.
# *Map of Ancient Alexandria*
## Second Half of First Century B.C.E.

*The Hellenistic city of Alexandria was built in the late fourth century* B.C.E. *by the Greek architect Dinocrates at the behest of Alexander the Great. It was one of the earliest attempts at urban planning and soon became the capital and administrative and economic center of the Ptolemaic Dynasty in Egypt. A super city, ormetropolis, its cosmopolitan culture and attractions attracted people of all backgrounds, races, and religions. Its library contained five hundred thousand scrolls, and the museum associated with it, which is dedicated to the Muses, is believed to have housed laboratories; observatories; a zoo; and lecture halls that attracted the leading poets, philosophers, and scientists of the time. The city's lighthouse, the tallest manmade structure of its time,*

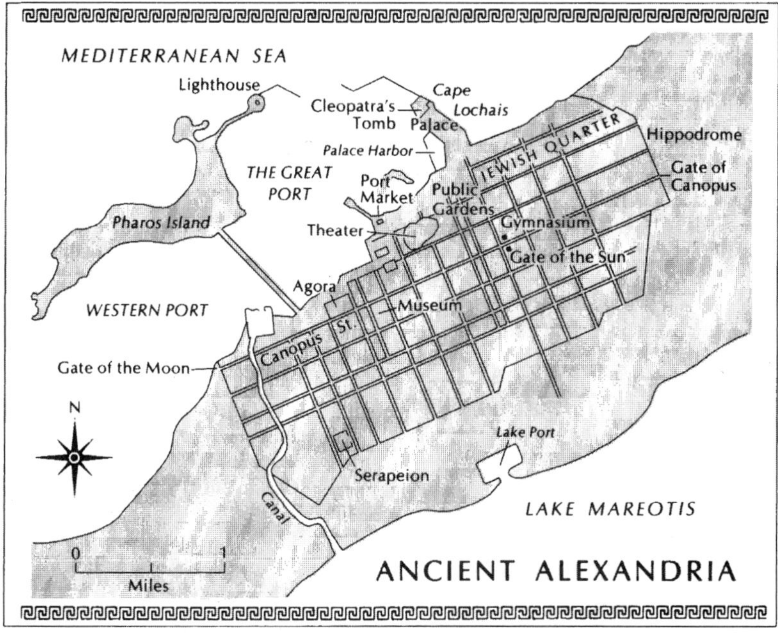


*The* Gate of Canopus, *located at the end of Canopus Street, is named after the second brightest star in the sky, often used for navigation.*
*The* Serapeion *was a cult temple dedicated to the god Sarapis, who had both Egyptian and Hellenistic attributes.*
*The* Hippodrome *was the arena for chariot races and other games.*
*The* Agora, *located on Canopus Street, was the marketplace.*
Courtesy Houghton Mifflin Company, Boston.

From Frank J. Frost, *Greek Society*, 5th ed. (Boston: Houghton Mifflin, 1997), 165.

*became known as one of the Seven Wonders of the Ancient World, while it served the practical function of bringing sailors to safe haven.*

### ■ Discussion Questions

1. Examine the city layout. How does the planning reflect the economic, social, and intellectual interests and occupations of its inhabitants and visitors? What can you determine about the population?
2. What kinds of entertainment or diversions did the city provide? What does this tell you about the planner's vision of what a city should be?
3. How would the city provide opportunities for social mobility not available in more traditional Greek city-states?
4. How does the city of Alexandria exemplify Alexander's vision of a Hellenistic world empire?

## 4.
## Epicurus
## *Letter to a Friend*
### Late Third Century B.C.E.

*Born on the island of Samos, Epicurus (c. 341–270 B.C.E.) earned a reputation as an accomplished teacher in Asia Minor that eventually led him to Athens in 306. In the tradition of the schools of philosophy of Plato and Aristotle, the "Garden" of Epicurus attracted a strong following. Although the adjective* Epicurean *has often been taken to mean the enjoyment of life's pleasures, Epicurus's actual philosophy was based on the pursuit of true, spiritual happiness. In his* Letter to a Friend, *Epicurus explores the meaning of happiness, and concludes that it is based on simple needs and a serene spirit.*

We must consider that of desires some are natural, others empty; that of the natural some are necessary, others not; and that of the necessary some are necessary for happiness, others for bodily comfort, and others for life itself. A right understanding of these facts enables us to direct all choice and avoidance toward securing the health of the body and tranquillity of the soul; this being the final aim of a blessed life. For the aim of all actions is to avoid pain and fear; and when this is once secured for us the tempest of the soul is entirely quelled, since the living animal no longer needs to wander as though in search of something he lacks, hunting for that by which he can fulfill some need of soul or body. We feel a need of plea-

From "Letter to Menoeceus," in *The Way of Philosophy,* trans. Philip Wheelwright (Upper Saddle River: Pearson Education, Inc., 1960).

sure only when we grieve over its absence; when we stop grieving we are in need of pleasure no longer. Pleasure, then, is the beginning and end of the blessed life. For we recognize it as a good which is both primary and kindred to us. From pleasure we begin every act of choice and avoidance; and to pleasure we return again, using the feeling as the standard by which to judge every good.

Now since pleasure is the good that is primary and most natural to us, for that very reason we do not seize all pleasures indiscriminately; on the contrary we often pass over many pleasures, when greater discomfort accrues to us as a result of them. Similarly we not infrequently judge pains better than pleasures, when the long endurance of a pain yields us a greater pleasure in the end. Thus every pleasure because of its natural kinship to us is good, yet not every pleasure is to be chosen; just as every pain also is an evil, yet that does not mean that all pains are necessarily to be shunned. It is by a scale of comparison and by the consideration of advantages and disadvantages that we must form our judgment on these matters. On particular occasions we may have reason to treat the good as bad, and the bad as good.

Independence of circumstance we regard as a great good: not because we wish to dispense altogether with external advantages, but in order that, if our possessions are few, we may be content with what we have, sincerely believing that those enjoy luxury most who depend on it least, and that natural wants are easily satisfied if we are willing to forego superfluities. Plain fare yields as much pleasure as a luxurious table, provided the pain of real want is removed; bread and water can give exquisite delight to hungry and thirsty lips. To form the habit of a simple and modest diet, therefore, is the way to health: it enables us to perform the needful employments of life without shrinking, it puts us in better condition to enjoy luxuries when they are offered, and it renders us fearless of fortune.

Accordingly, when we argue that pleasure is the end and aim of life, we do not mean the pleasure of prodigals and sensualists, as some of our ignorant or prejudiced critics persist in mistaking us. We mean the pleasure of being free from pain of body and anxiety of mind. It is not a continual round of drunken debauches and lecherous delights, nor the enjoyment of fish and other delicacies of a wealthy table, which produce a pleasant life; but sober reasoning, searching out the motives of choice and avoidance, and escaping the bondage of opinion, to which the greatest disturbances of spirit are due.

The first step and the greatest good is prudence—a more precious thing than philosophy even, for all the other virtues are sprung from it. By prudence we learn that we can live pleasurably only if we live prudently, honorably, and justly, while contrariwise to live prudently, honorably, and justly guarantees a life that is pleasurable as well. The virtues are by nature bound up with a pleasant life, and a pleasant life is inseparable from them in turn.

Is there any better and wiser man than he who holds reverent beliefs about the gods, is altogether free from the fear of death, and has serenely contemplated the basic tendencies *(telê)* of natural law? Such a man understands that the limit of good things is easy to attain, and that evils are slight either in duration or in intensity. He laughs at Destiny, which so many accept as all-powerful. Some things, he observes, occur of necessity, others by chance, and still others through our own agency. Necessity is irresponsible, chance is inconstant, but our own actions are free, and it is to them that praise and blame are properly attached. It would be better even to believe the myths about the gods than to submit to the Destiny which the natural philosophers teach. For the old superstitions at least offer some faint hope of placating the gods by worship, but the Necessity of the scientific philosophers is absolutely unyielding. As to chance, the wise man does not deify it as most men do; for if it were divine it would not be without order. Nor will he accept the view that it is a universal cause even though of a wavering kind; for he believes that what chance bestows is not the good and evil that determine a man's blessedness in life, but the starting-points from which each person can arrive at great good or great evil. He esteems the misfortune of the wise above the prosperity of a fool; holding it better that well chosen courses of action should fail than that ill chosen ones should succeed by mere chance.

Meditate on these and like precepts day and night, both privately and with some companion who is of kindred disposition. Thereby shall you never suffer disturbance, waking or asleep, but shall live like a god among men. For a man who lives constantly among immortal blessings is surely more than mortal.

### ■ Discussion Questions

1. According to Epicurus, what is the relationship between pleasure and pain? What is pleasure? Why might someone choose pain over pleasure?
2. What guidelines should a human being follow in making life choices?
3. How could someone best reconcile the fact that destiny, or chance, is beyond his or her control?

## 5.
## *The Book of I Maccabees, Chapter 8*
### Second Century B.C.E.

*Although Judaea was considered to be the Jewish homeland, after the third century* B.C.E. *it was ruled by the Seleucid dynasty in Syria. After Seleucid King Antiochus IV (r. 175–164* B.C.E.*) intervened in the selection of the high priest, who was regarded as the human authority of Judaism and as the center of human holiness and ritual purity, his candidate attempted to Hellenize the city. The Second Temple and treasury in Jerusalem were looted, and Jewish laws were officially abolished in favor of the Cult of the Lord of Heaven. In 165* B.C.E.*, anti-Greek Jews led by Judas Maccabaeus, whose family became known as Maccabees, conquered Jerusalem and purified and rededicated the Temple after defeating the enemy, an event celebrated in the Jewish feast of*

From *The Jerusalem Bible: Reader's Edition* (New York: Doubleday, 2000), 585–87.

*Chanukkah. As a result of internal power struggles in Syria, resistance continued for several decades. The following biblical account, which describes the Maccabees' alliance with Rome, conveys the foreign nature of Greek culture and the sanctity of the Second Temple.*

## A Eulogy of the Romans

8 Now, Judas had heard of the reputation of the Romans, their military strength and their benevolence towards all who made common cause with them; they wanted to establish friendly relations with anyone who approached them, •because of their military strength. He was told of their wars and of their prowess among the Gauls, whom they had conquered and put under tribute; •and of all they had done in the province of Spain to gain possession of the silver and gold mines there, •making themselves masters of the whole country by their determination and perseverance, despite its great distance from their own; of the kings who came from the ends of the earth to attack them, only to be crushed by them and overwhelmed with disaster, and of others who paid them annual tribute; •Philip, Perseus king of the Kittim,[1] and others who had dared to make war on them, had been defeated and reduced to subjection, •while Antiochus the Great, king of Asia,[2] who had advanced to attack them with a hundred and twenty elephants, cavalry, chariots and a very large army, had also suffered defeat at their hands; •they had taken him alive and imposed on him and his successors the payment of an enormous tribute, the surrender of hostages, and the cession •of the Indian territory, with Media, Lydia, and some of their best provinces, which they took from him and gave to King Eumenes.[3] •Judas was also told how, when the Greeks planned an expedition to destroy them, •the Romans got wind of it and sent against them a single general, fought a campaign in which they inflicted heavy casualties, carried off their women and children into captivity, pillaged their goods, subdued their country, tore down their fortresses and reduced them to a slavery lasting to this very day; •and how all other kingdoms and islands that had ever resisted them were also destroyed and enslaved.

But where their friends and those who relied on them were concerned, they had always stood by their friendship. They had subdued kings far and near, and all who heard their name went in terror of them. •One man, if they determined to help him and advance him to a throne, would certainly occupy it, while another, if they so determined, would find himself deposed, their influence was paramount. •In spite of all this not one of them had assumed a crown or put on the purple for his own aggrandizement. •They had set up a senate, where three hundred and twenty counselors deliberated daily, constantly debating how best to regulate

---

[1]Philip, King of Macedonia (221–179 B.C.E.).

[2]Antiochus IV.

[3]Eumenes II, ruler of Pergamum (197–159 B.C.E.).

public affairs. •They entrusted their government to one man for a year at a time, with absolute power over their whole empire, and this man was obeyed by all without any envy or jealousy.

## The Alliance between the Jews and Romans

Having chosen Eupolemus son of John, of the family of Accos, and Jason son of Eleazar, Judas sent them to Rome to make a treaty of friendship and alliance with these people, •who would surely lift the yoke from their shoulders once they understood that the kingdom of the Greeks was reducing Israel to slavery. •The envoys made the lengthy journey to Rome and presented themselves before the Senate with their formal proposal, •"Judas Maccabaeus and his brothers, with the Jewish people, have sent us to you to conclude a treaty of alliance and peace with you, and to enroll ourselves as your allies and friends." The proposal met with the approval of the senators, •and this is a copy of the rescript which they engraved on bronze tablets and sent to Jerusalem to be kept there by the Jews as a record of peace and alliance:

"Good fortune attend the Romans and the Jewish nation by sea and land for ever; may sword or enemy be far from them! •If war comes first to Rome or any of her allies throughout her dominions, •the Jewish nation is to take action as her ally, as occasion may require, and do it wholeheartedly. •They are not to give or supply to the aggressor any grain, arms, money or ships; this is the Roman decision, and they are to honor their obligations without recompense. In the same way, if war comes first to the Jewish nation the Romans are to support them energetically as occasion may offer, •and the aggressor shall not be furnished with grain, arms, money or ships; this is the Roman decision, and they will honor these obligations unreservedly. •These are the terms laid down by the Romans for the Jewish people. •If when they have come into force either party should wish to make any addition or deletion, they shall be free to do so, and any such addition or deletion shall be binding. . . .

### ■ Discussion Questions

1. What strengths and benefits did Judas Maccabaeus find in an alliance with republican Rome? What could the Jewish people offer in return for Roman support?
2. What specific Roman actions made the alliance so appealing to the Maccabees?
3. How is the Roman administration of government, both at home and abroad, described?

### ■ Comparative Questions

1. What evidence can you find in Zeno's records and the map of Alexandria of interactions between Greek and local indigenous traditions in the Hellenistic world?

2. In what ways did these interactions shape everyday political, cultural, and economic life?
3. Based on the book of I Maccabees, what challenges did Hellenistic kings face to their political dominance in the Mediterranean?
4. What are the similarities and differences between Epicurus's views of the human condition and those expressed in the inscriptions and epitaphs?

Chapter

# 4

# The Rise of Rome, c. 753–44 B.C.E.

WHEN THE ROMAN REPUBLIC was founded in 509 B.C.E., few could have foreseen its future as a mighty imperialist state. At the time, Greece was on the threshold of its Golden Age, which was soon followed by Macedonia's meteoric rise to power. Yet throughout this period, the Romans gradually expanded their territories and wealth so that by the end of the second century B.C.E., they controlled most of southern Europe, North Africa, and beyond. Victory came at a price, however, as Roman politicians and military leaders came to value their individual successes more than that of the republic. The documents in this chapter help us chart the republic's development from several different angles. Together, they reveal the pillars of the republic—law, tradition, and communal values—while providing a glimpse of their ultimate demise.

## 1.
## *The Twelve Tables*
### 451–449 B.C.E.

*Although Rome's elite successfully overthrew the Roman monarchy and established the republic in 509 B.C.E., more challenges lay ahead. For the next two centuries, the city's patricians and the rest of its citizens battled over the course the new government should take and their respective roles in it. Promulgated between 451 and 449 B.C.E., the Twelve Tables were a turning point in this struggle, marking the republic's first step toward establishing a fair system of justice. Surviving in fragments only, this code, the earliest in Roman law, was based largely on existing customs. The following excerpts illuminate not only the social and economic landscape of early Rome, but also the foundation of Roman jurisprudence.*

From *Ancient Rome Statutes*, trans. Allan Chester Johnson et al. (Austin: University of Texas Press, 1961), 9–17.

## TABLE I. PROCEEDINGS PRELIMINARY TO TRIAL

If the plaintiff summons the defendant to court the defendant shall go. If the defendant does not go the plaintiff shall call a witness thereto. Only then the plaintiff shall seize the defendant.

If the defendant attempts evasion or takes flight the plaintiff shall lay hand on him.

If sickness or age is an impediment he who summons the defendant to court shall grant him a vehicle. If he does not wish he shall not spread a carriage with cushions.

For a freeholder[1] a freeholder shall be surety;[2] for a proletary[3] anyone who wishes shall be surety.

There shall be the same right of bond and of conveyance with the Roman people for a steadfast person and for a person restored to allegiance.[4]

When the parties agree on the matter the magistrate shall announce it.

If they agree not on terms the parties shall state their case before the assembly in the meeting place or before the magistrate in the market place before noon. Both parties being present shall plead the case throughout together.

If one of the parties does not appear the magistrate shall adjudge the case, after noon, in favor of the one present.

If both parties are present sunset shall be the time limit of the proceedings. . . .

## TABLE II. TRIAL

The penal sum[5] in an action by solemn deposit shall be either 500 asses or 50 asses.[6] . . . It shall be argued by solemn deposit with 500 asses, when the property is valued at 1,000 asses or more, but with 50 asses, when the property is valued at less than 1,000 asses. But if the controversy is about the freedom of a person, although the person may be very valuable, yet the case shall be argued by a solemn deposit of 50 asses. . . .

---

[1]A taxpayer whose fortune is valued at not less than 1,500 asses.

[2]That is, for his appearance at trial.

[3]A "proletary" is a nontaxpayer whose fortune is rated at less than a freeholder's.

[4]This apparently allows the Latin allies who had revolted and later returned into allegiance to enjoy the same rights and to use the same legal formulas in contractual matters and in transferring property as those who had remained loyal.

[5]Each litigant deposited a sum with the court as a kind of "wager on oath" that his cause was right. The defeated party forfeited his deposit to the state. On account of the desire to show special favor to persons illegally held as slaves and claiming their freedom, the law made the deposit for them very low, typically only fifty asses in such cases.

[6]**asses:** Bronze coin. [Ed.]

## TABLE III. EXECUTION OF JUDGMENT

Thirty days shall be allowed by law for payment of confessed debt and for settlement of matters adjudged in court.

After this time the creditor shall have the right of laying hand on the debtor. The creditor shall hale the debtor into court.

Unless the debtor discharges the debt adjudged or unless someone offers surety for him in court the creditor shall take the debtor with him. He shall bind him either with a thong or with fetters of not less than fifteen pounds in weight, or if he wishes he shall bind him with fetters of more than this weight.

If the debtor wishes he shall live on his own means. If he does not live on his own means the creditor who holds him in bonds shall give him a pound of grits daily. If he wishes he shall give him more.

. . . Meanwhile they shall have the right to compromise, and unless they make a compromise the debtors shall be held in bonds for sixty days. During these days they shall be brought to the praetor[7] into the meeting place on three successive market days, and the amount for which they have been judged liable shall be declared publicly. Moreover, on the third market day they shall suffer capital punishment or shall be delivered for sale abroad across the Tiber River.

On the third market day the creditors shall cut shares. If they have cut more or less than their shares it shall be without prejudice.

## TABLE IV. PATERNAL POWER

A notably deformed child shall be killed immediately.

To a father . . . shall be given over a son the power of life and death.

If a father thrice surrenders a son for sale the son shall be free from the father.[8]

To repudiate his wife her husband shall order her . . . to have her own property for herself, shall take the keys, shall expel her.[9]

A child born within ten months of the father's death shall enter into the inheritance. . . .

---

[7]***praetor:*** A high elected official. [Ed.]

[8]In the early days of Rome, a Roman father could sell his son into slavery. If the buyer freed the son, the son reentered his father's control *(patria potestas)*.

[9]The formula for a valid repudiation of the other by either the husband or the wife is said to have contained the words "have (*or* manage) your own property for yourself." Dissolution of marriage by mutual consent is divorce *(divortium)*. In either event, an essential feature is the husband's return of the wife's dowry, if any, whose investment he had controlled during marriage.

## TABLE V. INHERITANCE AND GUARDIANSHIP

. . . Women, even though they are of full age,[10] because of their levity of mind shall be under guardianship . . . except vestal virgins, who . . . shall be free from guardianship. . . .

The conveyable possessions of a woman who is under guardianship of male agnates[11] shall not be acquired by prescriptive right unless they are transferred by the woman herself with the authorization of her guardian. . . .

According as a person has made bequest regarding his personal property or the guardianship of his estate so shall be the law.

If anyone who has no direct heir dies intestate the nearest male agnate shall have the estate.

If there is not a male agnate the male clansmen shall have the estate.

Persons for whom by will . . . a guardian is not given, for them . . . their male agnates shall be guardians.

If a person is insane authority over him and his personal property shall belong to his male agnates and in default of these to his male clansmen. . . .

If a Roman citizen freedman dies intestate without a direct heir, to his patron shall fall the inheritance . . . from said household . . . into said household. . . .

## TABLE VI. OWNERSHIP AND POSSESSION

. . . If any woman is unwilling to be subjected in this manner[12] to her husband's marital control she shall absent herself for three successive nights in every year and by this means shall interrupt his prescriptive right of each year.[13] . . .

One shall not take from framework timber fixed in buildings or in vineyard. . . . One shall be permitted neither to remove nor to claim stolen timber fixed in buildings or in vineyards, . . . but against the person who is convicted of having fixed such timber there an action for double damages shall be given. . . .

---

[10]For females "full age" was twenty-five years. According to the law of this period, a woman never has legal independence: if she is not in her father's power *(potestas)*, she is dependent on her husband's control *(manus)* or, if unmarried and fatherless, she is subject to her guardian's governance *(tutela)*.

[11]**agnates:** Relatives from the father's family. [Ed.]

[12]That is, by prescriptive right *(usus)*.

[13]This method, the so-called *ius trinoctii* (right of three nights; that is, the right acquired by an absence of three successive nights), enabled a wife to remain married to her husband and yet neither to come into nor to remain in his marital control. If the prescriptive right has been interrupted for three consecutive nights annually, the time of *usus* must commence afresh because the husband's previous possession is considered to be canceled.

## Table VII. Real Property

If a watercourse conducted through a public place does damage to a private person the said person shall have the right to bring an action . . . that security against damage may be given to the owner.

. . . Branches of a tree shall be pruned all around to a height of fifteen feet.

If a tree from a neighbor's farm has been felled by the wind over one's farm, . . . one rightfully can take legal action for that tree to be removed.

. . . It shall be lawful to gather fruit falling upon another's farm. . . .

A slave is ordered in a will to be a free man under this condition: "if he has given 10,000 asses to the heir"; although the slave has been alienated by the heir, yet the slave by giving the said money to the buyer shall enter into his freedom. . . .

## Table VIII. Torts or Delicts

. . . If anyone sings or composes an incantation that can cause dishonor or disgrace to another . . . he shall suffer a capital penalty.[14]

If anyone has broken another's limb there shall be retaliation in kind unless he compounds for compensation with him.

. . . If a person breaks a bone of a freeman with hand or by club, he shall undergo a penalty of 300 asses; or of 150 asses, if of a slave.

If one commits an outrage against another the penalty shall be twenty-five asses.

. . . One has broken. . . . One shall make amends.

If a quadruped is said to have caused damage an action shall lie therefore . . . either for surrendering that which did the damage to the aggrieved person . . . or for offering an assessment of the damage.

If fruit from your tree falls onto my farm and if I feed my flock off it by letting the flock onto it . . . no action can lie against me either on the statute concerning pasturage of a flock, because it is not being pastured on your land, or on the statute concerning damage caused by an animal. . . .

If anyone pastures on or cuts by night another's crops obtained by cultivation the penalty for an adult shall be capital punishment and after having been hung up, death as a sacrifice to Ceres. . . . A person below the age of puberty at the praetor's decision shall be scourged and shall be judged as a person either to be surrendered to the plaintiff for damage done or to pay double damages.

Whoever destroys by burning a building or a stack of grain placed beside a house . . . shall be bound, scourged, burned to death, provided that knowingly and consciously he has committed this crime; but if this deed is by accident, that is, by negligence, either he shall repair the damage or if he is unable he shall be corporally punished more lightly.

Whoever fells unjustly another's trees shall pay twenty-five asses for each tree.

[14]According to one ancient account the infliction of this penalty perhaps may have included clubbing to death.

If a thief commits a theft by night, if the owner kills the thief, the thief shall be killed lawfully.

By daylight . . . if a thief defends himself with a weapon . . . and the owner shall shout.

In the case of all other . . . thieves caught in the act freemen shall be scourged and shall be adjudged as bondsmen to the person against whom the theft has been committed provided that they have done this by daylight and have not defended themselves with a weapon; slaves caught in the act of theft . . . shall be whipped with scourges and shall be thrown from the rock;[15] but children below the age of puberty shall be scourged at the praetor's decision and the damage done by them shall be repaired. . . .

If a patron defrauds a client he shall be accursed.[16]

Unless he speaks his testimony whoever allows himself to be called as a witness or is a scales-bearer shall be dishonored and incompetent to give or obtain testimony. . . .

If anyone pastures on or cuts stealthily by night . . . another's crops . . . the penalty shall be capital punishment, and, after having been hung up, death as a sacrifice to Ceres, a punishment more severe than in homicide. . . .

## TABLE IX. PUBLIC LAW

Laws of personal exception shall not be proposed. Laws concerning capital punishment of a citizen shall not be passed . . . except by the Greatest Assembly. . . .

. . . Whoever incites a public enemy or whoever betrays a citizen to a public enemy shall be punished capitally.

For anyone whomsoever to be put to death without a trial and unconvicted . . . is forbidden.

## TABLE X. SACRED LAW

A dead person shall not be buried or burned in the city.[17] . . .

. . . Expenses of a funeral shall be limited to three mourners wearing veils and one mourner wearing an inexpensive purple tunic and ten flutists. . . .

Women shall not tear their cheeks or shall not make a sorrowful outcry on account of a funeral.

A dead person's bones shall not be collected that one may make a second funeral.

An exception is for death in battle and on foreign soil. . . .

---

[15]A southern spur of the Capitoline Hill, which overlooks the Forum.

[16]That is, declared forfeited to the lower gods and liable to be slain by anyone with impunity.

[17]Inhumation on a large scale and in a crowded community not only was insanitary but also took too much space. Cremation could involve hazards from fire.

### TABLE XI. SUPPLEMENTARY LAWS

. . . There shall not be intermarriage between plebeians and patricians.

### TABLE XII. SUPPLEMENTARY LAWS

It is forbidden to dedicate for consecrated use a thing concerning whose ownership there is a controversy; otherwise a penalty of double the value involved shall be suffered. . . .

### ■ Discussion Questions

1. What are the principal concerns expressed in this code?
2. What do these concerns suggest about Roman society at the time?
3. In what ways did these laws represent a triumph for the plebeian class?

## 2.
## *Etruscan Statuette of a Rider*
### c. 434–400 B.C.E.
## and
## *Roman Bust of Lucius Junius Brutus*
### c. 300 B.C.E.

*Within two decades of its foundation, the Roman Republic relied on an aggressive policy of territorial expansion in Italy and abroad to enhance its wealth and power. Unlike the practice of Greek city-states, the Romans absorbed conquered peoples into their population as citizens or allies. In the process, they were also exposed to new forms of art, literature, and language, which helped to shape Rome's own cultural development. The Etruscans were an especially important cross-cultural influence, as the two images that follow suggest. The first displays a bronze statuette of a male rider, dating from ca. 434–400* B.C.E. *A wealthy and urbanized people, the Etruscans were fine craftsmen as well as avid importers of luxury goods from throughout the Mediterranean, including Greece. The second, a bust thought to be of Lucius Junius Brutus, one of the founders of the republic, dates from c. 300* B.C.E.*, after the Roman conquest of Etruscan territory.*

From Detroit Institute of Arts; and Capitoline Museums (Palazzo dei Conservatori).

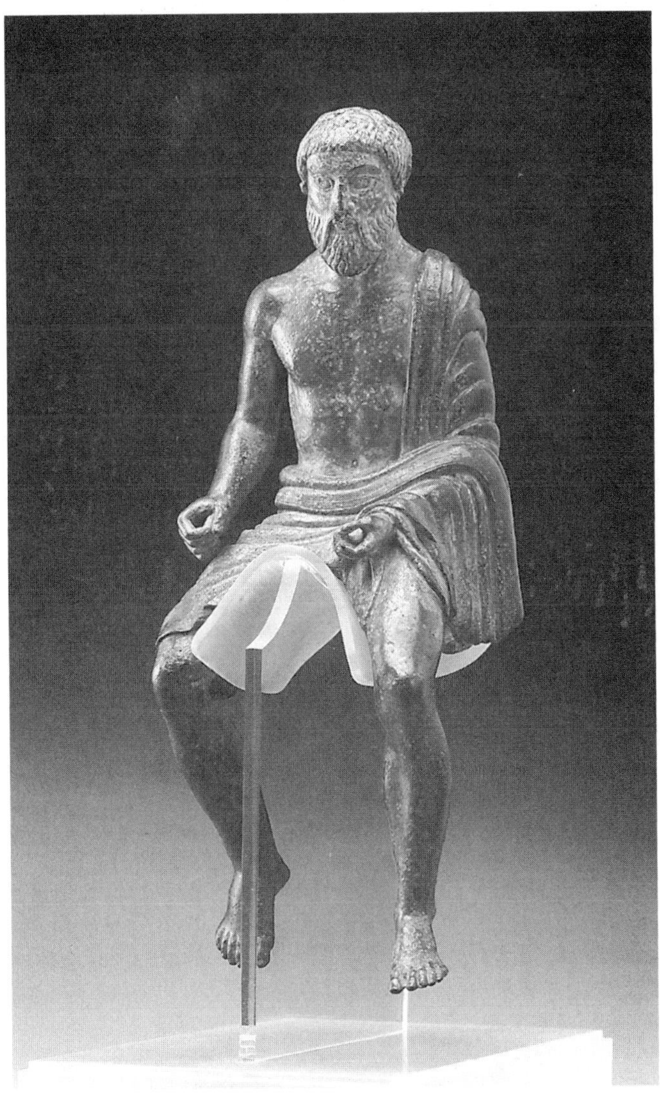

City of Detroit Purchase Photograph © 1985 The Detroit Institute of Arts

Scala/ Art Resource, NY

## Discussion Questions

1. How would you describe the facial features of the Etruscan rider? How do they compare to those of the bust of Brutus?
2. In choosing to portray human faces in this way, what emotions do you think the sculptors sought to provoke within the viewer?
3. Unlike the Etruscan statuette, the Roman bust probably depicts a known individual. How do you think this fact may have influenced the sculptor's design and why?

# 3.
# *Roman Women Demonstrate against the Oppian Law*
## 195 B.C.E.

*Women in ancient Rome were most valued as wives and mothers, yet sometimes they stepped outside the boundaries of family life to make their voices heard. In his* History of Rome, *the Roman historian Livy (59 B.C.E.–17 C.E.) reconstructs a heated debate that erupted on one such occasion. In 195 B.C.E., upper-class women from the city and its environs joined together to demonstrate publicly against the Oppian law, which had been passed during wartime and restricted the amount of finery women could wear and their use of carriages in an effort to reduce friction between rich and poor. Their demand for the law's repeal so that they could once again display their elite status sparked both disdain and sympathy among various leaders to whom they appealed for support. Each camp, represented here by the consul, Cato, and the tribune, Valerius, claimed to have tradition on its side.*

Amid the anxieties of great wars, either scarce finished or soon to come, an incident occurred, trivial to relate, but which, by reason of the passions it aroused, developed into a violent contention. Marcus Fundanius and Lucius Valerius, tribunes of the people, proposed to the assembly the abrogation of the Oppian law. The tribune Gaius Oppius had carried this law in the heat of the Punic War, in the consulship of Quintus Fabius and Tiberius Sempronius, that no woman should possess more than half an ounce of gold or wear a parti-coloured garment or ride in a carriage in the City or in a town within a mile thereof, except on the occasion of a religious festival. The tribunes Marcus and Publius Iunius Brutus were supporting the Oppian law, and averred that they would not permit its repeal; many distinguished men came forward to speak for and against it; the Capitoline was filled with crowds of supporters and opponents of the bill. The matrons could not be kept at home by advice or modesty or their husbands' orders, but blocked all the streets and approaches to the Forum, begging the men as they came down to the Forum that, in the prosperous condition of the state, when the private fortunes of all men were daily increasing, they should allow the women too to have their former distinctions restored. The crowd of women grew larger day by day; for they were now coming in from the towns and rural districts. Soon they dared even to approach and appeal to the consuls, the praetors, and the other officials, but one consul, at least, they found adamant, Marcus Porcius Cato, who spoke thus in favor of the law whose repeal was being urged.

"If each of us, citizens, had determined to assert his rights and dignity as a husband with respect to his own spouse, we should have less trouble with the sex

From Livy, *History of Rome,* vol. 9, trans. Evan T. Sage (Cambridge: Harvard University Press, 1961), 413–21, 425–39.

as a whole; as it is, our liberty, destroyed at home by female violence, even here in the Forum is crushed and trodden underfoot, and because we have not kept them individually under control, we dread them collectively. . . .

"For myself, I could not conceal my blushes a while ago, when I had to make my way to the Forum through a crowd of women. Had not respect for the dignity and modesty of some individuals among them rather than of the sex as a whole kept me silent, lest they should seem to have been rebuked by a consul, I should have said, 'What sort of practice is this, of running out into the streets and blocking the roads and speaking to other women's husbands? Could you not have made the same requests, each of your own husband, at home? Or are you more attractive outside and to other women's husbands than to your own? And yet, not even at home, if modesty would keep matrons within the limits of their proper rights, did it become you to concern yourselves with the question of what laws should be adopted in this place or repealed.' Our ancestors permitted no woman to conduct even personal business without a guardian to intervene in her behalf;[1] they wished them to be under the control of fathers, brothers, husbands; we (Heaven help us!) allow them now even to interfere in public affairs, yes, and to visit the Forum and our informal and formal sessions. What else are they doing now on the streets and at the corners except urging the bill of the tribunes and voting for the repeal of the law? Give loose rein to their uncontrollable nature and to this untamed creature and expect that they will themselves set bounds to their licence; unless you act, this is the least of the things enjoined upon women by custom or law and to which they submit with a feeling of injustice. It is complete liberty or, rather, if we wish to speak the truth, complete licence that they desire.

"If they win in this, what will they not attempt? Review all the laws with which your forefathers restrained their licence and made them subject to their husbands; even with all these bonds you can scarcely control them. What of this? If you suffer them to seize these bonds one by one and wrench themselves free and finally to be placed on a parity with their husbands, do you think that you will be able to endure them? The moment they begin to be your equals, they will be your superiors. . . . No law is entirely convenient for everyone; this alone is asked, whether it is good for the majority and on the whole. If every law which harms anyone in his private affairs is to be repealed and discarded, what good will it do for all the citizens to pass laws which those at whom they are aimed will at once annul? . . . What pretext, respectable even to mention, is now given for this insurrection of the women? 'That we may glitter with gold and purple,' says one, 'that we may ride in carriages on holidays and ordinary days, that we may be borne through the city as if in triumph over the conquered and vanquished law and over the votes which we have captured and wrested from you; that there may be no limits to our spending and our luxury.' . . .

[1]A woman was never independent and was not a person in the legal sense. If she was not under the power of a father or of a husband, a *tutor* was appointed to act for her in legal matters.

"She who can buy from her own purse will buy; she who cannot will beg her husband. Poor wretch that husband, both he who yields and he who yields not, since what he will not himself give he will see given by another man. Now they publicly address other women's husbands, and, what is more serious, they beg for a law and votes, and from sundry men they get what they ask. In matters affecting yourself, your property, your children, you, Sir, can be importuned; once the law has ceased to set a limit to your wife's expenditures you will never set it yourself. Do not think, citizens, that the situation which existed before the law was passed will ever return. It is safer for a criminal to go unaccused than to be acquitted; and luxury, left undisturbed, would have been more endurable then than it will be now, when it has been, like a wild beast, first rendered angry by its very fetters and then let loose. My opinion is that the Oppian law should on no account be repealed; whatever is your decision, I pray that all the gods may prosper it."

After this the tribunes of the people who had declared that they would veto the bill spoke briefly to the same effect, and then Lucius Valerius argued thus for the measure which he had proposed: . . . "Now, since that most influential man, the consul Marcus Porcius, has attacked our proposal not only with his authority, which unexpressed would have had enough of weight, but also in a long and carefully prepared speech, it is necessary to make a brief reply. And yet he used up more words in reproving the matrons than he did in opposing our bill, and, in fact, left it in doubt whether the conduct for which he rebuked the matrons was spontaneous or inspired by us. I propose to defend the measure rather than ourselves, at whom the consul directed his insinuations, more to have something to say than to make a serious charge. This gathering of women he called a sedition and sometimes 'a female secession,' because the matrons, in the streets, had requested you to repeal, in a time of peace and in a rich and prosperous commonwealth, a law that was passed against them in the trying days of a war. . . .

"What new thing, pray, have the matrons done in coming out into the streets in crowds in a case that concerned them? Have they never before this moment appeared in public? Let me unroll your own *Origines* against you.[2] Hear how often they have done it and always, indeed, for the general good. . . . These cases, you say, are different. It is not my purpose to prove them similar; it suffices if I prove that this is nothing new. But what no one wonders that all, men and women alike, have done in matters that concern them, do we wonder that the women have done in a case peculiarly their own? What now have they done? We have proud ears, upon my word, if, although masters do not scorn to hear the petitions of slaves, we complain that we are appealed to by respectable women. . . .

"Laws passed in time of peace, war frequently annuls, and peace those passed in times of war, just as in handling a ship some means are useful in fair weather

[2]Although Valerius pretends to quote from Cato's own historical work *Origines,* which discussed early Roman history, the work had not actually been written at the time of the women's demonstration. The scroll form of the ancient book explains the choice of the verb *revolvam.*

and others in a storm. Since they are so distinguished by nature, to which class, I ask, does the law which we are trying to repeal seem to belong? Well? Is it an ancient regal law, born with the City itself, or, what is next to that, one inscribed on the twelve tables by the decemvirs[3] appointed to codify the law? Is it a law without which our ancestors held that a matron's virtue could not be preserved, and which we too must fear to repeal lest along with it we repeal the modesty and purity of our women? Who is there, then, who does not know that this is a new law, passed twenty years ago, in the consulship of Quintus Fabius and Tiberius Sempronius? Since for so many years our matrons lived virtuous lives without it, what danger is there that when it is repealed they will rush into riotous luxury? . . .

"Who fails to see that the poverty and distress of the state wrote that law, since all private property had to be diverted to public use, and that the law was to remain in force so long as the cause of its enactment lasted?[4]

"All other orders, all men, will feel the change for the better in the state; shall our wives alone get no enjoyment from national peace and tranquillity? . . . By Hercules, there is mourning and anger among all when they see the wives of allies of the Latin confederacy permitted the ornaments which are refused to them, when they see them decked out in gold and purple, when they see them riding through the city, and themselves following on foot, as if dominion resided in the Latin towns and not in Rome. A thing like this would hurt the feelings even of men: what do you think is its effect upon weak women, whom even little things disturb? No offices, no priesthoods, no triumphs, no decorations, no gifts, no spoils of war can come to them; elegance of appearance, adornment, apparel—these are the woman's badges of honor; in these they rejoice and take delight; these our ancestors called the woman's world. What else do they lay aside in times of mourning than purple and jewelry? What do they put on when they have finished their time of mourning? What do they add save more splendid jewels in times of congratulations and thanksgiving? Of course, if you repeal the Oppian law, you will have no authority if you wish to forbid any of these things which now the law forbids; daughters, wives, even sisters of some will be less under control—never while their males survive is feminine slavery shaken off; and even they abhor the freedom which loss of husbands and fathers gives.[5] They prefer to have their finery under your control and not the law's; you too should keep them in control and guardianship and not in slavery, and should prefer the name of father or husband to that of master." . . .

---

[3]**decemvirs:** Roman lawmaker. [Ed.]

[4]Valerius argues that the Oppian law was merely one of a series of emergency measures by which all elements in the state were affected. To leave this one law in force would mean continued discrimination against only women, after the other methods had been abandoned.

[5]Under the stricter Roman law, a woman was throughout life under the *potestas* of her father or his representative or the *manus* of her husband. Valerius makes the point that this domestic authority will be resumed in full with the repeal of the law, and that the same restrictions that the law provided can be enforced if desired.

When these speeches against and for the bill had been delivered, the next day an even greater crowd of women appeared in public, and all of them in a body beset the doors of the Bruti, who were vetoing their colleagues' proposal, and they did not desist until the threat of veto was withdrawn by the tribunes. After that there was no question that all the tribes would vote to repeal the law. The law was repealed twenty years after it was passed.

### ■ Discussion Questions

1. Why did Cato object to repealing the Oppian law? What was the basis of his objections?
2. How did Valerius counter Cato's assertions? According to his view, what did finery symbolize to women?
3. What do both men reveal about contemporary attitudes toward women and their place in the republic?
4. What does this excerpt show about the republic's government?

## 4.
## *The Gracchan Reforms*
### 133 B.C.E.

*By the second century* B.C.E., *decades of war had exacted an economic toll on the Roman Republic. Despite the vast territories and riches of the elite, many Roman citizens struggled to survive, especially veterans who had been displaced from their farms. In 133* B.C.E., *the tribune newly elected by the plebs to protect their rights, Tiberius Gracchus (d. 133* B.C.E.*), initiated a reform program to relieve the people's plight, described here by his biographer, Plutarch (c. 50–120* C.E.*). As Plutarch vividly recounts, Tiberius's senatorial colleagues vehemently opposed him and viewed his efforts as a threat to their elite status and wealth. Tiberius paid for his reform initiative with his life, and thereby opened a new and violent chapter in Roman politics. Henceforth, Roman citizens became increasingly more divisive and polarized, which set the stage for civil war.*

But his brother Gaius has left it us in writing, that when Tiberius went through Tuscany to Numantia, and found the country almost depopulated, there being hardly any free peasants or shepherds, but for the most part only barbarian, imported slaves, he then first conceived the course of policy which in the sequel proved so fatal to his family. Though it is also most certain that the people themselves chiefly excited his zeal and determination in the prosecution of it, by setting

From *Plutarch's Lives,* vol. 4, rev. trans. A. H. Clough (Boston: Little, Brown, 1909), 514–21.

up writings upon the porches, walls, and monuments, calling upon him to reinstate the poor citizens in their former possessions.

However, he did not draw up his law without the advice and assistance of those citizens that were then most eminent for their virtue and authority; amongst whom were Crassus, the high-priest, Mucius Scaevola, the lawyer, who at that time was consul, and Claudius Appius, his father-in-law. Never did any law appear more moderate and gentle, especially being enacted against such great oppression and avarice. For they who ought to have been severely punished for transgressing the former laws, and should at least have lost all their titles to such lands which they had unjustly usurped, were notwithstanding to receive a price for quitting their unlawful claims, and giving up their lands to those fit owners who stood in need of help. But though this reformation was managed with so much tenderness, that, all the former transactions being passed over, the people were only thankful to prevent abuses of the like nature for the future, yet, on the other hand, the moneyed men, and those of great estates, were exasperated, through their covetous feelings against the law itself, and against the law giver, through anger and party spirit. They therefore endeavored to seduce the people, declaring that Tiberius was designing a general redivision of lands, to overthrow the government, and put all things into confusion.

But they had no success. For Tiberius, maintaining an honorable and just cause, and possessed of eloquence sufficient to have made a less creditable action appear plausible, was no safe or easy antagonist, when, with the people crowding around the hustings, he took his place, and spoke in behalf of the poor. "The savage beasts," said he, "in Italy, have their particular dens, they have their places of repose and refuge; but the men who bear arms, and expose their lives for the safety of their country, enjoy in the mean time nothing more in it but the air and light; and having no houses or settlements of their own, are constrained to wander from place to place with their wives and children." He told them that the commanders were guilty of a ridiculous error, when, at the head of their armies, they exhorted the common soldiers to fight for their sepulchres and altars; when not any amongst so many Romans is possessed of either altar or monument, neither have they any houses of their own, or hearths of their ancestors to defend. They fought indeed, and were slain, but it was to maintain the luxury and the wealth of other men. They were styled the masters of the world, but in the mean time had not one foot of ground which they could call their own. An harangue of this nature, spoken to an enthusiastic and sympathizing audience, by a person of commanding spirit and genuine feeling, no adversaries at that time were competent to oppose. Forbearing, therefore, all discussion and debate, they addressed themselves to Marcus Octavius, his fellow-tribune, who, being a young man of a steady, orderly character, and an intimate friend of Tiberius, upon this account declined at first the task of opposing him; but at length, over persuaded with the repeated importunities of numerous considerable persons, he was prevailed upon to do so, and hindered the passing of the law; it being the rule that any tribune has a power to hinder an act, and that all the rest can effect nothing, if only one of them dissents. . . .

When the day appointed was come, and the people summoned to give their votes, the rich men seized upon the voting urns, and carried them away by force; thus all things were in confusion. . . .

But when the senate assembled, and could not bring the business to any result, through the prevalence of the rich faction, he [Tiberius] then was driven to a course neither legal nor fair, and proposed to deprive Octavius of his tribuneship, it being impossible for him in any other way to get the law brought to the vote. . . .

He referred the whole matter to the people, calling on them to vote at once, whether Octavius should be deposed or not; and when seventeen of the thirty-five tribes had already voted against him, and there wanted only the votes of one tribe more for his final deprivation, Tiberius put a short stop to the proceedings, and once more renewed his importunities; he embraced and kissed him before all the assembly, begging, with all the earnestness imaginable, that he would neither suffer himself to incur the dishonor, nor him to be reputed the author and promoter of so odious a measure. Octavius, we are told, did seem a little softened and moved with these entreaties; his eyes filled with tears, and he continued silent for a considerable time. But presently looking towards the rich men and proprietors of estates, who stood gathered in a body together, partly for shame, and partly for fear of disgracing himself with them, he boldly bade Tiberius use any severity he pleased. The law for his deprivation being thus voted, Tiberius ordered one of his servants, whom he had made a freeman, to remove Octavius from the rostra, employing his own domestic freed servants in the stead of the public officers. And it made the action seem all the sadder, that Octavius was dragged out in such an ignominious manner. The people immediately assaulted him, whilst the rich men ran in to his assistance. Octavius, with some difficulty, was snatched away, and safely conveyed out of the crowd; though a trusty servant of his, who had placed himself in front of his master that he might assist his escape, in keeping off the multitude, had his eyes struck out, much to the displeasure of Tiberius, who ran with all haste, when he perceived the disturbance, to appease the rioters.

This being done, the law concerning the lands was ratified and confirmed, and three commissioners were appointed, to make a survey of the grounds and see the same equally divided. These were Tiberius himself, Claudius Appius, his father-in-law, and his brother, Caius Gracchus, who at this time was not at Rome, but in the army under the command of Scipio Africanus before Numantia. These things were transacted by Tiberius without any disturbance, none daring to offer any resistance to him. . . .

About this time, king Attalus, surnamed Philometor, died, and Eudemus, a Pergamenian, brought his last will to Rome, by which he had made the Roman people his heirs. Tiberius, to please the people, immediately proposed making a law, that all the money which Attalus left, should be distributed amongst such poor citizens as were to be sharers of the public lands, for the better enabling them to proceed in stocking and cultivating their ground; and as for the cities that were in the territories of Attalus, he declared that the disposal of them did not at all belong to the senate, but to the people, and that he himself would ask their pleasure herein. By this he offended the senate more than ever he had done before.

## Discussion Questions

1. According to Plutarch, what specific factors prompted Tiberius to take action in the people's favor?
2. In his address to the crowd, how does Tiberius characterize his opponents, and why?
3. As portrayed by Plutarch, what fundamental Roman values did Tiberius embody?

# 5.
# Julius Caesar
# *The Gallic War*
### 52 B.C.E.

*The violent failure of the Gracchan reforms marked the end of political cooperation among the Roman elite and, in the process, opened the door for a new kind of leader in the republic—the general-politician—who used his own troops to gain wealth and power. After securing a special command in Gaul, Julius Caesar (100–44 B.C.E.) exhibited just such a strategy through a combination of military genius and political savvyness. Between 58 and 50 B.C.E., he and his army pushed past Rome's northwest frontier, conquering much of modern-day France along the way. His success sparked a general rebellion among the peoples of central Gaul in 52 B.C.E., led by the tribal chief Vercingetorix (d. 46 B.C.E.). Caesar described the revolt and its climax at the fortress of Alesia in* The Gallic War, *excerpted below. In his account, he provides a glimpse of the realities of warfare and, at the same time, of how he won loyalty both at home and abroad. He used this loyalty as leverage in the civil war brewing in Rome, which ultimately destroyed the republic.*

. . . Now all his cavalry had fled, Vercingetorix withdrew his infantry force, which he had stationed in front of the three camps, and immediately began the march to Alesia, which is a town of the Mandubii. He issued orders for the baggage to be fetched quickly from the camps and to follow on behind. Caesar had his army's baggage taken to the nearest high ground and left two legions behind to guard it. He pursued Vercingetorix as long as the light lasted and killed about 3,000 of the enemy rearguard. The following day he pitched camp near Alesia. He reconnoitred the city's position and provoked panic in the enemy; then, after encouraging the soldiers for the task they faced, he set about the work of circumvallation.[1]

From Julius Caesar, *The Gallic War,* trans. Carolyn Hammond (New York and Oxford: Oxford University Press, 1996), 181, 183–84, 188–89, 191–94, 241–42.

[1]The construction of a fort for mounting weapons by a besieging army. The scale of the circumvallation at Alesia was so astonishing as to become the classic proof of Caesar's mastery of the art of generalship and command.

The actual stronghold of Alesia[2] was in an extremely lofty position on top of a hill, apparently impregnable except by means of a siege. On two sides the foot of this hill was washed by rivers, and for about three miles there stretched a plain in front of the town. Close by in every other direction more hills of equal height girded the town. Beneath the wall, where the hill faced east, the Gallic forces filled the entire space: they had constructed a ditch and a six-foot wall. The length of the siege-works which the Romans had started reached ten miles. Camps had been pitched at suitable locations and twenty-three forts built along the line. These forts were garrisoned in the daytime, to guard against unexpected sorties; at night sentries and reinforced patrols kept watch there. . . .

Vercingetorix now decided to send all his cavalry away by night before the Romans completed their siege-works. As they left, he told each of them to go to his own people and muster for battle all the men of an age to bear arms. He described the services he had done them and called upon them to take thought for his safety, and not to abandon him to the enemy's torments after he had done so much to secure the liberty of all. . . .

All these arrangements were relayed to Caesar by deserters and prisoners. He then decided to set up the following types of fortification. He had a twenty-foot-wide ditch dug, with vertical sides, so that the bottom of the ditch was as wide as its edges at the top. He fixed the position of all the other fortifications 400 paces back from the ditch, with the intention of preventing an unexpected or night-time onslaught on them by the enemy army, and of stopping the enemy aiming missiles at our men while they were busy on the siege-works; for the area he had enclosed was necessarily of considerable size, and it would be difficult to encircle the entire site with a cordon of soldiers. At this distance away, then, he extended two more ditches, of the same depth but fifteen feet across; he filled the inner one (which was on low-lying ground in the plain) with water diverted from the river. Behind them he constructed an earthwork with a rampart on top, twelve feet high; to this he attached a parapet and battlements, with large pointed stakes projecting at the joints where the parapet attached to the earthwork. This would slow down an enemy ascent. He placed towers all round the siege-works at intervals of eighty feet. . . .

Meanwhile Commius[3] and the other leaders entrusted with the supreme command reached Alesia with all their forces. They occupied a hill outside, less than a mile from our fortifications, and took up position there. The next day they brought their cavalry out of camp and filled the whole of the plain which we described earlier as being three miles across. They withdrew their infantry force a short distance and halted it on high ground. From the town of Alesia there was a clear view on to the plain. . . .

---

[2]The size of the forces on both sides is disputed: 50,000 has been suggested for Caesar's entire force, both cavalry and infantry, and 80,000 for the Gallic force inside Alesia.

[3]Before the uprising in Gaul, Commius had been an ally of Caesar's in Britain; in return, Caesar had made him King of the Atrebates. [Ed.]

Vercingetorix saw his men from the citadel of Alesia and marched out of the town, taking the wicker hurdles, poles, shelters, siege-hooks, and the rest of the equipment he had had made ready for the sortie. At one and the same moment there was fighting on every side, and every expedient was put to the test. Wherever a hint of weakness appeared, there they flocked to the attack. The Roman force was strung out along its extensive fortifications and found rallying to the defense difficult in many places. The shouting which arose behind them was effective in frightening our men as they fought, for they realized that the risk to themselves depended on the courage shown by others: after all, it is usually the case that what is unseen is more effective in disturbing men's minds.

Caesar took over a suitable spot and found out what was happening in every quarter; he sent help to those who were in difficulties. Both sides realized that this was the very moment for putting their utmost effort into the fight—the Gauls must despair of saving themselves unless they broke through the Roman defenses, and the Romans, if they held firm, were looking forward to the end of all their labors. . . . The unfavorable downward slope of the site played a crucial part. Some of the enemy threw missiles, others formed a "tortoise" and moved up close; exhausted troops were continually being replaced by fresh. They all threw earth on to the defenses, which gave the Gauls a means of ascent as well as covering over the devices which the Romans had hidden in the ground. Our men were now running out of weapons and of strength.

When he realized what was happening Caesar sent Labienus with six cohorts to help the men in trouble. He told him that if it was impossible to hold his ground he should withdraw his forces and then launch a counter-attack—but this was only to be done in an emergency. Caesar then approached the rest of the men in person, and urged them not to give up the struggle. He explained how the fruits of all their previous battles depended on that day, that hour. Inside the Roman lines the enemy abandoned hope of success on the level ground because of the size of the defenses; so they tried to climb one of the steep ascents to take it, and had all the equipment they had prepared conveyed there. A hail of missiles from the defenders on the towers scattered them, but they filled in the ditches with earth and hurdles, and started to tear down the rampart and parapet with grappling-hooks.

Caesar sent first the young Brutus[4] with some cohorts, then his legate Gaius Fabius with more. Finally, when the fighting grew more fierce, he came in person, leading fresh troops for reinforcements. The battle was renewed and the enemy forced back. Then Caesar made for the place where he had sent Labienus. He withdrew four cohorts from the nearest fort and ordered one section of the cavalry to follow him, the rest to move round the outer defenses and attack the enemy from the rear. Once Labienus had found that neither earthworks nor ditches could

[4]Decimus Junius Brutus Albinus commanded Caesar's fleet against the Veneti in 56 B.C.E. and later at Massilia in 49 B.C.E., following which he was made governor of Transalpine Gaul. He was also one of Caesar's assassins.

stand up to the enemy attack, he gathered eleven cohorts, which happened to be available after their withdrawal from the nearby guardposts. He then sent word to Caesar of what he thought needed to be done.

Caesar hurried to join in the fighting. The conspicuous color of the cloak[5] he habitually wore in battle proclaimed his arrival. Because the downward slopes were in clear view from the heights above, the enemy spotted the cavalry squadrons and cohorts he had ordered to follow him and joined battle. A shout went up from both sides, and was answered by another from the rampart and defense-works. Our men threw their spears, then fought with swords. Suddenly the cavalry was glimpsed in the rear: more cohorts were advancing. The enemy turned tail and the cavalry charged them as they fled. Massive slaughter followed. . . . Those in the town viewed the slaughter and the flight of their comrades: abandoning hope, they withdrew their forces from the defenses.

As soon as the news broke, the Gauls fled from their camp. If our men had not been exhausted after numerous relief efforts and all the struggles of the day they would have been able to wipe out the entire enemy army. The cavalry was sent out at around midnight and caught up with the enemy rearguard. Many of the enemy were taken and killed, and the rest fled to their home states.

The following day Vercingetorix called a council and argued that he had undertaken this war not in his own interests but for the liberty of all. Since they were forced to yield to fortune, he went on, he was putting himself in their hands, ready for either outcome, whether they wanted to make reparation to the Romans by putting him to death, or to hand him over alive.

They sent envoys to Caesar to discuss these options, and he ordered them to give up their weapons and bring out the ringleaders. Then he took his seat within the fortifications in front of his camp, and the ringleaders were brought to him there. Vercingetorix was handed over, and weapons were thrown down. Caesar had the Aedui and Arverni kept back, in case he could use them to win back their states' allegiance, and the rest of the prisoners he shared out as booty, one apiece, to his entire army.

Once this business was settled he set out for the territory of the Aedui and won back their nation. The Arvernian envoys who had been sent there pledged to carry out whatever he told them to do. . . .

## ■ Discussion Questions

1. What does Caesar's description of the siege of Alesia reveal about the technology of war at the time? How did Caesar use this technology to his advantage?
2. What does Caesar's portrait of Vercingetorix suggest about Roman attitudes toward non-Romans?
3. Although Caesar wrote *The Gallic War* to describe his own deeds, he uses "he" (the third person) instead of "I" (the first person) in telling his story. Why do

[5]A reference to the scarlet cloak worn by the *imperator.*

you think he made this choice? Does his use of "he" give you more confidence, or less, in the truth of his account?

4. In writing this account, how do you think Caesar intended to shape his public image and why?

## Comparative Questions

1. Although the Roman Republic was not a democracy, its nonelite citizens were an important political force. What evidence can you find in *Roman Women Demonstrating against the Oppian Law* and *The Gracchan Reforms* to support this claim?
2. How do the documents in this chapter lend support to the argument that the importance of law was a basic Roman value?
3. What do both Plutarch and Caesar reveal about the ways in which war shaped Roman society and politics?
4. Imagine that the sculptor of the Roman bust was designing a statue of Caesar. Based on Caesar's self-portrait in *The Gallic War* of his actions during the climax of the siege of Alesia (pp. 78–81), what features do you think the sculptor would include and why?

Chapter

# 5

# The Roman Empire, c. 44 B.C.E.–284 C.E.

THE CIVIL WARS SPARKED by the assassination of Julius Caesar in 44 B.C.E. may have marked the death of the Roman Republic, but they also signaled the birth of the Roman Empire. Through masterful political and military maneuvering, Caesar's heir Octavian (63 B.C.E.–14 C.E.) emerged from the wars as Rome's undisputed leader. In recognition of this fact, in 27 B.C.E., the Senate granted him special powers and a new title, Augustus ("divinely favored"). He thereupon forged a new system of government that laid the foundations for two hundred years of peace and prosperity. The documents in this chapter bring the empire to life both in the words of its emperors and in those of people living under Roman rule, from an official carrying out imperial orders to a prostitute advertising her services. The final documents hint at later troubles caused by challenges brought on by Jewish rebels and the emergence of a new religion, Christianity, which threatened traditional beliefs and practices.

## 1.
## Augustus
## *The Accomplishments of Augustus*
### 14 C.E.

*When Augustus assumed power in 27 B.C.E., he cast himself not as an innovator but rather as a guardian of tradition. In fact, over the next four decades, he used republican customs to create something new: a monarchical government in which he would reign supreme as a guardian of stability and order. In this document, Augustus describes how he achieved this goal and thereby transformed the republic into an empire. He composed the text to describe the course of his rule, and he ordered it to be engraved on bronze tablets upon his death and erected outside his mausoleum in Rome. That copy did not survive, but an almost complete one did, inscribed on the*

From Naphtali Lewis and Meyer Reinhold, eds., *Roman Civilization: Selected Readings*, 3d ed., vol. 1 (New York: Columbia University Press, 1990), 562–72.

*walls of a temple in modern-day Ankara, Turkey. Here Augustus commemorates the offices and honors bestowed upon him, his expenditures, and his triumphs in war and peace.*

At the age of nineteen, on my own initiative and at my own expense, I raised an army by means of which I liberated the Republic, which was oppressed by the tyranny of a faction.[1] For which reason the senate, with honorific decrees, made me a member of its order in the consulship of Gaius Pansa and Aulus Hirtius [43 B.C.E.], giving me at the same time consular rank in voting, and granted me the *imperium.*[2] It ordered me as propraetor, together with the consuls, to see to it that the state suffered no harm.[3] Moreover, in the same year, when both consuls had fallen in the war, the people elected me consul and a triumvir for the settlement of the commonwealth.

Those who assassinated my father[4] I drove into exile, avenging their crime by due process of law; and afterwards when they waged war against the state, I conquered them twice on the battlefield [the two battles of Phillippi (42 B.C.E.)].

I waged many wars throughout the whole world by land and by sea, both civil and foreign, and when victorious I spared all citizens who sought pardon. Foreign peoples who could safely be pardoned I preferred to spare rather than to extirpate. About 500,000 Roman citizens were under military oath to me. Of these, when their terms of service were ended, I settled in colonies or sent back to their own municipalities a little more than 300,000, and to all of these I allotted lands or granted money as rewards for military service. I captured 600 ships, exclusive of those which were of smaller class than triremes.[5]

Twice I celebrated ovations, three times curule triumphs, and I was acclaimed *imperátor* twenty-one times. When the senate decreed additional triumphs to me, I declined them on four occasions. I deposited in the Capitol laurel wreaths adorning my *fasces,* after fulfilling the vows which I had made in each war.[6] For successes achieved on land and on sea by me or through my legates

---

[1]Antony and his adherents are meant. The period referred to is late 44 to early 43 B.C.E., when Octavian (as Augustus was then known) was in coalition with the Senate against Antony.

[2]***imperium:*** Supreme administrative right or power to command (in military, religious, and judicial matters), held first by Roman kings and in the republic by chief officials. [Ed.]

[3]The formula for the "ultimate decree of the Senate." Augustus refers here to the war against Antony, which culminated in the two battles at Mutina in April of 43 B.C.E.

[4]Julius Caesar, his adoptive father. Yet in general Augustus sought to distance himself from the image and policies of Julius Caesar.

[5]The naval victories over Sextus Pompey (at Mylae and Naulochus), and over Antony and Cleopatra (at Actium) are meant.

[6]This is the well-known Republican custom, followed by victorious generals who were acclaimed *imperator,* of depositing laurelled *fasces* (symbolizing victory) in the Capitol in accordance with vows taken there before they set out for their provinces.

under my auspices the senate decreed fifty-five times that thanksgiving be offered to the immortal gods. Moreover, the number of days on which, by decree of the senate, such thanksgiving was offered, was 890. In my triumphs there were led before my chariot nine kings or children of kings. At the time I wrote this, I had been consul thirteen times, and I was in the thirty-seventh year of my tribunician power [14 C.E.].

The dictatorship offered to me in the consulship of Marcus Marcellus and Lucius Arruntius [22 B.C.E.] by the people and by the senate, both in my absence and in my presence, I refused to accept. In the midst of a critical scarcity of grain I did not decline the supervision of the grain supply, which I so administered that within a few days I freed the whole people from imminent panic and danger by my expenditures and efforts.[7] The consulship, too, which was offered to me at that time as an annual office for life, I refused to accept.

In the consulship of Marcus Vinicius and Quintus Lucretius, and again in that of Publius Lentulus and Gnaeus Lentulus, and a third time in that of Paullus Fabius Maximus and Quintus Tubero [in 19, 18, and 11 B.C.E.], though the Roman senate and people unitedly agreed that I should be elected sole guardian of the laws and morals with supreme authority, I refused to accept any office offered me which was contrary to the traditions of our ancestors.[8] The measures which the senate desired at that time to be taken by me I carried out by virtue of the tribunician power.[9] In this power I five times voluntarily requested and was given a colleague by the senate.[10] . . .

I was a member of the triumvirate for the settlement of the commonwealth for ten consecutive years.[11] I have been ranking senator for forty years, up to the day on which I wrote this document. I have been *pontifex maximus,* augur, member of the college of fifteen for performing sacrifices, member of the college of seven for conducting religious banquets, member of the Arval Brotherhood, one of the *Titii sodales,* and a fetial.[12]

In my fifth consulship I increased the number of patricians, by order of the people, the senate. Three times I revised the roll of senators. And in my sixth consulship,[13] with Marcus Agrippa as my colleague, I conducted a census of the

---

[7]This marks the beginning of the assumption by the Roman emperors of the *cura annonae* ("administration of the grain supply") of Rome as a permanent function of the imperial administration.

[8]In effect, Augustus was thus offered permanent dictatorship in a new guise.

[9]Augustus here refers to his moral and social legislation, the first installments of which were issued in 18 B.C.E.

[10]Marcus Agrippa, twice; Tiberius, three times.

[11]The triumvirate lasted officially from November 27, 43 B.C.E. to December 31, 33 B.C.E. The controversial question of the powers of Antony and Octavian in 32 B.C.E. has evoked heated scholarly discussion.

[12]All Roman emperors after Augustus held the first four of these priesthoods, the most important sacerdotal offices in the national religion.

[13]28 B.C.E. The last census had been taken in 70–69 B.C.E.

people. I performed the *lustrum*[14] after an interval of forty-two years. At this *lustrum* 4,063,000 Roman citizens were recorded. Then a second time, acting alone, by virtue of the consular power, I completed the taking of the census in the consulship of Gaius Censorinus and Gaius Asinius [8 B.C.E.]. At this *lustrum* 4,233,000 Roman citizens were recorded. And a third time I completed the taking of the census in the consulship of Sextus Pompeius and Sextus Appuleius [14 C.E.], by virtue of the consular power and with my son Tiberius Caesar as my colleague. At this *lustrum* 4,937,000 Roman citizens were recorded. By new legislation which I sponsored I restored many traditions of our ancestors which were falling into desuetude in our generation; and I myself handed down precedents in many spheres for posterity to imitate.

The senate decreed that vows for my health should be offered up every fifth year by the consuls and priests. In fulfillment of these vows, games were often celebrated during my lifetime, sometimes by the four most distinguished colleges of priests, sometimes by the consuls. Moreover, the whole citizen body, with one accord, both individually and as members of municipalities, prayed continuously for my health at all the shrines.

My name was inserted, by decree of the senate, in the hymn of the Salian priests. And it was enacted by law that I should be sacrosanct in perpetuity and that I should possess the tribunician power as long as I live.[15] I declined to become *pontifex maximus* in place of a colleague[16] while he was still alive, when the people offered me that priesthood, which my father had held. A few years later, in the consulship of Publius Sulpicius and Gaius Valgius, I accepted this priesthood, when death removed the man who had taken possession of it at a time of civil disturbance; and from all Italy a multitude flocked to my election such as had never previously been recorded at Rome.

To commemorate my return from Syria, the senate consecrated an altar to Fortune the Home-bringer before the temple of Honor and Virtue at the Porta Capena, on which alter it decreed that the pontiffs and Vestal Virgins should make a yearly sacrifice on the anniversary of the day in the consulship of Quintus Lucretius and Marcus Vinicius [19 B.C.E.] on which I returned to the city from Syria, and it designated that day *Augustalia* from my name.

On this occasion, by decree of the senate, a portion of the praetors and tribunes of the plebs, together with the consul Quintus Lucretius and the leading men, was sent to Campania to meet me, an honor which up to this time has been decreed to no one but myself. When I returned to Rome from Spain and Gaul in

[14]***lustrum:*** Purification ceremony, which brought the census officially to a close. [Ed.]

[15]Augustus was accorded the *sacrosanctitas,* inviolability, of a tribune in 36 B.C.E. Modified tribunician power was conferred upon him in 30 B.C.E., but it was only after the constitutional settlement of 23 B.C.E. that he began to date his regnal years by the number of years he had held this power in its complete form.

[16]Lepidus was deposed from the Second Triumvirate in 36 B.C.E. but was permitted to retain the office of *pontifex maximus.* Upon [Lepidus's] death in 13 B.C.E. Augustus was elected chief pontiff the following year. All subsequent emperors held this office.

the consulship of Tiberius Nero and Publius Quintilius [13 B.C.E.], after successfully settling the affairs of those provinces, the senate, to commemorate my return, ordered an altar of the Augustan Peace[17] to be consecrated in the Campus Martius, on which it decreed that the magistrates, priests, and Vestal Virgins should make an annual sacrifice.

The temple of Janus Quirinus,[18] which our ancestors desired to be closed whenever peace with victory was secured by sea and by land throughout the entire empire of the Roman people, and which before I was born is recorded to have been closed only twice since the founding of the city, was during my principate three times ordered by the senate to be closed.

My sons Gaius and Lucius Caesar,[19] whom fortune took from me in their youth, were, in my honor, made consuls designate by the Roman senate and people when they were fifteen years old, with permission to enter that magistracy after a period of five years. The senate further decreed that from the day on which they were introduced onto the Forum[20] they should attend its debates, Moreover, the whole body of Roman *equites* presented each of them with silver shields and spears and saluted each as *princeps iuventutis.*[21]

To the Roman plebs I paid 300 sesterces[22] apiece in accordance with the will of my father [i.e., Julius Caesar]; and in my fifth consulship [29 B.C.E.] I gave each 400 sesterces in my own name out of the spoils of war; and a second time in my tenth consulship [24 B.C.E.] I paid out of my own patrimony a largess of 400 sesterces to every individual; in my eleventh consulship [23 B.C.E.] I made twelve distributions of food out of grain purchased at my own expense; and in the twelfth year of my tribunician power [12 B.C.E.] for the third time I gave 400 sesterces to every individual. These largesses of mine reached never less than 250,000 persons. In the eighteenth year of my tribunician power and my twelfth consulship [5 B.C.E.] I gave sixty *denarii* to each of 320,000 persons of the urban plebs. And in my fifth consulship [29 B.C.E.] I gave out of the spoils of war 1,000 sesterces apiece to my soldiers settled in colonies. This largess on the occasion of my triumph was received by about 120,000 persons in the colonies. In my thirteenth consulship [2 B.C.E.] I gave sixty *denarii* apiece to those of the plebs who at that time were receiving public grain; the number involved was a little more than 200,000 persons.

[17]Extensive parts of the famous Altar of Peace, dedicated in 9 B.C.E., are extant. The whole monument has been reconstructed *in situ.*

[18]A small bronze shrine, with double doors on both ends, on the north side of the Forum.

[19]Grandsons of Augustus, the sons of Agrippa and Julia, adopted by him in 17 B.C.E. and marked out as his successors. But Gaius died in 4 C.E., Lucius in 2 C.E.

[20]That is, introduced to public life. This traditional Roman ceremony, which occurred at puberty, involved among other things the assumption of the *toga virilis* ("toga of manhood").

[21]That is, "leader of the youth." This title designated them as honorary heads of the young men of equestrian families who were organized in a kind of aristocratic Boy Scout movement.

[22]**sesterce:** Roman silver coin. [Ed.]

I reimbursed municipalities for the lands which I assigned to my soldiers in my fourth consulship, and afterwards in the consulship of Marcus Crassus and Gnaeus Lentulus the augur [30 and 14 B.C.E.]. The sums involved were about 600,000,000 sesterces which I paid for Italian estates, and about 260,000,000 sesterces which I paid for provincial lands. I was the first and only one to take such action of all those who up to my time established colonies of soldiers in Italy or in the provinces. And afterwards, in the consulship of Tiberius Nero and Gnaeus Piso, and likewise of Gaius Antistius and Decimus Laelius, and of Gaius Calvisius and Lucius Passienus, and of Lucius Lentulus and Marcus Messalla, and of Lucius Caninius and Quintus Fabricius [in 7, 6, 4, 3, and 2 B.C.E.], I granted bonuses in cash to the soldiers whom after the completion of their terms of service I sent back to their municipalities; and for this purpose I expended about 400,000,000 sesterces.

Four times I came to the assistance of the treasury with my own money, transferring to those in charge of the treasury 150,000,000 sesterces. And in the consulship of Marcus Lepidus and Lucius Arruntius [6 C.E.] I transferred out of my own patrimony 170,000,000 sesterces to the soldiers' bonus fund, which was established on my advice for the purpose of providing bonuses for soldiers who had completed twenty or more years of service.

From the year in which Gnaeus Lentulus and Publius Lentulus [18 B.C.E.] were consuls, whenever the provincial taxes fell short, in the case sometimes of 100,000 persons and sometimes of many more, I made up their tribute in grain and in money from my own grain stores and my own patrimony.

I built the following structures: the senate house and the Chalcidicum adjoining it; the temple of Apollo on the Palatine with its porticoes; the temple of the deified Julius; the Lupercal; the portico at the Circus Flaminius, which I allowed to be called Octavia after the name of the man who had built an earlier portico on the same site; the state box at the Circus Maximus; the temples of Jupiter the Smiter and Jupiter the Thunderer on the Capitoline; the temple of Quirinus; the temples of Minerva and Queen Juno and of Jupiter Freedom on the Aventine; the temple of the Lares at the head of the Sacred Way; the temple of the Penates on the Velia; the temple of Youth and the temple of the Great Mother on the Palatine.[23]

I repaired the Capitol and the theater of Pompey with enormous expenditures on both works, without having my name inscribed on them. I repaired the conduits of the aqueducts which were falling into ruin in many places because of age, and I doubled the capacity of the aqueduct called Marcia by admitting a new spring into its conduit. I completed the Julian Forum and the basilica which was between the temple of Castor and the temple of Saturn, works begun and far advanced by my father, and when the same basilica was destroyed by fire, I enlarged

[23]To identify for the reader each of the public works listed in this and the two following paragraphs would require a series of footnotes longer than the text. A convenient source of information on the various structures is E. Nash, *Pictorial Dictionary of Ancient Rome,* 2 vols. (New York: 1961–1962).

its site and began rebuilding the structure, which is to be inscribed with the names of my sons; and in case it should not be completed while I am still alive, I left instructions that the work be completed by my heirs. In my sixth consulship [28 B.C.E.] I repaired eighty-two temples of the gods in the city, in accordance with a resolution of the senate, neglecting none which at that time required repair. In my seventh consulship [27 B.C.E.] I reconstructed the Flaminian Way from the city as far as Ariminum, and also all the bridges except the Mulvian and the Minucian.

On my own private land I built the temple of Mars Ultor and the Augustan Forum from spoils of war. On ground bought for the most part from private owners I built the theater adjoining the temple of Apollo which was to be inscribed with the name of my son-in-law Marcus Marcellus. In the Capitol, in the temple of the deified Julius, in the temple of Apollo, in the temple of Vesta, and in the temple of Mars Ultor I consecrated gifts from spoils of war which cost me about 100,000,000 sesterces. In my fifth consulship [29 B.C.E.] I remitted to the municipalities and colonies of Italy 35,000 pounds of crown gold which they were collecting in honor of my triumphs; and afterwards, whenever I was acclaimed *imperator,* I did not accept the crown gold, though the municipalities and colonies decreed it with the same enthusiasm as before.

I gave a gladiatorial show three times in my own name, and five times in the names of my sons or grandsons; at these shows about 10,000 fought. Twice I presented to the people in my own name an exhibition of athletes invited from all parts of the world, and a third time in the name of my grandson. I presented games in my own name four times, and in addition twenty-three times in the place of other magistrates.[24] On behalf of the college of fifteen, as master of that college, with Marcus Agrippa as my colleague, I celebrated the Secular Games in the consulship of Gaius Furnius and Gaius Silanus. In my thirteenth consulship [2 B.C.E.] I was the first to celebrate the Games of Mars, which subsequently the consuls, in accordance with a decree of the senate and a law, have regularly celebrated in the succeeding years. Twenty-six times I provided for the people, in my own name or in the names of my sons or grandsons, hunting spectacles of African wild beasts in the circus or in the Forum or in the amphitheaters; in these exhibitions about 3,500 animals were killed.

I presented to the people an exhibition of a naval battle across the Tiber where the grove of the Caesars now is, having had the site excavated 1,800 feet in length and 1,200 feet in width. In this exhibition thirty beaked ships, triremes or biremes, and in addition a great number of smaller vessels engaged in combat. On board these fleets, exclusive of rowers, there were about 3,000 combatants.

When I was victorious I replaced in the temples of all the communities of the province of Asia the ornaments which my opponent [Mark Antony] in the war had seized for his private use after despoiling the temples. About eighty silver statues of myself, represented on foot, on horseback, or in a chariot, stood in the city; these I myself removed, and out of the money therefrom I set up golden offerings

[24]These were the games in the theatrical and circus shows.

in the temple of Apollo in my own name and in the names of those who had honored me with the statues.

I brought peace to the sea by suppressing the pirates.[25] In that war I turned over to their masters for punishment nearly 30,000 slaves who had run away from their owners and taken up arms against the state. The whole of Italy voluntarily took an oath of allegiance to me and demanded me as its leader in the war in which I was victorious at Actium.[26] The same oath was taken by the provinces of the Gauls, the Spains, Africa, Sicily, and Sardinia. More than 700 senators served at that time under my standards; of that number eighty-three attained the consulship and about 170 obtained priesthoods, either before that date or subsequently, up to the day on which this document was written.

I extended the frontiers of all the provinces of the Roman people on whose boundaries were peoples not subject to our empire.[27] I restored peace to the Gallic and Spanish provinces and likewise to Germany, that is to the entire region bounded by the Ocean from Gades to the mouth of the Elbe River. I caused peace to be restored in the Alps, from the region nearest to the Adriatic Sea as far as the Tuscan Sea, without undeservedly making war against any people. My fleet sailed the Ocean from the mouth of the Rhine eastward as far as the territory of the Cimbrians, to which no Roman previously had penetrated either by land or by sea. The Cimbrians, the Charydes, the Semnones, and other German peoples of the same region through their envoys sought my friendship and that of the Roman people.[28] At my command and under my auspices two armies were led almost at the same time into Ethiopia and into Arabia which is called Felix; and very large forces of the enemy belonging to both peoples were killed in battle, and many towns were captured. In Ethiopia a penetration was made as far as the town of Napata, which is next to Meroe; in Arabia the army advanced into the territory of the Sabaeans to the town of Mariba.[29]

I added Egypt to the empire of the Roman people.[30] Although I might have made Greater Armenia into a province when its king Artaxes was assassinated, I preferred, following the precedent of our ancestors, to hand over this kingdom, acting through Tiberius Nero, who was then my stepson, to Tigranes, son of King Artavasdes and grandson of King Tigranes. And afterwards, when this same people revolted and rebelled, after I subdued it through my son Gaius, I handed it over to the rule of King Ariobarzanes, son of Artabazus, king of the Medes, and after his

---

[25]The naval war with Sextus Pompey, which ended in 36 B.C.E.

[26]The war against Antony and Cleopatra, who were defeated at Actium in 31 B.C.E.

[27]The emphasis is on the frontier policy in the West. The eastern provinces were hardly as well stabilized under Augustus.

[28]The reference is to the campaign of 5 C.E., when Tiberius penetrated Germany as far as the Elbe River.

[29]This is the disastrous expedition of Aelius Gallus in 25–24 B.C.E. against Arabia Felix (Yemen); the punitive Ethiopian expedition under Gaius Petronius in 24–22 B.C.E. achieved greater success.

[30]On the death of Cleopatra in 30 B.C.E.

death to his son Artavasdes. When the latter was killed, I dispatched to that kingdom Tigranes, a scion of the royal family of Armenia. I recovered all the provinces extending beyond the Adriatic Sea eastward, and also Cyrenae, which were for the most part already in the possession of kings, as I had previously recovered Sicily and Sardinia, which had been seized in the slave war.[31]

I established colonies of soldiers in Africa, Sicily, Macedonia, in both Spanish provinces, in Achaea, Asia, Syria, Narbonese Gaul, and Pisidia. Italy, moreover, has twenty-eight colonies established by me, which in my lifetime have grown to be famous and populous.

A number of military standards lost by other generals I recovered, after conquering the enemy, from Spain, Gaul, and the Dalmatians. The Parthians I compelled to restore to me the spoils and standards of three Roman armies and to seek the friendship of the Roman people as suppliants.[32] The standards, moreover, I deposited in the inner shrine of the temple of Mars Ultor.

Through Tiberius Nero, who was then my stepson and legate, I conquered and subjected to the empire of the Roman people the Pannonian tribes, to which before my principate no army of the Roman people had ever penetrated; and I extended the frontier of Illyricum to the bank of the Danube River. An army of the Dacians which had crossed to our side of the river was conquered and destroyed under my auspices, and later on, my army crossed the Danube and compelled the Dacian tribes to submit to the orders of the Roman people.

Royal embassies from India, never previously seen before any Roman general, were often sent to me. Our friendship was sought through ambassadors by the Bastarnians and Scythians and by the kings of the Sarmatians, who live on both sides of the Don River, and by the kings of the Albanians and of the Iberians and of the Medes.[33]

The following kings fled to me as suppliants: Tiridates and afterwards Phraates son of King Phraates, kings of the Parthians; Artavasdes, king of the Medes; Artaxares, king of the Adiabenians; Dumnobellaunus and Tincommius, kings of the Britons; Maelo, king of the Sugumbrians, and Segimerus[?], king of the Marcomannian Suebians.[34] Phraates son of Orodes, king of the Parthians, sent to me in Italy all his sons and grandsons, not because he was conquered in war, but seeking our friendship through pledge of his children. Under my principate numerous other peoples, with whom previously there had existed no exchange of embassies and friendship, experienced the good faith of the Roman people.

---

[31]Provinces held by Antony and Sextus Pompey.

[32]These were the standards lost by Crassus at the battle of Carrhae in 53 B.C.E. and in Mark Antony's disastrous operations against the Parthians in 36 B.C.E. They were restored as the result of diplomatic negotiations; Augustus's version is calculated to salve Roman pride.

[33]The peoples named in this sentence inhabited the fringes of the Roman Empire from the Carpathians to the Caucasus.

[34]Adiabenia was a district of Assyria; the Sugumbrians and Marcomannian Suebians were Germanic tribes.

The peoples of the Parthians and of the Medes, through ambassadors who were the leading men of these peoples, received from me the kings for whom they asked: the Parthians, Vonones son of King Phraates, grandson of King Orodes; the Medes, Ariobarzanes son of King Artavasdes, grandson of King Ariobarzanes.

In my sixth and seventh consulships,[35] after I had put an end to the civil wars, having attained supreme power by universal consent, I transferred the state from my own power to the control of the Roman senate and the people. For this service of mine I received the title of Augustus by decree of the senate, and the doorposts of my house were publicly decked with laurels, the civic crown was affixed over my doorway, and a golden shield was set up in the Julian senate house, which, as the inscription on this shield testifies, the Roman senate and people gave me in recognition of my valor, clemency, justice, and devotion. After that time I excelled all in authority, but I possessed no more power than the others who were my colleagues in each magistracy.

When I held my thirteenth consulship,[36] the senate, the equestrian order, and the entire Roman people gave me the title of "father of the country" and decreed that this title should be inscribed in the vestibule of my house, in the Julian senate house, and in the Augustan Forum on the pedestal of the chariot which was set up in my honor by decree of the senate. At the time I wrote this document I was in my seventy-sixth year.

### ■ Discussion Questions

1. What does this document reveal about the ways in which Augustus used tradition to effect political change?
2. Upon what foundation does Augustus's power and success as a ruler seem to rest?
3. What do you think Augustus's primary goals were in composing this account of his political career?

[35]28 and 27 B.C.E. The reorganization of 28–27 B.C.E. put an end to the unlimited powers exercised by Augustus without legal title from the expiration of the triumvirate in 33 B.C.E. to that date. Augustus justifies his extralegal position by affirming that he held it "by universal consent."
[36]2 B.C.E.

## 2.
## *Notices and Graffiti Describing Life in Pompeii*
### First Century C.E.

*Among the remarkable features of the Roman Empire was its immense expanse and the many cities, both new and old, that dotted its landscape. The following messages,*

From Naphtali Lewis and Meyer Reinhold, eds., *Roman Civilization: Selected Readings,* 3d ed., vol. 2 (New York: Columbia University Press, 1990), 126–27, 237–38, 276–78.

*graffiti, and election notices from the Roman municipality of Pompeii illuminate the hustle and bustle of urban life in the first century of the empire. Located at the foot of Mount Vesuvius in southern Italy, Pompeii at the time was a thriving commercial city, with a fashionable resort nearby. In 79 C.E., Mount Vesuvius erupted, burying the city in cinders and ash. Although the local population was destroyed or fled, remarkably, the city's buildings were preserved, as were hundreds of announcements painted in red on white-washed walls, along with the scribbles of passersby. Here we see many facets of people's daily lives within the empire, from political appeals to lovesick lamentations.*

In the Arrius Pollio block owned by Gnaeus Alleius Nigidius Maius, to let from the fifteenth of next July, shops with their stalls, high-class second-story apartments, and a house. Prospective lessees may apply to Primus, slave of Gnaeus Alleius Nigidius Maius.

On the property owned by Julia Felix, daughter of Spurius, to let from the thirteenth of next August to the thirteenth of the sixth August hence, or five consecutive years, the élite Venus Baths, shops, stalls, and second-story apartments. Interested parties may apply to the lessor in the matter.

The fruit dealers together with Helvius Vestalis unanimously urge the election of Marcus Holconius Priscus as duovir[1] with judicial power.

The goldsmiths unanimously urge the election of Gaius Cuspius Pansa as aedile.[2]

I ask you to elect Gaius Julius Polybius aedile. He gets good bread [for us].

The muleteers urge the election of Gaius Julius Polybius as duovir.

The worshippers of Isis unanimously urge the election of Gnaeus Helvius Sabinus as aedile.

Proculus, make Sabinus aedile and he will do as much for you.

His neighbors urge you to elect Lucius Statius Receptus duovir with judicial power; he is worthy. Aemilius Celer, a neighbor, wrote this. May you take sick if you maliciously erase this!

Satia and Petronia support and ask you to elect Marcus Casellius and Lucius Albucius aediles. May we always have such citizens in our colony!

---

[1]**duovir:** One of two chief magistrates of Roman municipalities. [Ed.]
[2]**aedile:** Municipal administrator. [Ed.]

I ask you to elect Epidius Sabinus duovir with judicial power. He is worthy, a defender of the colony, and in the opinion of the respected judge Suedius Clemens and by agreement of the council, because of his services and uprightness, worthy of the municipality. Elect him!

If upright living is considered any recommendation, Lucretius Fronto is well worthy of the office.

Genialis urges the election of Bruttius Balbus as duovir. He will protect the treasury.

I ask you to elect Marcus Cerrinius Vatia to the aedileship. All the late drinkers support him. Florus and Fructus wrote this.

The petty thieves support Vatia for the aedileship.

I ask you to elect Aulus Vettius Firmus aedile. He is worthy of the municipality. I ask you to elect him, ballplayers. Elect him!

I wonder, O wall, that you have not fallen in ruins from supporting the stupidities of so many scribblers.[3]

Twenty pairs of gladiators of Decimus Lucretius Satrius Valens, life-time flamen[4] of Nero son of Caesar Augustus, and ten pairs of gladiators of Decimus Lucretius Valens, his son, will fight at Pompeii on April 8, 9, 10, 11, 12. There will be a full card of wild beast combats, and awnings [for the spectators]. Aemilius Celer [painted this sign], all alone in the moonlight.

Market days: Saturday in Pompeii, Sunday in Nuceria, Monday in Atella, Tuesday in Nola, Wednesday in Cumae, Thursday in Puteoli, Friday in Rome.

> 6th: cheese 1, bread 8, oil 3, wine 3[5]
> 7th: bread 8, oil 5, onions 5, bowl 1, bread for the slave[?] 2, wine 2
> 8th: bread 8, bread for the slave[?] 4, grits 3
> 9th: wine for the winner 1 *denarius,* bread 8, wine 2, cheese 2
> 10th: . . . 1 *denarius,* bread 2, for women 8, wheat 1 *denarius,* cucumber 1, dates 1, incense 1, cheese 2, sausage 1, soft cheese 4, oil 7

---

[3]Unlike the others, this inscription is a *graffito,* scratched on the wall.
[4]**flamen:** Priest. [Ed.]
[5]The initial number is the day of the months, the numbers following the items of food indicate expenditures in asses, except where *denarii* are specified. A *denarius* was a Roman silver coin originally valued at ten, and later sixteen, asses. It was the equivalent of the Greek drachma. [Ed.]

Pleasure says: "You can get a drink here for an *as*, a better drink for two, Falernian[6] for four.

A copper pot is missing from this shop. 65 sesterces reward if anybody brings it back, 20 sesterces if he reveals the thief so we can get our property back.

The weaver Successus loves the innkeeper's slave girl, Iris by name. She doesn't care for him, but he begs her to take pity on him. Written by his rival. So long.

[Answer by the rival:] Just because you're bursting with envy, don't pick on a handsomer man, a lady-killer and a gallant.

[Answer by the first writer:] There's nothing more to say or write. You love Iris, who doesn't care for you.

Take your lewd looks and flirting eyes off another man's wife, and show some decency on your face!

Anybody in love, come here. I want to break Venus' ribs with a club and cripple the goddess' loins. If she can pierce my tender breast, why can't I break her head with a club?

I write at Love's dictation and Cupid's instruction;
But damn it! I don't want to be a god without you.

[A prostitute's sign:] I am yours for two *asses* cash.

### ■ Discussion Questions

1. Based on these messages and notices, how would you describe life in Pompeii? What did the city look like?
2. What are some of the things people did for a living?
3. What do the election announcements reveal about the residents' political expectations and their role in local politics?

[6]One of the prized wines of the Italian countryside (named after a district in Campania), best known from the poems of Horace that sing its praises.

## 3.
## *Plan of Stabian Baths* and Seneca *Letters 56.1, 2*
### First Century C.E.

*Despite all its grandeur, city life in imperial Rome was noisy, crowded, and dirty. Public baths were one way for residents to keep clean while socializing with friends.*

---

From Jo-Ann Shelton, *As the Romans Did: A Sourcebook in Roman Social History* (New York and Oxford: Oxford University Press, 1988), 313–14.

*The plan of the Stabian Baths at Pompeii (shown here), the oldest of the city's public bath buildings, was built in the second century* B.C.E. *but was repaired and remodeled over the next two hundred years. The shops located along the walls were not affiliated with the public baths, but some may have sold oil, towels, and other related supplies. Similar baths existed in every sizable community in the empire. The Roman philosopher Seneca (4* B.C.E.*–65* C.E.*) wrote to a friend describing the commotion that he had to endure to keep up his studies while living in a rented apartment over a public bath. In this excerpt, he offers a lively picture of the range of people using and working in and around the bath, one of hundreds dotting the urban landscape.*

**Plan of Stabian Baths**

***Baths***

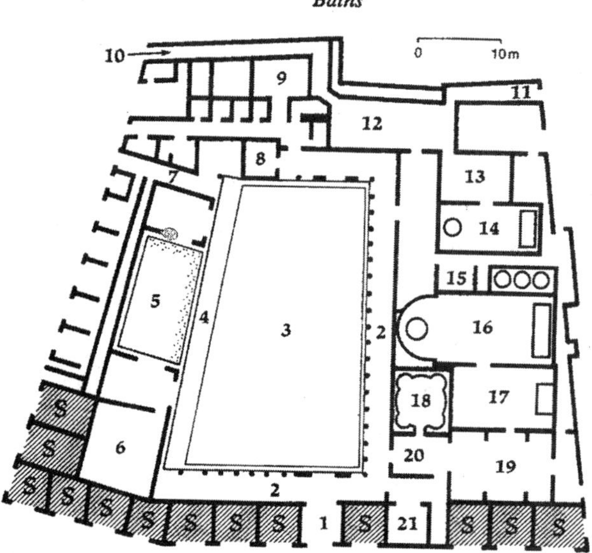


1. main entrance, men's baths
2. colonnade
3. palaestra (open-air exercise area)
4. bowling lane
5. swimming pool
6. dressing and massage room
7. side entrance, men's baths
8. office
9. toilets
10. entrance, women's baths
11. entrance, women's baths
12. apodyterium (dressing room), women's baths
13. tepidarium (warm room), women's baths
14. caldarium (hot room), with hot tub and basin, women's baths
15. furnace room, with three water tanks
16. caldarium, with hot tub and basin, men's baths
17. tepidarium, with warm tub, men's baths
18. frigidarium (cold room), men's baths
19. apodyterium, men's baths
20. vestibule
21. waiting room

S. shop

## SENECA, *Letters* 56.1, 2

If silence is as necessary as it seems for someone who wants seclusion to read and study, then I'm really in trouble. Here I am surrounded on all sides by a variety of noises. I live right over a public bath. Just imagine the whole range of voices which can irritate my ears. When the more muscular types are exercising and swinging about lead weights in their hands, and when they are straining themselves, or at least pretending to strain, I hear groans. And when they hold their breath for a while and then let it out, I hear hissing and very hoarse gasps. But when I have to put up with an unathletic fellow, one satisfied with a low-class rub-down, I hear the slap of a hand pummeling his shoulders (the sound varies somewhat, depending on whether the hand is flat or cupped). Now, if a ballplayer comes along and begins to count his score aloud, I'm definitely finished. Imagine also a quarrelsome drunk, or sometimes a thief caught in the act, or a man who loves to sing in the bath. And then imagine people diving into the pool with a great splash of water.

Besides these men, whose voices are, if nothing else, at least natural, imagine the hair plucker with his shrill and high-pitched voice, continually shrieking in order to be noticed; he's never quiet, except when he's plucking armpits and forcing his customer to shriek instead of him. I could wear myself out just listening to the variety of shouts among people selling drinks, sausages, and pastries; each restaurant or snack bar has its own huckster with his own recognizable jingle.

### ■ Discussion Questions

1. Based on the plan of the Stabian Baths and Seneca's letter, why do you think baths were so popular among men and women of all social classes throughout the Roman Empire? What activities and amenities did they provide?
2. What does Seneca's description reveal about housing conditions in ancient Rome?
3. What do these documents suggest about Roman attitudes toward the body?

## 4.
## Flavius Josephus
## *The Jewish War*
### 70 C.E.

*An independent kingdom under the descendants of Judas Maccabaeus after 142 B.C.E., Palestine came under Roman control in 63 B.C.E. Increasing intervention by Rome provoked rebellion during the first century. Joseph ben Matthias (37–100 C.E.)*

---

From *The Jewish War*, trans. G. A. Williamson; rev. E. Mary Smallwood (London: Penguin Books), 1959.

*was born into an upper-class Jewish priestly family. He adopted the Roman name Flavius Josephus after being captured by the emperor Vespasian (r. 69–79 C.E.). After giving information to the Romans, he enjoyed a privileged position in Rome. In spite of his earlier activities, Josephus was determined to prevent an insurrection by Jewish rebels, which he believed would be fatal for the Jewish people. He witnessed the events described in* The Jewish War, *which resulted in the destruction of the Second Temple in 70 C.E. by Vespasian's son Titus and in the eradication of all traces of Judaism in Jerusalem. The casualties were enormous, and tens of thousands more were sent into slavery in Egypt. This narrative is pro-Roman, intended to convince the Jews that Rome had been forced to take drastic measures as a result of the actions of a few Jewish fanatics.*

## [THE DESTRUCTION OF JERUSALEM]

As the legions charged in, neither persuasion nor threat could check their impetuosity: passion alone was in command. Crowded together round the entrances many were trampled by their friends, many fell among the still hot and smoking ruins of the colonnades and died as miserably as the defeated. As they neared the Sanctuary they pretended not even to hear Caesar's commands and urged the men in front to throw in more firebrands. The partisans were no longer in a position to help; everywhere was slaughter and flight. Most of the victims were peaceful citizens, weak and unarmed, butchered wherever they were caught. Round the Altar the heap of corpses grew higher and higher, while down the Sanctuary steps poured a river of blood and the bodies of those killed at the top slithered to the bottom. . . . Caesar therefore led his staff inside the building and viewed the Holy Place of the Sanctuary with its furnishings, which went far beyond the accounts circulating in foreign countries. . . . Titus dashed out and by personal efforts strove to persuade his men to put out the fire, instructing Liberalius, a centurion of his bodyguard of spearmen, to lay his staff across the shoulders of any who disobeyed. But their respect for Caesar and their fear of the centurion's staff were powerless against their fury, their detestation of the Jews, and an uncontrollable lust for battle. Most of them were also spurred on by the expectation of loot. . . . When Caesar dashed out to restrain the troops, that man pushed a firebrand into the hinges of the gate. Then from within a flame suddenly shot up, Caesar and his staff withdrew, and those outside were free to start what fires they liked. Thus the Sanctuary was set on fire in defiance of Caesar's wishes. . . .

While the Sanctuary was burning, looting went on right and left and all who were caught were put to the sword. There was no pity for age, no regard for rank; little children and old men, laymen and priests alike were butchered; every class was held in the iron embrace of war, whether they defended themselves or cried for mercy. Through the roar of the flames as they swept relentlessly on could be heard the groans of the falling: such were the height of the hill and the vastness of the blazing edifice that the entire city seemed to be on fire, while as for the noise, nothing could be imagined more shattering or more horrifying. There was the war-cry of the Roman legions as they converged; the yells of the partisans encircled with fire and sword; the panic flight of the people cut off above into the arms of the enemy, and their shrieks as the end approached. . . .

. . . The Temple Hill, enveloped in flames from top to bottom, appeared to be boiling up from its very roots; yet the sea of flame was nothing to the ocean of blood, . . .

The Romans, judging it useless to spare the outbuildings now that the Sanctuary was in flames, set fire to them all. . . . They also burnt the treasuries which housed huge sums of money, huge quantities of clothing, and other precious things. . . . Next they came to the last surviving colonnade of the outer court. On this women and children and a mixed crowd of citizens had found a refuge—6,000 in all. Before Caesar could reach a decision about them or instruct his officers, the soldiers, carried away by their fury, fired the colonnade from below; as a result some flung themselves out of the flames to their death, others perished in the blaze: of that vast number there escaped not one. . . .

## ■ Discussion Questions

1. How does Josephus portray Titus's behavior and feelings about ordering the destruction of Jerusalem and the Second Temple? What lesson does Josephus want to convey?
2. Because of the Roman respect for the antiquity of their traditions and beliefs, Jews had enjoyed relatively favored status from Rome before the revolt. What did Josephus and Titus fear so greatly that it resulted in the destruction of Jerusalem?
3. How might Josephus's account affect both Jews and Romans who read it?

# 5.
# Pliny the Younger
## *Letters*
### Early Second Century C.E.

*Although Augustus describes his rise to power and ensuing glories in vivid detail, he provides little insight into the mechanics of running a vast and diverse empire. These letters help to fill this gap. Pliny the Younger (61–62–c. 114 C.E.) wrote them while serving as governor of Bithynia, a Roman province in modern-day Turkey. More than one hundred pieces of Pliny's official correspondence regarding Bithynia exist, including his letters to Emperor Trajan (r. 98–117 C.E.), who had appointed him to the post, and the emperor's replies. As the letters reveal, upon his arrival in 111 C.E., Pliny faced an array of challenges, from fiscal mismanagement to a more novel menace,*

From *Pliny Letters and Panegyricus,* trans. Betty Radice, vol. 2 (Cambridge: Harvard University Press, 1969), 187, 189, 191, 207, 209, 213, 215, 217, 285, 287, 289, 291, 293.

*Christianity. Despite their minority status, Pliny perceived Christians' renunciation of traditional beliefs as a danger to peace and social order. Knowing of no precedent to guide him, he drew upon his administrative experience and authority in the hope of preserving the status quo. He wrote Trajan to ask if he had acted correctly, and his response established what passed for official policy concerning Christians in the early empire.*

## A

**Pliny to the Emperor Trajan:** I kept in excellent health, Sir, throughout my voyage to Ephesus, but I found the intense heat very trying when I went on to travel by road and developed a touch of fever which kept me at Pergamum. Then, when I had resumed my journey by coastal boat, I was further delayed by contrary winds, so that I did not reach Bithynia until 17 September. I had hoped to arrive earlier, but I cannot complain of the delay as I was in time to celebrate your birthday in my province, and this should be a good omen. (10.17a)

**Trajan to Pliny:** I wish you could have reached Bithynia without any illness yourself or in your party, and that your journey from Ephesus had been as easy as your voyage there. The date of your arrival in Bithynia, my dear Pliny, I have noted from your letter. The people there will appreciate, I think, that I am acting in their own interests, and you too will see that it is made clear to them that you were chosen as my representative for a special mission. Your first task must be to inspect the accounts of the various towns, as they are evidently in confusion. (10.18)

**Pliny to the Emperor Trajan:** While I was visiting another part of the province, a widespread fire broke out in Nicomedia which destroyed many private houses and also two public buildings (the Elder Citizens' Club and the Temple of Isis) although a road runs between them. It was fanned by the strong breeze in the early stages, but it would not have spread so far but for the apathy of the populace; for it is generally agreed that people stood watching the disaster without bestirring themselves to do anything to stop it. Apart from this, there is not a single fire engine anywhere in the town, not a bucket nor any apparatus for fighting a fire. These will now be provided on my instructions.

Will you, Sir, consider whether you think a company of firemen might be formed, limited to 150 members? I will see that no one shall be admitted who is not genuinely a fireman, and that the privileges granted shall not be abused: it will not be difficult to keep such small numbers under observation. (10.33)

**Trajan to Pliny:** You may very well have had the idea that it should be possible to form a company of firemen at Nicomedia on the model of those existing elsewhere, but we must remember that it is societies like these which have been responsible for the political disturbances in your province, particularly in its towns. If people assemble for a common purpose, whatever name we give them and for whatever reason, they soon turn into a political club. It is a better policy then to provide the equipment necessary for dealing with fires, and to instruct property owners to make use of it, calling on the help of the crowds which collect if they find it necessary. (10.34)

**Pliny to the Emperor Trajan:** The theater at Nicea, Sir, is more than half built but is still unfinished, and has already cost more than ten million sesterces, or so I am told—I have not yet examined the relevant accounts. I am afraid it may be money wasted. The building is sinking and showing immense cracks, either because the soil is damp and soft or the stone used was poor and friable. We shall certainly have to consider whether it is to be finished or abandoned, or even demolished, as the foundations and substructure intended to hold up the building may have cost a lot but look none too solid to me. There are many additions to the theater promised by private individuals, such as a colonnade on either side and a gallery above the auditorium, but all these are now held up by the stoppage of work on the main building which must be finished first.

The citizens of Nicaea have also begun to rebuild their gymnasium (which was destroyed by fire before my arrival) on a much larger and more extensive scale than before. They have already spent a large sum, which may be to little purpose, for the buildings are badly planned and too scattered. Moreover, an architect—admittedly a rival of the one who drew up the designs—has given the opinion that the walls cannot support the superstructure in spite of being twenty-two feet thick, as the rubble core has no facing of brick.

The people of Claudiopolis are also building, or rather excavating, an enormous public bath in a hollow at the foot of a mountain. The money for this is coming either from the admission fees already paid by the new members of the town council elected by your gracious favor, or from what they will pay at my demand. So I am afraid there is misapplication of public funds at Nicaea and abuse of your generosity at Claudiopolis, though this should be valued above any money. I am therefore compelled to ask you to send out an architect to inspect both theater and bath and decide whether it will be more practicable, in view of what has already been spent, to keep to the original plans and finish both buildings as best we can, or to make any necessary alterations and changes of site so that we do not throw away more money in an attempt to make some use of the original outlay. (10.39)

**Trajan to Pliny:** The future of the unfinished theater at Nicaea can best be settled by you on the spot. It will be sufficient for me if you let me know your decision. But, once the main building is finished, you will have to see that private individuals carry out their promises of adding to the theater.

These poor Greeks all love a gymnasium; so it may be that they were too ambitious in their plans at Nicaea. They will have to be content with one which suits their real needs.

As for the bath at Claudiopolis, which you say has been started in an unsuitable site, you must decide yourself what advice to give. You cannot lack architects: every province has skilled men trained for this work. It is a mistake to think they can be sent out more quickly from Rome when they usually come to us from Greece. (10.40)

**Pliny to the Emperor Trajan:** It is my custom to refer all my difficulties to you, Sir, for no one is better able to resolve my doubts and to inform my ignorance.

I have never been present at an examination of Christians. Consequently, I do not know the nature or the extent of the punishments usually meted out to them, nor the grounds for starting an investigation and how far it should be pressed. Nor am I at all sure whether any distinction should be made between them on the grounds of age, or if young people and adults should be treated alike; whether a pardon ought to be granted to anyone retracting his beliefs, or if he has once professed Christianity, he shall gain nothing by renouncing it; and whether it is the mere name of Christian which is punishable, even if innocent of crime, or rather the crimes associated with the name.

For the moment this is the line I have taken with all persons brought before me on the charge of being Christians. I have asked them in person if they are Christians, and if they admit it, I repeat the question a second and third time, with a warning of the punishment awaiting them. If they persist, I order them to be led away for execution; for, whatever the nature of their admission, I am convinced that their stubbornness and unshakeable obstinacy ought not to go unpunished. There have been others similarly fanatical who are Roman citizens. I have entered them on the list of persons to be sent to Rome for trial.

Now that I have begun to deal with this problem, as so often happens, the charges are becoming more widespread and increasing in variety. An anonymous pamphlet has been circulated which contains the names of a number of accused persons. Among these I considered that I should dismiss any who denied that they were or ever had been Christians when they had repeated after me a formula of invocation to the gods and had made offerings of wine and incense to your statue (which I had ordered to be brought into court for this purpose along with the images of the gods), and furthermore had reviled the name of Christ: none of which things, I understand, any genuine Christian can be induced to do.

Others, whose names were given to me by an informer, first admitted the charge and then denied it; they said that they had ceased to be Christians two or more years previously, and some of them even twenty years ago. They all did reverence to your statue and the images of the gods in the same way as the others, and reviled the name of Christ. They also declared that the sum total of their guilt or error amounted to no more than this: they had met regularly before dawn on a fixed day to chant verses alternately among themselves in honor of Christ as if to a god, and also to bind themselves by oath, not for any criminal purpose, but to abstain from theft, robbery and adultery, to commit no breach of trust and not to deny a deposit when called upon to restore it. After this ceremony it had been their custom to disperse and reassemble later to take food of an ordinary, harmless kind; but they had in fact given up this practice since my edict, issued on your instructions, which banned all political societies. This made me decide it was all the more necessary to extract the truth by torture from two slave-women, whom they call deaconesses. I found nothing but a degenerate sort of cult carried to extravagant lengths.

I have therefore postponed any further examination and hastened to consult you. The question seems to me to be worthy of your consideration, especially in view of the number of persons endangered; for a great many individuals of every age and class, both men and women, are being brought to trial, and this is likely to continue. It is not only the towns, but villages and rural districts too which are infected through contact with this wretched cult. I think though that it is still possible for it to be checked and directed to better ends, for there is no doubt that people have begun to throng the temples which had been almost entirely deserted for a long time; the sacred rites which had been allowed to lapse are being performed again, and flesh of sacrificial victims is on sale everywhere, though up till recently scarcely anyone could be found to buy it. It is easy to infer from this that a great many people could be reformed if they were given an opportunity to repent. (10.96)

**Trajan to Pliny:** You have followed the right course of procedure, my dear Pliny, in your examination of the cases of persons charged with being Christians, for it is impossible to lay down a general rule to a fixed formula. These people must not be hunted out; if they are brought before you and the charge against them is proved, they must be punished, but in the case of anyone who denies that he is a Christian, and makes it clear that he is not by offering prayers to our gods, he is to be pardoned as a result of his repentance however suspect his past conduct may be. But pamphlets circulated anonymously must play no part in any accusation. They create the worst sort of precedent and are quite out of keeping with the spirit of our age. (10.97)

## ■ Discussion Questions

1. What aspects of the local administration within Bithynia do Pliny and Trajan regard as problematic and why?
2. What do these letters reveal about the relationship between central and local authority in the Roman Empire?
3. What does Pliny reveal about the beliefs and rites of Christianity at this time, and how were they at odds with Roman traditions?
4. Do you think Pliny's treatment of the accused Christians reflects his administrative style and priorities in general? If so, how?

## ■ Comparative Questions

1. Based on his accomplishments, how would you describe Augustus's pattern for effective rule? How had imperial rule changed by the time Tacitus and Pliny were writing?
2. In what ways do these documents convey a similar image of the Roman emperor? How did Christians, as described in Document 5, challenge this image?
3. How does the graffiti from Pompeii offer a different perspective on Roman politics than the more official accounts and histories?

4. Compare the persecution of early Christians with the destruction of Jerusalem. What differences and similarities do you see in Roman attitudes toward the two groups? How might Roman actions have influenced the future of both Christianity and Judaism?
5. What do the Pompeii graffiti, the Roman bath documents, and Pliny's letters reveal about Roman social life? Do you see any similarities and/or differences to contemporary North American culture?

Chapter

6

# The Transformation of the Roman Empire, c. 284–600 C.E.

THE ROMAN EMPIRE had faced many challenges since its formation at the end of the first century B.C.E., but by the fourth century C.E., the forces of change proved too powerful to resist, as the documents in this chapter attest. Christianity was spreading far and wide, even gaining the allegiance of the emperor, Constantine (r. 306–337 C.E.), and attempting to define doctrine and combat heresy in the Nicene creed. It did not, however, end controversies. Although polytheism persisted, over the course of the fourth century Christianity gained the upper hand, which permanently transformed Roman culture and society. At the same time, waves of Germanic peoples penetrated the empire's borders and migrated westward, eventually establishing their own kingdoms that replaced imperial government. These new regimes became the heirs of Roman civilization in the West, setting the stage for the development of medieval Europe, whereas in the East the imperial legacy lived on in the Byzantine Empire.

## 1.
## Arius
## *Letter to Alexander, Bishop of Alexandria*
**c. 320 C.E.**
## and
## *The Nicene Creed*
**325 C.E.**

*Although Emperor Constantine (288–337 C.E.) had made Christianity a legal religion in the Roman Empire in 313 C.E., major controversies about doctrine and belief*

From J. Stevenson, *A New Eusebius: Documents Illustrating the History of the Church to AD 337*, rev. ed. (London: SPCK, 1987), 326–27; and Patrick V. Reid, *Readings in Western Religious Thought: The Ancient World* (New York: Paulist Press, 1987), 376.

*continued to rage. Arius (c. 260–336 C.E.), a priest and theologian of Alexandria, posed the most serious challenge to the developing church. Setting forth the belief that the Father and Son could not both be uncreated, Arius insisted that Jesus Christ was not God in the same manner as God the Father. He defended his views in the letter that follows, written circa 320 to the bishop of Alexandria after Arius's condemnation by the Synod of Egypt. As the doctrine of Arianism swept through the empire, sparking anger among many Christians, Constantine called the Council of Nicaea (325 C.E.) to resolve the issue. Two hundred to three hundred bishops attended the council, at which Arius was allowed to explain his position. It was rejected, and the council formulated a creed—one that is still used in slightly different forms in most Western Christian churches. Despite the creed's widespread acceptance, Arianism continued to spread and divide the church.*

## LETTER OF ARIUS TO ALEXANDER, BISHOP OF ALEXANDRIA

To our blessed Pope[1] and Bishop Alexander, the Presbyters and Deacons send greeting in the Lord.

Our faith from our forefathers, which we have learned also from thee, Blessed Pope, is this: We acknowledge One God, alone unbegotten, alone everlasting, alone unbegun, alone true, *alone having immortality,* alone wise, alone good, alone sovereign; judge, governor, and administrator of all, unalterable and unchangeable, just and good, God of Law and Prophets and New Testament; who begat an Only-begotten Son before eternal times, through whom he has made both the ages and the universe; and begat him not in semblance, but in truth: and that he made him subsist at his own will, unalterable and unchangeable; perfect creature of God, . . . created before times and before ages, and gaining life and being and his glories from the Father, who gave real existence to those together with him. For the Father did not, in giving to him the inheritance of all things, deprive himself of what he has ingenerately in himself; for he is the Fountain of all things. Thus there are three Subsistences *(hypostases).*[2] And God, being the cause of all things, is unbegun and altogether sole but the Son being begotten apart from time by the Father, and being created and found before ages, was not before his generation; but, being begotten apart from time before all things, alone was made to subsist by the Father. For he is not eternal or co-eternal or co-unoriginate with the Father, nor has he his being together with the Father, as some speak of relations, introducing two ingenerate beginnings, but God is before all things as being Monad and Beginning of all.

## THE NICENE CREED

We believe in one God, the Father Almighty, Maker of all things visible and invisible; and in one Lord Jesus Christ, the Son of God, the only-begotten of his Father,

[1]Papa, a title of respect for distinguished churchmen.
[2]***hypostases:*** Greek for "three or more Arian principles." [Ed.]

of the substance of the Father, God of God, Light of Light, very God of very God, begotten, not made, being of one substance *(homoousion)* with the Father. By whom all things were made, both which be in heaven and in earth. Who for us men and for our salvation came down [from heaven] and was incarnate and was made man. He suffered and the third day he rose again, and ascended into heaven. And he shall come again to judge both the quick and the dead.

And [we believe] in the Holy Ghost.

And whosoever shall say that there was a time when the Son of God was not, or that before he was begotten he was not, or that he was made of things that were not, or that he is of a different substance or essence [from the Father] or that he is a creature, or subject to change or conversion—all that so say, the Catholic and Apostolic Church anathematizes them.

### ■ Discussion Questions

1. What does Arius mean that Jesus is "not eternal or co-eternal or co-unoriginate with the Father"? How is this statement central to his and his followers' faith?
2. How does the Nicene Creed refute the Arian position while defining essential doctrinal beliefs about Christianity?
3. By defining "correct belief," how does the church put into place a mechanism for dealing with heresy?
4. How does the Nicene Creed illustrate the changes in the church as it grew from relatively small, illegal communities into a major hierarchical institution?

## 2.
## Quintas Aurelius Symmachus and St. Ambrose
## *The Altar of Victory Sparks a Religious Debate*
### 384 C.E.

*Although Christianity spread rapidly after Constantine's conversion in 312 C.E. and the promulgation of his edict of religious toleration in 313 C.E., the transformation from polytheist empire to Christian state did not come easily. Polytheism persisted, especially within elite social circles. These documents illuminate the conflict between paganism and Christianity with particular clarity. The emperor's removal of the Altar of Victory in 382 C.E. from the Senate house generated a heated response from prominent Roman politician Quintas Aurelius Symmachus (c. 345–402 C.E.), who demanded the altar's restoration in his memorial to Emperor Valentinian (c. 364–375 C.E.), excerpted here. When the prominent church leader St. Ambrose (339–397 C.E.) caught wind of the memorial, he voiced his opposing views to*

From *A Select Library of Nicene and Post-Nicene Fathers of the Christian Church,* 2d ser., vol. 10 (New York: Christian Literature Co., 1896), 411–15.

*Valentinian in the letter that follows. Ambrose's words foreshadowed the future. In 391 C.E., Christianity became the official religion of the empire.*

## THE MEMORIAL OF SYMMACHUS, PREFECT OF THE CITY

As soon as the most honorable Senate, always devoted to you, knew that crimes were made amenable to law, and that the reputation of late times was being purified by pious princes, it, following the example of a more favorable time, gave utterance to its long suppressed grief, and bade me be once again the delegate to utter its complaints. . . .

In the exercise, therefore, of a twofold office, as your Prefect I attend to public business, and as delegate I recommend to your notice the charge laid on me by the citizens. . . .

For to what is it more suitable that we defend the institutions of our ancestors, and the rights and destiny of our country, than to the glory of these times, which is all the greater when you understand that you may not do anything contrary to the custom of your ancestors? We demand then the restoration of that condition of religious affairs which was so long advantageous to the state. . . .

Who is so friendly with the barbarians as not to require an Altar of Victory? We will be careful henceforth, and avoid a show of such things. But at least let that honor be paid to the name which is refused to the goddess—your fame, which will last for ever, owes much and will owe still more to victory. Let those be averse to this power, whom it has never benefited. Do you refuse to desert a patronage which is friendly to your triumphs? That power is wished for by all, let no one deny that what he acknowledges is to be desired should also be venerated.

But even if the avoidance of such an omen were not sufficient, it would at least have been seemly to abstain from injuring the ornaments of the Senate House. Allow us, we beseech you, as old men to leave to posterity what we received as boys. . . .

Where shall we swear to obey your laws and commands? By what religious sanction shall the false mind be terrified, so as not to lie in bearing witness? All things are indeed filled with God, and no place is safe for the perjured, but to be urged in the very presence of religious forms has great power in producing a fear of sinning. That altar preserves the concord of all, that altar appeals to the good faith of each, and nothing gives more authority to our decrees than that the whole of our order issues every decree as it were under the sanction of an oath. . . .

Let us now suppose that Rome is present and addresses you in these words: "Excellent princes, fathers of your country, respect my years to which pious rites have brought me. Let me use the ancestral ceremonies, for I do not repent of them. Let me live after my own fashion, for I am free. This worship subdued the world to my laws, these sacred rites repelled Hannibal from the walls, and the Senones from the capitol. Have I been reserved for this, that in my old age I should be blamed? I will consider what it is thought should be set in order, but tardy and discreditable is the reformation of old age."

We ask, then, for peace for the gods of our fathers and of our country. It is just that all worship should be considered as one. We look on the same stars, the sky is common, the same world surrounds us. What difference does it make by what pains each seeks the truth? We cannot attain to so great a secret by one road.

## Ambrose's Response

Ambrose, Bishop, to the most blessed Prince and most Christian Emperor Valentinian.

As all men who live under the Roman sway engage in military service under you, the Emperors and Princes of the world, so too do you yourselves owe service to Almighty God and our holy faith. For salvation is not sure unless everyone worship in truth the true God, that is the God of the Christians, under Whose sway are all things; for He alone is the true God, Who is to be worshipped from the bottom of the heart; for "the gods of the heathen," as Scripture says, "are devils."

Now everyone is a soldier of this true God, and he who receives and worships Him in his inmost spirit, does not bring to His service dissimulation, or pretense, but earnest faith and devotion. And if, in fine, he does not attain to this, at least he ought not to give any countenance to the worship of idols and to profane ceremonies. For no one deceives God, to whom all things, even the hidden things of the heart, are manifest.

Since, then, most Christian Emperor, there is due from you to the true God both faith and zeal, care and devotion for the faith, I wonder how the hope has risen up to some, that you would feel it a duty to restore by your command altars to the gods of the heathen [polytheists], and furnish the funds requisite for profane sacrifices; for whatsoever has long been claimed by either the imperial or the city treasury you will seem to give rather from your own funds, than to be restoring what is theirs. . . .

If to-day any heathen Emperor should build an altar, which God forbid, to idols, and should compel Christians to come together thither, in order to be amongst those who were sacrificing, so that the smoke and ashes from the altar, the sparks from the sacrilege, the smoke from the burning might choke the breath and throats of the faithful; and should give judgment in that court where members were compelled to vote after swearing at the altar of an idol (for they explain that an altar is so placed for this purpose, that every assembly should deliberate under its sanction, as they suppose, though the Senate is now made up with a majority of Christians), a Christian who was compelled with a choice such as this to come to the Senate, would consider it to be persecution, which often happens, for they are compelled to come together even by violence. Are these Christians, when you are Emperor, compelled to swear at a heathen altar? What is an oath, but a confession of the divine power of Him Whom you invoke as watcher over your good faith? When you are Emperor, this is sought and demanded that you should command an altar to be built, and the cost of profane sacrifices to be granted.

But this cannot be decreed without sacrilege, wherefore I implore you not to decree or order it, nor to subscribe to any decrees of that sort. I, as a priest of

Christ, call upon your faith, all of us bishops would have joined in calling upon you, were not the report so sudden and incredible, that any such thing had been either suggested in your council, or petitioned for by the Senate. But far be it from the Senate to have petitioned this, a few heathen are making use of the common name. . . .

I call upon your own feelings not to determine to answer according to this petition of the heathen, nor to attach to an answer of such a sort the sacrilege of your subscription. Refer to the father of your Piety, the Emperor Theodosius, whom you have been wont to consult in almost all matters of greater importance. Nothing is greater than religion, nothing more exalted than faith. . . .

## ■ Discussion Questions

1. Why does Symmachus think that the restoration of the Altar of Victory is so important? What does the altar represent for him and his non-Christian colleagues?
2. Why is St. Ambrose opposed to Symmachus's petition? What does the Altar of Victory symbolize to him?
3. Based on Symmachus's and Ambrose's views, why might Christians and polytheists have been increasingly at odds during this period?

## 3.
## St. Jerome
## *Letter 107*
### 403 C.E.

*The Christianization of the Roman Empire extended beyond public debates into family life, as this letter elucidates. Biblical scholar and monk St. Jerome (c. 345–420 C.E.) wrote the letter in 403 C.E. in response to Laeta—a Christian woman in Rome—regarding how best to educate her daughter Paula. For Jerome, the answer was simple: send her to a monastery, where she would be trained to be a temple of God and shielded from the world's evils. St. Jerome's advice reveals the growing appeal of monasticism and its underlying ascetic ideals, which elevated virginity and sexual renunciation as the highest of Christian virtues. Monasticism thus offered women an identity outside the confines of their traditional roles as wives and mothers. Laeta heeded his advice, and Paula eventually succeeded her aunt and became the head of a female monastery in Bethlehem, where St. Jerome himself lived and worked.*

The blessed apostle Paul, writing to the Corinthians and instructing Christ's novice church in the ways of sacred discipline, among his other precepts laid

From *Select Letters of St. Jerome*, trans. F. A. Wright (Cambridge: Harvard University Press, 1963), 338–47, 351, 359, 363–67.

down also the following rule: "The woman that hath an husband that believeth not, and if he be pleased to dwell with her, let her not leave him. For the unbelieving husband is sanctified by the believing wife, and the unbelieving wife is sanctified by the believing husband; else were your children unclean, but now they are holy."[1] . . . You yourself are the child of a mixed marriage; but now you and my dear Toxotius are Paula's parents. Who would ever have believed that the granddaughter of the Roman pontiff Albinus would be born in answer to a mother's vows; that the grandfather would stand by and rejoice while the baby's yet stammering tongue cried "Alleluia"; and that even the old man would nurse in his arms one of Christ's own virgins? . . . Christians are not born but made. The gilded Capitol to-day looks dingy, all the temples in Rome are covered with soot and cobwebs, the city is shaken to its foundations, and the people hurry past the ruined shrines and pour out to visit the martyrs' graves. . . .

Even in Rome now heathenism [polytheism] languishes in solitude. Those who once were the gods of the Gentiles are left beneath their deserted pinnacles to the company of owls and night-birds. The army standards bear the emblem of the cross. The purple robes of kings and the jewels that sparkle on their diadems are adorned with the gibbet sign that has brought to us salvation. To-day even the Egyptian Serapis[2] has become a Christian: Marnas[3] mourns in his prison at Gaza, and fears continually that his temple will be overthrown. From India, from Persia and from Ethiopia we welcome crowds of monks every hour. The Armenians have laid aside their quivers, the Huns are learning the psalter, the frosts of Scythia are warmed by the fire of faith. The ruddy, flaxen-haired Getae carry tent-churches about with their armies; and perhaps the reason why they fight with us on equal terms is that they believe in the same religion. . . .

It was my intention, in answer to your prayers and those of the saintly Marcella, to direct my discourse to a mother, that is, to you, and to show you how to bring up our little Paula, who was consecrated to Christ before she was born, the child of prayers before the hour of conception. In our own days we have seen something such as we read of in the prophets: Hannah exchanged her barrenness for fruitful motherhood, you have exchanged a fertility bound up with sorrow for children who will live for ever. I tell you confidently that you who have given your first-born to the Lord will receive sons at His hand. The first-born are the offerings due under the Law. . . .

Thus must a soul be trained which is to be a temple of God. It must learn to hear nothing and to say nothing save what pertains to the fear of the Lord. It must have no comprehension of foul words, no knowledge of worldly songs, and its childish tongue must be imbued with the sweet music of the psalms. Let boys with their wanton frolics be kept far from Paula: let even her maids and attendants hold

---

[1] 1 Cor. 7:13.

[2] In 389 C.E., the temple of Serapis at Alexandria was torn down, and a Christian church was built on the site.

[3] The chief Syrian god in Gaza.

aloof from association with the worldly, lest they render their evil knowledge worse by teaching it to her. Have a set of letters made for her, of boxwood or of ivory, and tell her their names. Let her play with them, making play a road to learning, and let her not only grasp the right order of the letters and remember their names in a simple song, but also frequently upset their order and mix the last letters with the middle ones, the middle with the first. Thus she will know them all by sight as well as by sound. When she begins with uncertain hand to use the pen, either let another hand be put over hers to guide her baby fingers, or else have the letters marked on the tablet so that her writing may follow their outlines and keep to their limits without straying away. Offer her prizes for spelling, tempting her with such trifling gifts as please young children. Let her have companions too in her lessons, so that she may seek to rival them and be stimulated by any praise they win. You must not scold her if she is somewhat slow; praise is the best sharpener of wits. . . .

Her very dress and outward appearance should remind her of Him to whom she is promised. Do not pierce her ears, or paint with white lead and rouge the cheeks that are consecrated to Christ. Do not load her neck with pearls and gold, do not weigh down her head with jewels, do not dye her hair red and thereby presage for her the fires of hell. . . .

Let her every day repeat to you a portion of the Scriptures as her fixed task. A good number of lines she should learn by heart in the Greek, but knowledge of the Latin should follow close after. If the tender lips are not trained from the beginning, the language is spoiled by a foreign accent and our native tongue debased by alien faults. You must be her teacher, to you her childish ignorance must look for a model. Let her never see anything in you or her father which she would do wrong to imitate. Remember that you are a virgin's parents and that you can teach her better by example than by words. Flowers quickly fade; violets, lilies, and saffron are soon withered by a baleful breeze. Let her never appear in public without you, let her never visit the churches and the martyrs' shrines except in your company. Let no youth or curled dandy ogle her. Let our little virgin never stir a finger's breadth from her mother when she attends a vigil or an all-night service. I would not let her have a favorite maid into whose ear she might frequently whisper: what she says to one, all ought to know. . . .

If ever you visit the country, do not leave your daughter behind at Rome. She should have neither the knowledge nor the power to live without you, and should tremble to be alone. Let her not converse with worldlings [worldly people], nor associate with virgins who neglect their vows. Let her not be present at slaves' weddings, nor take part in noisy household games. I know that some people have laid down the rule that a Christian virgin should not bathe along with eunuchs or with married women, inasmuch as eunuchs are still men at heart, and women big with child are a revolting sight. For myself I disapprove altogether of baths in the case of a full-grown virgin. She ought to blush at herself and be unable to look at her own nakedness. If she mortifies and enslaves her body by vigils and fasting, if she desires to quench the flame of lust and to check the hot desires of youth by a cold chastity, if she hastens to spoil her natural beauty by a deliberate squalor, why should she rouse a sleeping fire by the incentive of baths?[4] . . .

You will answer: "How shall I, a woman of the world living in crowded Rome, be able to keep all these injunctions?" Do not then take up a burden which you cannot bear. . . . Let her be reared in a monastery amid bands of virgins, where she will learn never to take an oath, and to regard a lie as sacrilege. Let her know nothing of the world, but live like the angels; let her be in the flesh and without the flesh, thinking all mankind to be like herself.

## ■ Discussion Questions

1. What explicit signs of Christianity's triumph does St. Jerome describe in this letter written more than a decade after it had become the official religion of the empire?
2. How does Jerome think Paula should be raised, and why?
3. What do Jerome's views on Paula's education suggest about Christianity's attitudes toward women in general and toward female sexuality in particular?

[4]That is, the Roman, or as commonly known, "Turkish" baths.

# 4.
# *The Burgundian Code*
### c. 475–525 C.E.

*The migration of Germanic tribes into the West changed imperial politics and society just as profoundly as Christianity did. Members of these tribes gradually formed independent kingdoms based on a mixture of their own and Roman traditions, which soon superseded Roman provincial government. Law codes established by Germanic leaders from the fifth century on were a crucial component of their state-building efforts. Rome provided a powerful precedent in this regard, with its emphasis on written law as both the basis of social order and a manifestation of state authority. These excerpts are drawn from one of the most comprehensive early Germanic law codes, the Burgundian Code, compiled by the kings of the Burgundians, an East Germanic tribe, in the late fifth and early sixth centuries. At this time, they ruled over a large kingdom encompassing much of the former Roman province of Gaul. Early Frankish and Anglo-Saxon societies that were developing during this period were plagued by feuds that undermined political authority and perpetuated increasing cycles of violence. In an effort to curb personal vendettas and increase stability, many rulers established law codes based on* wergeld *("man money") that set fines based on the type of crime and a person's value in that society.*

From *The Burgundian Code,* trans. Katherine Fischer Drew (Philadelphia: University of Pennsylvania Press, 1972), 17–24, 30–33, 40–47.

## First Constitution

In the name of God in the second year of the reign of our lord the most glorious king Gundobad, this book concerning laws past and present, and to be preserved throughout all future time, has been issued on the fourth day before the Kalends of April (March 29) at Lyons. . . .

For the love of justice, through which God is pleased and the power of earthly kingdoms acquired, we have obtained the consent of our counts *(comites)* and leaders *(procures),* and have desired to establish such laws that the integrity and equity of those judging may exclude all rewards and corruptions from themselves.

Therefore all administrators *(administrantes)* and judges must judge from the present time on between Burgundians and Romans according to our laws which have been set forth and corrected by a common method, to the end that no one may hope or presume to receive anything by way of reward or emolument from any party as the result of the suits or decisions; but let him whose case is deserving obtain justice and let the integrity of the judge alone suffice to accomplish this. . . .

Therefore let all nobles *(obtimates),* counsellors *(consiliarii),* bailiffs *(domestici),* mayors of our palace *(maiores domus nostrae),* chancellors *(cancellarii),* counts *(comites)* of the cities or villages, Burgundian as well as Roman, and all appointed judges and military judges *(judices militantes)* know that nothing can be accepted in connection with those suits which have been acted upon or decided, and that nothing can be sought in the name of promise or reward from those litigating; nor can the parties (to the suit) be compelled by the judge to make a payment in order that they may receive anything (from their suit). . . .

Indeed if any judge, barbarian as well as Roman, shall not render decisions according to those provisions which the laws contain because he has been prevented by ignorance or negligence, and he has been diverted from justice for this reason, let him know that he must pay thirty solidi[1] and that the case must be judged again on behalf of the aggrieved parties. . . .

### Of Murders

If anyone presumes with boldness or rashness bent on injury to kill a native freeman of our people of any nation or a servant of the king, in any case a man of barbarian tribe, let him make restitution for the committed crime not otherwise than by the shedding of his own blood.

We decree that this rule be added to the law by a reasonable provision, that if violence shall have been done by anyone to any person, so that he is injured by blows of lashes or by wounds, and if he pursues his persecutor and overcome by grief and indignation kills him, proof of the deed shall be afforded by the act itself or by suitable witnesses who can be believed. Then the guilty party shall be compelled to pay to the relatives of the person killed half his wergeld according to the

[1]**solidi:** Gold coin. [Ed.]

status of the person: that is, if he shall have killed a noble of the highest class *(optimas nobilis),* we decree that the payment be set at one hundred fifty solidi, i.e., half his wergeld; if a person of middle class *(mediocris),* one hundred solidi; if a person of the lowest class *(minor persona),* seventy-five solidi.

If a slave unknown to his master presumes to kill a native freeman, let the slave be handed over to death, and let the master not be made liable for damages.

If the master knows of the deed, let both be handed over to death.

If the slave himself flees *(defuerit)* after the deed, let his master be compelled to pay thirty solidi to the relatives of the man killed for the value (wergeld) of the slave.

Similarly in the case of royal slaves, in accordance with the status of such persons, let the same condition about murderers be observed.

In such cases let all know this must be observed carefully, that the relatives of the man killed must recognize that no one can be pursued except the killer; because just as we have ordered the criminals to be destroyed, so we will suffer the innocent to sustain no injury. . . .

## Let Burgundians and Romans Be Held under the Same Condition in the Matter of Killing Slaves

If anyone kills a slave, barbarian by birth, a trained (select) house servant or messenger, let him compound sixty solidi; moreover, let the amount of the fine be twelve solidi. If anyone kills another's slave, Roman or barbarian, either ploughman or swineherd, let him pay thirty solidi.

Whoever kills a skilled goldsmith, let him pay two hundred solidi.
Whoever kills a silversmith, let him pay one hundred solidi.
Whoever kills a blacksmith, let him pay fifty solidi.
Whoever kills a carpenter, let him pay forty solidi. . . .

## Of the Stealing of Girls

If anyone shall steal a girl, let him be compelled to pay the price set for such a girl ninefold, and let him pay a fine to the amount of twelve solidi.

If a girl who has been seized returns uncorrupted to her parents, let the abductor compound six times the wergeld of the girl; moreover, let the fine be set at twelve solidi.

But if the abductor does not have the means to make the above-mentioned payment, let him be given over to the parents of the girl that they may have the power of doing to him whatever they choose.

If indeed, the girl seeks the man of her own will and comes to his house, and he has intercourse with her, let him pay her marriage price threefold; if moreover, she returns uncorrupted to her home, let her return with all blame removed from him.

If indeed a Roman girl, without the consent or knowledge of her parents, unites in marriage with a Burgundian, let her know she will have none of the property of her parents. . . .

## Of Succession

Among Burgundians we wish it to be observed that if anyone does not leave a son, let a daughter succeed to the inheritance of the father and mother in place of the son.

If by chance the dead leave neither son nor daughter, let the inheritance go to the sisters or nearest relatives.

It is pleasing that it be contained in the present law that if a woman having a husband dies without children, the husband of the dead wife may not demand back the marriage price *(pretium)* which had been given for her.

Likewise, let neither the woman nor the relatives of the woman seek back that which a woman pays when she comes to her husband if the husband dies without children.

Concerning those women who are vowed to God and remain in chastity, we order that if they have two brothers they receive a third portion of the inheritance of the father, that is, of that land which the father, possessing by the right of *sors* (allotment), left at the time of his death. Likewise, if she has four or five brothers, let her receive the portion due to her.

If moreover she has but one brother, let not a half, but a third part go to her on the condition that, after the death of her who is a woman and a nun, whatever she possesses in usufruct[1] from her father's property shall go to the nearest relatives, and she will have no power of transferring anything therefrom, unless perhaps from her mother's goods, that is, from her clothing or things of the cell *(res cellulae)*, or what she has acquired by her own labor.

We decree that this should be observed only by those whose fathers have not given them portions; but if they shall have received from their father a place where they can live, let them have full freedom of disposing of it at their will. . . .

## Of Burgundian Women Entering a Second or Third Marriage

If any Burgundian woman, as is the custom, enters a second or third marriage after the death of her husband, and she has children by each husband, let her possess the marriage gift *(donatio nuptialis)* in usufruct while she lives; after her death, let what his father gave her be given to each son, with the further provision that the mother has the power neither of giving, selling, or transferring any of the things which she received in the marriage gift.

If by chance the woman has no children, after her death let her relatives receive half of whatever has come to her by way of marriage gift, and let the relatives of the dead husband who was the donor receive half.

But if perchance children shall have been born and they shall have died after the death of their father, we command that the inheritance of the husband or children belong wholly to the mother. Moreover, after the death of the mother, we decree that what she holds in usufruct by inheritance from her children shall belong

---

[1]**usufruct:** The right to use another person's property as long as it is not damaged or altered. [Ed.]

to the legal heirs of her children. Also we command that she protect the property of her children dying intestate.

If any son has given his mother something by will or by gift, let the mother have the power of doing whatever she wishes therewith; if she dies intestate, let the relatives of the woman claim the inheritance as their possession.

If any Burgundian has sons (children?) to whom he has given their portions, let him have the power of giving or selling that which he has reserved for himself to whomever he wishes. . . .

## Of Knocking Out Teeth

If anyone by chance strikes out the teeth of a Burgundian of the highest class, or of a Roman noble, let him be compelled to pay fifteen solidi.

For middle-class freeborn people, either Burgundian or Roman, if a tooth is knocked out, let composition be made in the sum of ten solidi.

For persons of the lowest class, five solidi.

If a slave voluntarily strikes out the tooth of a native freeman, let him be condemned to have a hand cut off; if the loss which has been set forth above has been committed by accident, let him pay the price for the tooth according to the status of the person.

If any native freeman strikes out the tooth of a freedman, let him pay him three solidi. If he strikes out the tooth of another's slave, let him pay two solidi to him to whom the slave belongs. . . .

## Of Injuries Which Are Suffered by Women

If any native freewoman has her hair cut off and is humiliated without cause (when innocent) by any native freeman in her home or on the road, and this can be proved with witnesses, let the doer of the deed pay her twelve solidi, and let the amount of the fine be twelve solidi.

If this was done to a freedwoman, let him pay her six solidi.

If this was done to a maidservant, let him pay her three solidi, and let the amount of the fine be three solidi.

If this injury (shame, disgrace) is inflicted by a slave on a native freewoman, let him receive two hundred blows; if a freedwoman, let him receive a hundred blows; if a maidservant, let him receive seventy-five blows.

If indeed the woman whose injury we have ordered to be punished in this manner commits fornication voluntarily (i.e., if she yields), let nothing be sought for the injury suffered.

## Of Divorces

If any woman leaves (puts aside) her husband to whom she is legally married, let her be smothered in mire.

If anyone wishes to put away his wife without cause, let him give her another payment such as he gave for her marriage price, and let the amount of the fine be twelve solidi.

If by chance a man wishes to put away his wife, and is able to prove one of these three crimes against her, that is, adultery, witchcraft, or violation of graves, let him have full right to put her away: and let the judge pronounce the sentence of the law against her, just as should be done against criminals.

But if she admits none of these three crimes, let no man be permitted to put away his wife for any other crime. But if he chooses, he may go away from the home, leaving all household property behind, and his wife with their children may possess the property of her husband.

### Of the Punishment of Slaves Who Commit a Criminal Assault on Freeborn Women

If any slave does violence to a native freewoman, and if she complains and is clearly able to prove this, let the slave be killed for the crime committed.

If indeed a native free girl unites voluntarily with a slave, we order both to be killed.

But if the relatives of the girl do not wish to punish their own relative, let the girl be deprived of her free status and delivered into servitude to the king.

### ■ Discussion Questions

1. What do these laws reveal about the social and political structure of the Burgundian kingdom? For example, do the laws place the same value on all social groups?
2. What does the code reveal about Burgundian women and family life?
3. Historians regard the interaction between Germanic and Roman peoples as a key component of the process by which Germanic kingdoms replaced imperial government in western Europe. What evidence of such interaction can you find in this document?

## 5.
## Procopius
## *Buildings*
### c. 553–554 C.E.

*The emperors of the eastern Roman provinces successfully resisted the tides of change that engulfed the West. In the process, they forged a new empire, Byzantium. Its roots extended back to 293 C.E., when Emperor Diocletian reorganized imperial territory into four districts—two in the east and two in the west. In 395 C.E., the empire was formally divided into eastern and western halves. Emperor Justinian (r. 527–565 C.E.)*

From *Procopius,* vol. 7, trans. H. B. Dewing (Cambridge: Harvard University Press, 1961), 5–17, 27.

*played a pivotal role in shaping Byzantium's emerging identity as a bastion of Roman imperial glory and civilization. Here is a contemporary account of one of Justinian's most famous achievements—the reconstruction of the Church of the Holy Wisdom (Hagia Sophia) in the Byzantine capital, Constantinople. A courtier from Palestine, Procopius (c. 490/510–560s* C.E.*), included the description in his book* Buildings, *which he wrote to honor Justinian's architectural projects. Procopius sets the rebuilding of the church against the backdrop of the emperor's accomplishments as a whole, portraying the church as the embodiment of his power and divine favor.*

In our own age there has been born the Emperor Justinian, who, taking over the State when it was harassed by disorder, has not only made it greater in extent, but also much more illustrious, by expelling from it those barbarians who had from of old pressed hard upon it, . . . witness the way he has already added to the Roman domain many states which in his own times had belonged to others, and has created countless cities which did not exist before. And finding that the belief in God was, before his time, straying into errors and being forced to go in many directions, he completely destroyed all the paths leading to such errors, and brought it about that it stood on the firm foundation of a single faith. Moreover, finding the laws obscure because they had become far more numerous than they should be, and in obvious confusion because they disagreed with each other, he preserved them by cleansing them of the mass of their verbal trickery, and by controlling their discrepancies with the greatest firmness; as for those who plotted against him, he of his own volition dismissed the charges against them, and causing those who were in want to have a surfeit of wealth, and crushing the spiteful fortune that oppressed them, he wedded the whole State to a life of prosperity. Furthermore, he strengthened the Roman domain, which everywhere lay exposed to the barbarians, by a multitude of soldiers, and by constructing strongholds he built a wall along all its remote frontiers.

However, most of the Emperor's other achievements have been described by me in my other writings, so that the subject of the present work will be the benefits which he wrought as a builder. They do indeed say that the best king of whom we know by tradition was the Persian Cyrus, and that he was chiefly responsible for the founding of the kingdom of Persia for the people of his race. . . . But in the case of the king of our times, Justinian (whom one would rightly, I think, call a king by nature as well as by inheritance, since he is, as Homer says, "as gentle as a father"), if one should examine his reign with care, he will regard the rule of Cyrus as a sort of child's play. The proof of this will be that the Roman Empire, as I have just said, has become more than doubled both in area and in power generally. . . .

But now we must proceed, as I have said, to the subject of the buildings of this Emperor, so that it may not come to pass in the future that those who see them refuse, by reason of their great number and magnitude, to believe that they are in truth the works of one man. For already many works of men of former times which are not vouched for by a written record have aroused incredulity because of their surpassing merit. And with good reason the buildings in Byzantium, beyond all the rest, will serve as a foundation for my narrative. For "o'er a work's beginnings," as the old saying has it, "we needs must set a front that shines afar."

Some men of the common herd, all the rubbish of the city, once rose up against the Emperor Justinian in Byzantium, when they brought about the rising called the Nika Insurrection. . . . And by way of shewing that it was not against the Emperor alone that they had taken up arms, but no less against God himself, unholy wretches that they were, they had the hardihood to fire the Church of the Christians, which the people of Byzantium call "Sophia," an epithet which they have most appropriately invented for God, by which they call His temple; and God permitted them to accomplish this impiety, forseeing into what an object of beauty this shrine was destined to be transformed. So the whole church at that time lay a charred mass of ruins. But the Emperor Justinian built not long afterwards a church so finely shaped, that if anyone had inquired of the Christians before the burning if it would be their wish that the church should be destroyed and one like this should take its place, shewing them some sort of model of the building we now see, it seems to me that they would have prayed that they might see their church destroyed forthwith, in order that the building might be converted into its present form. At any rate the Emperor, disregarding all questions of expense, eagerly pressed on to begin the work of construction, and began to gather all the artisans from the whole world. . . . Indeed this also was an indication of the honor in which God held the Emperor, that He had already provided the men who would be most serviceable to him in the tasks which were waiting to be carried out. And one might with good reason marvel at the discernment of the Emperor himself, in that out of the whole world he was able to select the men who were most suitable for the most important of his enterprises.

So the church has become a spectacle of marvelous beauty, overwhelming to those who see it, but to those who know it by hearsay altogether incredible. For it soars to a height to match the sky, and as if surging up from amongst the other buildings it stands on high and looks down upon the remainder of the city, adorning it, because it is a part of it, but glorying in its own beauty, because, though a part of the city and dominating it, it at the same time towers above it to such a height that the whole city is viewed from there as from a watch-tower. Both its breadth and its length have been so carefully proportioned, that it may not improperly be said to be exceedingly long and at the same time unusually broad. And it exults in an indescribable beauty. For it proudly reveals its mass and the harmony of its proportions, having neither any excess nor deficiency, since it is both more pretentious than the buildings to which we are accustomed, and considerably more noble than those which are merely huge, and it abounds exceedingly in sunlight and in the reflection of the sun's rays from the marble. Indeed one might say that its interior is not illuminated from without by the sun, but that the radiance comes into being within it, such an abundance of light bathes this shrine. . . . And whenever anyone enters this church to pray, he understands at once that it is not by any human power or skill, but by the influence of God, that this work has been so finely turned. And so his mind is lifted up toward God and exalted, feeling that He cannot be far away, but must especially love to dwell in this place which He has chosen. And this does not happen only to one who sees the church for the first time, but the same experience comes to him on each successive occasion, as though the sight were new each time. Of this spectacle no one has ever had a surfeit, but when present in the church men rejoice in what they see, and when they leave it they take proud delight in conversing about it.

## ■ Discussion Questions

1. As described by Procopius, what were Justinian's most significant accomplishments?
2. What links does Procopius see between Justinian's accomplishments and his relationship with God?
3. What might have been Procopius's goals in writing this account?

## ■ Comparative Questions

1. The Nicene Creed was one of the earliest efforts to create a doctrinally unified Christianity. Based on later documents, how well did it work in the hundred years that followed?
2. When viewed together, what do the documents here reveal about the spread and institutional development of Christianity in the Roman Empire between the fourth and sixth centuries? How do these documents illuminate the interplay between politics and religion?
3. What parallels exist between Symmachus's and Procopius's expectations regarding the role that the emperor should play as protector of the empire's prosperity? What do these parallels suggest about the ways in which Byzantium preserved and perpetuated its Roman heritage?
4. According to Procopius, Justinian's efforts to codify imperial laws strengthened his authority and the stability of the empire. In what ways does the Burgundian Code reflect a similar attitude toward the function of law in government and society?

Chapter

7

# The Heirs of the Roman Empire, 600–750

THE SEVENTH AND EIGHTH centuries marked the beginning of a new era in Western civilization—the Middle Ages. By this period, the Roman Empire had fragmented into three different worlds: Byzantine, Muslim, and western European. Even so, these regions continued to share a common Roman heritage, which they adapted to their own interests and circumstances. The documents in this chapter reveal various dimensions of this process, beginning with the eastern empire, Byzantium. Although it inherited much from Rome, Byzantium forged its own political, cultural, and religious identity in response to the distinctive challenges it faced during this period, including the onslaught of foreign invaders. The newly founded Muslim state was extraordinarily successful on this front, and by 730 its warriors had conquered vast expanses of imperial territory. The second set of documents illuminates some of the fundamental beliefs uniting the Islamic community, while the third set demonstrates how the Muslim military conquests brought both change and continuity. The fourth pair of documents illuminates the development of the western kingdoms, where various barbarian peoples built new societies and cultures on the foundations of the Roman Empire. The final document illustrates the importance of women in the westward spread of Christianity and the personal values that were increasingly seen as desirable.

## 1.
## Theophanes Confessor
## *Chronicle*
### Ninth Century

*Although Byzantium resisted the effects of the Germanic migrations that changed the West, by 600 it had begun its own process of transformation. For the next one hundred fifty years, Byzantium was engaged in almost constant warfare with foreign*

From *The Chronicle of Theophanes Confessor*, trans. Cyril Mango and Roger Scott (Oxford: Clarendon Press, 1997), 559–61.

*peoples, especially Muslim Arabs. A historical chronicle written by a Greek monk, Theophanes Confessor (c. 759–818), in the early ninth century elucidates how war shaped two key facets of Byzantium's emerging identity: imperial autocracy and, concomitantly, the interdependency between the spiritual and political realms. In this passage, Theophanes recounts the coincidence of the Arab onslaught with the controversy over the question of icons during the reign of Emperor Leo III (r. 717–741). For Leo and his troops, the worship of sacred images was an abomination against God and a threat to Leo's unique status as God's earthly representative. For Theophanes and other Byzantines, however, icons were an essential source of divine intercession.*

In the summer season of the same year [726] a vapor as from a fiery furnace boiled up for a few days from the depth of the sea between the islands of Thera and Therasia. As it gradually became thicker and filled with stones because of the heat of the burning fire, all the smoke took on a fiery appearance. Then, on account of the density of the earthy substance, pumice stones as big as hills were thrown up against all of Asia Minor, Lesbos, Abydos, and coastal Macedonia, so that the entire surface of that sea was filled with floating pumice. In the midst of so great a fire an island that had not previously existed was formed and joined to the Sacred Island, as it is called; for, just as the aforementioned islands Thera and Therasia had once been thrown up, so was this one, too, in the present days of God's enemy Leo. Thinking that God's wrath was in his favor instead of being directed against him, he stirred up a more ruthless war on the holy and venerable icons. . . . The populace of the Imperial City were much distressed by the newfangled doctrines and meditated an assault upon him. They also killed a few of the emperor's men who had taken down the Lord's image that was above the great Bronze Gate, with the result that many of them were punished in the cause of the true faith by mutilation, lashes, banishment, and fines, especially those who were prominent by birth and culture. This led to the extinction of schools and of the pious education that had lasted from St. Constantine the Great until our days, but was destroyed, along with many other good things, by this Saracen-minded Leo. . . .

At the summer solstice . . . a multitude of Saracens led by two emirs was drawn up against Nicaea in Bithynia: Amer with 15,000 scouts led the van and surrounded the town which he found unprepared, while Mauias followed with another 85,000 men. After a long siege and a partial destruction of the walls, they did not overpower the town thanks to the acceptable prayers addressed to God by the holy Fathers who are honored there in a church (wherein their venerable images are set up to this very day and are honored by those who believe as they did). A certain Constantine, however, who was the *strator* of Artabasdos, on seeing an image of the Theotokos that had been set up, picked up a stone and threw it at her. He broke the image and trampled upon it when it had fallen down. He then saw in a vision the Lady standing beside him and saying to him: "See, what a brave thing you have done to me! Verily, upon your head have you done it." The next day, when the Saracens attacked the walls and battle was joined, that wretched man rushed to the wall like the brave soldier he was and was struck by a stone discharged from a siege engine, and it broke his head and face, a just reward for his impiety. After collecting many captives and much booty, the Arabs withdrew. In this manner God showed to the impious one that he had overcome his fellow-countrymen not on account of his piety, as he himself boasted, but for some divine cause and inscrutable judgment, whereby so great an Arab force was driven away from the city of the holy Fathers thanks to their intercession — on account of their most exact likenesses that are honored therein — and this, too, in reproof and unanswerable condemnation of the tyrant and in vindication of the true believers. Not only was the impious man in error concerning the relative worship of the holy icons, but also concerning the intercession of the all-pure Theotokos and all the saints, and he abominated their relics like his mentors, the Arabs. From this time on he impudently harassed the blessed Germanus, patriarch of Constantinople, blaming all the emperors, bishops, and Christian people who had lived before him for having committed idolatry in worshipping the holy and venerable icons, unable as he was to grasp the argument concerning relative veneration because of his lack of faith and crass ignorance.

### ■ Discussion Questions

1. To what does Theophanes attribute the Muslims' withdrawal from Nicaea? What does his explanation reveal about the role of icons in Byzantine religious devotion?
2. According to Theophanes, how did Emperor Leo III threaten the role of icons? Do you think Theophanes evaluated Leo's actions objectively?
3. Based on this passage, how would you describe the relationship between the Byzantine church and state?

## 2.
## *Qur'an*, Suras 1, 53, 98
### c. 610–632

*The remarkable rise of Islam during the seventh century had far-reaching consequences. Muhammad (c. 570–632), a merchant-turned-holy man from the Arabian city of Mecca, founded the new faith based on what he believed were direct revelations from God, which he first received around 610. The messages continued until his death and soon thereafter were written down and compiled into what became the* Qur'an, *the holy book of Islam. Comprising 114 hymnic chapters (suras), the* Qur'an *begins with the Fatihah ("opening"), which emphasizes God's oneness and the believer's*

From *Approaching the Qur'an: The Early Revelations,* trans. Michael Sells (Ashland: White Cloud Press, 1999), 35, 42, 44, 47, 104–06.

*recourse to God alone. The "road straight" is the path of right worship. The first eighteen verses of the Star, among the earliest of Muhammad's revelations, explicitly reveal his position in the divine plan, casting him as God's companion and servant. The final selection, the Testament, represents the later period of Muhammad's prophecy when he and his followers confronted the challenges posed by people who resisted the new religion.*

## 1
## THE OPENING

In the name of God
    the Compassionate the Caring
Praise be to God
    lord sustainer of the worlds
the Compassionate the Caring
master of the day of reckoning[1]
To you we turn to worship
    and to you we turn in time of need
Guide us along the road straight
the road of those to whom you are giving
    not those with anger upon them
    not those who have lost the way

## 53:1–18
## THE STAR

In the Name of God the Compassionate the Caring

By the star as it falls
Your companion[2] has not lost his way nor is he
    deluded
He does not speak out of desire
This is a revelation
taught him by one of great power
and strength that stretched out over

---

[1]The word translated here as *reckoning (dīn)* is related to a number of terms for borrowing and payment of debt, as well as to terms for religion and faith. The word for *day (yawm)* also can be a more general term for any length of time or a moment in time. The term has been translated as "day of judgment" and "day of accounting." But it also has an implication similar to the "moment of truth"—that is, a time of indeterminate duration in which each soul will encounter the fundamental reality that normal consciousness masks.
[2]"Your companion" is interpreted as Muhammad.

while on the highest horizon—
then drew near and came down
two bows' lengths or nearer
He revealed to his servant what he revealed
The heart did not lie in what it saw
Will you then dispute with him his vision?

He saw it[3] descending another time
at the lote tree of the furthest limit
There was the garden of sanctuary
when something came down over the
lote tree, enfolding
His gaze did not turn aside nor go too far
He had seen the signs of his lord, great signs

## 98
## THE TESTAMENT

In the Name of God the Compassionate the Caring

Those who denied the faith—
from the peoples of the book[4]
or the idolators—
could not stop calling it a lie
until they received the testament

A messenger of God
reciting pages that are pure

Of scripture that are sure

Those who were given the book
were not divided one against the other
until they received the testament

---

[3]When the Qur'an states "He saw it descending another time," the antecedent of the pronoun (*hu*, it/him) is unstated, and thus the referent of the "it" is not determinable from the passage. The identity of the referent became a matter of controversy, with the debate centering upon whether or not the deity can be seen in this world. Those for whom the vision of God can only occur in the afterlife tend to interpret the it/he as referring to the messenger-angel Gabriel.

[4]Those with written scriptures named in other passages of the Qur'an as the Jews, Christians, and Sabeans (the exact identity of whom has been a matter of controversy).

And all they were commanded
    was to worship God sincerely
    affirm oneness, perform the prayer
    and give a share of what they have
    That is the religion of the sure

Those who deny the faith—
    from the peoples of the book
    or the idolators—
    are in Jahannam's fire
    eternal there
    They are the worst of creation

Those who keep the faith
    and perform the prayer
    they are the best of creation

As recompense for them with their lord—
    gardens of Eden
    waters flowing underground
    eternal there forever

    God be pleased in them
    and they in God

    That is for those who hold their lord in awe

## ■ Discussion Questions

1. What do these excerpts reveal about the fundamental beliefs and practices of Islam?
2. How does the Star portray Muhammad? What does this portrait reveal about his role in Islam?
3. The rejection of Islam by many Jews and Christians ("peoples of the book") in Arabia surprised and disappointed Muhammad since he brought his message in the name of the tradition of Abraham, Moses, and Jesus. How does the Testament give expression to these feelings and, at the same time, defend the truth of Muhammad's revelations?
4. Do you see any differences in the concept of religion presented in the Opening and the Testament?

## 3.
## *Islamic Terms of Peace*
### 633–643

*Despite facing some resistance, Muhammad's revelations soon gained widespread adherence across the Arabian peninsula. Together his converts formed a community united by the worship of God, expressed not only in individual prayer but also in the collective duty to "strive" (jihad) against unbelievers, often in war. War was thus a central component of Islam, and by the eighth century Islamic warriors had conquered all of Persia and much of the Byzantine Empire. These letters dictate the terms of peace to conquered communities and illuminate the Muslims' method of conquest and rule in the decade following Muhammad's death. In exchange for the payment of a special tax* (jizya), *non-Muslim subjects were allowed to live much as they had before. Consequently, Islam became not the destroyer of Hellenistic and Roman traditions, but rather their heir.*

### BĀNQIYĀ AND BASMĀ (633)

In the name of God, the Merciful and the Compassionate.

This is a letter from Khālid ibn al-Walīd to Ṣalūba ibn Nasṭūnā and his people.

I have made a pact with you for *jizya* and defense for every fit man, for both Bānqiyā and Basmā, for 10,000 dinars, excluding coins with holes punched in them, the wealthy according to the measure of his wealth, the poor according to the measure of his poverty, payable annually. You have been made head of your people and your people are content with you. I, therefore, and the Muslims who are with me, accept you, and I [? you] and your people are content. You have protection [*dhimma*] and defense. If we defend you, the *jizya* is due to us; if we do not, it is not, until we do defend you.

Witnessed by Hishām ibn al-Walīd, al-Qa 'qā 'ibn 'Amr, Jarīr ibn 'Abdallāh al-Ḥimyarī and Ḥanẓala ibn al-Rabī'.

Written in the year 12, in Safar [April–May 633].

### JERUSALEM (636)

In the name of God the Merciful and the Compassionate.

This is the safe-conduct accorded by the servant of God 'Umar, the Commander of the Faithful, to the people of Aelia [Jerusalem].

He accords them safe-conduct for their persons, their property, their churches, their crosses, their sound and their sick, and the rest of their worship.

From Bernard Lewis, ed., *Islam from the Prophet Muhammad to the Capture of Constantinople*, vol. 1 (New York: Walker & Co., 1974), 234–36, 238–40.

Their churches shall neither be used as dwellings nor destroyed. They shall not suffer any impairment, nor shall their dependencies, their crosses, nor any of their property.

No constraint shall be exercised against them in religion nor shall any harm be done to any among them.

No Jew shall live with them in Aelia.

The people of Aelia must pay the *jizya* in the same way as the people of other cities.

They must expel the Romans and the brigands [?] from the city. Those who leave shall have safe-conduct for their persons and property until they reach safety. Those who stay shall have safe-conduct and must pay the *jizya* like the people of Aelia.

Those of the people of Aelia who wish to remove their persons and effects and depart with the Romans and abandon their churches and their crosses shall have safe-conduct for their persons, their churches, and their crosses, until they reach safety.

The country people who were already in the city before the killing of so-and-so may, as they wish, remain and pay the *jizya* the same way as the people of Aelia or leave with the Romans or return to their families. Nothing shall be taken from them until they have gathered their harvest.

This document is placed under the surety of God and the protection [*dhimma*] of the Prophet, the Caliphs and the believers, on condition that the inhabitants of Aelia pay the *jizya* that is due from them.

Witnessed by Khālid ibn al-Walīd, 'Amr ibn al-'Āṣ, 'Abd al-Raḥmān ibn 'Awf, Mu'āwiya ibn Abī Sufyān, the last of whom wrote this document in the year 15 [636].

## JURJĀN (639)

In the name of God, the Merciful and the Compassionate.

This is a letter from Suwayd ibn Muqarrin to Ruzbān Ṣūl ibn Ruzbān, the inhabitants of Dihistān, and the rest of the inhabitants of Jurjān.

You have protection and we must enforce it on the condition that you pay the *jizya* every year, according to your capacity, for every adult male. If we seek help from any of you, the help counts as his *jizya* in place of the payment. They have safe-conduct for themselves, their property, their religions, and their laws. There will be no change in what is due to them as long as they pay and guide the wayfarer and show good will and lodge the Muslims and do not spy or betray. Whoever stays with them shall have the same terms as they have, and whoever goes forth has safe-conduct until he reaches a place of safety, provided that if anyone insults a Muslim he is severely punished, and if he strikes a Muslim, his blood is lawful.

Witnessed by Sawād ibn Quṭba, Hind ibn 'Amr, Simāk ibn Makhrama, and 'Utayba ibn al-Naḥḥās.

Written in the year 18 [639].

### ■ Discussion Questions

1. Aside from the payment of a poll tax, what were some of the obligations Muslims imposed on their non-Muslim subjects?
2. What did the conquered people receive in exchange for the fulfillment of these obligations?
3. What does this system of exchange suggest about Muslim attitudes toward nonbelievers?

## 4.
## Pope Gregory the Great
## *Letters*
## 598–601

*Although Britain stood on the periphery of the empire, it, too, could not escape the turmoil of the late imperial period. After the Roman army was recalled to Italy, the Anglo-Saxons invaded the island in the 440s and replaced local traditions, including Christianity, with their own. In due course, however, Christianity was reintroduced from a variety of directions, of which Italy was among the most important. From here Pope Gregory I (r. 590–604) dispatched two groups of missionaries to establish Roman-style Christianity in England. The first group, sent in 595, was led by Augustine, who later became archbishop of Canterbury, and the second was sent in 601 by Mellitus; both were monks from Rome. In these letters, Gregory describes the mission's initial progress and then offers strategies for furthering its success. He points not only to the pope's growing influence in the West but also to the interaction between Roman and non-Roman customs.*

### TO EULOGIUS, BISHOP OF ALEXANDRIA

Gregory to Eulogius, &c.

Our common son, the bearer of these presents, when he brought the letters of your Holiness found me sick, and has left me sick; whence it has ensued that the scanty water of my brief epistle has been hardly able to exude to the large fountain of your Blessedness. But it was a heavenly boon that, while in a state of bodily pain, I received the letter of your Holiness to lift me up with joy for the instruction of the heretics of the city of Alexandria, and the concord of the faithful, to such an extent that the very joy of my mind moderated the severity of my suffering. And indeed we rejoice with new exultation to hear of your good doings, though at the same time we by no means suppose that it is a new thing for you to act thus

---

From *A Select Library of Nicene and Post-Nicene Fathers of the Christian Church,* 2d ser., vols. 12 and 13 (New York: Christian Literature Co., 1895 and 1898), 12:240, 13:84–85.

perfectly. For that the people of holy Church increases, that spiritual crops of corn for the heavenly garner are multiplied, we never doubted that this was from the grace of Almighty God which flowed largely to you, most blessed ones. . . .

But, since in the good things you do I know that you also rejoice with others, I make you a return for your favor, and announce things not unlike yours; for while the nation of the Angli, placed in a corner of the world, remained up to this time misbelieving in the worship of stocks and stones, I determined, through the aid of your prayers for me, to send to it, God granting it, a monk of my monastery for the purpose of preaching. And he, having with my leave been made bishop by the bishops of Germany, proceeded, with their aid also, to the end of the world to the aforesaid nation; and already letters have reached us telling us of his safety and his work; to the effect that he and those that have been sent with him are resplendent with such great miracles in the said nation that they seem to imitate the powers of the apostles in the signs which they display. Moreover, at the solemnity of the Lord's Nativity which occurred in this first indiction, more than ten thousand Angli are reported to have been baptized by the same our brother and fellow-bishop. This have I told you, that you may know what you are effecting among the people of Alexandria by speaking, and what in the ends of the world by praying. For your prayers are in the place where you are not, while your holy operations are shewn in the place where you are.

## TO MELLITUS, ABBOT

Gregory to Mellitus, Abbot in France.

Since the departure of our congregation, which is with thee, we have been in a state of great suspense from having heard nothing of the success of your journey. But when Almighty God shall have brought you to our most reverend brother the bishop Augustine, tell him that I have long been considering with myself about the case of the Angli; to wit, that the temples of idols in that nation should not be destroyed, but that the idols themselves that are in them should be. Let blessed water be prepared, and sprinkled in these temples, and altars constructed, and relics deposited, since, if these same temples are well built, it is needful that they should be transferred from the worship of idols to the service of the true God; that, when the people themselves see that these temples are not destroyed, they may put away error from their heart, and, knowing and adoring the true God, may have recourse with the more familiarity to the places they have been accustomed to. And, since they are wont to kill many oxen in sacrifice to demons, they should have also some solemnity of this kind in a changed form, so that on the day of dedication, or on the anniversaries of the holy martyrs whose relics are deposited there, they may make for themselves tents of the branches of trees around these temples that have been changed into churches, and celebrate the solemnity with religious feasts. Nor let them any longer sacrifice animals to the devil, but slay animals to the praise of God for their own eating, and return thanks to the Giver of all for their fulness, so that, while some joys are reserved to them outwardly, they may be able the more easily to incline their minds to inward joys. For it is undoubtedly impossible to cut away everything at once from hard hearts, since one who strives to ascend to the highest place must needs rise by steps or paces, and not by leaps. Thus to the people of Israel in Egypt the Lord did indeed make Himself known; but still He reserved to them in His own worship the use of the sacrifices which they were accustomed to offer to the devil, enjoining them to immolate animals in sacrifice to Himself; to the end that, their hearts being changed, they should omit some things in the sacrifice and retain others, so that, though the animals were the same as what they had been accustomed to offer, nevertheless, as they immolated them to God and not to idols, they should be no longer the same sacrifices. This then it is necessary for thy Love to say to our aforesaid brother, that he, being now in that country, may consider well how he should arrange all things.

### ■ Discussion Questions

1. Earlier in his papacy, Gregory had advised the destruction of pagan temples. How does Gregory reverse this decision in his letter to Mellitus, and why?
2. What does Gregory's change of approach suggest about the ways in which Latin Christianity adapted to non-Roman cultures?
3. Historians often refer to Gregory I as the "father of the medieval papacy" because of the role he played in transforming the papacy into the moral and spiritual head of the West. What evidence can you find in these letters to support this view?

## 5.
## *The Life of Lady Balthild, Queen of the Franks*
### Late Seventh Century

*With the collapse of imperial government in the West in the fifth and sixth centuries, the kings from the Frankish royal dynasty, the Merovingians, came to dominate Roman Gaul. Their queens also wielded power, as* The Life of Lady Balthild *demonstrates. Lady Balthild (d. c. 680) was an Anglo-Saxon captive sold as a slave to the mayor of the palace in the Frankish kingdom of Neustria. He eventually offered her in marriage to King Clovis II (r. 638–657). On the king's death in 657, Lady Balthild acted as regent until her eldest son came of age in 663 or 664. She thereupon retired from court to a monastery. Although the author is unknown, his or her intent is clear: to hold Lady Balthild up as a model of Christian piety. Religious motives aside, the book illuminates women's place in court life as well as the growing influence of Christianity in Merovingian culture.*

---

From Paul Fouracre and Richard A. Gerberding, eds., *Late Merovingian France: History and Hagiography, 640–720* (Manchester and New York: Manchester University Press, 1996), 119–127, 131–32.

## HERE BEGINS THE LIFE OF BLESSED QUEEN BALTHILD

Blessed be the Lord, *who wishes all men to be saved and to come to the recognition of truth,*[1] and *who causes them to will and to complete all in all.*[2] And therefore His praise must be deservedly sung first in the merits and miracles of the saints, He *who makes great men out of those of low station, indeed, He who raises the poor man out of the dunghill and makes him to sit with the princes of His people,*[3] just as He has raised the present great and venerable woman, Lady Balthild, the queen. Divine providence called her from lands across the sea[4] and this precious and best pearl of God arrived here, having been sold at a low price. She was acquired by the late Erchinoald,[5] the leader of the Franks and a man of illustrious standing, in whose service she dwelt as an adolescent most honorably so that her admirable and pious religious way of life pleased both the leader and all his servants. She was indeed kind in her heart, *temperate and prudent*[6] in her whole character, and provident. She contrived evil against no one. She was neither frivolous in her fine expression nor presumptuous in speaking, but most honorable in all her acts. And although she was from the race of the Saxons, the form of her body was pleasing, very slender, and beautiful to see. Her expression was cheerful and her gait dignified. And, since she was thus, *she was exceedingly pleasing to the prince and she found favor in his eyes.*[7] He engaged her to serve him the goblets in his chamber, and as a most honorable cupbearer she stood quite often present in his service. Nonetheless, from the favor of her position she derived no haughtiness but, based in humility, was loving and obedient to all her equals. With fitting honor she so served her seniors that she removed the shoes from their feet and washed and dried them. She fetched water for washing and promptly prepared their clothes. And she performed this service for them without muttering and with a good and pious heart.

. . .

And from her noble way of life, greatest praise and love among her companions accrued to her, and she earned such a favorable reputation that, when the wife of the above-mentioned prince Erchinoald died, he decided to join the most honorable virgin, Balthild, to himself in the matrimonial bed. And, having learned this thing, she secretly and earnestly withdrew herself from his sight. And when she was called to the bedchamber of the prince, she hid herself in an out-of-the-way corner and threw cheap rags over herself so that no one would have thought anyone to be hiding there. Indeed, she was then still a shrewd and prudent virgin

[1]I Timothy 2:4.
[2]This seems to be a combination of Phillipians 2:13 and I Corinthians 12:6. See also Ephesians 1:23.
[3]I Kings 2:8; Psalms 112:7–8.
[4]England.
[5]Neustrian mayor from 641 to about 659.
[6]I Timothy 3:11.
[7]Ester 7:3, 2:4 and 9, and 5:8. Ester was also a royal spouse of low origins.

fleeing empty high positions and seeking humility. She tried, as she was able, to avoid human marriage so that she might deserve to come to her spiritual and heavenly groom. But indeed, beyond doubt, it was accomplished by divine providence that the prince did not find her, whom he sought, and then joined another matron to himself in marriage. And then the girl Balthild was finally found so that, by the true will of God who had shunned the nuptials of the prince, she would later have Clovis,[8] son of the late King Dagobert,[9] in marriage so that He could thus raise her to a higher station through the merit of her humility. And in this station divine dispensation decided to honor her so that, seeing that she had refused a follower of the king, she might obtain union with the king and, from her, royal progeny might come forth.[10] And this has now come to pass, as it is obvious to everyone that the royal offspring reigning now is hers.

. . .

But as she had the grace of prudence conferred upon her by God, with watchful eagerness she obeyed the king as her lord, and to the princes she showed herself a mother, to the priests as a daughter, and to the young and the adolescents as the best possible nurse. And she was friendly to all, loving the priests as fathers, the monks as brothers, the poor as a faithful nurse does, and giving to each generous alms. She preserved the honor of the princes and kept their fitting counsel, always exhorting the young to religious studies and humbly and steadfastly petitioning the king for the churches and the poor. While still in secular dress, she desired to serve Christ; she prayed daily, tearfully commending herself to Christ, the heavenly king. And the pious king [Clovis], taking care of her faith and devotion, gave his faithful servant, Abbot Genesius, to her as support, and through his hands she served the priests and the poor, fed the hungry, clothed the naked with garments, and conscientiously arranged the burial of the dead. Through him she sent most generous alms of gold and silver to the monasteries of men and women. . . .

. . .

What more is there to say? At God's command, her husband, King Clovis, went forth from his body, leaving a lineage of sons with their mother. In his place after him, his son, the late King Clothar,[11] took the throne of the Franks and then also with the excellent princes, Chrodbert, bishop of Paris, Lord Audoin, and Ebroin, mayor of the palace, along with the other great magnates and very many of the rest.[12] And, indeed, the kingdom of the Franks was maintained in peace. Then indeed, a little while ago, the Austrasians peacefully received her son Childeric[13] as

---

[8]Clovis II, king of Neustria (638–57).

[9]Dagobert I, king of Austrasia (623–33) and Neustria (629–38).

[10]That is, Clothar III, king of Neustria (657–73); Childeric II, king of Austrasia (657–75) and Neustria (673–75); and Theuderic III, king of Neustria (673 and 675–90).

[11]Clothar III, king of Neustria, r. 657–73.

[12]Note how the author shows the broad base of the king's aristocratic support. This is the explanation for the peace in the realm.

[13]Childeric II, king of Austrasia 657–75 and of Neustria 673–75.

king in Austrasia by the arrangement of Lady Balthild and, indeed, through the advice of the great magnates. But the Burgundians and the Neustrians were united. And we believe that, with God guiding, and in accordance with the great faith of Lady Balthild, these three kingdoms kept the harmony of peace among themselves.

. . .

At that time it happened that the heresy of simony stained the Church of God with its depraved practice in which they received the rank of bishop by paying a price for it. By the will of God [acting] through her, and at the urging of the good priests, the above-mentioned Lady Balthild stopped this impious evil so that no one would set a price on the taking of holy orders. Through her, the Lord also arranged for another very evil and impious practice to cease, one in which many men were more eager to kill their offspring than to provide for them in order to avoid the royal exactions which were inflicted upon them by custom, and from which they incurred a very heavy loss of property. This the lady prohibited for her own salvation so that no one presumed to do it. Because of this deed, truly a great reward awaits her.

. . .

Who, then, is able to say how many and how great were the sources of income, the entire farms and the large forests she gave up by donating them to the establishments of religious men in order to construct cells or monasteries? And she also built as God's own and private houses a huge nunnery for women consecrated by God at Chelles, near Paris where she placed the religious handmaiden of God, the girl Bertila, in the position of the first mother. And in this place the venerable Lady Balthild in turn decided to dwell under the pure rule of religion and to rest in peace. And in truth she fulfilled this with a devoted will. . . .

. . .

Indeed, what else? To the religious man, Lord Filibert, at Jumièges, in order to build that monastery, she conceded both a large forest from the fisc where this monastery of brothers is located, and many gifts and pastures from the royal fisc.[14] Indeed, how many things, both a large villa and many talents of silver and gold, [did she concede] to Lord Laigobert for the monastery at Cobion?[15] Even her own royal belt, with which she was girded, she devotedly took from her holy loins and gave to the brothers in alms. All this she gave with a kind and joyous heart, for as Scripture says, *God loves the cheerful giver.*[16] Likewise, to both Saint-Wandrille[17] and Logium[18] she conceded much property. Indeed, how many things, both many

[14]The fisc was the great body of land the Merovingian kings inherited from their Roman predecessors or took by right of royal conquest. One of the reasons given for the weakening of the dynasty was the diminution of the fisc through concessions such as the one mentioned here to the point where the royal house lost its economic base.

[15]Saint-Moutiers-au-Perbe (Orne).

[16]II Corinthians 9:7.

[17]Today, Saint-Wandrille-Rançon.

[18]Logium was a monastery for women in that part of Neustria which is now Normandy.

large entire villas and innumerable sums of money, did she give to Luxeuil and to the other monasteries in Burgundy? What [did she give] to the monastery at Jouarre, whence she summoned the holy virgins with the above-mentioned Lady Bertila to her own monastery at Chelles? How many gifts of fields and how much money did she concede to that place? Likewise, she often gave large gifts to the monastery of Faremoutier. Near the city of Paris she conferred many large villas to the basilicas of the saints and to the monasteries, and she enriched them with many gifts. What more is there? As we said, we are not able to relate every one, not even with difficulty the half of them, and certainly all her good acts cannot be told by us. . . .

. . .

It was, however, her holy vow that she ought to dwell in the monastery of religious women which we mentioned above, that is, at Chelles, which she herself built. . . .

. . .

Indeed, with a most pious affection she loved her sisters as her own daughters, she obeyed their holy abbess as her mother, and rendered service to them as the lowest of handmaidens out of holy desire, just as [she had done] when she still ruled the royal palace and often visited her holy monastery. So strongly did she exhibit the example of great humility that she even served her sisters in the kitchen, and the lowest acts of cleaning, even the latrines, she herself did. All this she undertook with joy and a cheerful heart, in such humble service for Christ. For who would believe that the height of such power would serve in such lowly things if her most abundant and great love of Christ had not demanded it of her in every way? . . .

. . .

Indeed, we recall that other queens in the kingdom of the Franks have been noble and worshippers of God: Clothild, queen of the late King Clovis of old[19] and niece of King Gundobad,[20] who, by her holy exhortations, led both her very brave and pagan husband and many of the Frankish nobles to Christianity and brought them to the Catholic faith. She also was the first to construct the churches in honor of St Peter at Paris and St George in the little monastery for virgins at Chelles, and she founded many others in honor of the saints in order to store up her reward, and she enriched them with many gifts. The same is said of Ultrogoda, queen of the most Christian King Childebert,[21] because she was a comforter of the poor and a helper of the servants of God and of monks. And [it is said] also of Queen Radegund, truly a most faithful handmaiden of God, queen of the late elder King Clothar,[22] whom the grace of the Holy Spirit had so inflamed that she left her husband while he was still alive and consecrated herself to the Lord Christ under the holy veil, and, with Christ as her spouse, accomplished many good things. . . .

---

[19]Clovis I (481–511).
[20]King of the Burgundians.
[21]Childebert I (511–58).
[22]Clothar I (511–61).

But it is pleasing, nevertheless, to consider this about her whom it here concerns: the Lady Balthild. Her many good deeds were accomplished in our times, and that these things were done by her herself we have learned in the best manner. Concerning these things, we have here commemorated a few out of the many, and we do not think her to be the inferior in merits of those earlier [queens]; rather we know her to have outdone them in holy striving. After the many good things which she did before her evangelical perfection, she gave herself over to voluntary holy obedience and as a true nun she happily completed her blessed life under complete religious practice. Her holy death and her holy rites are celebrated on 30 January, and, having been interred, she rests in peace in her monastery at Chelles. Truly she reigns in glory with Christ in heaven in everlasting joy, not unmindful, we believe, of her own faithful friends. . . .

## Discussion Questions

1. Why does the author think that Lady Balthild's life is exemplary?
2. To whom do you think the author directed his or her message, and why?
3. What does this source suggest about women's role in Merovingian politics and the relationship between this role and Christian values?

## Comparative Questions

1. Based on these documents, in what ways did the Byzantine, Muslim, and western European worlds both perpetuate and diverge from the legacy of Rome?
2. What do the documents reveal about the relationship between religious beliefs and politics in this period in both Christian and Islamic culture?
3. In his letter to Mellitus, Gregory I recommends adapting Christian practices to local customs. How did this strategy differ from the Muslims' approach to other religions?
4. What similarities and/or differences do you see in the religious beliefs and principles enunciated in *The Life of Lady Balthild* and in suras 1, 53, and 98 of the Qur'an?

Chapter

# 8

# Unity and Diversity in Three Societies, 750–1050

THE FOLLOWING DOCUMENTS illuminate the forces of unity and fragmentation driving the development of western Europe, Byzantium, and Islam between 750 and 1050. During this period, the Carolingian king Charlemagne (r. 768–814) forged a vast kingdom, the scope of which had not been seen since Roman times. As the first document reveals, his success was based not simply on military victory but also on his ability to administer effectively the diverse regions under his rule. Although the division of Charlemagne's empire in 843 opened the door to local rule, his legacy endured and, as the second document suggests, enhanced Europe's distinctiveness from Byzantium. By that time, the Byzantine emperors had regained much of their lost luster, and they considered themselves to be the rightful successors of Rome. Against this backdrop, the Islamic world continued to forge a unified sense of identity even as it, like the West, fragmented into smaller political units (Documents 4 and 5).

## 1.
## *General Capitulary for the* Missi
## 802

*Although the Merovingians forged a powerful political polity on the demise of Roman provincial government, their success paled in comparison to that of the Carolingians, who deposed them in 751. By the 790s, the most famous Carolingian king, Charlemagne (r. 768–814), had created an empire across Europe, using imperial Rome as a model. He was crowned emperor in 800 by Pope Leo III (r. 795–816), which further exalted his power. To centralize his rule, Charlemagne dispatched officials, or* missi, *annually to every part of the empire to review local affairs and enforce royal legislation. The following document, known as a* capitulary, *provided basic guidelines for these an-*

From Dana Carleton Munro, ed., *Translations and Reprints from the Original Sources of European History,* vol. 6 (Philadelphia: University of Pennsylvania Press, 1898), 16–19, 23–24, 26–27.

*nual visits. Composed of regulatory articles, capitularies were typically compiled at general assemblies convened by Charlemagne to discuss important issues with his magnates. These excerpts illuminate the forces binding the empire together as well as those that ultimately broke it apart.*

First chapter. Concerning the embassy sent out by the lord emperor. Therefore, the most serene and most Christian lord emperor Charles has chosen from his nobles the wisest and most prudent men, both archbishops and some of the other bishops also, and venerable abbots and pious laymen, and has sent them throughout his whole kingdom, and through them by all the following chapters has allowed men to live in accordance with the correct law. Moreover, where anything which is not right and just has been enacted in the law, he has ordered them to inquire into this most diligently and to inform him of it; he desires, God granting, to reform it. And let no one, through his cleverness or astuteness, dare to oppose or thwart the written law, as many are wont to do, or the judicial sentence passed upon him, or to do injury to the churches of God or the poor or the widows or the wards or any Christian. But all shall live entirely in accordance with God's precept, justly and under a just rule, and each one shall be admonished to live in harmony with his fellows in his business or profession; the canonical clergy ought to observe in every respect a canonical life without heeding base gain, nuns ought to keep diligent watch over their lives, laymen and the secular clergy ought rightly to observe their laws without malicious fraud, and all ought to live in mutual charity and perfect peace. And let the *missi* themselves make a diligent investigation whenever any man claims that an injustice has been done to him by any one, just as they desire to deserve the grace of omnipotent God and to keep their fidelity promised to Him, so that entirely in all cases everywhere, in accordance with the will and fear of God, they shall administer the law fully and justly in the case of the holy churches of God and of the poor, of wards and widows and of the whole people. And if there shall be anything of such a nature that they, together with the provincial counts, are not able of themselves to correct it and to do justice concerning it, they shall, without any ambiguity, refer this, together with their reports, to the judgment of the emperor; and the straight path of justice shall not be impeded by any one on account of flattery or gifts from any one, or on account of any relationship, or from fear of the powerful.

Concerning the fidelity to be promised to the lord emperor. And he commanded that every man in his whole kingdom, whether ecclesiastic or layman, and each one according to his vow and occupation, should now promise to him as emperor the fidelity which he had previously promised to him as king; and all of those who had not yet made that promise should do likewise, down to those who were twelve years old. And that it shall be announced to all in public, so that each one might know, how great and how many things are comprehended in that oath; not merely, as many have thought hitherto, fidelity to the lord emperor as regards his life, and not introducing any enemy into his kingdom out of enmity, and not consenting to or concealing another's faithlessness to him; but that all may know that this oath contains in itself this meaning:

First, that each one voluntarily shall strive, in accordance with his knowledge and ability, to live wholly in the holy service of God in accordance with the precept of God and in accordance with his own promise, because the lord emperor is unable to give to all individually the necessary care and discipline.

Secondly, that no man, either through perjury or any other wile or fraud, on account of the flattery or gift of any one, shall refuse to give back or dare to abstract or conceal a serf of the lord emperor or a district or land or anything that belongs to him; and that no one shall presume, through perjury or other wile, to conceal or abstract his fugitive fiscaline serfs who unjustly and fraudulently say that they are free.

That no one shall presume to rob or do any injury fraudulently to the churches of God or widows or orphans or pilgrims; for the lord emperor himself, after God and His saints, has constituted himself their protector and defender.

That no one shall dare to lay waste a benefice of the lord emperor, or to make it his own property.

That no one shall presume to neglect a summons to war from the lord emperor; and that no one of the counts shall be so presumptuous as to dare to dismiss thence any one of those who owe military service, either on account of relationship or flattery or gifts from any one.

That no one shall presume to impede at all in any way a ban or command of the lord emperor, or to dally with his work or to impede or to lessen or in any way to act contrary to his will or commands. And that no one shall dare to neglect to pay his dues or tax.

That no one, for any reason, shall make a practice in court of defending another unjustly, either from any desire of gain when the cause is weak, or by impeding a just judgment by his skill in reasoning, or by a desire of oppressing when the cause is weak. But each one shall answer for his own cause or tax or debt unless any one is infirm or ignorant of pleading; for these the *missi* or the chiefs who are in the court or the judge who knows the case in question shall plead before the court; or if it is necessary, such a person may be allowed as is acceptable to all and knows the case well; but this shall be done wholly according to the convenience of the chiefs or *missi* who are present. But in every case it shall be done in accordance with justice and the law; and that no one shall have the power to impede justice by a gift, reward, or any kind of evil flattery or from any hindrance of relationship. And that no one shall unjustly consent to another in anything, but that with all zeal and goodwill all shall be prepared to carry out justice.

For all the above mentioned ought to be observed by the imperial oath.

That bishops and priests shall live according to the canons and shall teach others to do the same.

That bishops, abbots, abbesses, who are in charge of others, with the greatest veneration shall strive to surpass their subjects in this diligence and shall not oppress their subjects with a harsh rule or tyranny, but with sincere love shall carefully guard the flock committed to them with mercy and charity or by the examples of good works. . . .

That bishops, abbots and abbesses, and counts shall be mutually in accord, following the law in order to render a just judgment with all charity and unity of peace, and that they shall live faithfully in accordance with the will of God, so that always everywhere through them and among them a just judgment shall be rendered. The poor, widows, orphans and pilgrims shall have consolation and defense from them; so that we, through their good-will, may deserve the reward of eternal life rather than punishment. . . .

That counts and *centenarii*[1] shall compel all to do justice in every respect, and shall have such assistants in their ministries as they can securely confide in, who will observe law and justice faithfully, who will oppress the poor in no manner, who will not dare under any pretext, on account of flattery or reward, to conceal thieves, robbers, murderers, adulterers, magicians, wizards or witches, and all sacrilegious men, but instead will give them up that they may be punished and chastised in accordance with the law, so that, God granting it, all of these evils may be removed from the Christian people.

That judges shall judge justly in accordance with the written law, and not according to their own will.

And we command that no one in our whole kingdom shall dare to deny hospitality to rich or poor or pilgrims, that is, no one shall deny shelter and fire and water to pilgrims traversing our country in God's name, or to anyone traveling for the love of God or for the safety of his own soul. . . .

Concerning embassies coming from the lord emperor. That the counts and *centenarii* shall provide most carefully, as they desire the grace of the lord emperor, for the *missi* who are sent out, so that they may go through their departments without any delay; and he commands to all everywhere that they ought to see to it that no delay is encountered anywhere, but they shall cause them to go on their way in all haste and shall provide for them in such a manner as our *missi* may direct. . . .

And against those who announce the justice of the lord emperor, let no one presume to plot any injury or damage, or to stir up any enmity. But if any one shall have presumed, let him pay the imperial ban or, if he deserves a heavier punishment, it is commanded that he shall be brought to the emperor's presence. . . .

That all shall be fully and well prepared, whenever our order or proclamation shall come. But if any one shall then say that he was unprepared and shall have neglected our command, he shall be brought to the palace; and not only he, but also all who dare to transgress our ban or command. . . .

And that all shall be entirely of one mind with our *missi* in performing justice in every respect. And that they shall not permit the use of perjury at all, for it is necessary that this most evil crime shall be removed from the Christian people.

[1]A *centenarius* is the ruler of a subdivision of a province or county.

But if any one after this shall have been proved a perjurer, let him know that he shall lose his right hand; and they shall be deprived of their property until we shall render our decision. . . .

Lastly, therefore, we desire all our decrees to be known in our whole kingdom through our *missi* now sent out, either among the men of the church, bishops, abbots, priests, deacons, canons, all monks or nuns, so that each one in his ministry or profession may keep our ban or decree, or where it may be fitting to thank the citizens for their good will, or to furnish aid, or where there may be need still of correcting anything. Likewise also to the laymen and in all places everywhere, whether they concern the guardianship of the holy churches or of widows and orphans and the weaker; or the robbing of them; or the arrangements for the assembling of the army; or any other matters; how they are to be obedient to our precept and will, or how they observe our ban, or how each one strives in all things to keep himself in the holy service of God; so that all these good things may be well done to the praise of omnipotent God, and we may return thanks where it is fitting. But where we believe there is anything unpunished, we shall so strive to correct it with all our zeal and will that with God's aid we may bring it to correction, both for our own eternal glory and that of all our faithful. Likewise we desire all the above to be fruitfully known by our counts or *centenarii,* our ministerials.

### ■ Discussion Questions

1. What does this document reveal about Charlemagne's vision of himself and his empire? In what ways were his Christian beliefs central to both?
2. Why might Charlemagne have considered it necessary for all freemen to swear an oath of fidelity to him as emperor? How was the notion of fidelity crucial to the success of his government?
3. What do the articles suggest about the means by which Charlemagne sought to unify his empire?

## 2.
## Liutprand of Cremona
## *Report to Otto I*
### 968

*The successors of Carolingian King Charlemagne (r. 768–814) could not sustain his unifying vision. Wracked by family squabbles, the empire was divided into three kingdoms in 843. The imperial title lived on, however, in the Ottonian dynasty that succeeded the Carolingians in Germany in the tenth century. Fashioning himself in Charlemagne's image, Otto I (r. 936–973) was the most powerful of these rulers.*

From *The Works of Liudprand of Cremona,* trans. F. A. Wright (New York: E. P. Dutton, 1930), 235–43.

*Crowned emperor in 962, Otto treated his Byzantine counterpart as an equal. To enhance his status, Otto dispatched his ambassador, Liutprand (c. 920–972), a northern Italian bishop, to Constantinople in 968 to arrange the marriage of Otto's son to a Byzantine princess. With this goal in mind, Liutprand met with the Byzantine emperor Nicephorus Phocas (r. 963–969). As he describes in a report sent to Otto, excerpted here, his efforts were in vain, and the failed mission elucidates the widening gap between the emerging territorial kingdoms in the West and Byzantium.*

> That the Ottos, the invincible august emperors of the Romans and the most noble Adelaide the august empress, may always flourish, prosper and triumph, is the earnest wish, desire and prayer of Liudprand bishop of the holy church of Cremona.

On the fourth of June we arrived at Constantinople, and after a miserable reception, meant as an insult to yourselves, we were given the most miserable and disgusting quarters. The palace where we were confined was certainly large and open, but it neither kept out the cold nor afforded shelter from the heat. Armed soldiers were set to guard us and prevent my people from going out, and any others from coming in. This dwelling, only accessible to us who were shut inside it, was so far distant from the emperor's residence that we were quite out of breath when we walked there—we did not ride. To add to our troubles, the Greek wine we found undrinkable because of the mixture in it of pitch, resin and plaster. The house itself had no water and we could not even buy any to quench our thirst. All this was a serious "Oh dear me!" but there was another "Oh dear me" even worse, and that was our warden, the man who provided us with our daily wants. If you were to seek another like him, you certainly would not find him on earth; you might perhaps in hell. Like a raging torrent he poured upon us every calamity, every extortion, every expense, every grief and every misery that he could invent. . . .

On the fourth of June, as I said above, we arrived at Constantinople and waited with our horses in heavy rain outside the Carian gate until five o'clock in the afternoon. At five o'clock Nicephorus ordered us to be admitted on foot, for he did not think us worthy to use the horses with which your clemency had provided us, and we were escorted to the aforesaid hateful, waterless, draughty stone house. On the sixth of June, which was the Saturday before Pentecost, I was brought before the emperor's brother Leo, marshal of the court and chancellor; and there we tired ourselves with a fierce argument over your imperial title. He called you not emperor, which is Basileus in his tongue, but insultingly Rex, which is king in ours. I told him that the thing meant was the same though the word was different, and he then said that I had come not to make peace but to stir up strife. Finally he got up in a rage, and really wishing to insult us received your letter not in his own hand but through an interpreter. . . .

On the seventh of June, the sacred day of Pentecost, I was brought before Nicephorus himself in the palace called Stephana, that is, the Crown Palace. He is a monstrosity of a man, a dwarf, fat-headed and with tiny mole's eyes; disfigured by a short, broad, thick beard half going gray; disgraced by a neck scarcely an inch long; piglike by reason of the big close bristles on his head; in color an Ethiopian and, as the poet [Juvenal] says, "you would not like to meet him in the dark"; a big belly, a lean posterior, very long in the hip considering his short stature, small legs, fair sized heels and feet; dressed in a robe made of fine linen, but old, foul smelling, and discolored by age; shod with Sicyonian slippers; bold of tongue, a fox by nature, in perjury and falsehood a Ulysses. My lords and august emperors, you always seemed comely to me; but how much more comely now! Always magnificent; how much more magnificent now! Always mighty; how much more mighty now! Always clement; how much more clement now! Always full of virtues; how much fuller now! At his left, not on a line with him, but much lower down, sat the two child emperors, once his masters, now his subjects. He began his speech as follows:—

It was our duty and our desire to give you a courteous and magnificent reception. That, however, has been rendered impossible by the impiety of your master, who in the guise of a hostile invader has laid claim to Rome; has robbed Berengar and Adalbert of their kingdom contrary to law and right; has slain some of the Romans by the sword, some by hanging, while others he has either blinded or sent into exile; and furthermore has tried to subdue to himself by massacre and conflagration cities belonging to our empire. His wicked attempts have proved unsuccessful, and so he has sent you, the instigator and furtherer of this villainy, under pretense of peace to act *comme un espion,* that is, as a spy upon us.

To him I made this reply: "My master did not invade the city of Rome by force nor as a tyrant; he freed her from a tyrant's yoke, or rather from the yoke of many tyrants. Was she not ruled by effeminate debauchers, and what is even worse and more shameful, by harlots? Your power, methinks, was fast asleep then; and the power of your predecessors, who in name alone are called emperors of the Romans, while the reality is far different. If they were powerful, if they were emperors of the Romans, why did they allow Rome to be in the hands of harlots?" . . .

"Come, let us clear away all trickeries and speak the plain truth. My master has sent me to you to see if you will give the daughter of the emperor Romanos and the empress Theophano to his son, my master the august emperor Otto. If you give me your oath that the marriage shall take place, I am to affirm to you under oath that my master in grateful return will observe to do this and this for you. Moreover he has already given you, his brother ruler, the best pledge of friendship by handing over Apulia, which was subject to his rule. . . .

"It is past seven o'clock," said Nicephorus "and there is a church procession which I must attend. Let us keep to the business before us. We will give you a reply at some convenient season."

I think that I shall have as much pleasure in describing this procession as my masters will have in reading of it. . . .

As Nicephorus, like some crawling monster, walked along, the singers began to cry out in adulation: "Behold the morning star approaches: the day star rises: in his eyes the sun's rays are reflected: Nicephorus our prince, the pale death of the Saracens." And then they cried again: "Long life, long life to our prince Nicephorus.

Adore him, ye nations, worship him, bow the neck to his greatness." How much more truly might they have sung:—"Come, you miserable burnt-out coal; old woman in your walk, wood-devil in your look; clodhopper, haunter of byres, goat-footed, horned, double-limbed; bristly, wild, rough, barbarian, harsh, hairy, a rebel, a Cappadocian!" So, puffed up by these lying ditties, he entered St Sophia, his masters the emperors following at a distance and doing him homage on the ground with the kiss of peace. His armor bearer, with an arrow for pen, recorded in the church the era in progress since the beginning of his reign. So those who did not see the ceremony know what era it is.

On this same day he ordered me to be his guest. But as he did not think me worthy to be placed above any of his nobles, I sat fifteenth from him and without a table cloth. Not only did no one of my suite sit at table with me; they did not even set eyes upon the house where I was entertained. At the dinner, which was fairly foul and disgusting, washed down with oil after the fashion of drunkards and moistened also with an exceedingly bad fish liquor, the emperor asked me many questions concerning your power, your dominions and your army. My answers were sober and truthful; but he shouted out:—"You lie. Your master's soldiers cannot ride and they do not know how to fight on foot. The size of their shields, the weight of their cuirasses,[1] the length of their swords, and the heaviness of their helmets, does not allow them to fight either way." Then with a smile he added: "Their gluttony also prevents them. Their God is their belly, their courage but wind, their bravery drunkenness. Fasting for them means dissolution, sobriety, panic. Nor has your master any force of ships on the sea. I alone have really stout sailors, and I will attack him with my fleets, destroy his maritime cities and reduce to ashes those which have a river near them. Tell me, how with his small forces will he be able to resist me even on land?" . . .

I wanted to answer and make such a speech in our defense as his boasting deserved; but he would not let me and added this final insult: "You are not Romans but Lombards." He even then was anxious to say more and waved his hand to secure my silence, but I was worked up and cried: "History tells us that Romulus, from whom the Romans get their name, was a fratricide born in adultery. He made a place of refuge for himself and received into it insolvent debtors, runaway slaves, murderers and men who deserved death for their crimes. This was the sort of crowd whom he enrolled as citizens and gave them the name of Romans. From this nobility are descended those men whom you style 'rulers of the world.' But we Lombards, Saxons, Franks, Lotharingians, Bavarians, Swabians and Burgundians, so despise these fellows that when we are angry with an enemy we can find nothing more insulting to say than—'You Roman!' For us in the word Roman is comprehended every form of lowness, timidity, avarice, luxury, falsehood and vice. You say that we are unwarlike and know nothing of horsemanship. Well, if the sins of the Christians merit that you keep this stiff neck, the next war will prove what manner of men you are, and how warlike we."

---

[1]**cuirasses:** Armor for protecting the chest and back. [Ed.]

## ■ Discussion Questions

1. How would you characterize Liutprand as an observer of the Byzantine court?
2. At the time of Liutprand's visit, Byzantium was enjoying renewed power and influence. How might this have shaped the Byzantine court's attitudes toward Liutprand and his master, Otto I?
3. Why did the Byzantine emperor's brother refer to Otto I as "Rex"? Why did Liutprand find this so insulting? What does this suggest about the ways in which the West and Byzantium had grown different both politically and culturally?

## 3.
## *Digenis Akritas*
### Tenth or Eleventh Century

*In contrast to western Europe, Byzantium not only remained a unified state but also achieved new heights of power in the ninth and tenth centuries. During this period, Byzantine troops stemmed the Muslim advance and regained territory, to the benefit of both the emperor's prestige and treasury. Victory came at a price, however, as the military aristocracy charged with defending the empire increased their control in the countryside. Written in the tenth or eleventh century by an unknown poet, the Byzantine epic poem* Digenis Akritas *("two-blood border lord") celebrates the legendary exploits of Digenis, a member of the military elite born of an Arab mother and a Greek father. According to the legend, Digenis grew to be a fierce warrior who successfully battled against the Arabs on Byzantium's eastern frontier. In the following excerpt, Digenis meets the Byzantine emperor Basil the Blessed (who may or may not correspond with an actual emperor), for whom he has both praise and advice.*

On hearing of these deeds, the Emperor
Who at that time was governing the Romans,
Basil the Blesséd, the great trophy winner,
Whose imperial fame was buried with him,
Chanced to be on campaign against the Persians
In those same places where the boy [Digenis] was living,
And when he heard about it was amazed.
So wishing greatly he might see the youth,
He sent a letter to him with these words:
"We've learned the stories of your many exploits,

---

From *Digenis Akritas: The Two-Blood Border Lord,* trans. Denison B. Hull (Athens: Ohio University Press, 1972), 59–61.

My son, and we have much rejoiced in them,
And offered thanks to God who works with you.
Our purpose is to see you with our own eyes,
And give requital worthy of your deeds.
Come to us gladly, without hesitation,
And don't suspect you'll suffer hurt from us."
When he received this, he returned an answer:
"I am your majesty's most abject slave;
Indeed, I have no right to your good things.
Master, what deed of mine do you admire,
Who am so humble, base, and quite undaring?
Still, he who trusts in God can do all things.
Therefore, since you desire to see your servant,
Be by the Euphrates after a little while.
You'll see me all you wish, my sacred master.
Don't think that I refuse to come before you,
But you have certain inexperienced soldiers,
And if perhaps they say something they shouldn't,
I certainly would deprive you of such men,
For such things, master, happen to the young."
    The Emperor read his letter word by word,
Admired the humbleness of the boy's statement,
And understood with pleasure his high courage.
    Since he wished strongly to behold the youth,
He took along with him a hundred soldiers,
Some spearmen too, and went to the Euphrates,
Ordering all on no account to utter
A word offensive to the Border Lord.
Those posted to keep watch on his account
Shortly announced the Emperor's arrival
To the marvelous Two-Blood Border Lord.
The Two-Blood came out all alone to meet him,
And bowed his head down to the ground, and said,
"Hail, you who take imperial power from God,
And rule us all because of the heathen's sins.
Why has it happened that the whole world's master
Comes before me, who am of no account?"
The Emperor, astonished when he saw him,
Forgot the burden of his majesty,
Advanced a little from his throne, embraced him,
Joyfully kissed him, and admired his stature,
And the great promise of his well-formed beauty.
"My son," he said, "you've proof of all your deeds;
The way you're put together shows your courage.

Would that Romania [Byzantium] had four such men!
So speak, my son, freely and openly,
And then take anything you wish from us."
"Keep everything, my lord," the boy replied,
"Because your love alone is enough for me.
It's not more blesséd to receive than give;
You have immense expenses in your army.
So I beseech your glorious majesty:
Love him who is obedient, pity the poor,
Deliver the oppressed from malefactors,
Forgive those who unwittingly make blunders,
And heed no slanders, nor accept injustice,
Sweep heretics out, confirm the orthodox.
These, master, are the arms of righteousness
With which you can prevail over all foes.
To rule and reign are not part of that power
Which God and His right hand alone can give.
Vile as I am, I grant your majesty
To take what you once gave Iconium
As tribute, and as much again, from them.
Master, I'll make you carefree about this
Until my soul shakes off this mortal coil."
The Emperor was delighted at these words.
"O marvelous and excellent young man,"
He said, "we name you a patrician now,
And grant you all your grandfather's estates;
We give to you the power to rule the borders,
And will confirm this with a golden bull,
And furnish you with rich imperial raiment."

## ■ Discussion Questions

1. What does Digenis's conversation with the emperor reveal about the basis of imperial authority and prestige?
2. What advice does Digenis offer the emperor on the proper method of rule? What do his words suggest about the characteristics of an ideal emperor?
3. In this passage, it is the emperor, not Digenis, who arranges their meeting, at which the emperor pays homage to him. What does this imply about the status of warriors like Digenis in Byzantine society and the emperor's relationship to them?

# 4.
# Ahmad al-Ya'qūbī
# *Kitāb al-buldān*
## Ninth Century

*At the same time Carolingian emperor Charlemagne (r. 768–814) was forging his empire, Islamic leaders were strengthening their own. In 750, a new dynasty, the Abbasids, seized control of the Islamic state, which they brought to new heights of power and influence. The foundation of a new capital city, Baghdad, in 762 by the Abbasids physically embodied the revolutionary nature of their rule. In the first fifty years of their reign, they transformed Baghdad into the hub of the Islamic state. An early historian of Islam and descendant of the Abbasid family, Ahmad al-Ya'qūbī (d. 897), experienced the dynamism of the city firsthand during his travels as a young man, and he later included his observations in a geographical work,* Kitāb al-buldān, *which he wrote near the end of his life. Although composed after economic problems had begun to tarnish the Abbasids' luster,* Kitāb al-buldān *elucidates the cultural and economic forces binding the Islamic world together even at a time when the caliphate was fragmenting into separate political units.*

I begin with Iraq only because it is the center of this world, the navel of the earth, and I mention Baghdad first because it is the center of Iraq, the greatest city, which has no peer in the east or the west of the world in extent, size, prosperity, abundance of water, or health of climate, and because it is inhabited by all kinds of people, town-dwellers and country-dwellers. To it they come from all countries, far and near, and people from every side have preferred Baghdad to their own homelands. There is no country, the peoples of which have not their own quarter and their own trading and financial arrangements. In it there is gathered that which does not exist in any other city in the world. On its flanks flow two great rivers, the Tigris and the Euphrates, and thus goods and foodstuffs come to it by land and by water with the greatest ease, so that every kind of merchandise is completely available, from east and west, from Muslim and non-Muslim lands. Goods are brought from India, Sind, China, Tibet, the lands of the Turks, the Daylam, the Khazars, the Ethiopians, and others to such an extent that the products of the countries are more plentiful in Baghdad than in the countries from which they come. They can be procured so readily and so certainly that it is as if all the good things of the world are sent there, all the treasures of the earth assembled there, and all the blessings of creation perfected there.

Furthermore, Baghdad is the city of the Hashimites, the home of their reign, the seat of their sovereignty, where no one appeared before them and no kings but

From Bernard Lewis, ed., *Islam from the Prophet Muhammad to the Capture of Constantinople,* vol. 2 (New York: Walker & Co., 1974), 69–73.

they have dwelt. Also, my own forbears have lived there, and one of them was governor of the city.

Its name is famous, and its fame widespread. Iraq is indeed the center of the world, for in accordance with the consensus of the astronomers recorded in the writings of ancient scholars, it is in the fourth climate, which is the middle climate where the temperature is regular at all times and seasons. It is very hot in the summer, very cold in the winter, and temperate in autumn and in spring. The passage from autumn to winter and from spring to summer is gradual and imperceptible, and the succession of the seasons is regular. So, the weather is temperate, the soil is rich, the water is sweet, the trees are thriving, the fruit luscious, the seeds are fertile, good things are abundant, and springs are easily found. Because of the temperate weather and rich soil and sweet water, the character of the inhabitants is good, their faces bright, and their minds untrammeled. The people excel in knowledge, understanding, letters, manners, insight, discernment, skill in commerce and crafts, cleverness in every argument, proficiency in every calling, and mastery of every craft. There is none more learned than their scholars, better informed than their traditionists, more cogent than their theologians, more perspicuous than their grammarians, more accurate than their readers, more skillful than their physicians, more melodious than their singers, more delicate than their craftsmen, more literate than their scribes, more lucid than their logicians, more devoted than their worshippers, more pious than their ascetics, more juridical than their judges, more eloquent than their preachers, more poetic than their poets, and more reckless than their rakes.

In ancient days, that is to say in the time of the Chosroes and the Persians, Baghdad was not a city, but only a village in the district of Bādūrayā. The city in Iraq which the Chosroes had chosen for their capital was al-Madā'in, seven parasangs[1] from Baghdad. The audience chamber of Chosroes Anushirvan[2] is still there. At that time there was nothing in Baghdad but a convent situated at a place called Qarn al-Ṣarāt, at the confluence of the Ṣarāt and the Tigris. This convent is called al-Dayr al-'Atīq [the ancient convent] and is still standing at the present time. It is the residence of the Catholicos, the head of the Nestorian Christians.

Nor does Baghdad figure in the wars of the Arabs at the time of the advent of Islam, since the Arabs founded Basra and Kūfa. Kūfa was founded in the year 17 [638] by Sa'd ibn Abī Waqqās al-Zuhrī, one of 'Umar ibn al-Khaṭṭāb's governors. Basra, too, was founded in the year 17 by 'Utba ibn Ghazwān al-Māzinī of the tribe of Māzin of Qays, also a governor of 'Umar ibn al-Khaṭṭāb at that time. The Arabs settled down in these two places, but the important people, the notables, and the rich merchants moved to Baghdad.

The Umayyads lived in Syria and did not stay in Iraq. Mu'āwiya ibn Abī Sufyān, who had been governor of Syria in the name of 'Umar ibn al-Khaṭṭāb and then of 'Uthmān ibn 'Affān for twenty years, lived in Damascus with his family.

---

[1]**parasangs:** Ancient Persian units of distance equal to about 3.5 miles. [Ed.]
[2]**Chosroes Anushirvan:** Sixth-century Persian emperor. [Ed.]

When he seized power and sovereignty passed to him, he kept his residence and capital in Damascus, where he had his authority, his supporters, and his faction. The Umayyad kings after Mu'āwiya stayed in Damascus, since they were born there and knew no other place, and its people were their sole supporters.

Then the Caliphate came to the descendants of the paternal uncle of the Apostle of God, may God bless and save him and also his family, the line of 'Ab-bās ibn 'Abd al-Muṭṭālib. Thanks to clear discernment, sound intelligence, and perfect judgment, they saw the merits of Iraq, its magnificence, spaciousness, and central situation. They saw that it was not like Syria, with its pestilential air, narrow houses, rugged soil, constant diseases, and uncouth people; nor was it like Egypt, with changeable weather and many plagues, situated between a damp and fetid river, full of unhealthy mists that engender disease and spoil food, and the dry, bare mountains, so dry and salty and bad that no plant can grow nor any spring appear; nor like Ifrīqiya, far from the peninsula of Islam and from the holy house of God, with uncouth people and many foes; nor like Armenia, remote, cold and icy, barren, and surrounded by enemies; nor like the districts of the Jabal, harsh, rough, and snow-covered, the abode of the hard-hearted Kurds; nor like the land of Khurāsān, stretching to the east, surrounded on every side by rabid and war-like enemies; nor like the Ḥijāz where life is hard and means are few and the people's food comes from elsewhere, as Almighty God warned us in His book, through His friend Ibrāhīm, who said, "O Lord, I have given to my descendants as dwelling a valley without tillage" [Qur'an]; nor like Tibet, where, because of the foul air and food, the people are discolored, with stunted bodies and tufty hair.

When they understood that Iraq was the best of countries, the 'Abbasids decided to settle there. In the first instance the Commander of the Faithful, Abu'l-'Abbās, that is 'Abdallāh ibn Muḥammad ibn 'Alī ibn 'Abdallāh ibn 'Abbās ibn 'Abd al-Muṭṭalib, stayed in Kūfa. Then he moved to Anbār and built a city on the banks of the Euphrates which he called Hāshimiyya. Abu'l-'Abbās, may God be pleased with him, died before the building of this city was completed.

Then, when Abū Ja'far al-Manṣūr. succeeded to the Caliphate, he founded a new city between Kūfa and Ḥīra, which he also called Hāshimiyya. He stayed there for a while, until the time when he decided to send his son, Muḥammad al-Mahdī, to fight the Slavs in the year 140 [757–758]. He then came to Baghdad and stopped there, and asked, "What is the name of this place?" They answered, "Baghdad." "By God," said the Caliph, "this is indeed the city which my father Muḥammad ibn 'Alī told me I must build, in which I must live, and in which my descendants after me will live. Kings were unaware of it before and since Islam, until God's plans for me and orders to me are accomplished. Thus, the traditions will be verified and the signs and proofs be manifest. Indeed, this island between the Tigris in the east and the Euphrates in the west is a marketplace for the world. All the ships that come up the Tigris from Wāsiṭ, Basra, Ubulla, Ahwāz, Fārs, 'Umān, Yamāma, Baḥrayn, and beyond will anchor here; wares brought on ships down the Tigris from Mosul, Diyār-Rabī'a, Ādharbayjān, and Armenia, and along the Euphrates from Diyār-Muḍar, Raqqa, Syria, the border marches, Egypt, and North Africa, will be brought and unloaded here. It will be the highway for the people of the Jabal,

Iṣfahān, and the districts of Khurāsān. Praise be to God who preserved it for me and caused all those who came before me to neglect it. By God, I shall build it. Then I shall dwell in it as long as I live, and my descendants shall dwell in it after me. It will surely be the most flourishing city in the world."

### ■ Discussion Questions

1. Considering Ahmad al-Ya'qūbī's family connections, to what extent can we accept his view of Baghdad, and why?
2. What does Ahmad al-Ya'qūbī reveal about the geographical breadth and ethnic diversity of the Islamic empire?
3. As described here, how did trade help unify the Islamic empire at a time when it was beginning to fragment politically?

## 5.
## Fulbert of Chartres
## *Letter to William of Aquitaine*
## 1020

*Fragmented and under attack by outsiders, post-Carolingian Europe looked very different from the empire Charlemagne had envisioned. Counts and other local elites relied less on the king for new lands and offices and more on their own resources and networks. The glue binding these networks together was the notion of "fealty" by which local lords secured the personal loyalty and dependency of others, their "faithful men" (vassals). Duke William of Aquitaine, a very powerful lord in France who ruled from c. 995 to 1030, often found himself in conflict with his vassals. To clarify his and their obligations, he asked Fulbert, bishop of Chartres, to advise him on the matter. Fulbert's letter, written in 1020 and reproduced in full here, shows that many of the obligations were, like the Ten Commandments, negative ones.*

To William most glorious duke of the Aquitanians, bishop Fulbert the favor of his prayers.

Asked to write something concerning the form of fealty, I have noted briefly for you on the authority of the books the things which follow. He who swears fealty to his lord ought always to have these six things in memory; what is harmless, safe, honorable, useful, easy, practicable. Harmless, that is to say that he should not be injurious to his lord in his body; safe, that he should not be injurious to him in his secrets or in the defenses through which he is able to be secure; honorable, that he should not be injurious to him in his justice or in other matters

From *Translations and Reprints from the Original Sources of European History* (Philadelphia: University of Pennsylvania Press, 1898), vol. 4, no. 3, 23–24.

that pertain to his honor; useful, that he should not be injurious to him in his possessions; easy or practicable, that that good which his lord is able to do easily, he make not difficult, nor that which is practicable he make impossible to him.

However, that the faithful vassal should avoid these injuries is proper, but not for this does he deserve his holding; for it is not sufficient to abstain from evil, unless what is good is done also. It remains, therefore, that in the same six things mentioned above he should faithfully counsel and aid his lord, if he wishes to be looked upon as worthy of his benefice and to be safe concerning the fealty which he has sworn.

The lord also ought to act toward his faithful vassal reciprocally in all these things. And if he does not do this he will be justly considered guilty of bad faith, just as the former, if he should be detected in the avoidance of or the doing of or the consenting to them, would be perfidious and perjured.

I would have written to you at greater length, if I had not been occupied with many other things, including the rebuilding of our city and church which was lately entirely consumed in a great fire; from which loss though we could not for a while be diverted, yet by the hope of the comfort of God and of you we breathe again.

## ■ Discussion Questions

1. According to Fulbert, what are the mutual duties of vassals and lords?
2. What do these duties reveal about the basis of local rule in post-Carolingian society?
3. What does the fact that William of Aquitaine asked a bishop for advice suggest about the relationship between secular and religious authority at the time?

## ■ Comparative Questions

1. In what ways do Liutprand and Fulbert point to both the success and failure of Charlemagne's political vision as revealed in the capitulary for the *missi?*
2. Based on *Digenis Akritas* and Liutprand's report, how and why did Otto I's imperial image and claims to power compete with those of the Byzantine emperor?
3. How do Liutprand, Ahmad al-Ya'qūbī, and Digenis seek to enhance the image of their respective rulers? What does this suggest about the role of praise in both Eastern and Western culture during the tenth century?
4. When viewed together, what do these documents reveal about the development of Byzantium, Islam, and western Europe as distinctive societies with their own identities in the ninth and tenth centuries?

Chapter

# 9

# Renewal and Reform, 1050–1200

WESTERN EUROPE WAS ALIVE with change in the late eleventh and twelfth centuries. Trade and agricultural production were on the rise, promoting the development of a new cash-based economy. A great prevalence of wealth prompted a range of responses at all levels of medieval society. The first document set shows how economic growth refashioned the European landscape, as new municipalities were founded and old ones enlarged. With the economy booming, many ecclesiastical leaders feared that the church was becoming too entangled in its own web. The second document suggests how this fear helped spark a religious reform movement that elevated the papacy to new heights of power. The third and fourth documents illuminate how the vigor of the period found expression in new institutions and fiscally minded bureaucracies established by secular authorities seeking to enhance their authority and prestige. The final document unveils the spiritual manifestations of these currents of renewal, reform, and economic change.

## 1.
## *Urban Charters of Jaca, Spain*
### c. 1077
## *and Lorris, France*
### 1155

*Although cities were common in the Roman Empire, they featured less prominently in early medieval Europe, where wealth and power were derived largely from land. In the eleventh century, however, agricultural and commercial growth resulted in the development of new cities and towns across Europe as places where people congregated to live and work. The following documents attest to the rise of medieval urbanism*

---

From Olivia Remie Constable, ed., *Medieval Iberia,* (Philadelphia: University of Pennsylvania Press, 1997), 123–25; and Frederic Austin Ogg, *A Source Book of Mediaeval History* (New York: American Book Co., 1907), 328–30.

*and its economic and social implications. The first is a charter of laws and freedoms* (fuero) *bestowed on the community of Jaca in Christian Spain by Sancho I (r. 1063–1094), king of Aragon, around 1077. The second is another charter, this one granted by King Louis VII of France (r. 1137–1180) in 1155, which regulated the governance of the town of Lorris.*

## URBAN CHARTER OF JACA, SPAIN

[Emblem of Christ] In the name of our Lord Jesus Christ and of the undivided Trinity, Father and Son and Holy Spirit, amen. This is a charter of authority and confirmation which I Sancho, by the grace of God king of the Aragonese and Pamplonese, make to you.

Notice to all men who are even in the east and west and north and south that I wish to establish a city [*civitatem*] in my village [*villa*][1] which is called "Jaca."

First, I remit to you all bad *fueros* which you had until this day that I established Jaca to be a city; and so, because I wish it to be well settled, I concede and confirm to you and to all who settle in my city Jaca all the good *fueros* which you have asked of me in order that my city be well settled.

And each one may enclose his part as he can.

And if it happen that anyone of you comes to dispute and will strike anyone before me or in my palace when I am standing there, let him fine for 1000 s. or lose the fight.

And if anyone, whether knight or burgher or peasant, should strike another, and not in my presence nor in my palace although I be in Jaca, let him not pay the fine [*calonia*] except according to the *fuero* you have when I am not in the town.

And if it happen that someone be found killed in a robbery in Jaca or its district, you are not obligated to pay homicide.[2]

I give and concede to you and your successors with good will that you not go in the army [*hoste*] unless with bread for three days. And this should be in the name of battle in the field [*de lite campale*] or where I or my successors are surrounded by our enemies. And if the lord of the house does not wish to go there, let him substitute one armed footman.

And wherever you can buy anything in Jaca or outside of Jaca, or acquire any man's inheritance, you may have it free and unencumbered without any bad cut [*malo cisso*].[3]

And after you hold it undisturbed for a year and a day, anyone wishing to disturb them or take it away from you shall give me 60 s., and shall confirm your inheritance.

---

[1]The word *villa* does not always mean "village" in medieval Latin, but it does often refer to unwalled settlements in Mediterranean Europe.

[2]That is, the murder fine sometimes imposed by lords on communities.

[3]The "cut" was an arbitrary tax.

And as far as you can go and return in a day, everywhere, you may have pastures and woods, observing the boundaries of the men living there.

And that you should not have duel-war between you, unless agreeable to both; nor with men from elsewhere, unless with consent of the men of Jaca.

And that none of you should sit captive giving pledges of your foot [*de vestro pede*].[4]

And if any of you commits fornication with any willing woman, except a married one, you shall not pay calumny.[5] And if it happens that he forces her, let him give her a husband or receive her as his wife. And if the raped woman appeals on the first or second day, let her prove by truthful witnesses of Jaca. If she wishes to appeal after three days, it shall avail her nothing.

And if any of you goes against his neighbor in anger and armed with lance, sword, club, or knife, let him fine for it 1000 s. or lose the fight.

And if anyone kills another let him pay 500 s.

And if one strikes another in conflict or grabs him by the hair, let him pay 25 s. for it.

And if he falls to the ground, let him pay 250 s.

And if anyone enters his neighbor's house in anger, or makes seizures there, let him pay 20 s. to the lord of the house.

And that my agent [*merinus*] not receive calumny from any man of Jaca save with the approval of six better men [*vicinis*] of Jaca.

And none of all the men of Jaca should go to judgment anywhere but in Jaca.

And if anyone has false measure or weight, let him pay 60 s.

And that all men should go to mill in mills where they wish, except Jews and those who make bread for sale.

And you should not give or sell your honors to the church or to *infanzones.*[6]

And if any man is imprisoned for debt, let him who wishes to capture him do so with my agent; and let him put [him] in my palace, and let my jailer guard him; and after three days, he who took him should give him farthing's worth [*obolatam*]; and if he refuse to do [this], my jailer may release him.

And if any man seize as pledge the Saracen man or Saracen woman of his neighbor, let him put him in my palace; and the lord of the male and female Saracen shall give him bread and water, because he is a human being [*homo*] and should not starve like a beast.

And whoever wishes to disrupt this charter which I make to the settlers of Jaca, let him be excommunicated and anathematized for his cruelty and wholly separated from all God's faithful, whether he be of my stock or of another. Amen, amen, amen.

---

[4]Meaning unclear.

[5]*Calumny* was a payment exacted for slander.

[6]The *infanzones* were the lesser aristocracy of knights in Aragon.

## Urban Charter of Lorris, France

Every one who has a house in the parish of Lorris shall pay as *cens* sixpence only for his house, and for each acre of land that he possesses in the parish.[7]

No inhabitant of the parish of Lorris shall be required to pay a toll or any other tax on his provisions; and let him not be made to pay any measurage fee on the grain which he has raised by his own labor.[8]

No burgher shall go on an expedition, on foot or on horseback, from which he cannot return the same day to his home if he desires.[9]

No burgher shall pay toll on the road to Étampes, to Orleans, to Milly (which is in the Gâtinais), or to Melun.[10]

No one who has property in the parish of Lorris shall forfeit it for any offense whatsoever, unless the offense shall have been committed against us or any of our *hôtes*.[11]

No person while on his way to the fairs and markets of Lorris, or returning, shall be arrested or disturbed, unless he shall have committed an offense on the same day. . . .[12]

No one, neither we nor any other, shall exact from the burghers of Lorris any tallage, tax, or subsidy. . . .[13]

---

[7]This payment was made in recognition of the lordship of the king, the grantor of the charter. Aside from it, the burgher had full rights over his land.

[8]The burghers, who were often engaged in agriculture as well as commerce, are to be exempt from tolls on commodities bought for their own sustenance and from the ordinary fees due the lord for each measure of grain harvested.

[9]The object of this provision is to restrict the amount of military service due the king. The burghers of small places like Lorris were farmers and traders who made poor soldiers and who were ordinarily exempted from service by their lords. The provision for Lorris practically amounted to an exemption, for such service as was permissible under the charter was not worth much.

[10]The Gâtinais was the region in which Lorris was situated. The king's object in granting the burghers the right to carry goods to the towns specified without payment of tolls was to encourage commercial intercourse.

[11]This protects the landed property of the burghers against the crown and crown officials. With two exceptions, fine or imprisonment, not confiscation of land, is to be the penalty for crime. *Hôtes* denotes persons receiving land from the king and under his direct protection.

[12]This provision is intended to attract merchants to Lorris by placing them under the king's protection and assuring them that they would not be molested on account of old offenses.

[13]This safeguards the personal property of the burghers, as another section of the charter safeguards their land. Arbitrary imposts are forbidden and any of the inhabitants who as serfs had been paying arbitrary tallage are relieved of the burden. The nominal fee was to be the only regular payment due the king.

If a man shall have had a quarrel with another, but without breaking into a fortified house, and if the parties shall have reached an agreement without bringing a suit before the provost, no fine shall be due to us or our provost on account of the affair. . . .[14]

No inhabitant of Lorris is to render us the obligation of *corvée,* except twice a year, when our wine is to be carried to Orleans, and not elsewhere.[15]

No one shall be detained in prison if he can furnish surety that he will present himself for judgment.

Any burgher who wishes to sell his property shall have the privilege of doing so; and, having received the price of the sale, he shall have the right to go from the town freely and without molestation, if he so desires, unless he has committed some offense in it.

Any one who shall dwell a year and a day in the parish of Lorris, without any claim having pursued him there, and without having refused to lay his case before us or our provost, shall abide there freely and without molestation. . . .[16]

We ordain that every time there shall be a change of provosts in the town the new provost shall take an oath faithfully to observe these regulations; and the same thing shall be done by new sergeants[17] every time that they are installed.

## Discussion Questions

1. What do these excerpts reveal about the role of kings in promoting urban growth in medieval Europe?
2. What did Louis VII and Sancho I seek to gain in granting their respective charters? What similarities and differences do you see in each king's goals?
3. Based on these two charters, why might people have decided to move to newly established cities and towns? What did city life have to offer?

---

[14]An agreement outside of court was allowable in all cases except when there was a serious breach of the public peace. The provost was the chief officer of the town, and he was appointed by the crown and was charged chiefly with the administration of justice and the collection of revenues. All suits of the burghers were tried in the provost's court. They had no active part in their own government, as was generally true of the franchise towns.

[15]Another part of the charter specifies that only those burghers who owned horses and carts were expected to render the king even this service.

[16]This clause, which is common in the town charters of the twelfth century (especially in the case of towns on the royal domain), is intended to attract serfs from other regions and so to build up population. As a rule, the towns were places of refuge from seigniorial oppression, and the present charter undertakes to limit the time within which the lord might recover his serf who had fled to Lorris to a year and a day—except in cases where the serf should refuse to recognize the jurisdiction of the provost's court in the matter of the lord's claim.

[17]The sergeants were deputies of the provost.

# 2.
# Emperor Henry IV and Pope Gregory VII
## *Sources of the Investiture Conflict*
### 1076

*The commercial revolution helped spark not only economic changes but also religious ones. Pope Gregory VII (r. 1073–1085) became the driving force behind a movement for church reform, which strove to liberate the church from secular influence and wealth. His zeal brought him head-to-head with Emperor Henry IV (r. 1056–1106) who, claiming to be crowned by God, asserted the traditional right to oversee the church in his realm. These two documents illuminate each side of the debate. The first is a letter that Henry sent to the pope in January 1076 after Henry had denounced him for not obeying papal mandates prohibiting, among other things, laymen from "investing" (that is, appointing) church leaders. In response, the pope excommunicated and deposed Henry. The lines of the conflict were thus drawn, pitting imperial and papal claims of authority against each other. Although the battle ended in 1122 with a compromise, the papacy emerged as a more powerful force than ever before.*

## LETTER TO GREGORY VII FROM HENRY IV

Henry, King not by usurpation, but by the pious ordination of God, to Hildebrand, now not Pope, but false monk:

You have deserved such a salution as this because of the confusion you have wrought; for you left untouched no order of the Church which you could make a sharer of confusion instead of honor, of malediction instead of benediction.

For to discuss a few outstanding points among many: Not only have you dared to touch the rectors of the holy Church—the archbishops, the bishops, and the priests, anointed of the Lord as they are—but you have trodden them under foot like slaves who know not what their lord may do. In crushing them you have gained for yourself acclaim from the mouth of the rabble. You have judged that all these know nothing, while you alone know everything. In any case, you have sedulously used this knowledge not for edification, but for destruction, so greatly that we may believe Saint Gregory, whose name you have arrogated to yourself, rightly made this prophesy of you when he said: "From the abundance of his subjects, the mind of the prelate is often exalted, and he thinks that he has more knowledge than anyone else, since he sees that he has more power than anyone else."

And we, indeed, bore with all these abuses, since we were eager to preserve the honor of the Apostolic See. But you construed our humility as fear, and so you were emboldened to rise up even against the royal power itself, granted to us by

From *The Correspondence of Pope Gregory VII,* trans. Ephraim Emerton (New York: Columbia University Press, 1932), 90–91; and *Imperial Lives and Letters of the Eleventh Century,* trans. Theodor E. Mommsen and Karl F. Morrison (New York: Columbia University Press, 1962), 150–51.

God. You dared to threaten to take the kingship away from us—as though we had received the kingship from you, as though kingship and empire were in your hand and not in the hand of God.

Our Lord, Jesus Christ, has called us to kingship, but has not called you to the priesthood. For you have risen by these steps: namely, by cunning, which the monastic profession abhors, to money; by money to favor; by favor to the sword. By the sword you have come to the throne of peace, and from the throne of peace you have destroyed the peace. You have armed subjects against their prelates; you who have not been called by God have taught that our bishops who have been called by God are to be spurned; you have usurped for laymen the bishops' ministry over priests, with the result that these laymen depose and condemn the very men whom the laymen themselves received as teachers from the hand of God, through the imposition of the hands of bishops.

You have also touched me, one who, though unworthy, has been anointed to kingship among the anointed. This wrong you have done to me, although as the tradition of the holy Fathers has taught, I am to be judged by God alone and am not to be deposed for any crime unless—may it never happen—I should deviate from the Faith. For the prudence of the holy bishops entrusted the judgment and the deposition even of Julian the Apostate not to themselves, but to God alone. The true pope Saint Peter also exclaims, "Fear God, honor the king." You, however, since you do not fear God, dishonor me, ordained of Him.

Wherefore, when Saint Paul gave no quarter to an angel from heaven if the angel should preach heterodoxy, he did not except you who are now teaching heterodoxy throughout the earth. For he says, "If anyone, either I or an angel from heaven, preach any other gospel unto you than that which we have preached unto you, let him be accursed." Descend, therefore, condemned by this anathema and by the common judgment of all our bishops and of ourself. Relinquish the Apostolic See which you have arrogated. Let another mount the throne of Saint Peter, another who will not cloak violence with religion but who will teach the pure doctrine of Saint Peter.

I, Henry, King by the grace of God, together with all our bishops, say to you: Descend! Descend!

## EXCOMMUNICATION OF HENRY IV

O blessed Peter, prince of the Apostles, mercifully incline thine ear, we [*sic*] pray, and hear me, thy servant, whom thou hast cherished from infancy and hast delivered until now from the hand of the wicked who have hated and still hate me for my loyalty to thee. Thou art my witness, as are also my Lady, the Mother of God, and the blessed Paul, thy brother among all the saints, that thy Holy Roman Church forced me against my will to be its ruler. I had no thought of ascending thy throne as a robber, nay, rather would I have chosen to end my life as a pilgrim than to seize upon thy place for earthly glory and by devices of this world. Therefore, by thy favor, not by any works of mine, I believe that it is and has been thy will, that the Christian people especially committed to thee should render obedience to me, thy especially constituted representative. To me is given by thy grace the power of binding and loosing in Heaven and upon earth.

Wherefore, relying upon this commission, and for the honor and defense of thy Church, in the name of Almighty God, Father, Son and Holy Spirit, through thy power and authority, I deprive King Henry, son of the emperor Henry, who has rebelled against thy Church with unheard of audacity, of the government over the whole kingdom of Germany and Italy, and I release all Christian men from the allegiance which they have sworn or may swear to him, and I forbid anyone to serve him as king. For it is fitting that he who seeks to diminish the glory of thy Church should lose the glory which he seems to have.

And, since he has refused to obey as a Christian should or to return to the God whom he has abandoned by taking part with excommunicated persons, has spurned my warnings which I gave him for his soul's welfare, as thou knowest, and has separated himself from thy Church and tried to rend it asunder, I bind him in the bonds of anathema in thy stead and I bind him thus as commissioned by thee, that the nations may know and be convinced that thou art Peter and that upon thy rock the son of the living God has built his Church and the gates of hell shall not prevail against it.

### ■ Discussion Questions

1. What does Henry IV mean by denouncing the pope as a "false monk"?
2. What do the emperor's denunciations reveal about his conception of the source and the scope of his power?
3. How did Henry's self-image conflict with Gregory's understanding of his own authority as reflected in his excommunication and deposition of the emperor?

## 3.
## *The Anglo-Saxon Chronicle*
### (1085–1086)

*While the papacy was expanding its authority in the eleventh century, regional rulers were doing much the same. William I, duke of Normandy and king of England (r. 1066–1087), provides a case in point, and his efforts on this front helped to make his twelfth-century successors the mightiest kings in Europe. Upon conquering his rival to the throne in the battle of Hastings in 1066, William consolidated his rule by preserving existing institutions and establishing new ones. Among his achievements was the commission of a comprehensive survey of England's land, livestock, taxes, and population, which was conducted in 1086. Later condensed into two volumes, known as Domesday, the survey paints a detailed picture of England's agricultural and urban*

From *The Anglo-Saxon Chronicle*, trans. Dorothy Whitelock (New Brunswick: Rutgers University Press, 1961), 161–65.

*landscape. Here is a contemporary description of King William and his survey from the* Anglo-Saxon Chronicle, *a year-by-year account of English history from the birth of Christ to 1154, which bears witness to the king's immense resources and power.*

In this year people said and declared for a fact, that Cnut, king of Denmark, son of King Swein, was setting out in this direction and meant to conquer this country with the help of Robert, count of Flanders, because Cnut was married to Robert's daughter. When William, king of England, who was then in Normandy—for he was in possession of both England and Normandy—found out about this, he went to England with a larger force of mounted men and infantry from France and Brittany than had ever come to this country, so that people wondered how this country could maintain all that army. And the king had all the army dispersed all over the country among his vassals, and they provisioned the army each in proportion to his land. And people had much oppression that year, and the king had the land near the sea laid waste, so that if his enemies landed, they should have nothing to seize on so quickly. But when the king found out for a fact that his enemies had been hindered and could not carry out their expedition—then he let some of the army go to their own country, and some he kept in this country over winter.

Then at Christmas, the king was at Gloucester with his council, and held his court there for five days, and then the archbishop and clerics had a synod for three days. There Maurice was elected bishop of London, and William for Norfolk, and Robert for Cheshire—they were all clerics of the king.

After this, the king had much thought and very deep discussion with his council about this country—how it was occupied or with what sort of people. Then he sent his men over all England into every shire and had them find out how many hundred hides there were in the shire, or what land and cattle the king himself had in the country, or what dues he ought to have in twelve months from the shire.[1] Also he had a record made of how much land his archbishops had, and his bishops and his abbots and his earls—and though I relate it at too great length—what or how much everybody had who was occupying land in England, in land or cattle, and how much money it was worth. So very narrowly did he have it investigated, that there was no single hide nor virgate of land, nor indeed (it is a shame to relate but it seemed no shame to him to do) one ox nor one cow nor one pig which was there left out, and not put down in his record; and all these records were brought to him afterwards. . . .

This King William of whom we speak was a very wise man,[2] and very powerful and more worshipful and stronger than any predecessor of his had been. He was gentle to the good men who loved God, and stern beyond all measure to those people who resisted his will. In the same place where God permitted him to conquer England, he set up a famous monastery and appointed monks for it,[3] and

[1]This initiative resulted in Domesday. A hide was a unit of taxation. [Ed.]
[2]The account that follows was clearly written by a man who had attended William's court.
[3]Battle Abbey.

endowed it well. In his days the famous church at Canterbury was built,[4] and also many another over all England. Also, this country was very full of monks, and they lived their life under the rule of St. Benedict, and Christianity was such in his day that each man who wished followed out whatever concerned his order. Also, he was very dignified: three times every year he wore his crown, as often as he was in England. At Easter he wore it at Winchester, at Whitsuntide[5] at Westminster, and at Christmas at Gloucester, and then there were with him all the powerful men over all England, archbishops and bishops, abbots and earls, thegns[6] and knights. Also, he was a very stern and violent man, so that no one dared do anything contrary to his will. He had earls in his fetters,[7] who acted against his will. He expelled bishops from their sees, and abbots from their abbacies, and put thegns in prison, and finally he did not spare his own brother, who was called Odo; he was a very powerful bishop in Normandy (his cathedral church was at Bayeux) and was the foremost man next the king, and had an earldom in England. And when the king was in Normandy, then he was master in this country; and he [the king] put *him* in prison. Amongst other things the good security he made in this country is not to be forgotten—so that any honest man could travel over his kingdom without injury with his bosom full of gold; and no one dared strike[8] another, however much wrong he had done him. And if any man had intercourse with a woman against her will, he was forthwith castrated.

He ruled over England, and by his cunning it was so investigated that there was not one hide of land in England that he did not know who owned it, and what it was worth, and then set it down in his record.[9] Wales was in his power, and he built castles there, and he entirely controlled that race. In the same way, he also subdued Scotland to himself, because of his great strength. The land of Normandy was his by natural inheritance, and he ruled over the county called Maine; and if he could have lived two years more, he would have conquered Ireland by his prudence and without any weapons. Certainly in his time people had much oppression and very many injuries:

He had castles built
And poor men hard oppressed.
The king was so very stark
And deprived his underlings of many a mark
Of gold and more hundreds of pounds of silver,
That he took by weight and with great injustice
From his people with little need for such a deed.
Into avarice did he fall

[4]Lanfranc's rebuilding of Christ Church, Canterbury.
[5]**Whitsuntide:** Pentecost. [Ed.]
[6]**thegns:** King's officials; similar to knights. [Ed.]
[7]**fetters:** Shackles. [Ed.]
[8]Or "kill."
[9]Domesday.

And loved greediness above all.
He made great protection for the game
And imposed laws for the same,
That who so slew hart or hind
Should be made blind.

He preserved the harts and boars
And loved the stags as much
As if he were their father.
Moreover, for the hares did he decree that they should go free.
Powerful men complained of it and poor men lamented it,
But so fierce was he that he cared not for the rancor of them all,
But they had to follow out the king's will entirely
If they wished to live or hold their land,
Property or estate, or his favor great.
Alas! woe, that any man so proud should go,
And exalt himself and reckon himself above all men!
May Almighty God show mercy to his soul
And grant unto him forgiveness for his sins.

These things we have written about him, both good and bad, that good men may imitate their good points, and entirely avoid the bad, and travel on the road that leads us to the kingdom of heaven.

### ■ Discussion Questions

1. How does the *Anglo-Saxon Chronicle* present the Domesday survey as a reflection of William's method of rule in general?
2. According to the chronicle, from whom or what does William derive his authority?
3. Do you think that the author of this excerpt was an objective observer? Why or why not?

## 4.
## *Medieval University Life*
### Twelfth–Early Thirteenth Centuries

*The development of permanent centers of learning in the twelfth and thirteenth centuries in cities across Europe attests to the vitality of the age. As the following*

---

From Dana Carleton Munro, ed., *Translations and Reprints from the Original Sources of European History,* vol. 2, no. 3 (Philadelphia: University of Pennsylvania Press, 1898), 2–7; and *Wine, Women, and Song: Mediaeval Latin Students' Songs,* trans. John Addington Symonds (London: Chatto & Windus, 1907), 58–64.

*documents suggest, royal patronage and the formation of a sense of common identity among students were key to the rise of medieval universities as self-governing institutions. The first two documents consist of special privileges granted by King Frederick I (r. 1152–1190) of Germany in 1158 to all students within his domains, and by King Philip II of France (r. 1180–1223) in 1200 to students in Paris. In this way, students were enveloped within both rulers' growing bureaucracies as each strove to increase his power. The voices of students themselves are highlighted in the pair of anonymous poems written by students in the twelfth century describing the anxieties and pleasures of their way of life.*

## FROM KING FREDERICK I

After a careful consideration of this subject by the bishops, abbots, dukes, counts, judges, and other nobles of our sacred palace, we, from our piety, have granted this privilege to all scholars who travel for the sake of study, and especially, to the professors of divine and sacred laws, namely, that they may go in safety to the places in which the studies are carried on, both they themselves and their messengers, and may dwell there in security. For we think it fitting that, during good behavior, those should enjoy our praise and protection, by whose learning the world is enlightened to the obedience of God and of us, his ministers and the life of the subjects is molded; and by a certain special love we defend them from all injuries.

For who does not pity those who exile themselves through love for learning, who wear themselves out in poverty in place of riches, who expose their lives to all perils and often suffer bodily injury from the vilest men—this must be endured with vexation. Therefore, we declare by this general and ever to be valid law, that in the future no one shall be so rash as to venture to inflict any injury on scholars, or to occasion any loss to them on account of a debt owed by an inhabitant of their province—a thing which we have learned is sometimes done by an evil custom. And let it be known to the violators of this constitution, and also to those who shall at the time be the rulers of the places, that a four-fold restitution of property shall be exacted from all and that, the mark of infamy being affixed to them by the law itself, they shall lose their office forever. . . .

We also order this law to be inserted among the imperial constitutions under the title, *ne filius pro patre, etc.*

Given at Roncaglia, in the year of our Lord 1158, in the month of November. . . .

## FROM KING PHILIP II

In the Name of the sacred and indivisible Trinity, amen. Philip, by the grace of God, King of the French.

Concerning the safety of the students at Paris in the future, by the advice of our subjects we have ordained as follows: we will cause all the citizens of Paris to swear that if any one sees an injury done to any student by any layman, he will testify truthfully to this, nor will any one withdraw in order not to see [the act].

And if it shall happen that any one strikes a student, except in self-defense, especially if he strikes the student with a weapon, a club or a stone, all laymen who see [the act] shall in good faith seize the malefactor or malefactors and deliver them to our judge; nor shall they withdraw in order not to see the act, or seize the malefactor, or testify to the truth. Also, whether the malefactor is seized in open crime or not, we will make a legal and full examination through clerks or laymen or certain lawful persons; and our count and our judges shall do the same. And if by a full examination we or our judges are able to learn that he who is accused, is guilty of the crime, then we or our judges shall immediately inflict a penalty, according to the quality and nature of the crime; notwithstanding the fact that the criminal may deny the deed and say that he is ready to defend himself in single combat, or to purge himself by the ordeal by water.

Also, neither our provost nor our judges shall lay hands on a student for any offense whatever; nor shall they place him in our prison, unless such a crime has been committed by the student, that he ought to be arrested. And in that case, our judge shall arrest him on the spot, without striking him at all, unless he resists, and shall hand him over to the ecclesiastical judge, who ought to guard him in order to satisfy us and the one suffering the injury. And if a serious crime has been committed, our judge shall go or shall send to see what is done with the student. . . .

In order, moreover, that these [decrees] may be kept more carefully and may be established forever by a fixed law, we have decided that our present provost and the people of Paris shall affirm by an oath, in the presence of the scholars, that they will carry out in good faith all the above-mentioned. And always in the future, whosoever receives from us the office of provost in Paris, among the other initiatory acts of his office, namely, on the first or second Sunday, in one of the churches of Paris,—after he has been summoned for the purpose,—shall affirm by an oath, publicly in the presence of the scholars, that he will keep in good faith all the above-mentioned. And that these decrees may be valid forever, we have ordered this document to be confirmed by the authority of our seal and by the characters of the royal name, signed below.

## A WANDERING STUDENT'S PETITION

I, a wandering scholar lad,
Born for toil and sadness,
Oftentimes am driven by
Poverty to madness.

Literature and knowledge I
Fain would still be earning,
Were it not that want of pelf[1]
Makes me cease from learning.

[1]**pelf:** Money. [Ed.]

These torn clothes that cover me
    Are too thin and rotten;
Oft I have to suffer cold,
    By the warmth forgotten.

Scarce I can attend at church,
    Sing God's praises duly;
Mass and vespers both I miss,
    Though I love them truly.

Oh, thou pride of N—,
    By thy worth I pray thee
Give the suppliant help in need,
    Heaven will sure repay thee.
Take a mind unto thee now
    Like unto St. Martin;
Clothe the pilgrim's nakedness,
    Wish him well at parting.

So may God translate your soul
    Into peace eternal,
And the bliss of saints be yours
    In His realm supernal.

## A Song of the Open Road

We in our wandering,
Blithesome and squandering,
    Tara, tantara, teino![2]

Eat to satiety,
Drink with propriety;
    Tara, tantara, teino!

Laugh till our sides we split,
Rags on our hides we fit;
    Tara, tantara, teino!

Jesting eternally,
Quaffing infernally:
    Tara, tantara, teino!

[2]This refrain appears to be intended to imitate a bugle call.

Craft's in the bone of us,
Fear 'tis unknown of us:
    Tara, tantara, teino!

When we're in neediness,
Thieve we with greediness:
    Tara, tantara, teino!

Brother catholical,
Man apostolical,
    Tara, tantara, teino!

Say what you will have done,
What you ask 'twill be done!
    Tara, tantara, teino!

Folk, fear the toss of the
Horns of philosophy!
    Tara, tantara, teino!

Here comes a quadruple
Spoiler and prodigal!
    Tara, tantara, teino!

License and vanity
Pamper insanity:
    Tara, tantara, teino!

As the Pope bade us do,
Brother to brother's true:
    Tara, tantara, teino!

Brother, best friend, adieu!
Now, I must part from you!
    Tara, tantara, teino!

When will our meeting be?
Glad shall our greeting be!
    Tara, tantara, teino!

Vows valedictory
Now have the victory;
    Tara, tantara, teino!

Clasped on each other's breast,
Brother to brother pressed,
    Tara, tantara, teino!

## ■ Discussion Questions

1. Why might both Frederick I and Philip II have been concerned for students' welfare? What benefits do you think they gained from guaranteeing students certain privileges?
2. What do the kings' privileges reveal about the process of state building at the time? What role did official records, such as these, play in the process?
3. What picture of student life do the authors paint in the two poems? What similarities exist based on your own experiences as a student?
4. How do the student poems support the argument made by many historians that in the twelfth century, people became more aware of themselves as members of larger groups with similar concerns and objectives?

# 5.
# St. Francis and St. Clare of Assisi
# *Selected Writings*
## Thirteenth Century

*The church was very much entwined in the world of wealth, power, and splendor celebrated in the vernacular literature of the twelfth and early thirteenth centuries. A variety of new religious movements emerged in reaction against the church's perceived worldliness and neglect of its pastoral mission. St. Francis of Assisi (c. 1182–1226), the son of a wealthy merchant, founded what later became the most popular and largest of these movements in Europe, the Franciscans. These excerpts from his* Rule, *written in 1223, illuminate the fundamental principles guiding the order. The Franciscans' message of poverty, humility, and penance prompted people from all walks of life to follow their path, including St. Clare of Assisi (1194–1253). Upon hearing St. Francis preach in 1212, she established a community of pious women modeled after his ideals, which became the Order of the Sisters of St. Francis. Although the sisters were eventually cloistered, the following passages from Clare's* Testament *reveal not only how their ideals remained true to those of St. Francis, but also how medieval women played an important role in cultivating new forms of piety.*

From Ernest Henderson, ed., *Select Historical Documents of the Middle Ages* (London: G. Bell & Sons, 1921), 344–49; and *Francis and Clare: The Complete Works,* trans. Regis J. Armstrong and Ignatius C. Brady (New York: Paulist Press, 1982), 226–32.

## From *Rule*

This is the rule and way of living of the minorite brothers: namely to observe the holy Gospel of our Lord Jesus Christ, living in obedience, without personal possessions, and in chastity. Brother Francis promises obedience and reverence to our lord pope Honorius, and to his successors who canonically enter upon their office, and to the Roman Church. And the other brothers shall be bound to obey brother Francis and his successors.

If any persons shall wish to adopt this form of living, and shall come to our brothers, they shall send them to their provincial ministers; to whom alone, and to no others, permission is given to receive brothers. But the ministers shall diligently examine them in the matter of the catholic faith and the ecclesiastical sacraments. And if they believe all these, and are willing to faithfully confess them and observe them steadfastly to the end; and if they have no wives, or if they have them and the wives have already entered a monastery, or if they shall have given them permission to do so . . . the ministers shall say unto them the word of the holy Gospel, to the effect that they shall go and sell all that they have and strive to give it to the poor. But if they shall not be able to do this, their good will is enough. And the brothers and their ministers shall be on their guard and not concern themselves for their temporal goods; so that they may freely do with those goods exactly as God inspires them. . . . Afterwards there shall be granted to them the garments of probation: namely two gowns without cowls and a belt, and hose and a cape down to the belt; unless to these same ministers something else may at some time seem to be preferable in the sight of God. But, when the year of probation is over, they shall be received into obedience; promising always to observe that manner of living, and this Rule. . . .

I firmly command all the brothers by no means to receive coin or money, of themselves or through an intervening person. But for the needs of the sick and for clothing the other brothers, the ministers alone and the guardians shall provide through spiritual friends, as it may seem to them that necessity demands, according to time, place and cold temperature. This one thing being always regarded, that, as has been said, they receive neither coin nor money.

Those brothers to whom God has given the ability to labor, shall labor faithfully and devoutly; in such way that idleness, the enemy of the soul, being excluded, they may not extinguish the spirit of holy prayer and devotion; to which other temporal things should be subservient. As a reward, moreover, for their labor, they may receive for themselves and their brothers the necessaries of life, but not coin or money; and this humbly, as becomes the servants of God and the followers of most holy poverty.

The brothers shall appropriate nothing to themselves, neither a house, nor a place, nor anything; but as pilgrims and strangers in this world, in poverty and humility serving God, they shall confidently go seeking for alms. Nor need they be ashamed, for the Lord made Himself poor for us in this world. This is that height of most lofty poverty, which has constituted you my most beloved brothers heirs and kings of the kingdom of Heaven, has made you poor in possessions, has exalted you in virtues. . . .

All the brothers shall be bound always to have one of the brothers of that order as general minister and servant of the whole fraternity, and shall be firmly bound to obey him. . . .

The brothers may not preach in the bishopric of any bishop if they have been forbidden to by him. And no one of the brothers shall dare to preach at all to the people, unless he have been examined and approved by the general minister of this fraternity, and the office of preacher have been conceded to him. I also exhort those same brothers that, in the preaching which they do, their expressions shall be chaste and chosen, to the utility and edification of the people; announcing to them vices and virtues, punishment and glory, with briefness of discourse; for the words were brief which the Lord spoke upon earth.

The brothers who are the ministers and servants of the other brothers shall visit and admonish their brothers and humbly and lovingly correct them; not teaching them anything which is against their soul and against our Rule. But the brothers who are subjected to them shall remember that, before God, they have discarded their own wills. Wherefore I firmly command them that they obey their ministers in all things which they have promised God to observe, and which are not contrary to their souls and to our Rule. . . .

I firmly command all the brothers not to have suspicious intercourse or to take counsel with women. And, with the exception of those to whom special permission has been given by the Apostolic Chair, let them not enter nunneries. Neither may they become fellow god-parents with men or women, lest from this cause a scandal may arise among the brothers or concerning brothers.

Whoever of the brothers by divine inspiration may wish to go among the Saracens and other infidels, shall seek permission to do so from their provincial ministers. But to none shall the ministers give permission to go, save to those whom they shall see to be fit for the mission.

Furthermore, through their obedience I enjoin on the ministers that they demand from the lord pope one of the cardinals of the holy Roman Church, who shall be the governor, corrector and protector of that fraternity, so that, always subjected and lying at the feet of that same holy Church, steadfast in the catholic faith, we may observe poverty and humility, and the holy Gospel of our Lord Jesus Christ; as we have firmly promised.

## From *Testament*

*In the name of the Lord!*

Among all the other gifts which we have received and continue to receive daily from our benefactor, *the Father of mercies* (2 Cor. 1:3), and for which we must express the deepest thanks to our glorious God, our vocation is a great gift. Since it is the more perfect and greater, we should be so much more thankful to Him for it. For this reason the Apostle writes: "Acknowledge your calling" (1 Cor. 1:26).

The Son of God became for us *the Way* which our Blessed Father Francis, His true lover and imitator, has shown and taught us by word and example.

Therefore, beloved Sisters, we must consider the immense gifts which God has bestowed on us, especially those which He has seen fit to work in us through His beloved servant, our blessed Father Francis, not only after our conversion but also while we were still [living among] the vanities of the world.

For, almost immediately after his conversion, while he had neither brothers nor companions, when he was building the Church of San Damiano in which he was totally filled with divine consolation, he was led to abandon the world completely. This holy man, in the great joy and enlightenment of the Holy Spirit, made a prophecy about us which the Lord fulfilled later. Climbing the wall of that church he shouted in French to some poor people who were standing nearby: "Come and help me build the monastery of San Damiano, because ladies will dwell here who will glorify our heavenly Father throughout His holy Church by their celebrated and holy manner of life."

In this, then, we can consider the abundant kindness of God toward us. Because of His mercy and love, He saw fit to speak these words about our vocation and selection through His saint. And our most blessed Father prophesied not only for us, but also for those who were to come to this [same] holy vocation to which the Lord has called us.

With what solicitude and fervor of mind and body, therefore, must we keep the commandments of our God and Father, so that, with the help of the Lord, we may return to Him an increase of His *talents.* For the Lord Himself not only has set us as an example and mirror for others, but also for our [own] sisters whom the Lord has called to our way of life, so that they in turn will be a mirror and example to those living in the world. . . .

After the most high heavenly Father saw fit in His mercy and grace to enlighten my heart to do penance according to the example and teaching of our most blessed Father Francis, shortly after his own conversion, I, together with the few sisters whom the Lord had given me soon after my conversion, voluntarily promised him obedience, since the Lord had given us the Light of His grace through his holy life and teaching.

But when the Blessed Francis saw that, although we were physically weak and frail, we did not shirk deprivation, poverty, hard work, distress, or the shame or contempt of the world—rather, as he and his brothers often saw for themselves, we considered [all such trials] as great delights after the example of the saints and their brothers—he rejoiced greatly in the Lord. And moved by compassion for us, he promised to have always, both through himself and through his Order, the same loving care and special solicitude for us as for his own brothers.

And thus, by the will of God and our most blessed Father Francis, we went to dwell at the Church of San Damiano. There, in a short time, the Lord increased our number by His mercy and grace so that what He had predicted through His saint might be fulfilled. We had stayed in another place [before this], but only for a little while.

Later on he wrote a form of life for us, [indicating] especially that we should persevere always in holy poverty. And while he was living, he was not content to encourage us by many words and examples to love and observe holy poverty; [in addition] he also gave us many writings so that, after his death, we should in no way turn away from it. [In a similar way] the Son of God never wished to abandon this holy poverty while He lived in the world, and our most blessed Father Francis, following His footprints, never departed, either in example or teaching, from this holy poverty which he had chosen for himself and for his brothers.

Therefore, I, Clare, the handmaid of Christ and of the Poor Sisters of the Monastery of San Damiano—although unworthy—and the little plant of the holy Father, consider together with my sisters our most high profession and the command of so great a father. [We also take note] in some [sisters] of the frailty which we feared in ourselves after the death of our holy Father Francis, [He] who was our pillar of strength and, after God, our one consolation and support. [Thus] time and again, we bound ourselves to our Lady, most holy Poverty, so that, after my death, the Sisters present and to come would never abandon her.

And, as I have always been most zealous and solicitous to observe and to have the other sisters observe the holy poverty which we have promised the Lord and our holy Father Francis, so, too, the others who will succeed me in office should be bound always to observe it and have it observed by the other sisters. . . .

In the Lord Jesus Christ, I admonish and exhort all my sisters, both those present and those to come, to strive always to imitate the way of holy simplicity, humility, and poverty and [to preserve] the integrity of [our] holy manner of life, as we were taught by our blessed Father Francis from the beginning of our conversion to Christ. Thus may they always remain *in the fragrance* of a good name, both among those who are afar off and those who are near. [This will take place] not by our own merits but solely by the mercy and grace of our Benefactor, the *Father of mercies*. . . .

I also beg that sister who will have the office [of caring for] the sisters to strive to exceed others more by her virtues and holy life than by her office so that, encouraged by her example, the Sisters may obey her not so much out of duty but rather out of love. Let her also be prudent and attentive to her sisters just as a good mother is to her daughters; and especially, let her take care to provide for them according to the needs of each one from the things which the Lord shall give. Let her also be so kind and so available that all [of them] may reveal their needs with trust and have recourse to her at any hour with confidence as they see fit, both for her sake and that of her sisters.

But the sisters who are subjects should keep in mind that for the Lord's sake they have given up their own wills. Therefore I ask that they obey their mother as they have promised the Lord of their own free will so that, seeing the charity, humility, and unity they have toward one another, their mother might bear all the burdens of her office more lightly. Thus what is painful and bitter might be turned into sweetness for her because of their holy way of life. . . .

So that it may be observed better, I leave this writing for you, my dearest and most beloved Sisters, those present and those to come, as a sign of the blessing of the Lord and of our most blessed Father Francis and of my blessing—I who am your mother and servant.

## ■ Discussion Questions

1. Based on his *Rule,* how would you characterize St. Francis's spirituality and sense of mission? Why might he have appealed to so many people at the time?
2. How does St. Clare echo Francis's ideals in her *Testament?*
3. What goals did Francis and Clare share in composing the *Rule* and *Testament,* respectively?
4. What do both documents reveal about contemporary attitudes toward women?

## ■ Comparative Questions

1. Even though the number of cities in Europe was on the rise during the eleventh and twelfth centuries, most people at the time still lived in rural areas and farmed for a living. What evidence can you find of this fact in the urban charters and the *Anglo-Saxon Chronicle?*
2. How do you think Pope Gregory VII would have reacted to William I's relationship with the English church, as described in the *Anglo-Saxon Chronicle,* and why?
3. What do the urban charters, medieval university documents, Saint Francis's *Rule,* and Saint Clare's *Testament* reveal about the different ways in which medieval men and women shaped their identities?
4. What do the urban charters, *Anglo-Saxon Chronicle,* and the privileges granted to students reveal about the role of written documents in medieval governments? How does this role compare to Saint Francis's emphasis on preaching, and what does this suggest about the continued importance of the spoken word in medieval culture?

Chapter

# 10

# An Age of Confidence, 1200–1340

HARMONY, ORDER, AND UNITY were the ideals sought by people from all walks of life in the medieval world during the period from 1200 to 1340. The first three documents that follow reflect the artistic, religious, and literary search for meaning in a world in search of unity. However elusive, the signs were promising, as the fourth and fifth documents reveal: many monarchies consolidated their power, representative institutions developed, and the church appeared to be at its pinnacle. There was a new and hopeful vision of the world and the future. Yet there were cracks in this vision. Even as kings and popes wielded enormous authority, they were not invincible. This became all too clear when the Mongols captured the Russian city of Kiev in 1240, poised to move into the heart of Europe. The fifth document, a letter from the Mongol emperor addressed to Pope Innocent IV (r. 1243–1254), attests to the papacy's increased power as an international political force, while at the same time revealing its vulnerability.

## 1. Abbot Suger *The Abbey Church of St.-Denis* 1144

*The royal abbey of St.-Denis, on the northeast outskirts of Paris, sheltered the relics of the patron saint of France and served as the* necropolis *of its kings. Abbot Suger (1081–1151), a counselor and "biographer" of both King Louis VI and King Louis VII and regent for the latter during the Second Crusade, headed the abbey from 1122 until his death. He is generally credited with creating the Gothic style at St.-Denis, although elements of it had been present earlier. The rebuilding of St.-Denis began in 1137, according to Suger because it could not contain the crowds, and its inauguration was marked in 1144 by the attendance of Louis VII. The style of architecture,*

From Abbot Suger, *De Administratione,* trans. David Burr (http://www.fordham.edu/halsall/source/sugar.html).

*based on light and height, was intimately bound to new visions of religion and beauty: it reflected the sacral nature and power of French kingship as well as an increasing consciousness of other parts of Europe and the East.*

In the twenty-third year of our administration, on a certain day when we sat in general chapter conferring with our brethren about common and private matters, these same dear brothers and sons began to beg me vigorously and in love that I should not remain silent about the fruit of our past labors but rather with pen and ink should preserve for future memory the additions which the munificence of almighty God bestowed upon this church during the time of our leadership in the acquisition of new things, the recovery of lost ones, the multiplication of refurbished possessions, the construction of buildings, and the accumulation of gold, silver, precious gems and quality textiles. From this one thing they promised us two in return: Through this memorial we should earn the prayers of succeeding brothers for the salvation of our soul; and through this example we should arouse in them a zealous commitment to the proper maintenance of God's church. . . .

We managed to have the chapel of St. Romanus dedicated to the service of God and his holy angels by that venerable man Archbishop Hugh of Rouen and by many other bishops. Those who serve God there as if, even as they sacrifice, they dwell at least partly in heaven, know how secluded, hallowed and convenient for the celebration of divine rites this place is. At the same dedication ceremony, two chapels in the lower nave of the church—one for St. Hippolytus and his companions on one side and one for St. Nicholas on the other—were dedicated by those venerable men Manassas, Bishop of Meaux, and Peter, Bishop of Senlis. The single glorious procession of these three men went out through the door of Saint Eustace; then passed in front of the main doors with a throng of singing clergy and a crowd of rejoicing laymen, the bishops walking in front and carrying out the holy consecration; then, thirdly, they entered through the single door of the cemetery which had been transferred from the old building to the new. And when this festive work had been completed to the honor of almighty God and we, a bit tired, were preparing to officiate in the upper part, they revived us, very graciously encouraging us not to be depressed by consideration of the labor and funding problems that lay before us.

. . . [W]e erected the main doors, on which are represented the passion and resurrection or ascension of Christ, with great expense and heavy outlay for their gilding as befits such a noble portico. We also set up new ones on the right, and old ones on the left beneath the mosaic which, contrary to modern custom, we had placed in the tympanum. We also arranged to have the towers and upper crenelations of the front altered with an eye to beauty and, should circumstances require, to utility. We also ordered that, lest it be forgotten, the year of the consecration should be inscribed in copper-gilt letters in this way:

For the glory of the church which nurtured and raised him,
Suger strove for the glory of the church, Sharing with
you what is yours, oh martyr Denis. He prays that by your

prayers he should become a sharer in Paradise. The year
when it was consecrated was the one thousand, one
hundred and fortieth year of the Word.

Furthermore, the verses on the doors are these:

All you who seek to honor these doors,
Marvel not at the gold and expense but at the
craftsmanship of the work.
The noble work is bright, but, being nobly bright, the work
Should brighten the minds, allowing them to travel through the lights
To the true light, where Christ is the true door.
The golden door defines how it is imminent in these things.
The dull mind rises to the truth through material things,
And is resurrected from its former submersion when the light is seen.

And on the lintel was written,

Receive, stern Judge, the prayers of your Suger,
Let me be mercifully numbered among your sheep.

. . . For remembrance of the past is foresight of the future. Moreover, the most generous lord, who among other, greater things has provided the makers of our marvelous windows with opulent sapphire and ready cash of around seven hundred pounds or more, will not allow the project to remain incomplete through lack of funds. . . .

Lest forgetfulness, the rival of truth, should slip in and snatch away a good example for future behavior, we have thought it worthwhile to provide a description of the ornaments with which the hand of God has adorned the church, his chosen bride. We confess our lord the thrice-blessed Denis to be so generous and benevolent that, as we believe, he has intervened for us before God so strongly and so often, obtaining so many and so great benefits, that we could have done a hundred times more than we actually did for his church if human weakness, shifting circumstances and changing customs had not prevented it. Nevertheless, what we, by the gift of God, have collected for him is hereby listed. . . . Into this panel, which stands before his most sacred body, we estimate that we have put around forty-two marks of gold, a rich abundance of precious gems—hyacinths, rubies, sapphires, emeralds and topazes—and a variety of pearls, more than we ever hoped to find. You would see kings, princes and many outstanding men, imitating us, remove the rings from their fingers and order that the gold, gems and precious pearls of the rings be set in the panel. In the same way archbishops and bishops, depositing the rings of their investiture there for safekeeping, devoutly offered them up to God and his saints.

Of course the blessed Denis had lain in that same spot for five hundred years and more, from Dagobert's time to our own.

We do not wish to pass in silence over one humorous yet noble miracle which the Lord displayed to us in this connection. Just when I was in need of gems and unable to purchase enough (for rarity makes them more expensive), monks from three abbeys belonging to two different orders—that is, from Citeaux, from another abbey of the same order, and from Fontevrault—entered our little room adjoining the church and offered for sale a greater supply of gems than we would have hoped to find in ten years. They had obtained them as alms from Count Theobold, who had received them through his brother King Stephen of England from the treasury of his uncle the late King Henry. Theobold had stored them up throughout his life in marvelous vessels. . . .

We hastened to decorate the main altar of the blessed Denis, which had only a beautiful and sumptuous frontal panel from the time of Charles the Bald, the third emperor; for at this very altar we had been dedicated to the monastic life. We had it entirely covered, adding gold panels on each side. And a fourth, even more precious one, so that the whole altar would appear to be gold all the way around. On the sides we placed two candlesticks of King Louis, the son of Philip, so that they would not be stolen on some occasion. We added hyacinths, emeralds, and various other precious gems, ordering a diligent search for others which could be added.

I used to confer with Jerusalemites, and I was eager to learn from those who had seen the treasures of Constantinople and decorations of Hagia Sophia whether these here were worth anything in comparison. When some considered these here to be greater, it seemed to us that, through fear of the Franks, those marvelous objects of which we had once heard had been prudently put away lest by the impetuous greed of a few stupid people the friendship nurtured between Greek and Latin should suddenly change to sedition and warfare; for cunning is a preeminently Greek characteristic. Thus it may be that there is more displayed here, where it is safe, than there, where it is unsafe because of disorders. From many trustworthy men, and from Archbishop Hugh of Laon, we have heard wonderful and nearly incredible reports concerning the superior ornamentation of Hagia Sophia and other churches. If these reports are true—or more precisely, because we believe their testimony is indeed true—then such inestimable and incomparable treasures should be set out for the judgment of many people. "Let every man abound in his own sense" (Rom. 14:5).

To me, I confess, it always has seemed right that the most expensive things should be used above all for the administration of the holy eucharist. If golden vessels, vials and mortars were used to collect "the blood of goats or calves or the red heifer, how much more" should gold vases, precious stones and whatever is most valuable among created things be set out with continual reverence and full devotion "to receive the blood of Jesus Christ" (Heb. 9:1 3f).

. . . The date was that of the martyrdom of our lords the blessed martyrs, the eighth day before the ides of October. Archbishops and bishops of various provinces were there. They had come eagerly to bring devout prayers for this solemn celebration, as if paying their debt to the apostolate of Gaul. The archbishops of Lyons, Reims, Tours and Rouen were there, as were the bishops of Soissons,

Beauvais, Senlis, Meaux, Rennes, St. Malo and Vannes. There were also a large number of abbots, monks and clerics as well as an uncountable crowd of laity, male and female. . . .

We also discovered the reason why the relics had been deposited there. The Emperor Charles III, who lies gloriously interred beneath this altar, arranged by imperial edict that they be removed from the imperial repository and placed with him for the protection of his soul and body. We also found there evidence, sealed with his ring, which pleased us very much. . . .

We also erected the cross, admirable for its size, which is placed between the altar and Charles' tomb. According to tradition the most noble necklace of Queen Nanthilda, wife of King Dagobert, founder of the church, was affixed to the middle of this cross, while another (smaller but unequaled according to the testimony of the most experienced artisans) was affixed to the forehead of St. Denis. . . .

We also restored the noble throne of the glorious King Dagobert, on which, as tradition relates, the Frankish kings sat to receive the homage of their nobles after they had assumed power. We did so in recognition of its exalted function and because of the value of the work itself.

We also had the eagle in the middle of the choir regilded, for it had been rubbed bare of gold by the frequent touch of admirers.

We also had painted, by the hands of many masters sought out in various nations, a splendid variety of new windows below and above, from the first in the chevet representing the tree of Jesse to the one over the principal door of the entrance. . . .

Since their marvelous workmanship and the cost of the sapphire and painted glass makes these windows very valuable, we appointed a master craftsman for their protection and maintenance, just as we also appointed a skilled goldsmith for the gold and silver ornaments. These would receive their allowances and whatever was apportioned to them in addition, such as coins from the altar and flour from the common storehouse of the brethren, and they were never to neglect their duties.

We also had seven candlesticks of enameled and excellently gilded metalwork made, since the ones made by the emperor Charles for the blessed Denis seemed to be ruined by age. . . .

Moreover, with the devotion due to the blessed Denis, we acquired vessels of gold and precious stones for the service of the Lord's table, in addition to the ones already donated for this purpose by kings of the Franks and those devoted to the church. To be specific, we ordered a big gold chalice containing one hundred forty ounces of gold and decorated with precious gems (hyacinths and topazes) as a substitute for another which had been pawned during the time of our predecessor.

We also offered to the blessed Denis, along with some flowers from the empress' crown, another very precious vessel of praise, carved in the form of a boat, which King Louis, son of Philip, had left in pawn for nearly ten years. When it was offered for our inspection, we had purchased it with the king's permission for sixty marks of silver. This vessel, marvelous for both the quality and the quantity of its precious stones, is decorated with verroterie cloisonné work by St. Eloi and is considered by all goldsmiths to be very precious.

### ■ Discussion Questions

1. What was Suger's vision of holiness as exemplified in church architecture?
2. How is the French or Gothic style, which epitomized Western architecture for several centuries, intended to draw the viewer to God?
3. Suger inserts his own name in numerous inscriptions on parts of the abbey church. How does this reflect changing views of art and architecture in the twelfth century?
4. How does Suger intertwine his architectural vision with ideas of French kingship and its relationship with other kingdoms and the papacy?

## 2. Hadewijch of Brabant *Letters and Poems of a Female Mystic* 1220–1240

*The body of work written or dictated by women during the twelfth and thirteenth centuries is considerable—religious and mystical writings, poems, and courtly love literature, medical treatises, and songs. Often the line between the genres was blurred, especially in religious writing. Hadewijch of Brabant was one of many such women writers, and our knowledge of her comes primarily from her writings in her native Dutch, which include thirty-one letters, fourteen visions, forty-five stanzaic poems, and several other poems. Although criticized by members of her own, probably Beguine, community, Hadewijch nonetheless typifies many women writers of this period. She uses mystical and seemingly erotic language to describe a relationship with Christ. Although some Beguines bordered on the edge of unorthodoxy and were at times accused of heresy, most works by female mystics fit harmoniously with the writings of such church leaders as St. Bernard of Clairvaux (1090–1153) and Richard (1123–1173) and Hugh of St. Victor (1096–1141).*

### Letter 9

May God let you know, dear child, who He is and how He uses His servants and His handmaidens in particular, and may He consume you in Him. In the depth of His wisdom he shall teach you what He is and how wondrously sweet the beloved dwells in the other beloved, and how thoroughly one dwells in the other, so that

From "The Brabant Mystic: Hadewijch," in *Medieval Women Writers,* ed. Katherina M. Wilson (Athens: University of Georgia Press, 1984), 193–95, 198–201.

neither one nor the other knows themselves apart. But they possess and rejoice in each other mouth in mouth, heart in heart, body in body, soul in soul, and one sweet divine nature flows through them both, and both are one through themselves, yet remain themselves, and will always remain so. . . .

## LETTER 11

From the age of ten I have been overwhelmed with such passionate love that I would have died during the first two years of this experience if God had not granted me a power unknown to common people and made me recover with His own being. For He soon granted me reason, sometimes enlightened with many wonderful revelations, and I received many wonderful gifts from Him, when he let me feel His presence and showed Himself to me. I was aware of many signs that were between Him and me, as with friends who are used to concealing little and revealing much when their feelings for each other have grown most intimate, when they taste, eat, and drink and consume each other wholly. Through these many signs God, my lover, showed to me early in life, He made me gain much confidence in Him, and I often thought that no one loved him as dearly as I. . . . I do no longer believe that my love for Him is the dearest, nor do I believe that there is one alive who loves God as dearly as I. Sometimes I am so enlightened with love that I realize my failure to give my beloved what He deserves; sometimes when I am blinded with love's sweetness, when I am tasting and feeling her, I realize she is enough for me; and sometimes when I am feeling so fulfilled in her presence, I secretly admit to her that she is enough for me. . . .

## LETTER 20

In the fifth unspeakable hour love seduces the heart and the soul, and the soul is driven out of herself and out of love's nature and back into love's nature. The soul has then ceased to wonder about the power and darkness of love's designs, and has forgotten the pains of love. Then the soul knows love only through love herself, which may seem lower but is not. For where knowledge is most intimate the beloved knows least.

In the sixth unspeakable hour love despises reason and all that lies within reason and above it and below. Whatever belongs to reason stands against the blessed state of love. . . .

## STANZAIA POEM 8

Born is the new season as the old one that lasted so long is drawing to a close.

Those prepared to do love's service will receive her rewards: new comfort and new strength.

If they love her with the vigor of love, they will soon be one with love in love.

To be one with love is an awesome calling and those who long for it should spare no effort.

Beyond all reason they will give their all and go through all.

For love dwells so deep in the womb of the Father that her power will unfold only to those who serve her with utter devotion. . . .

Those who long to be one with love achieve great things, and shirk no effort.

They shall be strong and capable of any task that will win them the love of love, to help the sick or the healthy, the blind, the crippled, or the wounded.

For this is what the lover owes to love. . . .

Those who trust in love with all their being shall be given all they need.

For she brings comfort to the sad and guidance to those who cannot read.

Love will be pleased with the lover if he accepts no other comfort and trusts in her alone.

Those who desire to live in love alone with all their might and heart shall so dispose all things that they shall soon possess her all.

## Poem 12

Like the noble season born to bring us flowers in the fields, so the noble ones are called to bear the yoke, the bonds of love.

Faith grows forever in their deeds, and noble flowers blossom and their fruits.

The world is fashioned with faith, and the lover dwells in highest love, one with her in everlasting friendship. . . .

And outside love their truth cannot be known: to those who do not dwell in love the burden is not light but heavy, and they suffer fears unknown to love.

For the servants' law is fear but love is the law of sons.

What is this burden light in love, this yoke so sweet?

It is that noble thrust inside, that touch of love in the beloved which makes him one with her, one will, one being, one beyond revoke.

And ever deeper digs desire and all that is dug up is drunk by love, for love's demands on love surpass the mind of man.

These things are beyond the mind of man: how the lover whom love has overwhelmed with love beholds the beloved so full of love.

For he rests not an hour, before he sails with love through all that is and looks upon her splendor with devotion.

For in love's face he reads the designs she has for him, and in truth in love's face he sees clear and undeceived so many pains so sweet.

This he clearly sees: the lover must love in truth alone. . . .

All their secret veins will run into that stream where love gives love away, where love's friends are made drunk with love and filled with wonder at her passion.

And all this remains concealed to strangers, but to the wise it stands revealed. . . .

[T]heir life is free and undisturbed, and well may they say, "I am all of love and love is all of me."

For what will harm them when they claim the sun, the moon, and all the stars?

### POEM 28

Love be praised for the birds that rejoice now and were sad in winter, and soon the proud hearts will rejoice that dwelled in pain too long.

And in the fullness of her power she shall give them a reward that will surpass the mind of man. . . .

Burning desire is taught in the school of highest love.

She confounds the experienced, she brings happiness to the wretched, she makes them lords of all over which love holds sway.

Of this I am certain beyond all doubt.

To those who can serve love no more I give this good advice.

Let them still beg for her comfort if they falter and serve her with devotion according to her highest counsel.

Let them think how great love's power is, for only those near to death cannot be healed.

They have risen high that have received love's power, and in that power they shall read her judgment over them.

### ■ Discussion Questions

1. How does Hadewijch use gender imagery and language to express her feelings?
2. How would you describe Hadewijch's relationship with God and God's relationship with her?
3. What might have concerned some members of Hadewijch's community and some church authorities about her writings, as well as those of other female mystics? How did Hadewijch's approach challenge some accepted ways of thinking?
4. How does Hadewijch reflect the religious and cultural change of her times?

## 3.
## Dante Alighieri
## *Human and Divine Love*
### Late Thirteenth–Early Fourteenth Centuries

*Like many Florentines, Dante Alighieri (1265–1321) was heavily involved in politics, serving in the city government as envoy to Pope Boniface VIII (r. 1294–1303), and eventually suffering exile from his beloved city. But Dante is most celebrated as one of the world's greatest poets. Some of his writings are political, but it is in his vernacular*

From Dante Alighieri, *La Vita Nuova,* trans. Barbara Reynolds (New York: Penguin Books, 1980), 29, 31, 41, 46, 56; and Dante Alighieri, *The Comedy of Dante Alighieri the Florentine, Cantica III: Paradise,* trans. Dorothy L. Sayers and Barbara Reynolds (New York: Penguin Books, 1981), 53–56, 64, 73, 76, 84, 85, 90, 92, 93.

*writings, especially* The Divine Comedy *and* La Vita Nuova, *that his great genius lies. Dante, through his artistry, is widely credited with making Tuscan the language of Italy and spreading the use of the vernacular.* La Vita Nuova *(1292) is a celebration of human and divine love, written two years after the death of Beatrice Portinari, whom Dante tells us he met in 1274. Beatrice, who was married to a member of the rich and famous Bardi banking family, became in Dante's words his great love from the moment he first saw her when he was nine. His platonic/philosophical love for her—and what she represented—was in the purest courtly love tradition. It was love for the unattainable woman who teaches her "lover" about the mysteries of love.* The Divine Comedy, *consisting of the* Inferno, Purgatorio, *and* Paradiso, *was written between 1306 and 1320. Although the great Roman poet Virgil (70–19 B.C.E.) serves as Dante's guide in the nether regions, Beatrice allows him to glimpse the wonders of paradise as he journeys to understand the meaning of life.*

## *FROM* LA VITA NUOVA

Nine times the heaven of the light had revolved in its own movement since my birth and had almost returned to the same point when the woman whom my mind beholds in glory first appeared before my eyes. She was called Beatrice by many who did not know what it meant to call her this.... When exactly nine years had passed since this gracious being appeared to me, as I have described, it happened that on the last day of this intervening period this marvel appeared before me again,[1] dressed in purest white, walking between two other women of distinguished bearing, both older than herself. As they walked down the street she turned her eyes towards me where I stood in fear and trembling, and with her ineffable courtesy, which is now rewarded in eternal life, she greeted me; and such was the virtue of her greeting that I seemed to experience the height of bliss. It was exactly the ninth hour of day[2] when she gave me her sweet greeting. As this was the first time she had ever spoken to me, I was filled with such joy that, my senses reeling, I had to withdraw from the sight of others.... Whenever and wherever she appeared, in the hope of receiving her miraculous salutation I felt I had not an enemy in the world. Indeed, I glowed with a flame of charity which moved me to forgive all who had ever injured me; and if at that moment someone had asked me a question, about anything, my only reply would have been: "Love." ... And when this most gracious being[3] actually bestowed the saving power of her salutation, I do not say that Love as an intermediary could dim for me such unendurable bliss....

---

[1]May 1283, when Dante was eighteen.

[2]Numeric symbolism plays a key role in Dante's writing. Nine (the square of three, which represents the Trinity) is a mystical number symbolizing conversion. Dante is punning, contrasting his "new" *(nuova)* ninth (nine is *novem* in Latin) style to the oldness of an eighth *(octavo)* style of poetry.

[3]"This gracious being" indicates that Beatrice is something more than a mortal woman. *Grace* is the quality most commonly associated with the Virgin Mary.

I became like a person who does not know which road to take on his journey, who wants to set out but does not know where to start. . . .

One imperfection only Heaven has:
The lack of her; so now for her it pleads
And every saint with clamour intercedes,
Only compassion is our advocate.
God understands to whom their prayers relate
And answers them: "My loved ones, bear in peace
That she, your hope, remain until I please
Where one knows he must lose her, soon or late,
And who will say in Hell, 'Souls unconfessed!
I have beheld the hope of Heaven's blessed.' "
My lady is desired in highest heaven.

## *From* The Divine Comedy, Paradiso

O power divine, grant me in song to show
 The blest realm's image[4]—shadow though it be—
 Stamped on my brain; thus far thyself bestow,

. . .

When Beatrice, intent upon the sun,
 Turned leftward, and so stood and gazed before;
 No eagle e'er so fixed his eyes thereon.[5]
And, as the second ray doth evermore
 Strike from the just and dart back up again,
 Just as the peregrine will stoop and soar,
So through her eyes, her gesture, pouring in
 On my mind's eye, shaped mine; I stared wide-eyed
 On the sun's face, beyond the wont of men.

. . .

Beatrice stood, her eyes still riveted
 On the eternal wheels;[6] and, constantly,
 Turning mine thence, I gazed on her instead.

. . .

[4]The realms of Heaven.

[5]At noon Beatrice looks toward the sun, away from the darkness of Dante's hemisphere, to the south filled with light, signifying that she can lead Dante out of the darkness. Here Dante is presented with a choice—to live in the sun or die in darkness, for it was believed that young eagles who survived the bright sun were recognized by their mothers, while those who fell away died.

[6]Beatrice is gazing toward Heaven.

Whence she to whom my whole self open was
As to myself, to calm my troubled fit
Stayed not my question, but without pause
Opened her lips: "Thou dullest thine own wit
With false imagination, nor perceivest
That which thou wouldst perceive, being rid of it.
Thou art not still on earth, as thou believest;
Lightning from its sphere falling never matched
The speed which thou, returning there, achievest."[7]
But I, my first bewilderment despatched
By these few smiling words, was more perplexed
Now, by a new one which I promptly hatched.
I said: "I rest content, no longer vexed
By one great doubt; but how come I to fly
Through these light spheres? This doubt assails me next."
She turned on me, after a pitying sigh,
A look such as a mother's eyes let fall
Upon her infant, babbling feverishly.
Then she began: "All beings great and small
Are linked in order; and this orderliness
Is form, which stamps God's likeness on the All.
Herein the higher creatures see the trace
Of the Prime Excellence who is the end
For which that form was framed in the first place."[8]

. . .

Beatrice gazed on heav'n and I on her;
Then, while a quarrel might thud home, and wing,
And from the mocking-point unloose, as 'twere,
I found I'd come where a most wondrous thing
Enthralled my sight; whence she, being privy thus
To my whole thought and secret questioning,
Turning to me, as blithe as beautĕous:
"Lift up to God," said she, "thy grateful sense,
Who with the first star[9] now uniteth us.
Meseemed a cloud enclosed us, lucid, dense,
Solid, and smooth, like to the diamond stone
Smitten upon the sun's radiance.

---

[7]Lightning is the sphere of fire, but Dante is ascending to the sphere of Heaven, in which he was formed.

[8]Using analogies from Plato, Beatrice explains free will to Dante. The order of the universe is such that godlike bodies ascend upward, while brutish beasts descend to the lowest levels.

[9]Dante and Beatrice have ascended to the moon.

Into itself eternal union
    Received us both, as water doth receive
    A ray of light and still remains all one,

...

The sun that warmed my bosom first with love
    Had brought the beauteous face of truth to light,
    Unveiling it by proof and counter-proof.[10]
Corrected and convinced I must outright
    Confess me, and, the better to convey
    These sentiments, I raised my head upright;
But what I saw so carried me away
    To gaze on it, that ere I could confess,
    I had forgotten what I meant to say.

...

Toward Beatrice's self I moved me, turning;
    But on mine eyes her light at first so blazed,
    They could not bear the beauty and the burning;
And I was slow to question, being amazed.[11]

...

"O Loved," said I, "of the First Lover![12] O
    Most heavenly Lady, by whose words I live
    More and yet more, bathed in their quickening glow.
My love's whole store is too diminutive,
    Too poor in thanks to give back grace for grace;
    May he that sees, and has the power, so give!
That nothing save the light of truth allays
    Our intellect's disquiet I now see plain—
    God's truth, which holds all truth within its rays.[13]

...

This thought invites and makes me more secure
    To ask you, Lady, with all reverence due,
    About a further truth I find obscure.

---

[10]Beatrice was the first person with whom Dante fell in love on a human level. Now as a woman, she is showing him the source of the greatest love and truth, God, though he often does not understand.

[11]As Dante and Beatrice ascend heavenward, Beatrice's beauty increases as Dante gazes at her, signifying that he will be able to see God.

[12]The "First Lover" refers to God. This can be compared both to the scholastic Aristotelian definition of a creator as a First or Prime Mover and to the sentiments expressed by Hildegard, Hadewijch, and other female writers and poets.

[13]Because of Beatrice, Dante comes to understand that the human thirst for knowledge can only be satisfied by the truth, God. This was part of an ongoing debate begun in the twelfth century by mystics such as Bernard of Clairvaux (1090–1153), who believed faith led to understanding, and Peter Abelard (1079–1142), who insisted knowledge led to faith.

This would I know: can one atone to you
    For broken vows with other merchandise,
    Nor weigh too short upon your balance true?"
Beatrice looked at me, and lo! her eyes
    Grew so divine, with sparkling love alight,
    That I was lost in wonder and surprise,
My gaze downcast, my powers all put to flight.

. . .

"If in the fire of love I flame thus hot
    Upon thee, past all wont of mortal mood,
    Forcing thine eyes' surrender, marvel not.
This comes of perfect sight, with power endued
    To apprehend, and foot by foot to move
    Deeper into the apprehended good.[14]
Full well I see thine intellect give off
    Splendours already of the eternal light
    Which once to look upon is aye to love;
And if aught else your wandering loves invite,
    Still it is nothing but some gleams of this
    Which there shine through, though not yet known aright.[15]

[14]Platonic images show that the more perfect sight becomes, the closer one gets to God. As Dante gazes at Beatrice, representative of the Supreme Good, the closer he gets.
[15]Looking on the earthly Beatrice gives Dante a glimpse of heavenly beauty.

## 4.
## *Summons of Representatives of Shires and Towns to Parliament*
### 1295
## and
## *Rolls of Parliament, Petitions and Answers*
### 1290–1305

*The development of representative institutions in thirteenth- and fourteenth-century Europe points to two important features of the period: strong, bureaucratically minded kings and more clearly defined group identities within the population at large united by common aims and interests. From Spain to Poland, from England to Hungary, rulers turned to such groups to solidify and broaden royal support, gradually enmeshing them in the work of royal government. The documents that follow*

From *Translations and Reprints from the Original Sources of European History* (Philadelphia: University of Pennsylvania Press, 1897), vol. 1, no. 6, 35; and Basil Duke Henning et al., eds., *Crises in English History 1066–1945,* (New York: Holt, Rinehart and Winston, 1961), 62–64.

*illustrate this process in action in England. The first document is a royal writ issued by Edward I (r. 1272–1307) summoning representatives of counties and towns to Parliament in 1295. Although commoners had traditionally been excluded from royal assemblies, by this time they were becoming a regular fixture of Parliament along with the other two "estates," the clergy and nobility. Drawn from the official records of parliamentary proceedings, the second set of documents reveals that a key role of representatives sent to Parliament, regardless of their social station, was to present petitions to the king in the name of individuals and communities.*

## SUMMONS OF REPRESENTATIVES OF SHIRES AND TOWNS TO PARLIAMENT

The king to the sheriff of Northamptonshire. Since we intend to have a consultation and meeting with the earls, barons and other principal men of our kingdom with regard to providing remedies against the dangers which are in these days threatening the same kingdom, and on that account have commanded them to be with us on the Lord's day next after the feast of St. Martin, in the approaching winter, at Westminster, to consider, ordain, and do as may be necessary for the avoidance of these dangers, we strictly require you to cause two knights from the aforesaid county, two citizens from each city in the same county, and two burgesses from each borough, of those who are especially discreet and capable of laboring, to be elected without delay, and to cause them to come to us at the aforesaid time and place.

Moreover, the said knights are to have full and sufficient power for themselves and for the community of the aforesaid county, and the said citizens and burgesses for themselves and the communities of the aforesaid cities and boroughs separately, then and there for doing what shall then be ordained according to the common counsel in the premises, so that the aforesaid business shall not remain unfinished in any way for defect of this power. And you shall have there the names of the knights, citizens and burgesses and this writ.

Witness the king at Canterbury, on the third day of October. . . .

## ROLLS OF PARLIAMENT

### The Poor Men of England, 1305

To the petition of the poor men of the land of England, asking the King to give redress in the matter of the men serving on inquests, juries, and assizes, who are so commonly corrupted by gifts from the rich that no truth can be known from them, etc.; and also asking redress in the matter of the ordinaries [ecclesiastical judicial officers] who, to the prejudice of the Crown, strive to take cognizance of pleas of debt, transgressions, and other matters pertaining to the Crown, etc., and who take fines and payments therefore at their own will, etc.:—

It is answered thus: To the first, let them bring suit against jurors for convicting them by writ of attaint, etc. To the second, let them search diligently through the writs of prohibition in cases in which prohibition plays a part. . . .

### County of Hertford, 1290

The men of the county of Hertford beg that they may build a prison in the town of Hertford, from doing which William of Valence [Earl of Pembroke] hinders them, as it is said, to the King's loss and the county's vexation.

[Answer] The King granted it.

### County of Cumberland, 1305

To the petition of the community of Cumberland, seeking redress for that when the lord King by his writ commanded the sheriff of the county to provide the King's larder against the King's arrival in Scotland in the twenty-second year of his reign, the sheriff on pretext of the order took from the community a certain number of oats, and though he had an appropriation for them in his account, he paid nothing to the community:—

It is answered thus: Let suit be brought at the Exchequer, and if the sheriff has received an appropriation but has not paid, let him be punished by the established penalty and let him pay. But if otherwise let the treasurer ordain what is proper.

### Merchants of England, 1290

The merchants of England sought £2000 damages from the Count of Flanders, by virtue of the convention made with the king at Mustrel, which damages they suffered by the seizure and detention in Flanders of their chattels valued at £10,000.

[Answer] The King can do nothing except to ask him [the Count] by a letter (which he granted) to satisfy them and cause them to be indemnified; because it is not recorded that any convention was made or discussed for paying damages, and because the Count can seek his damages from the English in the same way.

### Religious Orders, 1292

Concerning the men of religious orders and others who seek to have their charters confirmed by the lord King and who present petitions for this purpose:—

The King orders that they all go to the Exchequer before the treasurer and barons, and let them make an end of the matter. Let the treasurer do what seems fitting to accomplish this, etc.

### Hospital of St. Katherine, 1290

The brothers and sisters of the hospital of St. Katherine petition that the King grant them the fifty shillings which King Henry, father of the present lord King, gave them annually, which they received for the soul of Sanchia, formerly Queen of Germany, that they might maintain a chapel in the Tower of London where they celebrate [masses] for her soul; and the arrears of the same for ten years back.

[Answer] It is not found at the Exchequer that they received any of the said fifty shillings either in the time of King Henry or in the time of the present King, . . . and nothing is to be done in the matter.

### Countess of Cornwall, 1298

Touching the lands of the Countess of Cornwall, which were assigned to her for her sustenance by her lord, and from which she claims that she was ejected: it seemed to the council that the *Curia Regis* can not interfere in any arrangement made between the Countess and her husband the Earl.

### Poor Alice, 1302

Alice de la Chapele of the Isle of Guernsey begs the magnanimity, grace, and compassion of our lord the King; for that she has taken thirty-five sheaves of various kinds of grain from the sharecrop of our lord the King, which sheaves were of little value, . . . so she begs in charity and compassion that grace be granted her upon her oath that she took them because of her poverty and to nourish her child.

[Answer] Let her have grace. Let the bailiffs certify the King concerning the cause and manner [of the theft], and if they find it as stated, the King concedes that it be done as is petitioned.

### ■ Discussion Questions

1. According to the summons, why did Edward I need to meet and consult with the "principal men" of his kingdom? What do these reasons suggest about his understanding of Parliament's functions in royal government?
2. Do you see any similarities and/or differences in these functions and those revealed in the parliamentary proceedings?
3. What do these proceedings reveal about everyday life in late thirteenth- and early fourteenth-century England?

## 5.
## Guyuk Khan
## *Letter to Pope Innocent IV*
## 1246

*Europeans' new sense of confidence and assertiveness in the thirteenth and early fourteenth centuries did not go unchallenged. To the east, the Mongols posed a significant threat both to Europe's territorial boundaries and its Christian identity. First united under the leadership of Chingiz Khan (c. 1162–1227), the Mongol army paved a path of destruction and conquest across northern China, and then turned westward with a series of well-orchestrated attacks in Russia, Poland, and Hungary. By the early 1240s, Pope Innocent IV (r. 1243–1254) was among the Western leaders who recognized the*

From Christopher Dawson, ed., *Mission to Asia* (Toronto: Medieval Academy of America, 1980), 85–86.

*urgent need to counter the Mongol advance. To this end, in 1245 he dispatched a mission to the Mongol emperor, urging him to cease his campaign of "savagery" and convert to Christianity. The mission arrived at the camp of the Mongol leader Guyuk in July 1246, just in time to see him enthroned as Great Khan. Guyuk Kahn formally responded to the pope's requests in the letter below, translated from Persian. In his choice of language, he illuminates the basis of the Mongol's own sense of identity while providing an outsider's perspective of European demands and interests.*

We, by the power of the eternal heaven,

Khan of the great Ulus[1]

Our command:—

This is a version sent to the great Pope, that he may know and understand in the [Muslim] tongue, what has been written. The petition of the assembly held in the lands of the Emperor [for our support], has been heard from your emissaries.

If he reaches [you] with his own report, Thou, who art the great Pope, together with all the Princes, come in person to serve us. At that time I shall make known all the commands of the *Yasa.*

You have also said that supplication and prayer have been offered by you, that I might find a good entry into baptism. This prayer of thine I have not understood. Other words which thou hast sent me: "I am surprised that thou hast seized all the lands of the Magyar and the Christians. Tell us what their fault is." These words of thine I have also not understood. The eternal God has slain and annihilated these lands and peoples, because they have neither adhered to Chingis Khan, nor to the Khagan,[2] both of whom have been sent to make known God's command, nor to the command of God. Like thy words, they also were impudent, they were proud and they slew our messenger-emissaries. How could anybody seize or kill by his own power contrary to the command of God?

Though thou likewise sayest that I should become a trembling Nestorian Christian, worship God and be an ascetic, how knowest thou whom God absolves, in truth to whom He shows mercy? How dost thou know that such words as thou speakest are with God's sanction? From the rising of the sun to its setting, all the lands have been made subject to me. Who could do this contrary to the command of God?

Now you should say with a sincere heart: "I will submit and serve you." Thou thyself, at the head of all the Princes, come at once to serve and wait upon us! At that time I shall recognize your submission.

---

[1]Ulus is a large or small social group, here consisting of all the peoples under the supreme ruler as a community.

[2]Khagan is the supreme ruler.

If you do not observe God's command, and if you ignore my command, I shall know you as my enemy. Likewise I shall make you understand. If you do otherwise, God knows what I know.

At the end of Jumada the second in the year 644.[3]

## THE SEAL

We, by the power of the eternal Tengri, universal Khan of the great Mongol Ulus—our command. If this reaches peoples who have made their submission, let them respect and stand in awe of it.

### ■ Discussion Questions

1. What does Guyuk Khan's letter suggest about the role of the papacy in European society at this time?
2. What reasons does Guyuk Khan give for rejecting this role?
3. What do these reasons reveal about the Khan's self-understanding as leader of the Mongol people?

### ■ Comparative Questions

1. What do Abbot Suger and the parliamentary documents suggest about the process of state building and the foundations of royal authority in France and England at the time?
2. In what ways do the first three documents share common assumptions about Europeans' religious and political identity?
3. How did the Mongol emperor's views, as expressed in his letter to the pope, challenge these assumptions?
4. How do Hadewijch and Dante express female spirituality? How does the female relationship with God compare with or differ from the male expression of female religious beliefs?
5. Compare and contrast the ways that Abbot Suger and Dante approach the search for God on earth.

[3]The date at the end of the document corresponds to November 1246.

Chapter

# 11

# Crisis and Renaissance, 1340–1500

CURRENTS OF BOTH CRISIS and renewal swept through medieval society in the years 1340–1500. On the one hand, throughout the fourteenth century Europeans faced a myriad of challenges, from pestilence to war to rebellions. On the other, the city-states of the northern Italian peninsula helped to spark a period of great creativity that historians often refer to as the Renaissance, which reached its peak in the 1400s. The documents in this chapter capture these twin themes, beginning with contemporary accounts of the catastrophic effects of the Black Death and the search for scapegoats, though many people viewed the plague as divine punishment. In its wake, the nobility sought to keep the people "in their place," adding restrictions and taxes that led to rebellions across Europe, including the English Peasants' Revolt of 1381, described in Document 2. At the same time, however, men of the upper classes in Italy defined themselves self-consciously as living in new times. For such men and a few women, this was a time of rebirth, distinct from what they viewed as the barbarism of a millennium and closer to the values and styles of antiquity. It was defined by the *studia humanitatis* (roughly, the liberal arts), from which the nineteenth-century term *humanism* derived. The third document illustrates the application and possibilities of humanism, while the fourth document demonstrates that the realities of Italian life often did match the ideals. The final source, by a Portuguese chronicler, details the quest for new lands and knowledge, which was an outward, geographical expression of the intellectual and cultural discoveries of the Renaissance.

## 1.
## *The Black Death*
### Fourteenth Century

*Few events in history have had such a shattering impact on every aspect of society as the plague, which reached Europe in 1347. The Black Death decimated a society*

From Rosemary Horrox, ed. and trans., *The Black Death* (Manchester: Manchester University Press, 1994), 16–21, 23, 207, 208, 219–22.

*already weakened by a demographic crisis, famines, and climatic disasters. It is estimated that one-third of Europe's population died in the first wave of plague, which was followed by repeated outbreaks. Some cities may have lost over half their people in 1347–1348 alone. Though the devastation was social, psychological, economic, political, and even artistic, many historians believe that in the long term the plague led to significant changes and even improvements in Western life. The following documents describe the arrival of the plague in various places and responses to it, including searches for its cause and people on whom to fix blame. The plague ultimately precipitated much of the crisis that characterized the fourteenth century.*

## FROM GABRIELE DE' MUSSIS (D. 1356), A LAWYER IN PIACENZA

In 1346, in the countries of the East, countless numbers of Tartars and Saracens were struck down by a mysterious illness which brought sudden death. . . . An eastern settlement under the rule of the Tartars called Tana, which lay to the north of Constantinople and was much frequented by Italian merchants, was totally abandoned after an incident there which led to its being besieged and attacked by hordes of Tartars who gathered in a short space of time. The Christian merchants, who had been driven out by force, were so terrified of the power of the Tartars that, to save themselves and their belongings, they fled in an armed ship to Caffa, a settlement in the same part of the world which had been founded long ago by the Genoese.

Oh God! See how the heathen Tartar races, pouring together from all sides, suddenly invested the city of Caffa and besieged the trapped Christians there for almost three years. There, hemmed in by an immense army, they could hardly draw breath, although food could be shipped in, which offered them some hope. But behold, the whole army was affected by a disease which overran the Tartars and killed thousands upon thousands every day. It was as though arrows were raining down from heaven to strike and crush the Tartars' arrogance. All medical advice and attention was useless; the Tartars died as soon as the signs of disease appeared on their bodies: swellings in the armpit or groin caused by coagulating humors, followed by a putrid fever.

The dying Tartars, stunned and stupefied by the immensity of the disaster brought about by the disease, and realizing that they had no hope of escape, lost interest in the siege. But they ordered corpses to be placed in catapults and lobbed into the city in the hope that the intolerable stench would kill everyone inside. What seemed like mountains of dead were thrown into the city, and the Christians could not hide or flee or escape from them, although they dumped as many of the bodies as they could in the sea. And soon the rotting corpses tainted the air and poisoned the water supply, and the stench was so overwhelming that hardly one in several thousand was in a position to flee the remains of the Tartar army. Moreover, one infected man could carry the poison to others, and infect people and places with the disease by look alone. No one knew, or could discover, a means of defense.

Thus almost everyone who had been in the East, or in the regions to the south and north, fell victim to sudden death after contracting this pestilential disease, as if struck by a lethal arrow which raised a tumor on their bodies. The scale of the mortality and the form which it took persuaded those who lived, weeping and lamenting, through the bitter events of 1346 to 1348—the Chinese, Indians, Persians, Medes, Kurds, Armenians, Cilicians, Georgians, Mesopotamians, Nubians, Ethiopians, Turks, Egyptians, Arabs, Saracens and Greeks (for almost all the East has been affected) that the last judgment had come. . . .

As it happened, among those who escaped from Caffa by boat were a few sailors who had been infected with the poisonous disease. Some boats were bound for Genoa, others went to Venice and to other Christian areas. When the sailors reached these places and mixed with the people there, it was as if they had brought evil spirits with them: every city, every settlement, every place was poisoned by the contagious pestilence. . . .

Scarcely one in seven of the Genoese survived. In Venice, where an inquiry was held into the mortality, it was found that more than 70% of the people had died, and that within a short period 20 out of 24 excellent physicians had died. The rest of Italy, Sicily and Apulia and the neighboring regions maintain that they have been virtually emptied of inhabitants. The people of Florence, Pisa and Lucca, finding themselves bereft of their fellow residents, emphasize their losses. The Roman Curia at Avignon, the provinces on both sides of the Rhône, Spain, France, and the Empire cry up their griefs and disasters—all of which makes it extraordinarily difficult for me to give an accurate picture.

By contrast, what befell the Saracens can be established from trustworthy accounts. In the city of Babylon alone (the heart of the Sultan's power), 480,000 of his subjects are said to have been carried off by the disease in less than three months in 1348—and this is known from the Sultan's register which records the names of the dead, because he receives a gold bezant for each person buried. . . .

I am overwhelmed, I can't go on. Everywhere one turns there is death and bitterness to be described. The hand of the Almighty strikes repeatedly, to greater and greater effect. The terrible judgment gains power as time goes by.

## FROM HERMAN GIGAS, A FRANCISCAN FRIAR IN GERMANY, WHOSE ACCOUNT GOES UNTIL 1349

In 1347 there was such a great pestilence and mortality throughout almost the whole world that in the opinion of well-informed men scarcely a tenth of mankind survived. The victims did not linger long, but died on the second or third day. . . . Some say that it was brought about by the corruption of the air; others that the Jews planned to wipe out all the Christians with poison and had poisoned wells and springs everywhere. And many Jews confessed as much under torture: that they had bred spiders and toads in pots and pans, and had obtained poison from overseas; and that not every Jew knew about this, only the more powerful ones, so that it would not be betrayed. . . . [M]en say that bags full of poison were found in many wells and springs.

## From Heinrich Truchess, a Former Papal Chaplain and Canon of Constance

The persecution of the Jews began in November 1348, and the first outbreak in Germany was at Sölden, where all the Jews were burnt on the strength of a rumor that they had poisoned wells and rivers, as was afterwards confirmed by their own confessions and also by the confessions of Christians whom they had corrupted.... Within the revolution of one year, that is from All Saints [1 November] 1348 until Michaelmas [29 September] 1349 all the Jews between Cologne and Austria were burnt and killed for this crime, young men and maidens and the old along with the rest. And blessed be God who confounded the ungodly who were plotting the extinction of his church.

## From the Councillors of Cologne to Conrad von Winterthur to the Bürgermeister and Councillors of Strassburg on 12 January 1349

Very dear friends, all sorts of rumors are now flying about against Judaism and the Jews prompted by this unexpected and unparalleled mortality of Christians, which, alas, has raged in various parts of the world and is still woefully active in several places. Throughout our city, as in yours, many-winged Fame clamors that this mortality was initially caused, and is still being spread, by the poisonings of springs and wells, and that the Jews must have dropped poisonous substances into them. When it came to our knowledge that serious charges had been made against the Jews in several small towns and villages on the basis of this mortality, we sent numerous letters to you and to other cities and towns to uncover the truth behind these rumors, and set a thorough investigation in train....

If a massacre of the Jews were to be allowed in the major cities (something which we are determined to prevent in our city, if we can, as long as the Jews are found to be innocent of these or similar actions) it could lead to the sort of outrages and disturbances which would whip up a popular revolt among the common people—and such revolts have in the past brought cities to misery and desolation. In any case we are still of the opinion that this mortality and its attendant circumstances are caused by divine vengeance and nothing else. Accordingly we intend to forbid any harassment of the Jews in our city because of these flying rumors, but to defend them faithfully and keep them safe, as our predecessors did—and we are convinced that you ought to do the same.

## Papal Bull *Sicut Judeis* of Clement VI Issued in July 1348

Recently, however, it has been brought to our attention by public fame—or more accurately, infamy—that numerous Christians are blaming the plague with which God, provoked by their sins, has afflicted the Christian people, on poisonings carried out by the Jews at the instigation of the devil, and that out of their own hot-headedness they have impiously slain many Jews, making no exception for age or sex; and that the Jews have been falsely accused of such outrageous behavior. . . . [I]t cannot be true that the Jews, by such a heinous crime, are the cause or occasion of the plague, because throughout many parts of the world the same plague, by the hidden judgment of God, has afflicted and afflicts the Jews themselves and many other races who have never lived alongside them.

We order you by apostolic writing that each of you upon whom this charge has been laid, should straitly command those subject to you, both clerical and lay . . . not to dare (on their own authority or out of hot-headedness) to capture, strike, wound or kill any Jews or expel them from their service on these grounds; and you should demand obedience under pain of excommunication.

### ■ Discussion Questions

1. What explanations are offered for the onset of plague? What is the understanding of the disease process?
2. What do the accounts by Mussis and the bull of Pope Clement VI have in common? How did different groups of people react to the plague?
3. Why might the city councillors or the pope have attempted to protect the Jews? Why was such protection of no avail in many places? Why might some Jews have confessed?

## 2.
## Thomas Walsingham
## *Peasant Rebels in London*
## 1381

*Thomas Walsingham (d. 1422) was the Benedictine author of six chronicles, including a portion of the famous "St. Alban's Chronicle." Although little is known of his life, his description of the Peasants' Revolt is a riveting and, by the standards of the time, reliable account of events early in the reign of King Richard II (r. 1377–1399). The revolt, one of the largest of its kind, was a response to noble demands on a population experiencing declining incomes as a result of the Black Death, the costs of war with France, and the realm's poor administration. The poll tax imposed on adult males in 1380 sparked a rebellion, led by Wat Tyler (d. 1381) and preacher John Ball, of townsmen and peasants in southeastern England. The larger causes can be found in the final breakdown of serfdom—a breakdown vigorously opposed by a nobility in decline and supported by a peasantry with new opportunities brought about by the scarcity of laborers.*

---

From Thomas Walsingham, "Historia Anglicana I," in R. B. Dobson, *The Peasants' Revolt of 1381*, 2d ed. (London: Macmillan, 1983), 169–76, 178–81.

On the next day [Corpus Christi] the rebels went in and out of London and talked with the simple commons of the city about the acquiring of liberty and the seizure of the traitors, especially the duke of Lancaster whom they hated most of all; and in a short time easily persuaded all the poorer citizens to support them in their conspiracy. And when, later that day, the sun had climbed higher and grown warm and the rebels had tasted various wines and expensive drinks at will and so had become less drunk than mad (for the great men and common people of London had left all their cellars open to the rebels), they began to debate at length about the traitors with the more simple men of the city. Among other things they assembled and set out for the Savoy, the residence of the duke of Lancaster, unrivaled in splendor and nobility within England, which they then set to the flames. . . . This news so delighted the common people of London that, thinking it particularly shameful for others to harm and injure the duke before themselves, they immediately ran there like madmen, set fire to the place on all sides and so destroyed it. In order that the whole community of the realm should know that they were not motivated by avarice, they made a proclamation that no one should retain for his own use any object found there under penalty of execution. Instead they broke the gold and silver vessels, of which there were many at the Savoy, into pieces with their axes and threw them into the Thames or the sewers. They tore the golden cloths and silk hangings to pieces and crushed them underfoot; they ground up rings and other jewels inlaid with precious stones in small mortars, so that they could never be used again. . . .

After these malicious deeds, the rebels destroyed the place called the "Temple Bar" (in which the more noble apprentices of the law lived) because of their anger . . . and there many muniments which the lawyers were keeping in custody were consumed by fire. Even more insanely they set fire to the noble house of the Hospital of St. John at Clerkenwell so that it burnt continuously for the next seven days. . . .

For who would ever have believed that such rustics, and most inferior ones at that, would dare (not in crowds but individually) to enter the chamber of the king and of his mother with their filthy sticks; and undeterred by any of the soldiers, to stroke and lay their uncouth and sordid hands on the beards of several most noble knights. Moreover, they conversed familiarly with the soldiers asking them to be faithful to the ribalds and friendly in the future. . . . [They] gained access singly and in groups to the rooms in the Tower, they arrogantly lay and sat on the king's bed while joking; and several asked the king's mother to kiss them. . . . The rebels, who had formerly belonged to the most lowly condition of serf, went in and out like lords; and swineherds set themselves above soldiers. . . .

When the archbishop finally heard the rebels coming, he said to his men with great fortitude: "Let us go with confidence, for it is better to die when it can no longer help to live. At no previous time of my life could I have died in such security of conscience." A little later the executioners entered crying, "Where is that traitor to the kingdom? Where the despoiler of the common people?" . . . [They] dragged the archbishop along the passages by his arms and hood to their fellows once outside the gates on Tower Hill. . . . Words could not be heard among their horrible shrieks but rather their throats sounded with the bleating of sheep, or, to be more accurate, with the devilish voices of peacocks. . . .

Scarcely could the archbishop finish [his] speech before the rebels broke out with the horrible shout that they feared neither an interdict nor the Pope; all that remained for him, as a man false to the community and treasonable to the realm was to submit his neck to the executioners' swords. The archbishop now realized that his death was imminent and inevitable. . . . He was first struck severely but not fatally in the neck. He put his hand to the wound and said: "Ah! Ah! this is the hand of God." As he did not move his hand from the place of sorrow the second blow cut off the top of his fingers as well as severing part of the arteries. But the archbishop still did not die, and only on the eighth blow, wretchedly wounded in the neck and on the head, did he complete what we believe is worthy to be called his martyrdom. . . .

Nor did they show any reverence to any holy places but killed those whom they hated even if they were within churches and in sanctuary. I have heard from a trustworthy witness that thirty Flemings were violently dragged out of the church of the Austin Friars in London and executed in the open street. . . .

On the next day, Saturday 15 June (the feasts of Saints Vitus and Modestus), behold, the men of Kent showed themselves no less persistent in their wicked actions than on the previous day: they continued to kill men and to burn and destroy houses. The king sent messengers to the Kentishmen telling them that their fellows had left to live in peace henceforward and promising that he would give them too a similar form of peace if they would accept it. The rebels' greatest leader was called "Walter Helier" or "Tylere" (for such names had been given to him because of his trade), a cunning man endowed with much sense if he had decided to apply his intelligence to good purposes. . . .

On this the king, although a boy and of tender age, took courage and ordered the mayor of London to arrest Tyler. The mayor, a man of incomparable spirit and bravery, arrested Tyler without question and struck him a blow on the head which hurt him badly. Tyler was soon surrounded by the other servants of the king and pierced by sword thrusts in several parts of his body. His death, as he fell from his horse to the ground, was the first incident to restore to the English knighthood their almost extinct hope that they could resist the commons. . . .

But the king, with marvelous presence of mind and courage for so young a man, spurred his horse towards the commons and rode around them, saying, "What is this, my men? What are you doing? Surely you do not wish to fire on your own king? Do not attack me and do not regret the death of that traitor and ruffian. For I will be your king, your captain and your leader. Follow me into the field where you can have all the things you would like to ask for." . . .

The commons were allowed to spend the night under the open sky. However the king ordered that the written and sealed charter which they had requested should be handed to them in order to avoid more trouble at that time. He knew that Essex was not yet pacified nor Kent settled; and the commons and rustics of both counties were ready to rebel if he failed to satisfy them quickly. . . .

Once they had this charter, the commons returned to their homes. But still the earlier evils by no means ceased.

## ■ Discussion Questions

1. How does Thomas Walsingham's class and position affect his recording of events? How does he describe the different classes of society?
2. What does the account suggest about economic and political conditions in late fourteenth-century England?
3. How did the rebels choose their targets, both human and material? What were they seeking? Against what were they protesting?
4. What was the rebels' attitude toward religious authority? What might explain their actions in this regard?

# 3.
# Giovanni Pico della Mirandola
# *Oration on the Dignity of Man*
## 1496

*The work of Giovanni Pico della Mirandola (1463–1494), a Neoplatonic thinker and Dominican friar, epitomizes in many ways the philosophical beliefs of humanism. The* Oration on the Dignity of Man, *part of a series of nine hundred theses written when Pico was twenty-three, is in many ways a manifesto of the Renaissance. Steeped in both the Aristotelian and Platonic traditions, Pico knew Latin, Greek, Hebrew, and Italian. He was also deeply interested in Hebrew mysticism, pre-Socratic thought, and occult knowledge attributed at the time to a supposed ancient god/teacher, Hermes Trismegistus. The discovery of truth from many different sources is known as* syncretism. *Not surprisingly, some of Pico's ideas were deemed heretical by Pope Innocent VIII (r. 1484–1492). Although Pico was arrested, he lived under the protection of Lorenzo de' Medici (1449–1492) until he died at the age of thirty-one. The* Oration, *first published in 1496, revolves around the concept of free will—the human ability to choose, for good or ill.*

I have read in the ancient annals of the Arabians, most reverend Fathers, that when asked what on the world's stage could be considered most admirable, Abdala the Saracen answered that there is nothing more admirable to be seen than man. In agreement with this opinion is the saying of Hermes Trismegistus: "What a great miracle, O Asclepius, is man!"

When I had thought over the meaning of these maxims, the many reasons for the excellence of man advanced by many men failed to satisfy me. . . .

At last, it seems to me that I have understood why man is the most fortunate living thing worthy of all admiration and precisely what rank is his lot in the

From Julia Conaway Bondanella and Mark Musa, eds., *The Italian Renaissance Reader* (New York: Meridian, 1987), 180–83.

universal chain of being, a rank to be envied not only by the brutes but even by the stars and by minds beyond this world. It is a matter past faith and extraordinary! . . .

God the Father, the supreme Architect, had already built this cosmic home which we behold, this most majestic temple of divinity, in accordance with the laws of a mysterious wisdom. He had adorned the region above the heavens with intelligences, had quickened the celestial spheres with eternal souls and had filled the vile and filthy parts of the lower world with a multitude of animals of every kind. But when the work was completed, the Maker kept wishing that there were someone who could examine the plan of so great an enterprise, who could love its beauty, who could admire its vastness. On that account, when everything was completed, as Moses and Timaeus both testify, He finally took thought of creating man. However, not a single archetype remained from which he might fashion this new creature, not a single treasure remained which he might bestow upon this new son, and not a single seat remained in the whole world in which the contemplator of the universe might sit. All now was complete; all things had been assigned to the highest, the middle, and the lowest orders. But it was not in the nature of the Father's power to fail in this final creative effort, as though exhausted; nor was it in the nature of His wisdom to waver in such a crucial matter through lack of counsel; and it was not in the nature of His Beneficent Love that he who was destined to praise God's divine generosity in regard to others should be forced to condemn it in regard to himself. At last, the Supreme Artisan ordained that the creature to whom He could give nothing properly his own should share in whatever He had assigned individually to the other creatures. He therefore accepted man as a work of indeterminate nature, and placing him in the center of the world, addressed him thus:

"O Adam, we have given you neither a place nor a form nor any ability exclusively your own, so that according to your wishes and your judgment, you may have and possess whatever place, form, or abilities you desire. The nature of all other beings is limited and constrained in accordance with the laws prescribed by us. Constrained by no limits, in accordance with your own free will, in whose hands we have placed you, you shall independently determine the bounds of your own nature. We have placed you at the world's center, from where you may more easily observe whatever is in the world. We have made you neither celestial nor terrestrial, neither mortal nor immortal, so that with honor and freedom of choice, as though the maker and molder of yourself, you may fashion yourself in whatever form you prefer. You shall have the power to degenerate into the inferior forms of life which are brutish; you shall have the power, through your soul's judgment, to rise to the superior orders which are divine." . . .

In man alone, at the moment of his creation, the Father placed the seeds of all kinds and the germs of every way of life. Whatever seeds each man cultivates will mature and bear their own fruit in him; if vegetative, he will be like a plant; if sensitive, he will become a brute; if rational, he will become a celestial being; if intellectual, he will be an angel and the son of God. . . .

Who would not admire this our chameleon? Or who could admire any other being more greatly than man? Asclepius the Athenian justly says that man was symbolized in the mysteries by the figure of Proteus because of his ability to change his character and transform his nature. This is the origin of those metamorphoses or transformations celebrated among the Hebrews and the Pythagoreans. For the occult theology of the Hebrews sometimes transforms the holy Enoch into an angel of divinity and sometimes transforms other people into other divinities. The Pythagoreans transform impious men into beasts and, if Empedocles is to be believed, even into plants. Echoing this, Mohammed often had this saying on his lips: "He who deviates from divine law becomes a beast," and he was right in saying so. For it is not the bark that makes the beast of burden but its irrational and sensitive soul; neither is it the spherical form which makes the heavens, but their undeviating order; nor is it the freedom from a body which makes the angel but its spiritual intelligence. . . .

Are there any who will not admire man? In the sacred Mosaic and Christian writings, man, not without reason, is sometimes described by the name of "all flesh" and sometimes by that of "every creature," since man molds, fashions, and transforms himself according to the form of all flesh and the character of every creature. For this reason, the Persian Evantes, in describing Chaldean theology, writes that man does not have an inborn and fixed image of himself but many which are external and foreign to him; whence comes the Chaldean saying: "Man is a being of varied, manifold, and inconstant nature."

But why do we reiterate all these things? To the end that from the moment we are born we are born into the condition of being able to become whatever we choose.

## ■ Discussion Questions

1. What, according to Pico, are man's abilities? Why were these abilities and possibilities given to him?
2. What kinds of sources does Pico use to support his ideas? What is their importance as part of his philosophy?
3. Why might the words and ideas Pico used to describe God and how God went about the process of creation have been considered dangerous?
4. What makes this document a "statement" of Renaissance thought?

# 4.
# Bernardino of Siena
## *An Italian Preacher: Sins against Nature*
### 1380–1444

*At the same time that the great orators, civic humanists, and artists of the Renaissance were attempting to distance themselves from the perceived "barbarity" of earlier times,*

---

From Franco Mormando, *The Preacher's Demons: Bernardino of Siena and the Social Underworld of Early Renaissance Italy* (Chicago and London: University of Chicago Press, 1999), 119–20, 124, 128, 130, 138, 139, 147–48, 152.

*religion continued to play an enormous role in everyday life. The famous preacher Bernardino of Siena (1380–1444) exemplifies the continuing great importance of religion during this period. One of the most popular preachers of his day, Bernardino was an itinerant Franciscan, canonized only six years after his death. He preached throughout northern Italy and was active in efforts to unify the Roman and Greek churches at the Council of Florence in 1439. His greatest fame, however, came as a preacher of moral reform. Besides discussing the typical subjects one might find in sermons, Bernardino devotes special attention to "problems" he finds in his day, especially sodomy, sorcery, vanity, and the Jews. These excerpts are from several sermons.*

Oooo! Have I heard stories. . . . Aooo! Once I was in a certain place where some man had taken as his wife a beautiful young woman. They lived together for six years, and she was still a virgin. That is, she had been with him in all those years in a state of most grave sin against nature. Oh, what disorder, oh, what grievous shame! Ooo, ooo, ooo! Do you know what this poor little thing was reduced to? She was all wasted, pale, pasty, sallow. She begged me for the love of God to help her if I could in any way. She said she had been to the bishop about this matter and even to the mayor; but they answered her that they needed proof of what she was charging. O what ignorance is this to need proof and witnesses for these kinds of things! I'll tell you what is needed: a bonfire, a bonfire. . . .

O ladies, make sure you don't send your sons [where there are sodomites]; send instead your daughters, because there's no danger for them if you send them among such people. They will not be contaminated by anything; and even if they were seized and violated, at least there wouldn't be as much danger and as much sin as there would be [if your sons were violated]. If there is no other way, I would permit it as the lesser evil. . . .

Don't you see that you are showing yourself to be against God, who said to the man and the woman, our first mother and father: "*Crescite et multiplicamini, et replete terram?* Increase and multiply, and fill the earth?" O sodomite of the Devil, what are you doing? It's as if you're saying to God: "I want to spite you; I don't want anyone to be born." . . .

And what do you say? "Oh, it's completely harmless, no one's going to get hurt, he's just a boy, after all." If he were a girl, perhaps you wouldn't be doing this, because she could get herself pregnant this way. And since he can't get pregnant, you're happy and offer up your "flatcake" to the "queen of heaven." And you just keep on doing such things so much that you are provoking the wrath of God; and God, seeing this and all the other vices, is threatening you and says: "My wrath will come down over your head." Do you know what he will do? He will send you wars, plagues, and famines in order to punish the sodomites, so much so that you won't be left with either livestock, or farms or gardens or money or even your very population. In all these ways, God will show his wrath. . . .

They aren't even dry behind the ears and they're already contaminated and sodomites! Just look at them, fathers and mothers, it's astounding: At such a tender age and they're already contaminated by sodomy! . . .

I've heard about those [boys] who paint themselves up and go around bragging about their sodomizers and make it into a profession and incite others to do likewise. . . .

[T]hese types are never satisfied. Oh, woman, take note, if he's trapped in this vice, you'll never be able to satisfy him! He always complains about everything you do, always. When he comes home, he comes in turmoil, with a head full of frenzy, and nothing does he care for the judgment of God or honor in this world. He's always cranky and agitated, he's afraid — he's afraid of falling out of favor with his wicked little boy. . . . He obeys the boy like a servant and does everything he can to grant his wishes. . . .

[In Venice] I saw three things happening together. I saw [the sodomite] placed at the stake, and tied all the way up. [I saw] a keg of pitch, brushwood, and fire, and an executor who set him on fire, and a lot of people, all around, watching. The sodomite felt the smoke and the fire, and he burned to death; the executioner felt only the smoke, and whoever was standing around watching saw nothing but smoke and fire. What this stands for is that: in hell the sodomites will burn with smoke and fire [while] their torturers down there will get the smoke. . . . Those who stand watching [represent] the blessed spirits in paradise who see the punishment of the sodomites and rejoice over it because they see the justice of God shining forth from it.

### ■ Discussion Questions

1. Why might Bernardino have directed many of his comments to women? How would you compare his views of men and women?
2. Bernardino refers to the "population" at a number of points. To whom is he referring? Why might this have been a concern?
3. How does Bernardino exhibit an increasing repression of sexuality?

## 5.
## Gomes Eanes de Zurara
## *Chronicle of the Discovery of Guinea*
### c. 1453

*While Italian Renaissance thinkers were rediscovering the ancient past, the fall of Constantinople in 1453 to the Turks, blocking access to trade in the East, led to the so-called Age of Discovery or Exploration. As intellectual horizons expanded, so did geographical ones, sometimes with disastrous consequences for native peoples. In his* Discovery of Guinea, *official chronicler Zurara (c. 1410–1474) continued the work of his predecessors in writing histories of the kings of Portugal. Recognized as one of*

From George Kish, ed., *A Source Book in Geography* (Cambridge and London: Harvard University Press, 1978), 295–97.

*the first historiographers to provide an account of the initial exploration of the western coast of Africa, Zurara relied on earlier chroniclers as well as oral reports from Portuguese sailors and soldiers from 1433 to 1448. His chronicle offers information about Prince Henry the Navigator (1394–1460) whose circle at the port of Lagos in southern Portugal comprised astronomers, geographers, and navigators. Henry's desire to find a route to the East led to important advances in technology and geographical knowledge, and ultimately led to the Portuguese slave trade. In the following excerpt, Zurara describes early encounters and descriptions of the people of Guinea and a critique of those who had feared exploration.*

## HOW THOSE CARAVELS ARRIVED AT THE RIVER OF NILE, AND OF THE GUINEAS THAT THEY TOOK

Now these caravels having passed by the land of Sahara, as hath been said, came in sight of the two palm trees that Dinis Diaz[1] had met with before, by which they understood that they were at the beginning of the land of the Negroes. And at this sight they were glad indeed, and would have landed at once, but they found the sea so rough upon that coast that by no manner of means could they accomplish their purpose. And some of those who were present said afterwards that it was clear from the smell that came off the land how good must be the fruits of that country, for it was so delicious that from the point they reached, though they were on the sea, it seemed to them that they stood in some gracious fruit garden ordained for the sole end of their delight. And if our men showed on their side a great desire of gaining the land, no less did the natives of it show their eagerness to receive them into it; but of the reception they offered I do not care to speak, for according to the signs they made to our men from the first, they did not intend to abandon the beach without very great loss to one side or the other. Now the people of this green land are wholly black, and hence this is called Land of the Negroes, or Land of Guinea. . . . They understood right well that they were close to the river of Nile. . . .

It is well that we should here leave these matters at rest for a space and treat of the limits of those lands through the which our people journeyed in the labors of which we have spoken, in order that you may have an understanding of the delusion in which our forefathers ever lived who were affrighted to pass that Cape for fear of those things of which we have told in the beginning of this book; and also that you may see how great praise our Prince deserveth, by bringing their doubts before the presence not only of us who are now living, but also of all others who will be born in the time to come. And because one of the things which they alleged

[1]Dinis Diaz had "discovered" Cape Verde, fifteen hundred miles down the African coast, in 1445.

to be a hindrance to the passage into these lands consisted of the very strong currents that were there, on account of which it was impossible for any ship to navigate those seas, you now have a clear knowledge of their former error in that you have seen vessels come and go as free from danger as in any part of the other seas. They further alleged that the lands were all sandy and without any inhabitants, and true it is that in the matter of the sands they were not altogether deceived, but these were not so great as they thought; while as to the inhabitants, you have clearly seen the contrary to be the fact, since you witness the dwellers in those parts each day before your eyes, although their inhabited places are chiefly villages and very few towns. For from the Cape of Bojador to the kingdom of Tunis there will not be in the whole, what with towns and places fortified for defense, as many as fifty. They were no less at fault as regards the depth of the sea, for they had it marked on their charts that the shores were so shallow that at the distance of a league from the land there was only a fathom of water; but this was found not to be so, for the ships have had and have sufficient depth for their management, except for certain shoals; and thus dwellings were made that exist on certain sandbanks, as you will find now in the navigating charts which the Infant caused to be prepared.

In the land of the Negroes there is no walled place save that which they call Oadem, nor are there any settlements except some by the water's edge, of straw houses, the which were emptied of their dwellers by those that went there in the ships of this land. True it is that the whole land is generally peopled, but their mode of living is only in tents and carts, such as we use here when our princes do happen to go on a warlike march, and those who were captured there gave testimony of this, and also John Fernandez, of whom we have already spoken, related much concerning the same. All their principal study and toil is in guarding their flocks, to wit, cows and sheep and goats and camels, and they change their camp almost every day, for the longest they can rest in one spot will be eight days. And some of their chief men possess tame mares, of which they breed horses, though very few.

Their food consisteth for the great part of milk, and sometimes a little meat and the seeds of wild herbs that they gather in those mountains. . . . And those that live by the sea shore eat nothing save fish, and all for the most part without either bread or anything else, except the water that they drink, and they generally eat their fish raw and dried. Their clothing consisteth of a skin vest and breeches of the same, but some of the more honorable wear bournouses; and some preeminent men, who are almost above all the others, have good garments. . . .

The women wear bournouses which are like mantles, with the which they only cover their faces, and by that they think they have covered all their shame, for they leave their bodies quite naked. "For sure," saith he who compiled this history, "this is one of the things by the which one may discern their great bestiality, for if they had some particle of reason they would follow nature, and cover those parts only which by its shewing ought to be covered. . . . And the wives of the most honorable men wear rings of gold in their nostrils and ears, as well as other jewels.

## Discussion Questions

1. How do the Portuguese first describe the land of Guinea?
2. Although Zurara does not go into detail, how do the native peoples react to the Portuguese? Why might account for their reactions?
3. How does Zurara describe the men and women of Guinea? What characteristics does he single out in an attempt to convince his readers of the native peoples' inferiority?
4. How might this source have been seen as a work of political propaganda for increasingly strong states?

## Comparative Questions

1. What connections can you draw between the plague and the peasant rebellions that swept over Europe during the decades after 1347?
2. Compare the visions of both the human being and the state as described by Pico della Mirandola with those of Bernardino of Siena. In what ways do they differ? How might you account for this difference?
3. One of historian Jacob Burckhardt's chapters in *The Civilization of the Renaissance* is entitled "The Discovery of Man and the World." Based on the documents in this chapter and your understanding of the period, what is "new" about the Renaissance? What could be considered a continuation of medieval ideas?
4. Pico della Mirandola wrote nearly fifty years after Zurara. How might Pico's references to a wide range of sources, many non-Christian, have been affected by Europeans' expanding knowledge of other parts of the world?

Chapter

# 12

# Struggles over Beliefs, 1500–1648

THE SIXTEENTH THROUGH the mid-seventeenth centuries were a time of turmoil and change for people from all walks of life, as the following documents illustrate. Despite the ending of the Great Schism in 1417, serious damage had been done to the authority of the Catholic Church. Many within the church tried to institute reforms, but change was slow in coming. Increasing numbers of laymen and women turned to individual avenues of devotion, including an evangelicalism that was given new life with the advent of the printing press. The problems of the church, joined with the spirit and methods of the Renaissance, ushered in a period known as the Reformation, which forever shattered European religious unity. With the possibility of religious choice came violence, fueled by both ecclesiastical and lay leaders' belief that political and social stability depended on religious conformity. As the violence escalated, however, some people argued successfully that peace could come only if state interests took precedence over religious ones. Europeans' views of the earth and heavens also changed because of the rise of new scientific methods and topics of inquiry. At the same time, the lure of traditional beliefs remained strong within communities struggling to make sense of the upheavals occurring around them.

## 1.
## Martin Luther
## *Freedom of a Christian*
## 1520

*German monk Martin Luther's attempt to reform the Catholic Church from within developed into a new branch of Christianity known as Protestantism. After his excommunication by Pope Leo X in 1520, Luther published several treatises that attacked church authority, clerical celibacy, and the sacraments while elucidating his*

From Martin Luther, *Christian Liberty*, ed. Harold J. Grimm (Philadelphia: Fortress Press, 1957), 6–10.

*evangelical theology. He set forth the guiding principles of his beliefs with particular clarity in* Freedom of a Christian. *Although originally written in Latin and addressed to the pope, the tract was soon translated into German and widely circulated among Luther's ever-growing number of followers. In the excerpt that follows, Luther defined what became a central tenet of the reform movement: faith in Christ and his promise of salvation is all that a Christian needs to be saved from sin.*

Many people have considered Christian faith an easy thing, and not a few have given it a place among the virtues. They do this because they have not experienced it and have never tasted the great strength there is in faith. It is impossible to write well about it or to understand what has been written about it unless one has at one time or another experienced the courage which faith gives a man when trials oppress him. But he who has had even a faint taste of it can never write, speak, meditate, or hear enough concerning it. It is a living "spring of water welling up to eternal life," as Christ calls it in John 4 [:14].

As for me, although I have no wealth of faith to boast of and know how scant my supply is, I nevertheless hope that I have attained to a little faith, even though I have been assailed by great and various temptations; and I hope that I can discuss it, if not more elegantly, certainly more to the point, than those literalists and subtile disputants have previously done, who have not even understood what they have written....

First, let us consider the inner man to see how a righteous, free, and pious Christian, that is, a spiritual, new, and inner man, becomes what he is. It is evident that no external thing has any influence in producing Christian righteousness or freedom ... It does not help the soul if the body is adorned with the sacred robes of priests or dwells in sacred places or is occupied with sacred duties or prays, fasts, abstains from certain kinds of food, or does any work that can be done by the body and in the body....

One thing, and only one thing, is necessary for Christian life, righteousness, and freedom. That one thing is the most holy Word of God, the gospel of Christ, as Christ says, John 11 [:25], "I am the resurrection and the life; he who believes in me, though he die, yet shall he live"; and John 8 [:36], "So if the Son makes you free, you will be free indeed"; and Matt. 4 [:4], "Man shall not live by bread alone, but by every word that proceeds from the mouth of God." Let us then consider it certain and firmly established that the soul can do without anything except the Word of God and that where the Word of God is missing there is no help at all for the soul. If it has the Word of God it is rich and lacks nothing since it is the Word of life, truth, light, peace, righteousness, salvation, joy, liberty, wisdom, power, grace, glory, and of every incalculable blessing....

You may ask, "What then is the Word of God, and how shall it be used, since there are so many words of God?" I answer: The Apostle explains this in Romans 1. The Word is the gospel of God concerning his Son, who was made flesh, suffered, rose from the dead, and was glorified through the Spirit who sanctifies. To preach Christ means to feed the soul, make it righteous, set it free, and save it, provided it believes the preaching. Faith alone is the saving and efficacious use of the Word of God . . . Therefore it is clear that, as the soul needs only the Word of God for its life and righteousness, so it is justified by faith alone and not any works . . .

When you have learned this you will know that you need Christ, who suffered and rose again for you so that, if you believe in him, you may through this faith become a new man in so far as your sins are forgiven and you are justified by the merits of another, namely, of Christ alone. . . .

### ■ Discussion Questions

1. According to Luther, what is faith and where does it come from?
2. How can an individual Christian become a "new man" through such faith?
3. By defining faith alone as essential to salvation, in what ways does Luther undermine basic Catholic teachings?
4. What authority does Luther draw upon to defend his point of view? What does this reveal about the basis of his theology?

## 2.
## St. Ignatius of Loyola
## *A New Kind of Catholicism*
### 1546, 1549, 1553

*The interests of Ignatius of Loyola (1491–1556), born of a Spanish noble family, centered more on chivalry than religion before his serious injury at the Battle of Pamplona in 1520. While recovering, he experienced a conversion when he began reading the only books available to him,* The Golden Legend *(about saints' lives) and the* Life of Christ. *After spending time at the monastery of Montserrat, where he devoted himself to prayer, fasting, and self-reflection, he began work on* The Spiritual Exercises, *a manual of discernment for the pilgrim journeying to God. After studying at the University of Paris, Ignatius, Francis Xavier (1506–1552), and other friends made vows of chastity and poverty, determining to travel to Jerusalem. When this became impossible, they went to Italy. The Society of Jesus (the Jesuits), founded by Ignatius and his early companions, was officially recognized by Pope Paul III in 1540 as a new order directly under the papacy. Its spirituality would be expressed most prominently in teaching and missionary work. The following letters of Ignatius reveal a new form of Catholic spiritual expression that was active and apostolic in its orientation. It was less a "response" to Protestantism than a model for Catholic life and work. Along with the works of other early Jesuits, it embodied a new spirit that so many had sought but not found in the late medieval church.*

---

From Joseph A. Munitiz and Philip Endean, eds. and trans., *Saint Ignatius of Loyola, Personal Writings: Reminiscences, Spiritual Diary, Select Letters, Including the Text of* The Spiritual Exercises (New York: Penguin Books, 1996), 165, 166, 230, 233–34, 257, 259, 262–63.

## CONDUCT AT TRENT: ON HELPING OTHERS, 1546

Our main aim [to God's greater glory] during this undertaking at Trent is to put into practice (as a group that lives together in one appropriate place) preaching, confessions and readings, teaching children, giving good example, visiting the poor in the hospitals, exhorting those around us, each of us according to the different talents he may happen to have, urging on as many as possible to greater piety and prayer. . . .

In their preaching they should not refer to points of conflict between Protestants and Catholics, but simply exhort all to upright conduct and to ecclesiastical practice, urging everyone to full self-knowledge and to greater knowledge and love of their Creator and Lord, with frequent allusions to the Council. At the end of each session, they should (as has been mentioned) lead prayers for the Council.

They should do the same with readings as with sermons, trying their best to influence people with greater love of their Creator and Lord as they explain the meaning of what is read; similarly, they should lead their hearers to pray for the Council. . . .

They should spend some time, as convenient, in the elementary teaching of youngsters, depending on the means and disposition of all involved, and with more or less explanation according to the capacity of the pupils. . . . Let them visit the almshouses once or twice a day, at times that are convenient for the patients' health, hearing confessions and consoling the poor, if possible taking them something, and urging them to the sort of prayers mentioned above for confession. If there are three of ours in Trent, each should visit the poor at least once every four days.

When they are urging people in their dealings with them to go to confession and communion, to say mass frequently, to undertake the Spiritual Exercises and other good works, they should also be urging them to pray for the Council.

It was said that there are advantages in being slow to speak and measured in one's statements when doctrinal definitions are involved. The opposite is true when one is urging people to look to their spiritual progress. Then one should be eloquent and ready to talk, full of sympathy and affection.

## SPREADING GOD'S WORD IN A GERMAN UNIVERSITY, 1549

The aim that they should have above all before their eyes is that intended by the Supreme Pontiff who has sent them: to help the University of Ingolstadt, and as far as is possible the whole of Germany, in all that concerns purity of faith, obedience to the Church, and firmness and soundness of doctrine and upright living. . . .

They must be very competent in them, and teach solid doctrine without many technical terms (which are unpopular), especially if these are hard to understand. The lectures should be learned yet clear, sustained in argument yet not long-winded, and delivered with attention to style. . . . Besides these academic lectures, it seems opportune on feast days to hold sermons on Bible readings, more calculated to move hearts and form consciences than to produce learned minds. . . . They should make efforts to attract their students into a friendship of spiritual quality, and if possible towards confession and making the Spiritual Exercises, even in the full form, if they seem suitable to join the Society....

On occasion they should give time to works of mercy of a more visible character, such as in hospitals and prisons and helping other kinds of poor; such works arouse a "sweet fragrance" in the Lord. Opportunity may also arise to act as peacemakers in quarrels and to teach basic Christian doctrine to the uneducated. Taking account of local conditions and the persons concerned, prudence will dictate whether they should act themselves or through others.

They should make efforts to make friends with the leaders of their opponents, as also with those who are most influential among the heretics or those who are suspected of it yet seem not absolutely immovable. They must try to bring them back from their error by sensitive skill and signs of love.... All must try to have at their finger-tips the main points concerning dogmas of faith that are subjects of controversy with heretics, especially at the time and place when they are present, and with those persons with whom they are dealing. Thus they will be able, whenever opportunity arises, to put forward and defend the Catholic truth, to refute errors and to strengthen the doubtful and wavering, whether by lectures and sermons or in the confessional and in conversations....

It will be helpful to lead people, as far as possible, to open themselves to God's grace, exhorting them to a desire for salvation, to prayer, to alms, and to everything that conduces to receiving grace or increasing it....

Let [the duke] understand also what glory it will mean for him if he is the first to introduce into Germany seminaries in the form of such colleges, to foster sound doctrine and religion.

## The Final Word on Obedience, 1553, to the Brothers in Portugal

To form an idea of the exceptional intrinsic value of this obedience in the eyes of God Our Lord, one should weigh both the worth of the noble sacrifice offered, involving the highest human power, and the completeness of the self-offering undertaken, as one strips oneself of self, becoming a "living victim" pleasing to the Divine Majesty. Another indication is the intensity of the difficulty experienced as one conquers self for love of God, opposing the natural human inclination felt by us all to follow our own opinions....

Let us be unpretentious and let us be gentle! God Our Lord will grant the grace to enable you, gently and lovingly, to maintain constantly the offering you have made to Him....

All that has been said does not exclude your bringing before your superiors a contrary opinion that may have occurred to you, once you have prayed about the matter and you feel that it would be proper and in accord with your respect for God to do so.... Such is the model on which divine Providence "gently disposes all things," so that the lower via the middle, and the middle via the higher, are led to their final ends.... The same can be seen upon the earth with respect to all secular constitutions that are duly established, and with respect to the ecclesiastical hierarchy, which is subordinated to you in virtue of holy obedience to select among the many routes open to you that which will bring you back to Portugal as soon and as safely as possible. So I order you in the name of Christ Our Lord to do this, even if it will be so as to return soon to India. . . . Firstly, you are well aware how important for the upkeep and advancement of Christianity in those lands, as also in Guinea and Brazil, is the good order that the King of Portugal can grant from his kingdom. When a prince of such Christian desires and holy intentions as is the King of Portugal receives information from someone of your experience about the state of affairs in those parts, you can imagine what influence this will have on him to do much more in the service of God Our Lord and for the good of those countries that you will describe to him. . . .

You are also aware how important it is for the good of the Indies that the persons sent there should be suitable for the aim that one is pursuing in those and in other lands. . . . Quite apart from all these reasons, which apply to furthering the good of India, it seems to me that you would fire the King's enthusiasm for the Ethiopian project, which has been planned for so many years without anything effective having been seen. Similarly, with regard to the Congo and Brazil, you could give no small help from Portugal, which you cannot do from India as there are not the same commercial relations. If people in India consider that your presence is important given your post, you can continue to act as superior no less from Portugal than from Japan or China, and probably much better. Just as you have gone away on other occasions for longer periods, do the same now.

### ■ Discussion Questions

1. What does the Catholic life mean to Ignatius?
2. What advice does Ignatius offer about dealing with the problem of heresy?
3. What role will Jesuits play throughout Europe and the rest of the world according to Ignatius's instructions?
4. How does Ignatius think political leaders can be enlisted to support the aims of the reform movement?

## 3.
## Hans Jacob Christoffel von Grimmelshausen
## *The Adventures of a Simpleton*
### 1668–1669

*Lutheranism was not the only challenge posed to the Catholic Church. A second wave of reform gained momentum under the influence of Frenchman John Calvin (1509–1564). Calvin had embraced the reform movement while studying in Paris in*

From Hans Jacob Christoffel von Grimmelshausen, *The Adventures of Simplicius Simplicissimus,* trans. George Schulz-Behrend (Columbia: Camden House, 1993), 6–7.

*1533–1534. Fleeing a government crackdown on Protestantism, Calvin eventually settled in Geneva, where he worked to build a godly city, making it a haven for reformers and a training ground for preachers. From here, Calvin's own brand of evangelical doctrine spread across Europe. The addition of Calvinism into the already heady mix of religious conflict fueled the last and most destructive war of religion, the Thirty Years War (1618–1648), which began in the Holy Roman Empire but eventually involved most European states. Hans Jacob Christoffel von Grimmelshausen (c. 1621–1676) experienced the war firsthand and then wrote about it in his novel,* The Adventures of a Simpleton *(published in six books in 1668–1669). He had been a Lutheran schoolboy when Swedish troops pillaged his town, described in this excerpt. Later he served as a musketeer in the Catholic imperial armies and converted to Catholicism. In the novel, he writes from the point of view of a "simpleton," a naïve peasant who does not understand what is happening around him when in fact he had a keen eye for describing the horrors of war.*

Though I hadn't intended to take the peace-loving reader into my father's home and farm along with these merry cavalrymen, the orderly progress of my tale requires me to make known to posterity the sort of abysmal and unheard-of cruelties occasionally perpetrated in our German war, and to testify by my own example that all these evils were necessarily required for our own good by the kindness of our Lord. For, my dear reader, who would have told me that there is a God in heaven if the warriors hadn't destroyed my knan's house, if they hadn't forced me to be among the people who taught me well enough? Shortly before this event I could neither know nor imagine but that my knan, mother and Ursula, myself and the hired hands were the only humans on earth, for no people or dwellings were known to me except my knan's house, where I went in and out daily. But I soon discovered where people come from, and that they have no permanent abode, but often have to move on again before they can look around. I had been human in shape alone, and a Christian in name only; in reality I was an animal! But the Almighty looked upon my ignorance with forgiving eyes, and wanted me to come to the recognition of both Him and myself. And though he had a thousand different ways for this purpose, undoubtedly he wanted to use as an example to others the manner in which my knan and mother were punished for my negligent upbringing.

The first thing these horsemen did in the nice black rooms of the house was to put in their horses. Then everyone took up a special job, a job having to do with death and destruction. Although some began butchering, heating water, and rendering lard, as if to prepare for a banquet, others raced through the house, ransacking upstairs and down; not even the privy chamber was safe, as if the golden fleece of Colchis might be hidden there. Still others bundled up big bags of cloth, household goods, and clothes, as if they wanted to hold a rummage sale somewhere. What they did not intend to take along they broke and spoiled. Some ran their swords into the hay and straw, as if there hadn't been hogs enough to stick. Some shook the feathers out of beds and put bacon slabs, hams, and other stuff in the ticking, as if they might sleep better on these. Others knocked down the hearth and broke the windows, as if announcing an everlasting summer. They flattened out copper and pewter dishes and baled the ruined goods. They burned up bedsteads, tables, chairs, and benches, though there were yards and yards of dry firewood outside the kitchen. Jars and crocks, pots and casseroles all were broken, either because they preferred their meat broiled or because they thought they'd eat only one meal with us. In the barn, the hired girl was handled so roughly that she was unable to walk away, I am ashamed to report. They stretched the hired man out flat on the ground, stuck a wooden wedge in his mouth to keep it open, and emptied a milk bucket full of stinking manure drippings down his throat; they called it a Swedish cocktail. He didn't relish it and made a very wry face. By this means they forced him to take a raiding party to some other place where they carried off men and cattle and brought them to our farm. Among these were my knan, mother, and Ursula.

Then they used thumbscrews, which they cleverly made out of their pistols, to torture the peasants, as if they wanted to burn witches. Though he had confessed to nothing as yet, they put one of the captured hayseeds in the bake-oven and lighted a fire in it. They put a rope around someone else's head and tightened it like a tourniquet until blood came out of his mouth, nose, and ears. In short, every soldier had his favorite method of making life miserable for peasants, and every peasant had his own misery. My knan was, as I thought, particularly lucky because he confessed with a laugh what others were forced to say in pain and martyrdom. No doubt because he was the head of the household, he was shown special consideration; they put him close to a fire, tied him by his hands and feet, and rubbed damp salt on the bottom of his soles. Our old nanny goat had to lick it off and this so tickled my knan that he could have burst laughing. This seemed so clever and entertaining to me—I had never seen or heard my knan laugh so long—that I joined him in laughter, to keep him company or perhaps to cover up my ignorance. In the midst of such glee he told them the whereabouts of hidden treasure much richer in gold, pearls, and jewelry than might have been expected on a farm.

I can't say much about the captured wives, hired girls, and daughters because the soldiers didn't let me watch their doings. But I do remember hearing pitiful screams from various dark corners and I guess that my mother and our Ursula had it no better than the rest. Amid all this horror I was busy turning a roasting spit and didn't worry about anything, for I didn't know the meaning of it. In the afternoon I helped water the horses and that way got to see our hired girl in the barn. She looked wondrously messed up and at first I didn't recognize her. In a sickly voice she said, "Boy, get out of this place, or the soldiers will take you with them. Try to get away; you can see they are up to no good!" That is all she could say.

## ■ Discussion Questions

1. Grimmelshausen's novel was very popular, appearing in six editions during his lifetime. Based on this passage, why do you think contemporary audiences found the book so appealing?

2. In what ways did Grimmelshausen's religious beliefs shape his account? What does this suggest about his understanding of the novel's broader function?
3. What does his account reveal about the methods of war at the time, and their impact on everyday life?

# 4. Henry IV *Edict of Nantes* 1598

*The promulgation of the Edict of Nantes in 1598 by King Henry IV (r. 1589–1610) marked the end of the French Wars of Religion by recognizing French Protestants as a legally protected religious minority. Drawing largely on earlier edicts of pacification, the Edict of Nantes comprised ninety-two general articles, fifty-six secret articles, and two royal warrants. The two series of articles represented the edict proper and were registered by the highest courts of law in the realm* (parlements). *The following excerpts from the general articles reveal the triumph of political concerns over religious conformity on the one hand, and the limitations of religious tolerance in early modern France on the other.*

Henry, By the Grace of God, King of *France,* and *Navarre,* To all Present, and to Come, greeteth. Among the infinite Mercies that God hath pleased to bestow upon us, that most Signal and Remarkable is, his having given us Power and Strength not to yield to the dreadful Troubles, Confusions, and Disorders, which were found at our coming to this Kingdom, divided into so many Parties and Factions, that the most Legitimate was almost the least, enabling us with Constancy in such manner to oppose the Storm, as in the end to surmount it, reducing this Estate to Peace and Rest. . . . For the general difference among our good Subjects, and the particular evils of the soundest parts of the State, we judged might be easily cured, after the Principal cause (the continuation of the Civil Wars) was taken away, in which we have, by the blessing of God, well and happily succeeded, all Hostility and Wars through the Kingdom being now ceased, and we hope he will also prosper us in our other affairs, which remain to be composed, and that by this means we shall arrive at the establishment of a good Peace, with tranquility and rest. . . . Amongst our said affairs . . . one of the principal hath been, the many complaints we received from divers of our Provinces and Catholick Cities, for that the exercise of the Catholick Religion was not universally re-established, as is provided by Edicts or Statutes heretofore made for the Pacification of the Troubles

From Henry IV, "Edict of Nantes" in Edmund Everard, *The Great Pressures and Grievances of the Protestants in France* (London: 1681); reprinted in *The Assassination of Henry IV,* trans. Joan Spencer (New York: Scribner, 1973), 316–25, 333, 343, 347.

arising from Religion; as also the Supplications and Remonstrances which have been made to us by our Subjects of the reformed Religion, as well upon the execution of what hath been granted by the said former Laws, as that they desire to have some addition for the exercise of their Religion, the liberty of their Consciences and the security of their Persons and Fortunes; presuming to have just reasons for desiring some inlargement of Articles, as not being without great apprehensions, because their Ruine hath been the principal pretext and original foundation of the late Wars, Troubles, and Commotions. Now not to burden us with too much business at once, as also that the fury of War was not compatible with the establishment of Laws, how good soever they might be, we have hitherto deferred from time to time giving remedy herein. But now that it hath pleased God to give us a beginning of enjoying some Rest, we think we cannot imploy our self better, than to apply to that which may tend to the glory and service of his holy name, and to provide that he may be adored and prayed unto by all our Subjects: and if it hath not yet pleased him to permit it to be in one and the same form of Religion, that it may at the least be with one and the same intention, and with such rules that may prevent amongst them all troubles and tumults. . . . For this cause . . . we have upon the whole judged it necessary to give to all our said Subjects one general Law, Clear, Pure, and Absolute, by which they shall be regulated in all differences which have heretofore risen among them, or may hereafter rise, wherewith the one and other may be contented, being framed according as the time requires: and having had no other regard in this deliberation than solely the Zeal we have to the service of God, praying that he would henceforward render to all our subjects a durable and Established peace. . . . We have by this Edict or Statute perpetual and irrevocable said, declared, and ordained, saying, declaring, and ordaining;

That the memory of all things passed on the one part and the other, since the beginning of the month of *March,* 1585. Until our coming to the Crown, and also during the other precedent troubles, and the occasion of the same, shall remain extinguished and suppressed, as things that had never been. . . .

We prohibit to all our Subjects of what State and Condition soever they be, to renew the memory thereof, to attaque, resent, injure, or provoke one the other by reproaches for what is past, under any pretext or cause whatsoever, by disputing, contesting, quarrelling, reviling, or offending by factious words; but to contain themselves, and live peaceably together as Brethren, Friends, and fellow-Citizens, upon penalty for acting to the contrary, to be punished for breakers of Peace, and disturbers of the public quiet.

We ordain, that the Catholick Religion shall be restored and re-established in all places, and quarters of this Kingdom and Countrey under our obedience, and where the exercise of the same hath been intermitted, to be there again, peaceably and freely exercised without any trouble or impediment. . . .

And not to leave any occasion of trouble and difference among our Subjects, we have permitted and do permit to those of the Reformed Religion, to live and dwell in all the Cities and places of this our Kingdom and Countreys under our obedience, without being inquired after, vexed, molested, or compelled to do any thing in Religion, contrary to their Conscience. . . .

We permit also to those of the said Religion to hold, and continue the Exercise of the same in all the Cities and Places under our obedience, where it hath by them been Established and made public by many and divers times, in the Year 1586, and in 1597, until the end of the Month of *August*. . . .

In like manner the said Exercise may be Established, and re-established in all the Cities and Places where it hath been established, or ought to be by the Statute of Pacification, made in the Year 1577. . . .

As also not to exercise the said Religion in our Court, nor in our Territories and Countries beyond the Mountains, nor in our City of *Paris,* nor within five Leagues of the said City. . . .

We prohibit all Preachers, Readers, and others who speak in public, to use any words, discourse, or propositions tending to excite the People to Sedition; and we enjoin them to contain and comport themselves modestly, and to say nothing which shall not be for the instruction and edification of the Auditors, and maintaining the peace and tranquillity established by us in our said Kingdom. . . .

They [French Protestants] shall also be obliged to keep and observe the Festivals of the Catholick Church, and shall not on the same dayes work, sell, or keep open shop, nor likewise the Artisans shall not work out of their shops, in their chambers or houses privately on the said Festivals, and other dayes forbidden, of any trade, the noise whereof may be heard without by those that pass by, or by the Neighbors. . . .

We ordain, that there shall not be made any difference or distinction upon the account of the said Religion, in receiving Scholars to be instructed in the Universities, Colledges, or Schools, nor of the sick or poor into Hospitals, sick houses or public Almshouses. . . .

We Will and Ordain, that all those of the Reformed Religion, and others who have followed their party, of what State, Quality or Condition soever they be, shall be obliged and constrained by all due and reasonable wayes, and under the penalties contained in the said Edict or Statute relating thereunto, to pay tythes to the Curates, and other Ecclesiasticks, and to all others to whom they shall appertain. . . .

To the end to re-unite so much the better the minds and good will of our Subjects, as is our intention, and to take away all complaints for the future; We declare all those who make or shall make profession of the said Reformed Religion, to be capable of holding and exercising all Estates, Dignities, Offices, and public charges whatsoever. . . .

We declare all Sentences, Judgments, Procedures, Seisures, Sales, and Decrees made and given against those of the Reformed Religion, as well living as dead, from the death of the deceased King *Henry* the Second our most honored Lord and Father in Law, upon the occasion of the said Religion, Tumults and Troubles since happening, as also the execution of the same Judgments and Decrees, from henceforward cancelled, revoked, and annulled. . . .

Those also of the said Religion shall depart and desist henceforward from all Practices, Negotiations, and Intelligences, as well within as without our Kingdom; and the said Assemblies and Councels established within the Provinces, shall readily separate, and also all the Leagues and Associations made or to be made under what pretext soever, to the prejudice of our present Edict, shall be cancelled and annulled, . . . prohibiting most expresly to all our Subjects to make henceforwards any Assesments or Leavy's of Money, Fortifications, Enrolments of men, Congregations and Assemblies of other than such as are permitted by our present Edict, and without Arms. . . .

We give in command to the People of our said Courts of Parliaments, Chambers of our Courts, and Courts of our Aids, Bayliffs, Chief-Justices, Provosts and other our Justices and Officers to whom it appertains, and to their Leivetenants, that they cause to be read, published, and Registred this present Edict and Ordinance in their Courts and Jurisdictions, and the same keep punctually, and the contents of the same to cause to be injoyned and used fully and peaceably to all those to whom it shall belong, ceasing and making to cease all troubles and obstructions to the contrary, for such is our pleasure: and in witness hereof we have signed these presents with our own hand; and to the end to make it a thing firm and stable for ever, we have caused to put and indorse our Seal to the same. Given at *Nantes* in the Month of *April* in the year of Grace 1598. and of our Reign the ninth

Signed

HENRY

### ■ Discussion Questions

1. What are the edict's principal objectives?
2. In what ways does the edict balance the demands of both French Catholics and Protestants?
3. What limits does the edict place on Protestants' religious rights?
4. Did Henry IV regard this edict as a permanent solution to the religious divisions in the realm? Why or why not?

## 5.
## Galileo
## *Letter to the Grand Duchess Christina*
### 1615

*Italian-born and educated, Galileo Galilei (1564–1642) was among the most illustrious proponents of the new science in the seventeenth century. Early in his studies, he embraced the theory held by Nicolaus Copernicus (1473–1543) that the sun, not the earth, was at the center of the universe. Having improved on the newly invented telescope in 1609, Galileo was able to substantiate the heliocentric view through his observations of*

From *Discoveries and Opinions of Galileo,* trans. Stillman Drake (New York: Doubleday, 1957), 175–86.

*the moon and planets. Because Galileo's work challenged both traditional religious and scientific views, it sparked considerable controversy. In the letter excerpted here, written in 1615 to the Grand Duchess Christina of Tuscany, an important Catholic patron of learning, Galileo defends the validity of his findings while striving to separate scriptural authority from the study of natural phenomena.*

## GALILEO GALILEI TO THE MOST SERENE GRAND DUCHESS MOTHER:

Some years ago, as Your Serene Highness well knows, I discovered in the heavens many things that had not been seen before our own age. The novelty of these things, as well as some consequences which followed from them in contradiction to the physical notions commonly held among academic philosophers, stirred up against me no small number of professors—as if I had placed these things in the sky with my own hands in order to upset nature and overturn the sciences. . . .

Well, the passage of time has revealed to everyone the truths that I previously set forth. . . . But some, besides allegiance to their original error, possess I know not what fanciful interest in remaining hostile not so much toward the things in question as toward their discoverer. No longer being able to deny them, these men now take refuge in obstinate silence, but being more than ever exasperated by that which has pacified and quieted other men, they divert their thoughts to other fancies and seek new ways to damage me. . . .

Persisting in their original resolve to destroy me and everything mine by any means they can think of, these men are aware of my views in astronomy and philosophy. They know that as to the arrangement of the parts of the universe, I hold the sun to be situated motionless in the center of the revolution of the celestial orbs while the earth rotates on its axis and revolves about the sun. . . .

Now as to the false aspersions which they so unjustly seek to cast upon me, I have thought it necessary to justify myself in the eyes of all men, whose judgment in matters of religion and of reputation I must hold in great esteem. I shall therefore discourse of the particulars which these men produce to make this opinion detested and to have it condemned not merely as false but as heretical. To this end they make a shield of their hypocritical zeal for religion. They go about invoking the Bible, which they would have minister to their deceitful purposes. Contrary to the sense of the Bible and the intention of the holy Fathers, if I am not mistaken, they would extend such authorities until even in purely physical matters—where faith is not involved—they would have us altogether abandon reason and the evidence of our senses in favor of some biblical passage, though under the surface meaning of its words this passage may contain a different sense. . . .

The reason produced for condemning the opinion that the earth moves and the sun stands still is that in many places in the Bible one may read that the sun moves and the earth stands still. Since the Bible cannot err, it follows as a necessary consequence that anyone takes an erroneous and heretical position who maintains that the sun is inherently motionless and the earth movable.

With regard to this argument, I think in the first place that it is very pious to say and prudent to affirm that the holy Bible can never speak untruth—whenever its true meaning is understood. But I believe nobody will deny that it is often very abstruse, and may say things which are quite different from what its bare words signify. Hence in expounding the Bible if one were always to confine oneself to the unadorned grammatical meaning, one might fall into error. Not only contradictions and propositions far from true might thus be made to appear in the Bible, but even grave heresies and follies. Thus it would be necessary to assign to God feet, hands, and eyes, as well as corporeal and human affections, such as anger, repentance, hatred, and sometimes even the forgetting of things past and ignorance of those to come. These propositions uttered by the Holy Ghost were set down in that manner by the sacred scribes in order to accommodate them to the capacities of the common people, who are rude and unlearned. For the sake of those who deserve to be separated from the herd, it is necessary that wise expositors should produce the true senses of such passages, together with the special reasons for which they were set down in these words. This doctrine is so widespread and so definite with all theologians that it would be superfluous to adduce evidence for it.

Hence I think that I may reasonably conclude that whenever the Bible has occasion to speak of any physical conclusion (especially those which are very abstruse and hard to understand), the rule has been observed of avoiding confusion in the minds of the common people which would render them contumacious toward the higher mysteries. Now the Bible, merely to condescend to popular capacity, has not hesitated to obscure some very important pronouncements, attributing to God himself some qualities extremely remote from (and even contrary to) His essence. Who, then, would positively declare that this principle has been set aside, and the Bible has confined itself rigorously to the bare and restricted sense of its words, when speaking but casually of the earth, of water, of the sun, or of any other created thing? Especially in view of the fact that these things in no way concern the primary purpose of the sacred writings, which is the service of God and the salvation of souls—matters infinitely beyond the comprehension of the common people.

This being granted, I think that in discussions of physical problems we ought to begin not from the authority of scriptural passages, but from sense-experiences and necessary demonstrations; for the holy Bible and the phenomena of nature proceed alike from the divine Word, the former as the dictate of the Holy Ghost and the latter as the observant executrix of God's commands. It is necessary for the Bible, in order to be accommodated to the understanding of every man, to speak many things which appear to differ from the absolute truth so far as the bare meaning of the words is concerned. But Nature, on the other hand, is inexorable and immutable; she never transgresses the laws imposed upon her, or cares a whit whether her abstruse reasons and methods of operations are understandable to men. For that reason it appears that nothing physical which sense-experience sets before our eyes, or which necessary demonstrations prove to us, ought to be called in question (much less condemned) upon the testimony of biblical passages which may have some different meaning beneath their words. For the Bible is not chained in every expression to conditions as strict as those which govern all physical effects; nor is God any less excellently revealed in Nature's actions than in the sacred statements of the Bible. . . .

From this I do not mean to infer that we need not have an extraordinary esteem for the passages of holy Scripture. On the contrary, having arrived at any certainties in physics, we ought to utilize these as the most appropriate aids in the true exposition of the Bible and in the investigation of those meanings which are necessarily contained therein, for these must be concordant with demonstrated truths. I should judge that the authority of the Bible was designed to persuade men of those articles and propositions which, surpassing all human reasoning, could not be made credible by science, or by any other means than through the very mouth of the Holy Spirit.

Yet even in those propositions which are not matters of faith, this authority ought to be preferred over that of all human writings which are supported only by bare assertions or probable arguments, and not set forth in a demonstrative way. This I hold to be necessary and proper to the same extent that divine wisdom surpasses all human judgment and conjecture.

But I do not feel obliged to believe that that same God who has endowed us with senses, reason, and intellect has intended to forgo their use and by some other means to give us knowledge which we can attain by them. He would not require us to deny sense and reason in physical matters which are set before our eyes and minds by direct experience or necessary demonstrations. This must be especially true in those sciences of which but the faintest trace (and that consisting of conclusions) is to be found in the Bible. Of astronomy, for instance, so little is found that none of the planets except Venus are so much as mentioned, and this only once or twice under the name of "Lucifer." If the sacred scribes had had any intention of teaching people certain arrangements and motions of the heavenly bodies, or had they wished us to derive such knowledge from the Bible, then in my opinion they would not have spoken of these matters so sparingly in comparison with the infinite number of admirable conclusions which are demonstrated in that science. . . .

From these things it follows as a necessary consequence that, since the Holy Ghost did not intend to teach us whether heaven moves or stands still, whether its shape is spherical or like a discus or extended in a plane, nor whether the earth is located at its center or off to one side, then so much the less was it intended to settle for us any other conclusion of the same kind. And the motion or rest of the earth and the sun is so closely linked with the things just named, that without a determination of the one, neither side can be taken in the other matters. Now if the Holy Spirit has purposely neglected to teach us propositions of this sort as irrelevant to the highest goal (that is, to our salvation), how can anyone affirm that it is obligatory to take sides on them, and that one belief is required by faith, while the other side is erroneous? Can an opinion be heretical and yet have no concern with the salvation of souls? Can the Holy Ghost be asserted not to have intended teaching us something that does concern our salvation? I would say here something that was heard from an ecclesiastic of the most eminent degree: "That the intention of the Holy Ghost is to teach us how one goes to heaven, not how heaven goes." . . .

From this it is seen that the interpretation which we impose upon passages of Scripture would be false whenever it disagreed with demonstrated truths. And therefore we should seek the incontrovertible sense of the Bible with the assistance of demonstrated truth, and not in any way try to force the hand of Nature or deny experiences and rigorous proofs in accordance with the mere sound of words that may appeal to our frailty. . . .

To that end they would forbid him the use of reason, divine gift of Providence, and would abuse the just authority of holy Scripture—which, in the general opinion of theologians, can never oppose manifest experiences and necessary demonstrations when rightly understood and applied. If I am correct, it will stand them in no stead to go running to the Bible to cover up their inability to understand (let alone resolve) their opponents' arguments.

### ■ Discussion Questions

1. What do you think Galileo's goal in writing this letter to the Grand Duchess was?
2. What is the basis of the attacks by Galileo's critics?
3. According to Galileo, what role should the Bible play in scientific inquiry?
4. How does this document lend support to historians who have credited Galileo for helping to popularize the principles and methods of the new science?

## 6.
## *The Trial of Suzanne Gaudry*
### 1652

*Even as the new science gained support, most Europeans continued to believe in demonic "black magic," especially at this time of religious wars, economic decline, and social strife. This belief found violent expression in a wave of witchcraft persecutions across Europe between 1560 and 1640. The following selections from the trial records of Suzanne Gaudry attest to the predominant notion that witches were agents of the devil. Although conducted at a time when the number of witch hunts and persecutions were in decline, her trial attests to the persistence of a deeply felt fear among many people regarding the presence of diabolical forces in everyday life.*

---

From Alan C. Kors and Edward Peters, eds., *Witchcraft in Europe, 1100–1700: A Documentary History* (Philadelphia: University of Pennsylvania Press, 1972), 266–75.

*At Ronchain, May 28, 1652. . . . Interrogation of Suzanne Gaudry, prisoner at the court of Rieux.* Questioned about her age, her place of origin, her mother and father.

—Said that she is named Suzanne Gaudry, daughter of Jean Gaudry and Marguerite Gerné, both natives of Rieux, but that she is from Esgavans, near Odenarde, where her family had taken refuge because of the wars, that she was born the day that they made bonfires for the Peace between France and Spain, without being able otherwise to say her age.

Asked why she has been taken here.

—Answers that it is for the salvation of her soul.

—Says that she was frightened of being taken prisoner for the crime of witchcraft.

Asked for how long she has been in the service of the devil.

—Says that about twenty-five or twenty-six years ago she was his lover, that he called himself Petit-Grignon, that he would wear black breeches, that he gave her the name Magin, that she gave him a pin with which he gave her his mark on the left shoulder, that he had a little flat hat; said also that he had his way with her two or three times only.

Asked how many times she has been at the nocturnal dance.

—Answers that she has been there about a dozen times, having first of all renounced God, Lent and baptism; that the site of the dance was at the little marsh of Rieux, understanding that there were diverse dances. The first time, she did not recognize anyone there, because she was half blind. The other times, she saw and recognized there Noelle and Pasquette Gerné, Noelle the wife of Nochin Quinchou and the other of Paul Doris, the widow Marie Nourette, not having recognized others because the young people went with the young people and the old people with the old. [ . . . ]

Interrogated on how and in what way they danced.

—Says that they dance in an ordinary way, that there was a guitarist and some whistlers who appeared to be men she did not know; which lasted about an hour, and then everyone collapsed from exhaustion.

Inquired what happened after the dance.

—Says that they formed a circle, that there was a king with a long black beard dressed in black, with a red hat, who made everyone do his bidding, and that after the dance he made a . . . [the word is missing in the text], and then everyone disappeared. . . .

Questioned if she has abused the Holy Communion.

—Says no, never, and that she has always swallowed it. Then says that her lover asked her for it several times, but that she did not want to give it to him.

After several admonitions were sent to her, she has signed this

Mark
X
Suzanne Gaudry

## Second Interrogation, May 29, 1652, in the Presence of the Afore-mentioned

This prisoner, being brought back into the chamber, was informed about the facts and the charges and asked if what she declared and confessed yesterday is true.
—Answers that if it is in order to put her in prison it is not true; then after having remained silent said that it is true.
Asked what is her lover's name and what name has he given himself.
—Said that his name is Grinniou and that he calls himself Magnin.
Asked where he found her the first time and what he did to her.
—Answers that it was in her lodgings, that he had a hide, little black breeches, and a little flat hat; that he asked her for a pin, which she gave to him, with which he made his mark on her left shoulder. Said also that at the time she took him oil in a bottle and that she had thoughts of love.
Asked how long she has been in subjugation to the devil.
—Says that it has been about twenty-five or twenty-six years, that her lover also then made her renounce God, Lent, and baptism, that he has known her carnally three or four times, and that he has given her satisfaction. And on the subject of his having asked her if she wasn't afraid of having a baby, says that she did not have that thought.
Asked how many times she found herself at the nocturnal dance and carol and who she recognized there.
—Answers that she was there eleven or twelve times, that she went there on foot with her lover, where the third time she saw and recognized Pasquette and Noelle Gerné, and Marie Homitte, to whom she never spoke, for the reason that they did not speak to each other. And that the sabbat took place at the little meadow. . . .

Asked what occurred at the dance and afterwards.
—Says that right after the dance they put themselves in order and approached the chief figure, who had a long black beard, dressed also in black, with a red hat, at which point they were given some powder, to do with it what they wanted; but that she did not want to take any.
Charged with having taken some and with having used it evilly.
—Says, after having insisted that she did not want to take any, that she took some, and that her lover advised her to do evil with it; but that she did not want to do it.
Asked if, not obeying his orders, she was beaten or threatened by him, and what did she do with this powder.
—Answers that never was she beaten; she invoked the name of the Virgin [and answered] that she threw away the powder that she had, not having wanted to do any evil with it.
Pressed to say what she did with this powder. Did she not fear her lover too much to have thrown it away?
—Says, after having been pressed on this question, that she made the herbs in her garden die at the end of the summer, five to six years ago, by means of the powder, which she threw there because she did not know what to do with it. [ . . . ]

Charged once more with having performed some malefice with this powder, pressed to tell the truth.
—Answers that she never made any person or beast die; then later said that she made Philippe Cornié's red horse die, about two or three years ago, by means of the powder, which she placed where he had to pass, in the street close to her home.
Asked why she did that and if she had had any difficulty with him.
—Says that she had had some difficulty with his wife, because her cow had eaten the leeks.[ . . . ]

After having been admonished to think of her conscience, was returned to prison after having signed this

Mark
X
Suzanne Gaudry

## DELIBERATION OF THE COURT OF MONS—JUNE 3, 1652

The under-signed advocates of the Court of Mons have seen these interrogations and answers. They say that the aforementioned Suzanne Gaudry confesses that she is a witch, that she has given herself to the devil, that she has renounced God, Lent, and baptism, that she has been marked on the shoulder, that she has cohabited with him and that she has been to the dances, confessing only to have cast a spell upon and caused to die a beast of Philippe Cornié; but there is no evidence for this, excepting a prior statement. For this reason, before going further, it will be necessary to become acquainted with, to examine and to probe the mark, and to hear Philippe Cornié on the death of the horse and on when and in what way he died. . . .

## DELIBERATION OF THE COURT OF MONS—JUNE 13, 1652

[The Court] has reviewed the current criminal trial of Suzanne Gaudry, and with it the trial of Antoinette Lescouffre, also a prisoner of the same office.

It appeared [to the Court] that the office should have the places probed where the prisoners say that they have received the mark of the devil, and after that, they must be interrogated and examined seriously on their confessions and denials, this having to be done, in order to regulate all this definitively. . . .

## DELIBERATION OF THE COURT OF MONS—JUNE 22, 1652

The trials of Antoinette Lescouffre and Suzanne Gaudry having been described to the undersigned, advocates of the Court of Mons, and [the Court] having been told orally that the peasants taking them to prison had persuaded them to confess in order to avoid imprisonment, and that they would be let go, by virtue of which it could appear that the confessions were not so spontaneous:

They are of the opinion that the office, in its duty, would do well, following the two preceding resolutions, to have the places of the marks that they have taught us about probed, and if it is found that these are ordinary marks of the devil, one can proceed to their examination; then next to the first confessions, and if they deny [these], one can proceed to the torture, given that they issue from bewitched relatives, that at all times they have been suspect, that they fled to avoid the crime [that is to say, prosecution for the crime of witchcraft], and that by their confessions they have confirmed [their guilt], notwithstanding that they have wanted to revoke [their confessions] and vacillate. . . .

## THIRD INTERROGATION, JUNE 27, IN THE PRESENCE OF THE AFORE-MENTIONED

This prisoner being led into the chamber, she was examined to know if things were not as she had said and confessed at the beginning of her imprisonment.
—Answers no, and that what she has said was done so by force.
Asked if she did not say to Jean Gradé that she would tell his uncle, the mayor, that he had better be careful . . . and that he was a Frank.
—Said that that is not true.
Pressed to say the truth, that otherwise she would be subjected to torture, having pointed out to her that her aunt was burned for this same subject.
—Answers that she is not a witch.
Interrogated as to how long she has been in subjection to the devil, and pressed that she was to renounce the devil and the one who misled her.
—Says that she is not a witch, that she has nothing to do with the devil thus that she did not want to renounce the devil, saying that he has not misled her, and upon inquisition of having confessed to being present at the carol, she insisted that although she had said that, it is not true, and that she is not a witch.
Charged with having confessed to having made a horse die by means of a powder that the devil had given her.
—Answers that she said it, but because she found herself during the inquisition pressed to say that she must have done some evil deed; and after several admonitions to tell the truth:

She was placed in the hands of the officer of the *haultes oeuvres* [the officer in charge of torture], throwing herself on her knees, struggling to cry, uttering several exclamations, without being able, nevertheless, to shed a tear. Saying at every moment that she is not a witch.

## THE TORTURE

On this same day, being at the place of torture.

This prisoner, before being strapped down, was admonished to maintain herself in her first confessions and to renounce her lover.
—Said that she denies everything she has said, and that she has no lover. Feeling herself being strapped down, says that she is not a witch, while struggling to cry.
Asked why she fled outside the village of Rieux.

—Says that she cannot say it, that God and the Virgin Mary forbid her to; that she is not a witch. And upon being asked why she confessed to being one, said that she was forced to say it.

Told that she was not forced, that on the contrary she declared herself to be a witch without any threat.

—Says that she confessed it and that she is not a witch, and being a little stretched [on the rack] screams ceaselessly that she is not a witch, invoking the name of Jesus and of Our Lady of Grace, not wanting to say any other thing.

Asked if she did not confess that she had been a witch for twenty-six years.

—Says that she said it, that she retracts it, crying Jésus-Maria, that she is not a witch.

Asked if she did not make Philippe Cornié's horse die, as she confessed.

—Answers no, crying Jésus-Maria, that she is not a witch.

The mark having been probed by the officer, in the presence of Doctor Bouchain, it was adjudged by the aforesaid doctor and officer truly to be the mark of the devil.

Being more tightly stretched upon the torture-rack, urged to maintain her confessions.

—Said that it was true that she is a witch and that she would maintain what she had said.

Asked how long she has been in subjugation to the devil.

—Answers that it was twenty years ago that the devil appeared to her, being in her lodgings in the form of a man dressed in a little cow-hide and black breeches.

Interrogated as to what her lover was called.

—Says that she said Petit-Grignon, then, being taken down [from the rack] says upon interrogation that she is not a witch and that she can say nothing.

Asked if her lover has had carnal copulation with her, and how many times.

—To that she did not answer anything; then, making believe that she was ill, not another word could be drawn from her.

As soon as she began to confess, she asked who was alongside of her, touching her, yet none of those present could see anyone there. And it was noticed that as soon as that was said, she no longer wanted to confess anything.

Which is why she was returned to prison.

## Verdict

### July 9, 1652

In the light of the interrogations, answers and investigations made into the charge against Suzanne Gaudry, coupled with her confessions, from which it would appear that she has always been ill-reputed for being stained with the crime of witchcraft, and seeing that she took flight and sought refuge in this city of Valenciennes, out of fear of being apprehended by the law for this matter; seeing how her close family were also stained with the same crime, and the perpetrators executed; seeing by her own confessions that she is said to have made a pact with the devil, received the mark from him, which in the report of *sieur* Michel de Roux was judged by the medical doctor of Ronchain and the officer of *haultes oeuvres* of Cambrai, after having proved it, to be not a natural mark but a mark of the devil, to which they have sworn with an oath; and that following this, she had renounced God, Lent, and baptism and had let herself be known carnally by him, in which she received satisfaction. Also, seeing that she is said to have been a part of nocturnal carols and dances. Which are crimes of divine lèse-majesty:

For expiation of which the advice of the under-signed is that the office of Rieux can legitimately condemn the aforesaid Suzanne Gaudry to death, tying her to a gallows, and strangling her to death, then burning her body and burying it there in the environs of the woods.

At Valenciennes, the 9th of July, 1652. To each [member of the Court] 4 *livres*, 16 *sous*. . . . And for the trip of the aforementioned Roux, including an escort of one soldier, 30 *livres*.

## ■ Discussion Questions

1. According to the trial record, why was Suzanne Gaudry targeted for persecution? What does this reveal about contemporary beliefs in witches and their powers?
2. How would you characterize the legal procedures used in this trial? How might the procedures help to explain the widespread consistency in the content of confessions throughout the period of witchcraft persecutions?
3. What does this document suggest about the religious anxieties of the times?

## ■ Comparative Questions

1. What similarities and/or differences do you see between Luther and Ignatius's models of Christian life?
2. What do *The Adventures of a Simpleton* and the witchcraft trial suggest about the role of violence in seventeenth-century European society and culture?
3. How do the Edict of Nantes and Galileo's letter support scholars who argue that amid the conflicts of this period, many European leaders and thinkers increasingly gave precedence to secular concerns over religious ones?
4. Despite a gradual trend toward secularization in seventeenth-century Europe, what do *The Adventures of a Simpleton*, the Edict of Nantes, Galileo's letter, and Suzanne Gaudry's trial records reveal about the continued importance of religion in shaping Europeans' understanding of the everyday world?
5. In what ways is Galileo's emphasis on the value of observation and personal experience reflected in the procedures of the Gaudry trial? What does this suggest about the impact of the new science on traditional beliefs?

Chapter

# 13

# State Building and the Search for Order, 1648–1690

THE WARS OVER RELIGION not only had left bitter memories in late seventeenth-century Europe but also had ruined economies and weakened governments. In response, many people sought to impose order on the turbulent world in a variety of ways. As the first four documents reveal, politically, the quest for stability fueled the development of two rival systems of state building—absolutism and constitutionalism—with France and England, respectively, taking the lead. Despite their differences, rulers within both systems centralized power and expanded bureaucracies, casting an increasingly wide net over their subjects' lives. Although not everyone submitted willingly to the expansion of state power, such resistance was typically fruitless. Even so, as the final document suggests, the emergence of a new literary genre—the novel—during this period points to other, less overt forces countering the search for order.

## 1.
## Louis de Rouvroy, Duke of Saint-Simon
## *Memoirs*
## 1694–1723

*A nobleman and godson of King Louis XIV (r. 1643–1715), Louis de Rouvroy (1675–1755), the Duke of Saint-Simon, was raised at the royal palace of Versailles. He recorded his life and impressions of the court for almost three decades, beginning at the age of nineteen. The result was his multivolume* Memoirs, *which painted an intimate portrait of Louis XIV and the workings of the absolutist state. Louis de Rouvroy was not an entirely objective observer, however. Having never achieved great success within the court, he often viewed it through the lens of his own resentment. The excerpt here provides insight into both the reasons behind Louis XIV's move to Versailles and his method of rule there.*

From *The Memoirs of the Duke of Saint Simon,* vol. II, trans. Bayle St. John (Philadelphia: Gebbie and Co., 1890), 363–69.

Let me touch now upon some other incidents in his career, and upon some points in his character.

He early showed a disinclination for Paris. The troubles that had taken place there during the minority made him regard the place as dangerous; he wished, too, to render himself venerable by hiding himself from the eyes of the multitude; all these considerations fixed him at St. Germains soon after the death of the Queen, his mother. It was to that place he began to attract the world by fêtes and gallantries, and by making it felt that he wished to be often seen.

His love for Madame de la Vallière, which was at first kept secret, occasioned frequent excursions to Versailles, then a little card castle, which had been built by Louis XIII.—annoyed, and his suite still more so, at being frequently obliged to sleep in a wretched inn there, after he had been out hunting in the forest of Saint Leger. That monarch rarely slept at Versailles more than one night, and then from necessity; the King, his son, slept there, so that he might be more in private with his mistress; pleasures unknown to the hero and just man, worthy son of Saint Louis, who built the little château.

These excursions of Louis XIV. by degrees gave birth to those immense buildings he erected at Versailles; and their convenience for a numerous court, so different from the apartments at St. Germains, led him to take up his abode there entirely shortly after the death of the Queen. He built an infinite number of apartments, which were asked for by those who wished to pay their court to him; whereas at St. Germains nearly everybody was obliged to lodge in the town, and the few who found accommodation at the château were strangely inconvenienced.

The frequent fêtes, the private promenades at Versailles, the journeys, were means on which the King seized in order to distinguish or mortify the courtiers, and thus render them more assiduous in pleasing him. He felt that of real favors he had not enough to bestow; in order to keep up the spirit of devotion, he therefore unceasingly invented all sorts of ideal ones, little preferences and petty distinctions, which answered his purpose as well.

He was exceedingly jealous of the attention paid him. Not only did he notice the presence of the most distinguished courtiers, but those of inferior degree also. He looked to the right and to the left, not only upon rising but upon going to bed, at his meals, in passing through his apartments, or his gardens of Versailles, where alone the courtiers were allowed to follow him; he saw and noticed everybody; not one escaped him, not even those who hoped to remain unnoticed. He marked well all absentees from the court, found out the reason of their absence, and never lost an opportunity of acting towards them as the occasion might seem to justify. With some of the courtiers (the most distinguished), it was a demerit not to make the court their ordinary abode; with others 'twas a fault to come but rarely; for those who never or scarcely ever came it was certain disgrace. When their names were in any way mentioned, "I do not know them," the King would reply haughtily. Those who presented themselves but seldom were thus characterized: "They are people I never see"; these decrees were irrevocable. He could not bear people who liked Paris.

Louis XIV took great pains to be well informed of all that passed everywhere; in the public places, in the private houses, in society and familiar intercourse. His spies and tell-tales were infinite. He had them of all species; many who were ignorant that their information reached him; others who knew it; others who wrote to him direct, sending their letters through channels he indicated; and all these letters were seen by him alone, and always before everything else; others who sometimes spoke to him secretly in his cabinet, entering by the back stairs. These unknown means ruined an infinite number of people of all classes who never could discover the cause; often ruined them very unjustly; for the King, once prejudiced, never altered his opinion, or so rarely, that nothing was more rare. He had, too, another fault, very dangerous for others and often for himself, since it deprived him of good subjects. He had an excellent memory; in this way, that if he saw a man who, twenty years before, perhaps, had in some manner offended him, he did not forget the man, though he might forget the offense. This was enough, however, to exclude the person from all favor. The representations of a minister, of a general, of his confessor even, could not move the King. He would not yield.

The most cruel means by which the King was informed of what was passing—for many years before anybody knew it—was that of opening letters. The promptitude and dexterity with which they were opened passes understanding. He saw extracts from all the letters in which there were passages that the chiefs of the post-office, and then the minister who governed it, thought ought to go before him; entire letters, too, were sent to him, when their contents seemed to justify the sending. Thus the chiefs of the post, nay, the principal clerks were in a position to suppose what they pleased and against whom they pleased. A word of contempt against the King or the government, a joke, a detached phrase, was enough. It is incredible how many people, justly or unjustly, were more or less ruined, always without resource, without trial, and without knowing why. The secret was impenetrable; for nothing ever cost the King less than profound silence and dissimulation. . . .

He liked splendor, magnificence, and profusion in everything: you pleased him if you shone through the brilliancy of your houses, your clothes, your table, your equipages. Thus a taste for extravagance and luxury was disseminated through all classes of society; causing infinite harm, and leading to general confusion of rank and to ruin.

## ■ Discussion Questions

1. How did Louis XIV use court etiquette as a form of power?
2. Why might nobles have resided at Versailles? What benefits did they gain?
3. What is Saint-Simon's attitude toward Louis XIV's style of governing?
4. In what ways did court life embody the principles of absolutism?

## 2.
## British Parliament
## *The English Bill of Rights*
### 1689

*King Louis XIV (r. 1643–1715) had many admirers in Europe, including King James II (r. 1685–1688) of England. Unlike Louis, however, James faced a major challenge to his power: Parliament. James and Parliament had been at odds for decades concerning the nature of royal authority, and James's absolutist policies proved too much for Parliament to bear. As a result, in 1688 they ousted the king and offered the throne to Prince William of Orange (1650–1702) and his wife, Mary (1662–1694), the eldest of James's adult daughters. In exchange, William and Mary agreed to accept the Bill of Rights, which legally defined the role of Parliament as the monarchy's partner in government. The bill not only marked the victory of constitutionalism over absolutism in England but also formed the cornerstone of the idea that government should ensure certain rights by law to protect its citizens from the dangers of arbitrary power.*

Whereas the said late King James II having abdicated the government, and the throne being thereby vacant, his Highness the prince of Orange (whom it hath pleased Almighty God to make the glorious instrument of delivering this kingdom from popery and arbitrary power) did (by the advice of the lords spiritual and temporal, and diverse principal persons of the Commons) cause letters to be written to the lords spiritual and temporal, being Protestants, and other letters to the several counties, cities, universities, boroughs, and Cinque Ports, for the choosing of such persons to represent them, as were of right to be sent to parliament, to meet and sit at Westminster upon the two and twentieth day of January, in this year 1689, in order to such an establishment as that their religion, laws, and liberties might not again be in danger of being subverted; upon which letters elections have been accordingly made.

And thereupon the said lords spiritual and temporal and Commons, pursuant to their respective letters and elections, being now assembled in a full and free representation of this nation, taking into their most serious consideration the best means for attaining the ends aforesaid, do in the first place (as their ancestors in like case have usually done), for the vindication and assertion of their ancient rights and liberties, declare:

1. That the pretended power of suspending laws, or the execution of laws, by regal authority, without consent of parliament is illegal.

2. That the pretended power of dispensing with the laws, or the execution of law by regal authority, as it hath been assumed and exercised of late, is illegal.

---

From Great Britain, *The Statutes,* vol. II, rev. ed. (London: Eyre and Spottiswoode, 1871), 10–12.

3. That the commission for erecting the late court of commissioners for ecclesiastical causes, and all other commissions and courts of like nature, are illegal and pernicious.

4. That levying money for or to the use of the crown by pretense of prerogative, without grant of parliament, for longer time or in other manner than the same is or shall be granted, is illegal.

5. That it is the right of the subjects to petition the king, and all commitments and prosecutions for such petitioning are illegal.

6. That the raising or keeping a standing army within the kingdom in time of peace, unless it be with consent of parliament, is against law.

7. That the subjects which are Protestants may have arms for their defense suitable to their conditions, and as allowed by law.

8. That election of members of parliament ought to be free.

9. That the freedom of speech, and debates or proceedings in parliament, ought not to be impeached or questioned in any court or place out of parliament.

10. That excessive bail ought not to be required, nor excessive fines imposed, nor cruel and unusual punishments inflicted.

11. That jurors ought to be duly impaneled and returned, and jurors which pass upon men in trials for high treason ought to be freeholders.

12. That all grants and promises of fines and forfeitures of particular persons before conviction are illegal and void.

13. And that for redress of all grievances, and for the amending, strengthening, and preserving of the laws, parliament ought to be held frequently.

And they do claim, demand, and insist upon all and singular the premises, as their undoubted rights and liberties: and that no declarations, judgments, doings, or proceedings, to the prejudice of the people in any of the said premises, ought in any wise to be drawn hereafter into consequence or example.

To which demand of their rights they are particularly encouraged by the declaration of his Highness the prince of Orange, as being the only means for obtaining a full redress and remedy therein.

Having therefore an entire confidence that his said Highness the prince of Orange will perfect the deliverance so far advanced by him, and will still preserve them from the violation of their rights, which they have here asserted, and from all other attempt upon their religion, rights, and liberties:

The said lords spiritual and temporal, and commons, assembled at Westminster, do resolve that William and Mary, prince and princess of Orange, be, and be declared, king and queen of England, France, and Ireland, the dominions thereunto belonging, to hold the crown and royal dignity of the said kingdoms and dominions to them the said prince and princess during their lives. . . .

Upon which their said Majesties did accept the crown and royal dignity of the kingdoms of England, France, and Ireland, and the dominions thereunto belonging, according to the resolution and desire of the said lords and commons contained in the said declaration.

## Discussion Questions

1. In what ways does the Bill of Rights limit the powers of the crown?
2. What role does the bill grant Parliament in government?
3. How does the bill give weight to the attitude of some members of Parliament at the time that they had "made" the new king and queen?

# 3.
# Ludwig Fabritius
# *The Revolt of Stenka Razin*
## 1670

*Despite its geographical and cultural isolation from the rest of Europe, Russia followed France's lead down the path of absolutism. In the process, Tsar Alexei (r. 1645–1676) legally combined millions of slaves and free peasants into a single serf class bound to the land and their aristocratic masters. Not everyone passively accepted this fate, however. In 1667, a Cossack named Stenka Razin (c. 1630–1671) led a revolt against serfdom that gained considerable support among people whose social and economic status was threatened by the tsar's policies, including soldiers from peasant stock. Razin's ultimate defeat at the hands of the tsar explains the close ties between the Russian government's enhanced power and the enforcement of serfdom. A Dutch soldier, Ludwig Fabritius (1648–1729), who lived in Russia from 1660 to 1677 while employed as a military expert in the Russian army, wrote the following account of one stage of the revolt.*

Then Stenka with his company started off upstream, rowing as far as Tsaritsyn, whence it took him only one day's journey to Panshin, a small town situated on the Don. Here he began straightaway quietly gathering the common people around him, giving them money, and promises of great riches if they would be loyal to him and help to exterminate the treacherous boyars.[1]

This lasted the whole winter, until by about spring he had assembled 4,000 to 5,000 men. With these he came to Tsaritsyn and demanded the immediate surrender of the fortress; the rabble soon achieved their purpose, and although the governor tried to take refuge in a tower, he soon had to give himself up as he was deserted by one and all. Stenka immediately had the wretched governor hanged; and all the goods they found belonging to the Tsar and his officers as well as to the merchants were confiscated and distributed among the rabble.

---

From Anthony Glenn Cross, ed., *Russia under Western Eyes, 1517–1825* (London: Elek Books, 1971), 120–23.

[1]This term refers to a class of noblemen.

Stenka now began once more to make preparations. Since the plains are not cultivated, the people have to bring their corn from Nizhniy-Novgorod and Kazan down the Volga in big boats known as *nasady,* and everything destined for Astrakhan has first to pass Tsaritsyn. Stenka Razin duly noted this, and occupied the whole of the Volga, so that nothing could get through to Astrakhan. Here he captured a few hundred merchants with their valuable goods, taking possession of all kinds of fine linen, silks, striped silk material, sables, soft leather, ducats, talers, and many thousands of rubles in Russian money and merchandise of every description. . . .

In the meantime four regiments of *streltsy* [sharpshooters] were dispatched from Moscow to subdue these brigands. They arrived with their big boats and as they were not used to the water, were easily beaten. Here Stenka Razin gained possession of a large amount of ammunition and artillery-pieces and everything else he required. While the above-mentioned [sharpshooters] were sent from Moscow, about 5,000 men were ordered up from Astrakhan by water and by land to capture Stenka Razin. As soon as he had finished with the former, he took up a good position, and, being in possession of reliable information regarding our forces, he left Tsaritsyn and came to meet us half way at Chernyy Yar, confronting us before we had suspected his presence or received any information about him. We stopped at Chernyy Yar for a few days and sent out scouts by water and by land, but were unable to obtain any definite information. On 10 July [*sic:* June] a council of war was held at which it was decided to advance and seek out Stenka. The next morning, at 8 o'clock, our look-outs on the water came hurriedly and raised the alarm as the Cossacks were following at their heels. We got out of our boats and took up battle positions. General Knyaz Semen Ivanovich Lvov went through the ranks and reminded all the men to do their duty and to remember the oath they had taken to His Majesty the Tsar, to fight like honest soldiers against these irresponsible rebels, whereupon they all unanimously shouted: "Yes, we will give our lives for His Majesty the Tsar, and will fight to the last drop of our blood."

In the meantime Stenka prepared for battle and deployed on a wide front; to all those who had no rifle he gave a long pole, burnt a little at one end, and with a rag or small hook attached. They presented a strange sight on the plain from afar, and the common soldiers imagined that, since there were so many flags and standards, there must be a host of people. They [the common soldiers] held a consultation and at once decided that this was the chance for which they had been waiting so long, and with all their flags and drums they ran over to the enemy. They began kissing and embracing one another and swore with life and limb to stand together and to exterminate the treacherous boyars, to throw off the yoke of slavery, and to become free men.

The general looked at the officers and the officers at the general, and no one knew what to do; one said this, and another that, until finally it was decided that they and the general should get into the boats and withdraw to Astrakhan. But the rascally [sharpshooters] of Chernyy Yar stood on the walls and towers, turning their weapons on us and opened fire; some of them ran out of the fortress and cut us off from the boats, so that we had no means of escape. In the meantime those curs of ours who had gone over to the Cossacks came up from behind. We numbered about eighty men, officers, noblemen, and clerks. Murder at once began. Then, however, Stenka Razin ordered that no more officers were to be killed, saying that there must be a few good men among them who should be pardoned, whilst those others who had not lived in amity with their men should be condemned to well-deserved punishment by the Ataman and his *Krug*. A *Krug* is a meeting convened by the order of the Ataman, at which the Cossacks stand in a circle with the standard in the center; the Ataman then takes his place beside his best officers, to whom he divulges his wishes, ordering them to make these known to the common brothers and to hear their opinion on the matter. . . .

A *Krug* was accordingly called and Stenka asked through his chiefs how the general and his officers had treated the soldiers under their command. Thereupon the unscrupulous curs [sharpshooters], as well as soldiers, unanimously called out that there was not one of them who deserved to remain alive, and they all asked that their father Stepan Timofeyevich Razin should order them to be cut down. This was granted with the exception of General Knyaz Semen Ivanovich Lvov, whose life was specially spared by Stenka himself. The officers were now brought in order of rank out of the tower, into which they had been thrown bound hand and foot the previous day, their ropes were cut and they were led outside the gate. When all the bloodthirsty curs had lined up, each was eager to deal his former superior the first blow, one with the sword, another with the lance, another with the scimitar, and others again with martels, so that as soon as an officer was pushed into the ring, the curs immediately killed him with their many wounds; indeed, some were cut to pieces and straightaway thrown into the Volga. My stepfather, Paul Rudolf Beem, and Lt. Col. Wundrum and many other officers, senior and junior, were cut down before my eyes.

My own time had not yet come: this I could tell by the wonderful way in which God rescued me, for as I—half-dead—now awaited the final blow, my [former] orderly, a young soldier, came and took me by my bound arms and tried to take me down the hill. As I was already half-dead, I did not move and did not know what to do, but he came back and took me by the arms and led me, bound as I was, through the throng of curs, down the hill into the boat and immediately cut my arms free, saying that I should rest in peace here and that he would be responsible for me and do his best to save my life. . . . Then my guardian angel told me not to leave the boat, and left me. He returned in the evening and brought me a piece of bread which I enjoyed since I had had nothing to eat for two days.

The following day all our possessions were looted and gathered together under the main flag, so that both our bloodthirsty curs and the Cossacks got their share.

## ■ Discussion Questions

1. What do you think motivated Razin and his followers to take action?
2. Why were Razin and his forces able to defeat the tsar's soldiers?
3. With whom do you think Fabritius's sympathies lay, and why?

# 4.
# *A True and Exact Relation of the Raising of the Siege of Vienna*
## 1683

*As the decision by Tsar Alexei (r. 1645–1676) to enserf millions of Russian peasants suggests, rulers in central and eastern Europe developed their own form of absolutism, which reflected the conditions and challenges specific to their regions. The following anonymous eyewitness account of the raising of the siege of the Austrian capital, Vienna, in 1683 provides an example of just how formidable the conditions and challenges could be. Although the Holy Roman Emperor Leopold I (r. 1658–1705) had expanded his authority over the patchwork of ethnic groups under his rule, he still faced the growing presence of the Ottoman Turks to the east. As they pushed into the heart of Austrian Habsburg territory and surrounded Vienna in 1683, the Turks seemed poised for victory. All appeared lost for the Austrian troops until a Polish detachment under the leadership of King Jan Sobieski (r. 1674–1696) arrived. Together they took the Turkish army by surprise and saved the beleaguered city. For the eyewitness, the impact of this "signal victory" extended far beyond the walls of Vienna, opening the door for Austrian dominance of eastern Europe. His optimism was not unfounded, for by 1699, the Turkish sultan had relinquished almost all of Hungary to the Austrians.*

## SEPTEMBER 12TH

After a Siege of Sixty days, accompanied with a Thousand Difficulties, Sicknesses, Want of Provisions, and great Effusion of Blood, after a Million of Cannon and Musquet Shot, Bombs, Granadoes, and all sorts of Fire Works, which has changed the Face of the fairest and most flourishing City in the World, disfigured and ruined most part of the best Palaces of the same, and chiefly those of the Emperor; and damaged in many places the Beautiful Tower and Church of St. *Stephen,* with many Sumptuous Buildings. After a Resistance so vigorous, and the Loss of so many brave Officers and Soldiers, whose Valor and Bravery deserve Immortal Glory. After so many Toils endured, so many Watchings and so many Orders so prudently distributed by Count *Staremburgh,* and so punctually executed by the other Officers.

After so many new Retrenchments, Pallizadoes, Parapets, new Ditches in the Ravelins, Bastions, Courtins, and principal Streets and Houses in the Town: Finally, after a Vigorous Defense and a Resistance without parallel, Heaven favorably heard the Prayers and Tears of a Cast-down and Mournful People, and retorted

---

From "A True and Exact Relation of the Raising of the Siege of Vienna and the Victory Obtained Over the Ottoman Army" (London: 1683), 59–62, 65–66.

the Terror on a powerful Enemy, and drove him from the Walls of *Vienna,* who since the Fifteenth of *July* last early in the Morning, to the Twelfth of *September,* had so Vigorously attacked it with Two hundred thousand Men; and by endless Workings, Trenchings, and Minings, reduced it almost to its last gasp.

Count *Staremburgh,* who sustained this great Burden, assisted by so many Gallant Officers, having given Notice to the Christian Army, by Discharge of Musquets from the Tower of St. *Stephen,* of the Extremity whereto the City was reduced, they discovered on the Twelfth of this Month, early in the Morning, the Christian Troops marching down the Neighboring Mountains of *Kalemberg,* and heard continually the Discharges of their Artillery against the *Turks,* who being advanced thither, were fortified with Parapets of Earth and great Stones, to hinder the Descent of the Christian Army from the Mountains, who notwithstanding did advance. The Vanguard of the Horse and Foot, seconded by the Polish Horse, had a long Skirmish with the *Turks,* disputing every Foot of Ground; but seeing themselves totally vanquished by the Christian Forces, who had surmounted all the Difficulties of the Mountains, and drawn down their Cannon in spight of them, they retired Fighting, leaving to the Christians all their Camps full of Pavillions, Tents, Barracks, and Eight Pieces of Cannon (with which they had raised a Battery on that side Four days before) and retreated towards their Principal Camp, between the Villages of *Hernalls, Haderkling* and *Jezing;* but as they passed by the Bastion of *Melck* they fired their Cannon furiously on them: The Christians being ravish'd with the Victory, pursued them with so much heat, that they were not only forced to leave their great Camps, but likewise all their others; flying towards *Hungary:* And it is certain, had not the Night come on, they had totally defeated and routed the *Ottoman Army.* [. . .]

In the Night the Christians made themselves Masters of all the *Turks* Camp. Afterwards Four Companies of our Foot entered into the Enemies Approaches with Torches and lighted Straw, but found nothing but Dead Bodies; they took possession of the Enemies Artillery, some whereof were brought into the City. All the night long we saw Fires at a distance, the *Turk* having fired as many of their Camps as so sudden a flight would give them leave, and retreated from the *Island* by favor of a Bridge which they had made below the River, upon one of the Arms of the *Danube,* the Christians having seized the Bridge above, on the same River.

On Monday Morning we saw all the Camps and Fields covered with Soldiers as well *Poles* as *Germans.* The *City* was relieved on *Sunday* about Five of the Clock in the Afternoon, and every bodies' curiosity carried them to see the Camp, after they had been shut up above two Months.

The King of *Poland* having in the mean time with the greatest Vigor repulsed the Enemy on his side and put them to flight, leaving the Plunder of their Camp behind them, which consisted of a very Rich Tent of the Grand Visier, his Colors, Two Poles with the Horse Tails, their usual Signal of War, and his Guidon or Standard, set with Diamonds, his Treasure designed for the Payment of the Army, and in short, all his Equipage was possess'd by the *Polanders.* As for the rest of the Tents, Baggage, Artillery, Ammunition, and Provisions enough to load Eight thousand Waggons, was divided among our Army.

Night coming on, we could no longer pursue, having followed the Enemy about a Mile from their Camp, and our Army having been all that time without Eating and Drinking, we were forced to found a Retreat to refresh them. We had all that Night to rest in, and the Enemy to save themselves. The next day being the Thirteenth we continued not the pursuit for the same reason, which without doubt we might have done with great advantage, since they fled in much disorder toward St. *Godart* to get over the River *Raab.* We are building a Bridge at *Alltemburgh* in *Hungary,* and our Armies will march very suddenly. On Sunday Night, after the Battle, his Imperial Majesty came to *Cloister Nuburgh,* Four hours from *Vienna,* from whence he sent the next day to compliment the King of *Poland* and the Electors upon their good success the day before.

On the Fourteenth, Count *Staremburgh* came to his Imperial Majesty (who received him with all manner of demonstrations of Affection and Esteem) and gave him a Relation of several considerable passages during the Siege: A short time after the Emperor embarked on the *Danube,* and landed above the Bridge before the Town, and entered the City at the *Stuben Gate,* at Landing he was received by the Electors of *Bavaria* and *Saxony,* who were attended by their Guards and a great many Noble Men. It being impossible to remove in so short a time such a number of Dead Bodies, both *Turks, Christians,* and *Horses,* whereof the stench was so great on the Road, that it was enough to have caused an Infection. [. . .]

## SEPTEMBER 19TH

The Emperor is gone this day to Lintz: We are now beginning to cleanse the City of its Rubbish, and carry off the Dead Carcasses of Man and Beast. The *Turks* had a *French Engineer* in their Camp, who hath done very much hurt to this City, and ruin'd us 50 Pieces of Cannon: There was also a great many *French* among the *Janizaries,* and many were found among the Dead with *French* Silver and Gold in their Pockets. There are daily brought in a great number of *Turks* Prisoners since the flight of the Grand Visier. It is intended to set the *Turks* that are already, and shall be hereafter taken, at Work on the reparation of our *Bastions* and *Courtins.* The Sieur *Kaunitz,* the Emperors Resident at the Port, who was found in the *Grand Visier* Tent, is now in this City.

This moment comes the News that *Friday* last the *17th,* a part of the *Turks Army* fled away in such haste, within sight of *Raab,* as if ours were at their backs; the Officer who brought it, added that on his way from *Raab* he met with but two *Turks,* whom he brought Prisoners to *Bruckham* of *Ceytha,* where he sold them for four Pecks of Oats. All the Enemies or Rebels who had got into the Isle of *Schut,* are retired thence. There are gone down from hence some Boats full of Infantry towards *Hungary.* We are in hopes to hear shortly of some great Enterprize on the *Turks.* Here are daily brought in abundance of young Children whom the *Turks* had taken Captive; they ravish'd the young Maids and Women, and cut off the Heads of the old Men and Women.

Here is News from *Gratz,* That Count *Budiani* (who hath desired Count *Strasoldo* to intercede for him to the Emperor) had commanded 8000 *Hussars* of his Troops, under the Command of his Son and the Count *Nadasti,* to fall on 2000 *Turks* encamped near *Canisa,* and that they have put them all to the Sword. *Baron Buroni* is dead, and his Son revolted from the Rebels, and begs the Emperor's Pardon. The *Turks* who are Prisoners, unanimously affirm, That the Grand Visier hath caused *Ibrahim Bassa* Visier of *Buda* to be strangled for first giving Ground at the Battle before *Vienna.* Part of the *Ottoman Army* is arrived near *Greekish Weissenberg.*

Since this Signal Victory obtained by the Christian Army (who some days had refreshed themselves) we are certainly informed they passed *Presbourgh* the 23rd of *September,* in pursuit of the scattered Forces of the Ottoman Army, who fled to *Stollweissembourgh;* so that a few days will bring us an Accompt of what has passed between them. This Victory hath already given this advantage to our Affairs, that the Count of *Trausmondorse* [Trautmannsdorf] had taken and confiscated the Castles and Revenues of those who had done Homage to the *Turk;* and it was resolved to do the like in *Hungary.*

### ■ Discussion Questions

1. What does this account reveal about military technology and tactics at the time?
2. How does the eyewitness portray Leopold I? What does this portrayal suggest about his method of rule?
3. How do the religious differences between the two camps shape the content and tone of this account of the raising of the siege?

## 5.
## Madame de Lafayette
## *The Princess of Clèves*
## 1678

*Like the Duke of Saint-Simon, French author Marie-Madeline de La Vergne (b. 1634), Countess of Lafayette, was well acquainted with the court of Louis XIV (r. 1643–1715). She also had close ties to intellectual circles in Paris, where she cultivated her formidable writing talents. In 1678, she published anonymously* The Princess of Clèves, *which was an overnight literary sensation. The following letters help explain why. Set during the reign of King Henry II (r. 1547–1559), the book centers on the character of Mademoiselle de Chartres, who, upon captivating the court with her wit and beauty, weds the Prince of Clèves. Their union proves an unhappy one, and the princess falls in love with another man, Nemours. She never succumbs to her desire, however, even after her husband's death. The book's portrayal of her emotional struggle scandalized many readers by challenging conventional notions of marriage and proper aristocratic behavior. At*

From Marie-Madeleine de Lafayette, *The Princess of Clèves,* trans. and ed. John D. Lyons (New York: Norton, 1994), 121–22.

*the same time, the book abandoned the idealized and lengthy style of the romantic genre, giving birth to a new literary form, the novel.*

## MADAME DE LAFAYETTE TO JOSEPH MARIE DE LESCHERAINE

13 April 1678

A little book which appeared fifteen years ago and that people attributed to me makes them want to credit me with *The Princess of Clèves*. But I assure you that I had nothing to do with it and that M. de La Rochefoucauld, to whom the book has also been attributed, had as little to do with it as I did. He declared this under oath so many times that he cannot be doubted, especially about something that could be admitted without shame. As for me, I am flattered that people suspect me of being the author, and I believe that I would acknowledge the book as mine if I could be sure that the author would never show up and ask for it back. I find it a very pleasant work, well written without being perfectly polished, so full of admirably subtle details that it has to be read more than once. And most of all, I find in it a perfect representation of the world of the court and of the way one lives there. The book does not seem like a romance, and there is nothing overdone in it. Assuredly it is not a romance but rather a book of memoirs, and I have been told that such was its title, but they changed it.

So there, Monsieur, is my opinion of *Madame de Clèves*. I would ask yours as well. People are so divided over this book that they could come to blows. Some condemn what others admire in it. So, no matter what you say, don't be afraid of being the only one to say it.

## ROGER DE BUSSY-RABUTIN TO MARIE DE SÉVIGNÉ

26 June 1678

But I forgot to tell you that I have finally given *The Princess of Clèves* an impartial reading, not at all prejudiced by the good and bad things people have written. I found the first part admirable; the second didn't seem as good. In the first volume, except a few words that are repeated too often—just a small number—everything is pleasing, everything is natural, nothing is stilted. In the second part, Madame de Clèves's confession is preposterous, and could only be told in a true history; but when one is making a story up it is absurd to depict the heroine as having a sentiment that is so out of the ordinary. The author, by doing so, was thinking of ways to be different from the old romances and was not paying attention to common sense. A wife rarely tells her husband that a man is in love with her and *never* tells her husband that she is in love with another man, and especially not by throwing herself at his feet, a gesture that can make him think she has committed the ultimate offense. Besides, it is implausible that passionate love and virtue should remain for a long time equal in strength. In court society if a woman hasn't completely rejected a suitor in two or three weeks, or at most a month, she is only trying to make herself appear more desirable. And if, against all the odds and in spite of custom, the conflict between love and virtue should last until her husband's death, she would be delighted to harmonize virtue and love by marrying a man of his [Nemours's] quality, the handsomest gallant of his day. The first incident in the gardens at Coulommiers is not plausible and smacks of romance. It is very a calculated arrangement that when the Princess confesses to her husband that she loves another man, M. de Nemours, at just the right moment, is behind the fence listening to them; I don't even see why he had to know her confession, and in any event it should have been arranged so that he learned about [it] in some other way. It's like a romance, as well, when people talk to themselves. Besides the fact that it is not customary for people to talk to themselves, it isn't possible to know what someone says to herself unless she writes her own story: and even then she would say only what she thought. The letter to the Vidame is also like the letters in a romance, obscure, too long, and not at all natural. Just the same, in this second volume everything is just as well narrated, and the turns of phrase are just as beautiful as in the first volume.

Roger de Rabutin, comte de Bussy

## ■ Discussion Questions

1. In the first letter, how does Madame de Lafayette confront the prejudice that it was improper in seventeenth-century France for noblewomen to publish their writings and use it to her advantage?
2. Why is Roger de Bussy-Rabutin critical of *The Princess of Clèves* in the second letter?
3. What do Roger de Bussy-Rabutin's criticisms suggest about the development of the novel as a new type of literature?

## ■ Comparative Questions

1. What do both Saint-Simon and Roger de Bussy-Rabutin reveal about court culture during the reign of Louis XIV?
2. Based on the first three documents, what comparisons could be drawn about the relationship between the individual and the state in England, France, and Russia? What do these comparisons suggest about the basis of authority in constitutional and absolutist governments?
3. What do the accounts of Stenka Razin's revolt and the raising of the siege of Vienna suggest about the role of the military in the growth of absolutism in central and eastern Europe?

Chapter

# 14

# The Atlantic System and Its Consequences, 1690–1740

THE GROWTH OF EUROPEAN domestic economies and overseas colonization during the eighteenth century infused Europe with money, new products, and a new sense of optimism about the future. Yet, as the first document here illustrates, the good times came at a horrible price for the millions of African slaves who formed the economic backbone of the colonial system. Changes were also underway on the political front, with the stabilization of the European state system. Consequently, states such as Russia shone more brightly over the political landscape while others lost their luster. The second document brings Russia's new prominence to life in its leader's own words. The third and fourth documents that follow reveal that intellectual circles were also ablaze with change as scholars and writers cast political, social, and religious issues in a new critical and secular light. Yet at the same time, the final document attests that religion continued to assert a powerful hold on Europeans, many of whom yearned for a renewal of Christian beliefs and practices.

## 1.
## Olaudah Equiano
## *The Interesting Narrative of the Life of Olaudah Equiano Written by Himself*
**1789**

*The autobiography of Olaudah Equiano (c. 1745–1797) puts a human face on the eighteenth-century Atlantic slave trade and its human consequences. As he describes, he was born in what is now Nigeria and was captured by local raiders and sold into slavery in his early teens. He gained his freedom in 1766 and soon thereafter became a vocal supporter of the English abolitionist movement. He published his autobiography in 1789, a best seller in its day, with numerous editions published in Britain and*

From Paul Edwards, ed., *Equiano's Travels: His Autobiography,* abridged (London: Heinemann, 1967), 25–32.

*America. In the following excerpt, Equiano recounts his journey on the slave ship that took him away from his homeland, his freedom, and his very identity. Millions of others shared this same fate. Scholars have recently challenged this account, pointing to new evidence that suggests Equiano was born a slave in South Carolina, so probably early parts of his autobiography drew on the oral history of other slaves rather than on Equiano's personal experience. Regardless of where the truth lies, his book is invaluable as one of the very few texts written in English during the eighteenth century by a person of African descent.*

The first object which saluted my eyes when I arrived on the coast was the sea, and a slave ship which was then riding at anchor and waiting for its cargo. These filled me with astonishment, which was soon converted into terror when I was carried on board. I was immediately handled and tossed up to see if I were sound by some of the crew, and I was now persuaded that I had gotten into a world of bad spirits and that they were going to kill me. Their complexions too differing so much from ours, their long hair and the language they spoke (which was very different from any I had ever heard) united to confirm me in this belief. Indeed such were the horrors of my views and fears at the moment that, if ten thousand worlds had been my own, I would have freely parted with them all to have exchanged my condition with that of the meanest slave in my own country. When I looked round the ship too and saw a large furnace or copper boiling and a multitude of black people of every description chained together, every one of their countenances expressing dejection and sorrow, I no longer doubted of my fate; and quite overpowered with horror and anguish, I fell motionless on the deck and fainted. When I recovered a little I found some black people about me, who I believed were some of those who had brought me on board and had been receiving their pay; they talked to me in order to cheer me, but all in vain. I asked them if we were not to be eaten by those white men with horrible looks, red faces, and loose hair. They told me I was not, and one of the crew brought me a small portion of spirituous liquor in a wine glass, but being afraid of him I would not take it out of his hand. One of the blacks therefore took it from him and gave it to me, and I took a little down my palate, which instead of reviving me, as they thought it would, threw me into the greatest consternation at the strange feeling it produced, having never tasted such any liquor before. Soon after this the blacks who brought me on board went off, and left mc abandoned to despair.

I now saw myself deprived of all chance of returning to my native country or even the least glimpse of hope of gaining the shore, which I now considered as friendly; and I even wished for my former slavery in preference to my present situation, which was filled with horrors of every kind, still heightened by my ignorance of what I was to undergo. I was not long suffered to indulge my grief; I was soon put down under the decks, and there I received such a salutation in my nostrils as I had never experienced in my life: so that with the loathsomeness of the stench and crying together, I became so sick and low that I was not able to eat, nor had I the least desire to taste anything. I now wished for the last friend, death, to relieve me; but soon, to my grief, two of the white men offered me eatables, and on my refusing to eat, one of them held me fast by the hands and laid me across I think the windlass, and tied my feet while the other flogged me severely. I had never experienced anything of this kind before, and although, not being used to the water, I naturally feared that element the first time I saw it, yet nevertheless could I have got over the nettings I would have jumped over the side, but I could not; and besides, the crew used to watch us very closely who were not chained down to the decks, lest we should leap into the water: and I have seen some of these poor African prisoners most severely cut for attempting to do so, and hourly whipped for not eating. This indeed was often the case with myself. In a little time after, amongst the poor chained men I found some of my own nation, which in a small degree gave ease to my mind. I inquired of these what was to be done with us; they gave me to understand we were to be carried to these white people's country to work for them. I then was a little revived, and thought if it were no worse than working, my situation was not so desperate: but still I feared I should be put to death, the white people looked and acted, as I thought, in so savage a manner; for I had never seen among my people such instances of brutal cruelty, and this not only shewn towards us blacks but also to some of the whites themselves. One white man in particular I saw, when we were permitted to be on deck, flogged so unmercifully with a large rope near the foremast that he died in consequence of it; and they tossed him over the side as they would have done a brute. This made me fear these people the more, and I expected nothing less than to be treated in the same manner. . . . At last, when the ship we were in had got in all her cargo, they made ready with many fearful noises, and we were all put under deck so that we could not see how they managed the vessel. But this disappointment was the last of my sorrow. The stench of the hold while we were on the coast was so intolerably loathsome that it was dangerous to remain there for any time, and some of us had been permitted to stay on the deck for the fresh air; but now that the whole ship's cargo were confined together it became absolutely pestilential. The closeness of the place and the heat of the climate, added to the number in the ship, which was so crowded that each had scarcely room to turn himself, almost suffocated us. This produced copious perspirations, so that the air soon became unfit for respiration from a variety of loathsome smells, and brought on a sickness among the slaves, of which many died, thus falling victims to the improvident avarice, as I may call it, of their purchasers. This wretched situation was again aggravated by the galling of the chains, now become insupportable, and the filth of the necessary tubs, into which the children often fell and were almost suffocated. The shrieks of the women and the groans of the dying rendered the whole a scene of horror almost inconceivable. Happily perhaps for myself I was soon reduced so low here that it was thought necessary to keep me almost always on deck, and from my extreme youth I was not put in fetters. In this situation I expected every hour to share the fate of my companions, some of whom were almost daily brought upon deck at the point of death, which I began to hope would soon put an end to my miseries. . . . At last we came in sight of the island of Barbados, at which the whites on board gave a great shout and made many signs of joy to us.

We did not know what to think of this, but as the vessel drew nearer we plainly saw the harbour and other ships of different kinds and sizes, and we soon anchored amongst them off Bridgetown. Many merchants and planters now came on board, though it was in the evening. They put us in separate parcels and examined us attentively. They also made us jump, and pointed to the land, signifying we were to go there. . . . We were not many days in the merchant's custody before we were sold after their usual manner, which is this: On a signal given, (as the beat of a drum) the buyers rush at once into the yard where the slaves are confined, and make choice of that parcel they like best. The noise and clamor with which this is attended and the eagerness visible in the countenances of the buyers serve not a little to increase the apprehensions of the terrified Africans, who may well be supposed to consider them as the ministers of that destruction to which they think themselves devoted. In this manner, without scruple, are relations and friends separated, most of them never to see each other again. I remember in the vessel in which I was brought over, in the men's apartment there were several brothers who, in the sale, were sold in different lots; and it was very moving on this occasion to see and hear their cries at parting. O, ye nominal Christians! might not an African ask you, Learned you this from your God who says unto you, Do unto all men as you would men should do unto you?

### ■ Discussion Questions

1. What are Equiano's impressions of the white men on the ship and their treatment of the slaves? How does this treatment reflect the slave traders' primary concerns?
2. What message do you think Equiano sought to convey to his readers? Based on this message, to whom do you think his book especially appealed?

## 2.
## Tsar Peter I
## *Letter to His Son, Alexei*
### October 11, 1715
## and
## *Alexei's Response*
### October 31, 1715

*During the eighteenth century, European states turned much of their attention to the political and military scene burgeoning within Europe, vying to keep one step ahead*

From *A Source Book for Russian History from Early Times to 1917*, vol. II (New Haven and London: Yale University Press, 1972), 338–39.

*of their rivals. Russian Tsar Peter I (r. 1689–1725) was especially successful at this game, transforming Russia into a great European power with all the trappings of a Western absolutist state, including a strong army and centralized bureaucracy, during his reign. Peter wrote the following letter to Alexei, who was then his only son and heir, during the Great Northern War against Sweden, which Peter ultimately won to Russia's great advantage. The letter explains the tsar's relentless drive toward greatness on the European stage. Alexei's response reveals not only the striking differences in personality between the two men but also the tension that marked their tumultuous relationship.*

[Peter to Alexei, October 11, 1715:]

Declaration to my son:

Everyone knows how, before the beginning of this war, our people were hemmed in by the Swedes, who not only stole the essential ports of our fatherland . . . but cut us off from communication with the whole world. And also later, in the beginning of this war (which enterprise was and is directed by God alone), oh, what great persecution we had to endure from those eternal enemies of ours because of our incompetence in the art of war, and with what sorrow and endurance we went to this school and, with the help of the above-mentioned guide, achieved a creditable degree [of effectiveness]. We were thus found worthy of looking on this enemy now trembling before us, trembling, perhaps, even more than we did before him. All this has been accomplished with the help of God through my modest labors and through those of other equally zealous and faithful sons of Russia.

However, when, considering this great blessing given by God to our fatherland, I think of my successor, a grief perhaps as strong as my joy gnaws me, when I see you, my heir, unfit for the management of state affairs (for it is not the fault of God, who has not deprived you of mind or health; for although not of a very strong constitution, you are not very weak either). But above all, you have no wish to hear anything about military affairs, which opened to us the way from darkness to light, so that we who were unknown before are now honored. I do not teach you to be inclined to wage war without a just cause, but to love this art and to endow and learn it by all means, for it is one of the two activities necessary for government: order and defense.

I have no wish to give you many examples, but I will mention only the Greeks, who are of the same religion as we. Did they not perish because they laid their arms aside, and were they not vanquished because of their peaceableness? Desirous of tranquil living, they always gave way to their enemy, who changed their tranquillity into endless servitude to tyrants. Perhaps you think that it can all be left to the generals; but this is really not so, for everyone looks up to his chief, to comply with his desires, which is an obvious fact. Thus, in the days of my brother's reign [Theodore, 1676–82], everyone liked clothes and horses above all things, and now they like arms. They may not be really interested in one or the other; but in what the chief is interested all take an interest, and to what he is indifferent, all are indifferent. And if they turn away so lightly from the frivolous pastimes, which are only a pleasure to man, how much more easily will they abandon so burdensome a game as war!

Furthermore, you do not learn anything because you have no desire to learn it, and you have no knowledge of military affairs. Lacking all knowledge, how can you direct these affairs? How can you reward the diligent and punish the negligent when you yourself do not understand their work? You will be forced to look into people's mouths like a young bird. Do you pretend to be unfit for military work because of weak health? But that is no reason. I ask of you not work, but good will, which no malady can destroy. Ask anyone who remembers my brother whom I spoke of but now, who was, beyond comparison, sicklier than you and could not ride spirited horses, but he had a great liking for them and was always looking at them and kept them before his eyes.... So you see, not everything is done by great labor, but also by a strong desire. You say to yourself, perhaps, that many rulers do not themselves go to war, and yet campaigns are still carried on. This is true when, although not going themselves, they have a desire for it, as had the late French king [Louis XIV], who went to war himself but little, and who yet had a great taste for it and showed such magnificent deeds in war that his wars were called the theater and school for the whole world. But he had a taste not only for war, but also for other affairs and for manufactures, through all of which he procured glory for his state more than anybody else.

Now that I have gone into all this, I return again to my original point, thinking of you. I am a man, and subject to death. To whom shall I leave all this sowing, done with God's help, and that harvest which has already grown? To one who, like the idle slave in the Gospel, buried his talent in the ground (which means that he threw away everything that God had given him)? I also keep thinking of your wicked and stubborn disposition; for how many times I used to scold you for that, and not only scold but beat you, and also how many years I have now gone without speaking to you, and all without success!...

I have pondered this with much grief, and, seeing that I can in no wise dispose you toward good, I have deemed it appropriate to write to you this last admonition, and to wait a short time for you to mend your ways, and that *not hypocritically* [Peter's emphasis]. If you do not, know that I shall totally disinherit you like a gangrenous member; and do not imagine that, because you are my only son, I write this only to frighten you; I will do it indeed (with God's consent), because I have never spared my own life for my fatherland and people, nor do I now; therefore how can I spare you, unworthy one? Better a good stranger than an unworthy kinsman.

Peter
October 11, 1715
Saint Petersburg

[Alexei to Peter, October 31, 1715:]

Most gracious sovereign and father:

I have read [the letter] that was given me on your behalf on October 27, 1715, after the funeral of my wife. I have nothing to say about it, except that if you wish to disinherit me of the Russian crown because of my worthlessness, let it be as you will. Most humbly I ask you for this very thing, Sire, for I consider myself unqualified and unfit for this task, being most deficient in memory (without which it is impossible to accomplish anything). All my mental and physical capacities are weakened by various illnesses, and I have become unfit to rule such a people, which task requires a man less rotten than I. Therefore, I do not make a claim, nor will I make claim in the future, to the inheritance of the Russian throne after you —God give you health for many years—even if I did not have a brother (but now, thank God, I have one [note: Prince Peter, born to Peter and Catherine on October 29, 1715], God give him health); let God be my witness [in this matter], and to show that I testify truthfully I write this with my own hand.

I entrust my children to your will and ask only for maintenance for myself to the end of my life. This is submitted to your decision and merciful will.

Your most humble slave and son Alexei
Saint Petersburg
October 31, 1715

## ■ Discussion Questions

1. Why do you think Peter regarded the "art of war" as so important to government, and what did he gain by practicing it?
2. In what ways was Peter critical of his son, and why?
3. Whom does Peter single out as a political role model, and why is this significant?
4. What do these letters reveal about the tsar's personality?

# 3.
# Montesquieu
# *Persian Letters: Letter 37*
## 1721

*As Europe's economy expanded, so did its intellectual horizons with the birth of the Enlightenment in the 1690s. Charles-Louis de Secondat, Baron of Montesquieu (1689–1755), was an especially important literary figure on this front. In 1721 he*

From Montesquieu, *Persian Letters,* vol. I, trans. John Davidson (London: Privately printed, 1892), 85–86.

*published* Persian Letters, *in which he uses fictional characters to explore an array of topics with the critical, reasoning spirit characteristic of the period. Letter 37 points to one of his and other Enlightenment authors' main targets: the French king Louis XIV (r. 1643–1715) and his absolutist state. Written by one of the book's two main characters, a Persian traveler in France named Usbek, to a friend back home, the letter explicitly criticizes the king's vanity, ostentation, and life at court. The letter implicitly passes even more serious judgment on the aging ruler in noting his esteem for "oriental policies." Montesquieu condemns these same policies elsewhere in his letters as inhumane and unjust.*

## USBEK TO IBBEN, AT SMYRNA

The King of France is old. We have no examples in our histories of such a long reign as his. It is said that he possesses in a very high degree the faculty of making himself obeyed: he governs with equal ability his family, his court, and his kingdom: he has often been heard to say, that, of all existing governments, that of the Turks, or that of our august Sultan, pleased him best: such is his high opinion of Oriental statecraft.[1]

I have studied his character, and I have found certain contradictions which I cannot reconcile. For example, he has a minister who is only eighteen years old,[2] and a mistress [Madame de Maintenon] who is fourscore; he loves his religion, and yet he cannot abide those [the Jansenists] who assert that it ought to be strictly observed; although he flies from the noise of cities, and is inclined to be reticent, from morning till night he is engaged in getting himself talked about; he is fond of trophies and victories, but he has as great a dread of seeing a good general at the head of his own troops, as at the head of an army of his enemies. It has never I believe happened to anyone but himself, to be burdened with more wealth than even a prince could hope for, and yet at the same time steeped in such poverty as a private person could ill brook.

He delights to reward those who serve him; but he pays as liberally the assiduous indolence of his courtiers, as the labors in the field of his captains; often the man who undresses him, or who hands him his serviette at table, is preferred before him who has taken cities and gained battles; he does not believe that the greatness of a monarch is compatible with restriction in the distribution of favors; and, without examining into the merit of a man, he will heap benefits upon him, believing that his selection makes the recipient worthy; accordingly, he has been

[1]When Louis XIV was in his sixteenth year, some courtiers discussed in his presence the absolute power of the Sultans, who dispose as they like of the goods and the lives of their subjects. "That is something like being a king," said the young monarch. Marshal d'Estrées, alarmed at the tendency revealed in that remark, rejoined, "But, sire, several of these emperors have been strangled even in my time." [Ed.]

[2]Barbezieux, son of Louvois, Louis's youngest minister, held office at twenty-three, not eighteen; and he was dead in 1713. [Ed.]

known to bestow a small pension upon a man who had run off two leagues from the enemy, and a good government on another who had gone four.

Above all, he is magnificent in his buildings; there are more statues in his palace gardens [at Versailles] than there are citizens in a large town. His bodyguard is as strong as that of the prince before whom all the thrones of the earth tremble;[3] his armies are as numerous, his resources as great, and his finances as inexhaustible.

Paris, the 7th of the moon of Maharram, 1713.

## ■ Discussion Questions

1. What contradictions does Usbek see in Louis's character, and what do they reveal about his method of rule?
2. In what ways does this letter reflect Montesquieu's general interest in the foundation of good government?
3. Based on this letter, why do you think that scholars regard Montesquieu as a herald of the Enlightenment?

[3]The Shah of Persia. [Ed.]

# 4.
# Mary Astell
# *Reflections upon Marriage*
## 1706

*Like Montesquieu, English author Mary Astell (1666–1731) helped to usher in the Enlightenment by surveying society with a critical eye. First published anonymously in 1700,* Reflections upon Marriage, *one of her best-known books, highlights Astell's keen interest in the institution of marriage, education, and relations between the sexes. Only the third edition (published in 1706) divulged her gender, but still not her name. As the following excerpt reveals, Astell held a dim view of women's inequality in general and of their submissive role in marriage in particular. She argues that one should abhor the use of arbitrary power within the state, and so, too, within the family. Among the book's principal goals was to present spinsterhood as a viable alternative to marriage. Perhaps not surprisingly, Astell herself never married.*

These Reflections being made in the Country, where the Book that occasion'd them came but late to Hand, the *Reader* is desir'd to excuse their Unseasonableness as well as other Faults; and to believe that they have no other Design than to Correct some Abuses, which are not the less because Power and Prescription seem

From Bridget Hill, ed., *The First English Feminist: Reflections upon Marriage and Other Writings by Mary Astell* (New York: St. Martin's Press, 1986), 69–76.

to Authorize them. If any are so needlessly curious as to inquire from what Hand they come, they may please to know, that it is not good Manners to ask, since the Title-Page does not tell them: We are all of us sufficiently Vain, and without doubt the Celebrated Name of *Author,* which most are so fond of, had not been avoided but for very good Reasons: To name but one; *Who will care to pull upon themselves an Hornet's nest?* 'Tis a very great Fault to regard rather who it is that Speaks, than what is Spoken; and either to submit to Authority, when we should only yield to Reason; or if Reason press too hard, to think to ward it off by Personal Objections and Reflections. Bold Truths may pass while the Speaker is Incognito, but are not endur'd when he is known; few Minds being strong enough to bear what Contradicts their Principles and Practices without Recriminating when they can. And tho' to tell the Truth be the most Friendly Office, yet whosoever is so hardy as to venture at it, shall be counted an Enemy for so doing.

Thus far the old Advertisement, when the Reflections first appear'd, A.D.1700.

But the *Reflector,* who hopes *Reflector* is not bad English, now Governor is happily of the feminine Gender, had as good or better have said nothing; For People by being forbid, are only excited to a more curious Inquiry. A certain Ingenuous Gentleman (as she is inform'd) had the Good-Nature to own these Reflections, so far as to affirm that he had the Original M.S. in his Closet, a Proof she is not able to produce, and so to make himself responsible for all their Faults, for which she returns him all due Acknowledgment. However, the Generality being of Opinion, that a Man would have had more Prudence and Manners than to have Publish'd such unseasonable Truths, or to have betray'd the *Arcana Imperii* of his Sex, she humbly confesses, that the Contrivance and Execution of this Design, which is unfortunately accus'd of being so destructive to the government, of the Men I mean, is entirely her own. She neither advis'd with Friends, nor turn'd over Antient or Modern Authors, nor prudently submitted to the Correction of such as are, or such as *think* they are good Judges, but with an *English* Spirit and Genius, set out upon the Forlorn Hope, meaning no hurt to any body, nor designing any thing but the Public Good, and to retrieve, if possible, the Native Liberty, the Rights and Privileges of the Subject.

Far be it from her to stir up Sedition of any sort, none can abhor it more; and she heartily wishes that our Masters wou'd pay their Civil and Ecclesiastical Governors the same Submission, which they themselves extract from their Domestic Subjects. Nor can she imagine how she any way undermines the Masculine Empire, or blows the Trumpet of Rebellion to the Moiety of Mankind. Is it by exhorting Women, not to expect to have their own Will in any thing, but to be entirely Submissive, when once they have made choice of a Lord and Master, tho' he happen not to be so Wise, so Kind, or even so Just a Governor as was expected? She did not indeed advise them to think his Folly Wisdom, nor his Brutality that Love and Worship he promised in his Matrimonial Oath, for this required a Flight of Wit and Sense much above her poor Ability, and proper only to Masculine Understandings. However she did not in any manner prompt them to Resist, or to Abdicate the Perjur'd Spouse, tho' the Laws of GOD and the Land make special Provision for it, in a case wherein, as is to be fear'd, few Men can truly plead Not Guilty.

Tis true, thro' Want of Learning, and of that Superior Genius which Men as Men lay claim to, she was ignorant of the *Natural Inferiority* of our Sex, which our Masters lay down as a Self-Evident and Fundamental Truth.[1] She saw nothing in the Reason of Things, to make this either a Principle or a Conclusion, but much to the contrary; it being Sedition at least, if not Treason to assert it in this Reign. For if by the Natural Superiority of their Sex, they mean that every Man is by Nature superior to every Woman, which is the obvious meaning, and that which must be stuck to if they would speak Sense, it wou'd be a Sin in *any* Woman to have Dominion over *any* Man, and the greatest Queen ought not to command but to obey her Footman, because no Municipal Laws can supersede or change the Law of Nature; so that if the dominion of the Men be such, the *Salique Law*,[2] as unjust as *English Men* have ever thought it, ought to take place over all the Earth, and the most glorious Reigns in the *English, Danish, Castilian,* and other Annals, were wicked Violations of the Law of Nature!

If they mean that *some* Men are superior to *some* Women, this is no great Discovery; had they turn'd the Tables they might have seen that *some* Women are Superior to *some* Men. Or had they been pleased to remember their Oaths of Allegiance and Supremacy, they might have known that *One* Woman is superior to *All* the Men in these Nations, or else they have sworn to very little purpose. And it must not be suppos'd, that their Reason and Religion wou'd suffer them to take Oaths, contrary to the Law of Nature and Reason of things.

By all which it appears, that our Reflector's Ignorance is very pitiable, it may be her Misfortune but not her Crime, especially since she is willing to be better inform'd, and hopes she shall never be so obstinate as to shut her Eyes against the Light of Truth, which is not to be charg'd with Novelty, how late soever we may be bless'd with the Discovery. Nor can Error, be it as Antient as it may, ever plead Prescription against Truth. And since the only way to remove all Doubts, to answer all Objections, and to give the Mind entire Satisfaction, is not by *Affirming,* but by *Proving,* so that every one may see with their *own* Eyes, and Judge according to the best of their *own* Understandings, She hopes it is no Presumption to insist on this Natural Right of Judging for her self, and the rather, because by quitting it, we give up all the Means of Rational Conviction. Allow us then as many Glasses as you please to help our Sight, and as many good Arguments as you can afford to Convince our Understandings: But don't exact of us we beseech you, to affirm that we see such things as are only the Discovery of Men who have quicker Senses; or that we understand and Know what we have by Hearsay only, for to be so excessively Complaisant, is neither to see nor to understand.

---

[1]Possibly a reference to William Nichols, D.D., *The Duty of Inferiours Towards Their Superiours in Five Practical Discourses* (1701), in which he argued that man possesses "a higher state of natural perfection and dignity, and thereupon puts in a just claim of superiority, which everything which is of more worth has a right to, over that which has less" (pp. 87–88). [Ed.]

[2]***Salique Law:*** A law excluding women from the throne of France. [Ed.]

That the Custom of the World has put Women, generally speaking, into a State of Subjection, is not deny'd; but the Right can no more be prov'd from the Fact, than the Predominancy of Vice can justifie it. A certain great Man has endeavour'd to prove by Reasons not contemptible, that in the Original State of things the Woman was the Superior, and that her Subjection to the Man is an Effect of the Fall, and the Punishment of her Sin. And that Ingenious Theorist Mr. *Whiston*[3] asserts, That before the Fall there was a greater equality between the two Sexes. However this be 'tis certainly no Arrogance in a Woman to conclude, that she was made for the Service of GOD, and that this is her End. Because GOD made all Things for Himself, and a Rational Mind is too noble a Being to be Made for the Sake and Service of any Creature. The Service she at any time becomes oblig'd to pay to a Man, is only a Business by the Bye. Just as it may be any Man's Business and Duty to keep Hogs; he was not Made for this, but if he hires himself out to such an Employment, he ought conscientiously to perform it. Nor can any-thing be concluded to the contrary from St. *Paul's* Argument, *I Cor. II.* For he argues only for Decency and Order, according to the present Custom and State of things. Taking his Words strictly and literally, they prove too much, in that *Praying and Prophecying in the Church* are allow'd the Women, provided they do it with their Head Cover'd, as well as the Men; and no inequality can be inferr'd from hence, their Reverence to the Sacred Oracles who engage them in such Disputes. And therefore the blame be theirs, who have unnecessarily introduc'd them in the present Subject, and who by saying that the *Reflections* were not agreeable to Scripture, oblige the Reflector to shew that those who affirm it must either mistake her Meaning, or the Sense of Holy Scripture, or both, if they think what they say, and do not find fault merely because they resolve to do so. For had she ever writ any thing contrary to those sacred Truths, she wou'd be the first in pronouncing its Condemnation.

But what says the Holy Scripture? It speaks of Women as in a State of Subjection, and so it does of the *Jews* and *Christians* when under the Dominion of the *Chaldeans* and *Romans*, requiring of the one as well as of the other a quiet submission to them under whose Power they liv'd. But will any one say that these had a *Natural Superiority* and Right to Dominion? that they had a superior Understanding, or any Pre-eminence, except what their greater Strength acquir'd? Or that the other were subjected to their Adversaries for any other Reason but the Punishment of their sins, and in order to their Reformation? Or for the Exercise of their Vertue, and because the Order of the World and the Good of Society requir'd it?

If Mankind had never sinn'd, Reason wou'd always have been obey'd, there wou'd have been no struggle for Dominion, and Brutal Power wou'd not have pre-

[3]William Whiston (1667–1752), divine, mathematician and Newtonian. Author of many works including *A New Theory of the Earth* (1696). He succeeded Newton as the Lucasian Professor and did much to popularize Newton's ideas. In 1710 he was deprived of his chair for casting doubt on the doctrine of the Trinity. [Ed.]

vail'd. But in the laps'd State of Mankind, and now that Men will not be guided by their Reason but by their Appetites, and do not what they *ought* but what they *can*, the Reason, or that which stands for it, the Will and Pleasure of the Governor is to be the Reason of those who will not be guided by their own, and must take place for Order's sake, altho' it shou'd not be conformable to right Reason. Nor can there be any Society great or little, from Empires down to private Families, with a last Resort, to determine the Affairs of that Society by an irresistible Sentence. Now unless this Supremacy be fix'd somewhere, there will be a perpetual Contention about it, such is the love of Dominion, and let the Reason of things be what it may, those who have least Force, or Cunning to supply it, will have the Disadvantage. So that since Women are acknowledg'd to have least Bodily strength, their being commanded to obey is in pure kindness to them and for their Quiet and Security, as well as for the Exercise of their Vertue. But does it follow that Domestic Governors have more Sense than their Subjects, any more than that other Governors have? We do not find that any Man thinks the worse of his own Understanding because another has superior Power; or concludes himself less capable of a Post of Honor and Authority, because he is not Prefer'd to it. How much time wou'd lie on Men's hands, how empty wou'd the Places of Concourse be, and how silent most Companies, did Men forbear to Censure their Governors, that is in effect to think themselves Wiser. Indeed Government wou'd be much more desirable than it is, did it invest the Possessor with a superior Understanding as well as Power. And if mere Power gives a Right to Rule, there can be no such thing as Usurpation; but a Highway-Man so long as he has strength to force, has also a Right to require our Obedience.

Again, if Absolute Sovereignty be not necessary in a State, how comes it to be so in a family? or if in a Family why not in a State; since no Reason can be alledg'd for the one that will not hold more strongly for the other? If the Authority of the Husband so far as it extends, is sacred and inalienable, why not of the Prince? The Domestic Sovereign is without Dispute Elected, and the Stipulations and Contract are mutual, is it not then partial in Men to the last degree, to contend for, and practice that Arbitrary Dominion in their Families, which they abhor and exclaim against in the State? For if Arbitrary Power is evil in itself, and an improper Method of Governing Rational and Free Agents, it ought not to be Practis'd any where; Nor is it less, but rather more mischievous in Families than in Kingdoms, by how much 100,000 Tyrants are worse than one. What tho' a Husband can't deprive a Wife of Life without being responsible to the Law, he may however do what is much more grievous to a generous Mind, render Life miserable, for which she has no Redress, scarce Pity which is afforded to every other Complainant. It being thought a Wife's Duty to suffer everything without Complaint. *If all Men are born free*, how is it that all Women are born slaves? as they must be if the being subjected to the *inconstant, uncertain, unknown, arbitrary Will* of Men, be the *perfect Condition of Slavery?* and if the Essence of Freedom consists, as our Masters say it does, in having a *standing Rule to live by?* And why is Slavery so much condemn'd and strove against in one Case, and so highly applauded, and held so necessary and so sacred in another?

## ■ Discussion Questions

1. According to Mary Astell, what is women's customary status in society, and why? What evidence does Astell present to challenge this status?
2. What does the language Astell uses reveal about her style of thinking and basic intellectual beliefs?
3. Why do you think scholars characterize *Reflections upon Marriage* as a "feminist" work?

# 5.
# *Pietist Spiritual Songbook*
## 1705

*Even as the new secular spirit of the Enlightenment began to emerge in the 1690s, most Europeans remained sincere Christians. Some people sought to deepen their faith further still during this period, giving rise to various religious revivals, including the Protestant movement known as* Pietism. *Although Pietism first appeared in Lutheran Germany in the late seventeenth century, its concerns spread rapidly to Protestant denominations in Holland, Switzerland, and Scandinavia. In its most basic form, Pietism opposed the rigidity of academic theology in favor of practical and experiential piety. Its success was fueled in part by the popularity of a printing program in the Prussian town of Halle, which was also an important center of pietist study. By making inexpensive and readable editions of books available to the public, the Halle program offered the laity hands-on spiritual and moral guidance imbued with pietist ideals. The songbook excerpted here was published in Halle in 1705, with a preface by Johann Anastasius Freylinghausen (1670–1739).*

## Preface

*Dear Reader:*

The Old and the New Testaments, all of church history, and experience itself testifies that it is always a mark of special grace by which God visits his people or promises to visit them in the future, when and wherever spiritual loving hymns flow out from the mouths of spiritual children in songs of praise. . . .

[This can be seen in the songs sung by the children of Israel, by David and Solomon, by the prophets, by the Magnificat of Mary, and the Benedictus of Zacharias, by the songs indicated in the New Testament as sung by the apostolic communities, and by the songs sung thereafter, in particular by the hymns gathered by the Bohemian brethren.]

---

From Peter C. Erb, ed., *Pietists: Selected Writings* (New York: Paulist Press, 1983), 167–68, 172–75.

All the examples given to this point demonstrate the truth of the proposition that God visits his people in song; this can be demonstrated even more strongly by the experience of our own times in which the good hand of God has led us. In the last few years he has allowed the preaching of repentance and of the gospel, in particular in Germany, to ring forth with new strength, and he has sealed this not insignificant fruit. Not to acknowledge this or not to wish to acknowledge this is an indication of the most dangerous blindness. Likewise God has placed a new song in the hearts and mouths of many of his children and servants so that they might praise him with this song and by it elevate both present and coming grace. [The results of these new songs can be seen in the many songbooks of our day.]

Just as one does with all other good things, so also in the appropriation and use of this gift one is not to remain hanging to the wretched and petty instruments of this world, but is to look up to God the Father of light from whom all good and all perfect gifts come from above and who grants through the one spirit the many gifts for the improvement and building up of the body of Jesus Christ. One is to acknowledge and praise this same wisdom and faithful concern which God demonstrates toward his congregation and to use it for teaching and instruction, particularly for daily encouragement and a walking in faith, love, and hope, as well as for consolation and all struggle and suffering in this short pilgrim journey. One is to do this in humility and out of a simple heart.

For this end the present new songbook of the saints, elect and beloved of God, has been published in the good hope that through the grace of the Lord this end will be reached. . . .

## HYMN

Praise God! one step toward eternity
Is once again completed.
In the movement of this time
My heart ardently turns to you
O source, out of which my heart flows
And all grace flows
Into my soul as life.

I count the hours, days, and years,
And time seems never-ending
Until I completely
Embrace you, O life.
Then what is mortal in me
Will be completely swallowed up in you
And I will be immortal.

With the fire of love
My heart glows so that it ignites
What is in me, and my mind

Binds itself so to you
That you in me and I in you
And I yet always more
Will press nearer into you.

Oh, that you would come quickly;
I count the moments.
Ah, come, before my heart grows cold
And turns to death.
Come, in your glory.
Behold, your bride has prepared herself;
The loins are girded.

And since the oil of the Spirit
Is poured out upon me,
You are closer to me in my interior,
And I have flowed into you.
Thus, the light of life enlightens me,
And my lamp is prepared
To receive you joyously.

"Come" is the voice of your bride.
"Come" calls your pious beloved.
She calls and shouts loudly.
Come quickly, Jesus, come.
So come then, my bridegroom;
You know me, O lamb of God,
That I am betrothed to you.

But the proper time and hour
Are totally left to you.
I know that it is pleasing to you
That I with heart and tongue
Promise to come to you, and, therefore,
From now on direct my way
Toward you.

I am satisfied that nothing
Can separate me from your love
And that free before every man
I dare call you the bridegroom,
And you, O true prince of life,
will be wedded to me there
And give me your inheritance.
Therefore, I praise you with thanks

That the day (night, hour, year) is ended
And that from this time
one more step is completed.
I step forth again speedily
Until I come to the gate
Of Jerusalem above.
When hands are careless
And knees shake,

Offer me your hands quickly
In the chest of my faith
So that through your strength, my heart
Might be strengthened, and heavenwards
I might rise up without intermission.

Go, soul, fresh in faith
And be not now afraid.
Do not be enticed from the true path
by the desires of the world.
If you think you are too slow,
Hasten, as the eagle flys
with wings of sweet love.

O Jesus, my soul
Has already flown up to you.
You have, because you are totally love,
Completely exhausted me.
Leave off, what are times and hours,
I am already in eternity
Because I live in Jesus.

## ■ Discussion Questions

1. According to the preface, why is singing important to Christians in general and Pietists in particular?
2. In what ways does the hymn reflect this importance? What message does it convey?
3. What kind of emotional effect do you think the hymn may have had on a congregation, and why?

## ■ Comparative Questions

1. Both Louis XIV and Peter I cast themselves as absolute rulers. Do the documents support this claim? If so, how?
2. In what ways does Astell's discussion of the evils of arbitrary power foreshadow Montesquieu's concerns?

3. Although *Persian Letters* and Equiano's narrative belong to different literary genres, how do they adopt similar methods to describe eighteenth-century Europeans and their customs?

4. In what ways do Equiano, Astell, and Freylinghausen challenge conventional Christian authority and beliefs? What does this suggest about the place of Christianity in European society and culture at the time?

## *Acknowledgments (continued)*

**Chapter 1**

King Hammurabi. *The Code of Hammurabi* (Early Eighteenth Century B.C.E.) in *Ancient Near Eastern Texts Relating to the Old Testament,* Third Edition with Supplement, edited by James B. Pritchard. Copyright © 1950, 1955, 1969, and renewed 1978 by Princeton University Press. Reprinted by permission of Princeton University Press.

*The Book of Exodus, Chapters 19–24* (c. Tenth–Sixth Centuries B.C.E.). From *The Jerusalem Bible* by Alexander Jones, ed. Copyright © 1966 by Darton, Longman & Todd, Ltd. and Doubleday, a Division of Random House, Inc. Used by permission of Doubleday, a division of Random House, Inc.

*Inscription Honoring Cyrus, King of Persia* (r.c. 557–530 B.C.E.). From *Ancient Near Eastern Texts Relating to the Old Testament,* Third Edition with Supplement, edited by James B. Pritchard. Copyright © 1950, 1955, 1969, and renewed 1978 by Princeton University Press. Reprinted by permission of Princeton University Press.

Tyrtaeus of Sparta and Solon of Athens. *Poems* (Seventh–Sixth Centuries B.C.E.). From *Early Greek Lyric Poetry,* translated by David Mulroy (pp. 48–49, 68–69). Copyright © 1992. Reprinted by permission of the University of Michigan Press.

Sappho of Lesbos. *Poems* (Sixth Century B.C.E.). From *Women's Life in Greece and Rome: A Source Book in Translation* by Mary R. Lefkowitz and Maureen B. Fant, eds., pp. 2–4. © 1992 by Mary R. Lefkowitz and Maureen B. Fant. Reprinted with permission of The Johns Hopkins University Press.

**Chapter 2**

Thucydides. *The Funeral Oration of Pericles* (429 B.C.E.). From *The Peloponnesian Wars,* translated by Benjamin Jowett. Revised and abridged with Introduction by P. A. Brunt. Twayne Publishers, Inc. (1963).

Plato. *The Apology of Socrates* (399 B.C.E.). From *Dialogues of Plato,* translated by Benjamin Jowett and edited by J. D. Kaplan, pp. 5–14, 21–24, 39–40. Copyright © 1950, 2001 by Simon & Schuster, Inc. Reprinted and edited with the permission of Pocket Books, an imprint of Simon & Schuster Adult Publishing Group. All rights reserved.

Euphiletus. *A Husband Speaks in His Own Defense* (c. 400 B.C.E.). From *The Murder of Herodes And Other Trials from the Athenian Law Courts* edited by Kathleen Freeman. Copyright © 1946. Reprinted by permission of Hackett Publishing Company, Inc. All rights reserved.

*Overhead Views of a House on the Slope of the Areopagus* (Fifth Century B.C.E.). From "Women and Housing in Classical Greece: The Archeological Evidence," in *Images of Women in Antiquity,* ed. Averil Cameron and Amélie Kuhrt (London: Routledge, 1983) 87. Reproduced by permission of International Thompson Publishing Services Ltd. on behalf of Routledge. Courtesy Crook Helm, London.

Aristophanes. *Lysistrata* (411 B.C.E.). From *Greek Literature in Translation* by Whitney Jennings Oates and Charles T. Murphy. Copyright © 1944 by Longman Publishing Group. Reprinted by permission.

**Chapter 3**

Zeno, Egyptian Official. *Records* (259–250 B.C.E.). From *Select Papyri,* translated by A. S. Hunt and C. C. Edgar, vol. 1, pp. 269–77, 397–99, 409–15. Copyright © 1932. Reprinted by permission.

*Funerary Inscriptions and Epitaphs* (Fifth–First Centuries B.C.E.). From *Women's Life in Greece and Rome: A Source Book in Translation* edited by Mary R. Lefkowitz and Maureen B.

Fant. © 1992 by Mary R. Lefkowitz and Maureen B. Fant. Reprinted with permission of The Johns Hopkins University Press.

Epicurus. *Letter to a Friend* (Late Third Century B.C.E.). From *The Way of Philosophy* translated by Philip Wheelwright. Copyright © 1960. Reprinted by permission of Pearson Education, Upper Saddle River, NJ.

*The Book of I Maccabees, Chapter 8* (Sixth Century B.C.E.). From *The Jerusalem Bible* by Alexander Jones, ed. Copyright © 1966 by Darton, Longman & Todd, Ltd. and Doubleday, a Division of Random House, Inc. Used by permission of Doubleday, a division of Random House, Inc.

**Chapter 4**

*The Twelve Tables* (451–449 B.C.E.). From *Ancient Roman Statutes: A Translation with Introduction, Commentary, Glossary, and Index,* translated by Allan Chester Johnson, Paul Robinson, Coleman-Norton, Frank Card Bourne. Copyright © 1961. Courtesy of the University of Texas Press.

*Roman Women Demonstrate Against the Oppian Law* (195 B.C.E.). From *Livy: Volume IX, Loeb Classical Library* Volume #L295, translated by Evan T. Sage. Copyright © 1935. The Loeb Classical Library® is a registered trademark of the President and Fellows of Harvard College. Reprinted by permission of the publishers and Trustees of the Loeb Classical Library.

Julius Caesar. *The Gallic War* (52 B.C.E.). From *The Gallic War,* translated by Carolyn Hammond. Copyright © 1996. Reprinted by permission of Oxford University Press.

**Chapter 5**

Augustus. *The Accomplishments of Augustus* (14 C.E.). From *Roman Civilization: Selected Readings,* Third Edition, Volume I, edited by Naphatali Lewis and Meyer Reinhold. Copyright © 1990 Columbia University Press. Reprinted with permission of the publisher.

*Notices and Graffiti Describing Life in Pompeii* (First Century C.E.). From *Roman Civilization: Selected Readings,* Third Edition, Volume 1, edited by Naphatali Lewis and Meyer Reinhold. Copyright © 1990 Columbia University Press. Reprinted with permission of the publisher.

*Plan of Stabian Baths* and Seneca, *Letters 56.1, 2* (First Century C.E.). From *As the Romans Did: A Sourcebook in Roman Social History* by Jo-Ann Shelton. Copyright © 1988.

Flavius Josephus. *The Jewish War* (7 C.E.). From *The Jewish War,* translated by G. A. Williamson. Revised by E. Mary Smallwood. Penguin Classics, 1959. Revised edition 1981. Copyright © G. A. Williamson, 1959. Reprinted by permission of Penguin (UK).

Pliny the Younger. *Letters* (Early Second Century C.E.). From *Pliny Letters and Panegyricus,* Volume 2, translated by Betty Radice. Copyright © 1969 by the President and Fellows of Harvard College. The Loeb Classical Library® is a registered trademark of the President and Fellows of Harvard College. Reprinted by permission of the publishers and the Trustees of the Loeb Classical Library.

**Chapter 6**

Arius. *Letter to Alexander, Bishop of Alexandria* (c. 320 C.E.). From *A New Eusebius: Documents Illustrating the History of the Church to AD 337,* Revised edition, by J. Stevenson. Copyright © 1987 by J. Stevenson. Reprinted by permission of SPCK.

*The Nicene Creed* (325 C.E.). From *Readings in Western Religious Thought: The Ancient World* by Patrick V. Reid, editor. Copyright © 1987 by Paulist Press, Inc. Used with permission of Paulist Press. www.paulistpress.com.

St. Jerome. *Letter 107* (403 C.E.). From *Select Letters of St. Jerome LCL 262,* translated by F. A. Wright. Harvard University Press, 1933. The Loeb Classical Library® is a registered trademark of the President and Fellows of Harvard College. Reprinted by permission of the publishers and the Trustees of the Loeb Classical Library.

Excerpt from *The Burgundian Code* (c. 475–525 C.E.), translated by Katherine Fischer Drew. Copyright © 1972 University of Pennsylvania Press. Reprinted by permission of the University of Pennsylvania Press.

Procopius. *Buildings* (c. 553–554 C.E.). From *Procopius LCL 343,* Volume VII, translated by H. B. Dewing. Copyright © 1940 by the President and Fellows of Harvard College. The Loeb Classical Library® is a registered trademark of the President and Fellows of Harvard College. Reprinted by permission of the publishers and the Trustees of the Loeb Classical Library.

**Chapter 7**

Theophanes Confessor. *Chronicle* (Ninth Century). From *The Chronicle of Theophanes Confessor: Byzantine and Near Eastern History AD 284–813,* translated with Introduction and Commentary by Cyril Mango and Roger Scott. © Cyril Mango and Roger Scott 1997. Reprinted by permission of Oxford University Press (UK).

*Qur'an,* Suras 1, 53, 98 (c. 610–632). From *Approaching the Qur'an: The Early Revelations,* translated by Michael Sells. Copyright © 1999 by Michael Sells. Reprinted by permission of the publisher, White Cloud Press.

*Islamic Terms of Peace* (633–643). From *Islam from the Prophet Muhammad to the Capture of Constantinople,* volume 1: *Politics and War,* edited and translated by Bernard Lewis. Copyright © 1974 . Reprinted by permission of Walker & Company.

*The Life of Lady Balthild, Queen of the Franks* (Late Seventh Century). From *Late Merovingian France: History and Hagiography,* 640–720, ed. Paul Fouracre and Richard A. Gerberding. Published by Manchester University Press, 1996. Reprinted by permission of the authors.

**Chapter 8**

Liudprand of Cremona. *Report to Otto I* (968). Excerpts from *The Works of Liudprand of Cremona,* translated by F. A. Wright. Copyright © 1930 F. A. Wright. Published by G. Routledge & Sons (UK) and E. P. Dutton (NY), 1930. Reproduced by permission of Taylor & Francis Books UK.

*Digenis Akritas* (Tenth or Eleventh Century). From *Digenis Akritas: The Two-Blood Border Lord,* translated by Denison B. Hull. Copyright © 1986 Ohio University Press. Reprinted with the permission of Ohio State University Press, Athens, Ohio.

Ahmad al-Ya'qubi. *Kitāb al-buldān* (Ninth Century). From *Islam from the Prophet Muhammad to the Capture of Constantinople,* volume 2: *Politics and War,* edited and translated by Bernard Lewis. Copyright © 1974. Reprinted by permission of Walker & Company.

Fulbert of Chartres. *Letter to William of Aquitaine* (1020). From *Translations and Reprints from the Original Sources of European History.* Published by the University of Pennsylvania Press, 1898, vol. 4, no. 3. Courtesy of the publisher.

**Chapter 9**

*Urban Charters of Jaca, Spain* (c. 1077) *and Lorris, France* (1155). From *Medieval Iberia: Readings from Christian, Muslim, and Jewish Sources,* translated by Thomas N. Bisson and edited by Olivia Remie Constable. Copyright © 1997 by The University of Pennsylvania Press. Reprinted with the permission of the publisher.

Emperor Henry IV and Pope Gregory VII. *Sources* of the Investiture of Conflict (1076). From *The Correspondence of Pope Gregory VII,* translated by Ephriam Emerton. Copyright © 1932 Columbia University Press. From *Imperial Lives and Letters of the Eleventh Century,* translated by Theodor E. Mommsen and Karl F. Morrison. Copyright © 1962 Columbia University Press. Reprinted with permission of the publisher.

*The Anglo-Saxon Chronicle* (1085–1086). From *The Anglo-Saxon Chronicle: A Revised Translation* edited by Dorothy Whitelock. Copyright © 1961 by Dorothy Whitelock and David Douglas. Reprinted with the permission of Rutgers University Press.

*Medieval University Life* (Twelfth–Early Thirteenth Centuries). From *Translations and Reprints* from the *Original Sources of European History,* vol. 2, no 3, edited by Dana Carleton Munro. University of Pennsylvania Press, 1898. From *Wine, Women and Song: Mediaeval Latin Students' Songs,* translated by John Addington Symouds. Chatto & Windus, 1907.

St. Francis and St. Clare of Assisi. *Selected Writings* (Thirteenth Century). From *Select Historical Documents of the Middle Ages,* edited by Ernest Henderson (1921). *Francis and Clare: The Complete Works.* The Classics of Western Spirituality Series, translated by Regis J. Armstrong, O.M.F., CAP and Ignatius C. Brady, O.M.F. Copyright © 1982 by Paulist Press, Inc., New York, Mahwah, NJ. Used with permission of Paulist Press. www.paulistpress.com.

**Chapter 10**

Abbot Suger. *The Abbey Church of St.-Denis* (1144). From *De Administratione,* translated by David Burr. www.fordham.edu.

Hadewijch of Brabant. *Letters and Poems of a Female Mystic* (1220–1240). From *Medieval Women Writers,* edited by Katharina M. Wilson. Copyright © 1984 by The University of Georgia Press. Reprinted by permission of the University of Georgia Press.

Dante Alighieri. *Human and Divine Love* (Late Thirteenth–Early Fourteenth Centuries). From *La Vita Nuova,* translated by Barbara Reynolds. Copyright © 1980 Barbara Reynolds. Published by Penguin Books (1980). *The Comedy of Dante Alighieri the Florentine, Cantica III: Paradise,* translated by Dorothy L. Sayers and Barbara Reynolds. Copyright © 1981 by Dorothy L. Sayers and Barbara Reynolds. Published by Penguin Books (1981). Reprinted with permission of David Higham Associates Limited.

*Summons of Representatives of Shires and Towns to Parliament* (1295). From *Translations and Reprints from the Original Sources of European History.* University of Pennsylvania Press, 1897, vol. 1, no 6, 35, doc 4. Reprinted by permission of the University of Pennsylvania Press.

*Rolls of Parliament,* Petitions and Answers (1290–1305). From *Crises in English History 1066–1945,* edited by Basil Duke Henning et al. Holt, Rinehart and Winston, 1961. Copyright © 1961 Basil Duke Henning. Reprinted with permission.

Guyuk Khan. *Letter to Pope Innocent IV* (1246). From *Mission to Asia,* edited by Christopher Dawson. Medieval Academy of America, 1980. Courtesy of the publisher.

**Chapter 11**

*The Black Death* (Fourteenth Century). From *The Black Death* edited and translated by Rosemary Horrox. Copyright © 1994 by Rosemary Harrox. Reprinted with the permission of Manchester University Press.

Thomas Walsingham. *Peasant Rebels in London* (1381). From *The Peasants' Revolt of 1381,* 2nd edition, R. B. Dobson. Published by Macmillan Press (1983). Courtesy of the publisher.

Giovanni Pico della Mirandola. *Oration on the Dignity of Man* (1496). From *The Italian Renaissance Reader* edited by Julia Conaway Bondanella and Mark Musa. Copyright © 1987 by Julia Conaway Bondanella and Mark Musa. Used by permission of Dutton Signet, a division of Penguin Group (USA) Inc.

Bernardino of Siena. *An Italian Preacher: Sins against Nature* (1380–1444). From *The Preacher's Demons: Bernardino of Siena and the Social Underworld of Early Renaissance Italy* by Franco Mormando. Copyright © 1986. Reprinted by permission of the University of Chicago Press.

Gomes Eanes de Zurara. *Chronicle of the Discovery of Guinea* (c. 1453). From *A Source Book in Geography* edited by George Kish. Copyright © 1978. Reprinted with permission of the University of Harvard Press. Originally published by the Hakluyt Society, #95, 1896, translated by C. R. Beazley and Edgar Prestage.

**Chapter 12**

Martin Luther. *Freedom of a Christian* (1520). From *Christian Liberty,* edited by Harold J. Grimm. Copyright © 1957 by Harold J. Grimm. Reprinted by permission of Fortress Press.

Saint Ignatius of Loyola. *A New Kind of Catholicism* (1546, 1549, 1553). From *St. Ignatius of Loyola, Personal Writing: Reminiscences, Spiritual Diary, Select Letters, Including the Text of the Spiritual Exercises.* Translated and edited by Joseph A. Munitiz and Philip Endean. Copyright © 1996 Joseph A. Munitiz and Philip Endean. Used by permission of Penguin Books (UK).

Hans Jacob Christoffel von Grimmelshausen. *The Adventures of a Simpleton* (1668–1669). From *The Adventures of a Simplicius Simplicissimus,* translated by George Schulz-Behrend. Published by Camden House (1991). Courtesy of the publisher.

Henry IV. *Edict of Nantes* (1598). From *The Great Pressures and Grievances of the Protestants in Prison.* Edited by Edmund Everand. Reprinted by permission of Faber & Faber, Ltd.

Galileo. *Letter to the Grand Duchess Christina* (1615). From *Discoveries and Opinions of Galileo,* translated by Stillman Drake. Copyright © 1957 by Stillman Drake. Used by permission of Doubleday, a division of Random House, Inc.

*The Trial of Suzanne Gaudry* (1652). From *Witchcraft in Europe 1100–1700: A Documentary History,* edited by Alan C. Kors and Edward Peters. Copyright © 1972. Reprinted by permission of the University of Pennsylvania Press.

**Chapter 13**

Madame de Lafayette. *The Princess of Clèves* (1678). From *The Princess of Cleves NCE,* edited by John D. Lyons. Copyright © 1994 by W. W. Norton and Company, Inc. Used by permission of W. W. Norton & Company, Inc.

**Chapter 14**

Olaudah Equiano. *The Interesting Narrative of the Life of Olaudah Equiano Written by Himself* (1789). From *Equiqno's Travels: His Autobiography,* abridged. Published by Heinemann, 1967. Courtesy of the publisher.

Tsar Peter I. *Letter to His Son, Alexei* (October 22, 1715); and *Alexei's Response* (October 31, 1715). From *Sourcebook of Russian History* by Vermadsky. Copyright © 1972. Reprinted by permission of Yale University Press.

Mary Astell. *Reflections upon Marriage* (1706). From *The First English Feminist: Reflections upon Marriage and Other Writings by Mary Astell* edited by Bridget Hill. Reprinted by permission of the author.

*Pietist Spiritual Songbook* (1705). From *Pietists: Selected Writings* edited by Peter C. Erb. Copyright © 1983 Paulist Press, Inc. Reprinted by permission of Paulist Press. www.paulistpress.com.